Jīvanmukti in Transformation

Jīvanmukti in Transformation

Embodied Liberation in Advaita and Neo-Vedanta

Andrew O. Fort

State University of New York Press

Published by
State University of New York Press, Albany

Printed in the United States of America

For information, address State University of New York
Press, State University Plaza, Albany, N.Y. 12246

Production by E. Moore
Marketing by Nancy Farrell

Library of Congress Cataloging-in-Publication Data

Fort, Andrew O.
Jivanmukti in transformation : embodied liberation in Advaita and
neo-Vedanta / by Andrew O. Fort
p. cm.
Includes bibliographical references and index.
ISBN 0-7914-3903-8 (hardcover : alk. paper). — ISBN 0-7914-3904-6
(pbk. : alk. paper)
1. Mokṣa. 2. Advaita. 3. Vedanta. I. Title.
BL1213.58.F67 1998
181'.482—dc21 97-39409
CIP

10 9 8 7 6 5 4 3 2 1

To Sam and Meredith, joys of my life, and
to Wilhelm Halbfass, for his scholarly inspiration

Contents

Preface and Acknowledgments

This book has had a long gestation. I first started thinking about *jīvanmukti* in Advaita in 1987 and organized a panel for the American Academy of Religion on Living Liberation in Hindu Thought in 1989. That panel eventuated in the 1996 State University of New York (SUNY) Press book of the same name, co-edited with Patricia Mumme. While that and this book are not a "matching set," each informed the other. As I read more in the scholastic Advaita tradition, I became aware that the ostensibly Advaitic *Yogavāsiṣṭha* and *Jīvanmuktiviveka* presented a different, "Yogic Advaita" version of *jīvanmukti*. My interest in "neo-Vedanta" came later, as I noticed the transformation of the traditional conceptions of *jīvanmukti* to a more ecumenical and "socially conscious" model in post–British times. This interest was part of a more general inquiry, prompted especially by Wilhelm Halbfass's work, into the impact of Western ideas on modern Indian thinkers and into the possibilities of genuine cross-cultural understanding.

An earlier version of parts of chapter 1 appears in "Going or Knowing? The Development of the Idea of Living Liberation in the *Upaniṣads*," *Journal of Indian Philosophy* 22 (December 1994): 379–90, and chapter 2 is a revision of "Knowing *Brahman* While Embodied: Śaṅkara on *Jīvanmukti*," *Journal of Indian Philosophy* 19 (December 1991): 369–89. Both appear here with kind permission from Kluwer Academic Publishers. The above-mentioned book, *Living Liberation in Hindu Thought*, includes a chapter called "Liberation While Living in the *Jīvanmuktiviveka:* Vidyāraṇya's *Yogic Advaita*"; it appears here in revised form as chapter 8 by permission of the State University of New York Press. Finally, an earlier version of chapter 12 appears in *Beyond Orientalism: The Work of Wilhelm Halbfass and Its Impact on Indian and Cross-Cultural Studies,* edited by Eli Franco and Karin Preisendanz, Poznan Studies in the Philosophy of Sciences and Humanities, No. 59, Amsterdam/Atlanta: Editions Rodopi, 1997.

It is a pleasure to acknowledge those who helped me bring this book into being. I benefitted greatly from an American Institute of Indian Studies (AIIS) senior research fellowship in 1990, particularly from the assistance of the AIIS officer in Madras, Pappu Venugopala Rao. I also received significant assistance from the staff of the Kuppuswami Shastri Research Institute, directed by S. S. Janaki. Dr. Janaki introduced me to Dr. R. Krishnamurti Sastry of the Madras Sanskrit College, who was of critical importance in helping me understand the views of traditional Advaita thinkers on *jīvanmukti*. Others in India who helped me better comprehend various Advaitins on liberation while living include Drs. R. Balasubramanian, P. K. Sundaram, N. Veezhinathan, K. Kunjunni Raja, and Arabinda Basu. I also learned a great deal from the members of the Sriramana (Maharshi) Ashram and from the *Śaṅkarācāryas* of Kanchipuram and Sringeri. Stateside, I am grateful to Professors Mackenzie Brown, William Cenkner, and Lance Nelson for conversations about and insights into *jīvanmukti*. Finally, Texas Christian University has been supportive in many ways, from grants to visit India to a congenial and collegial department in which to work.

Abbreviations

BāU	*Bṛhadāraṇyaka Upaniṣad*
BS	*Brahmasūtras* (of Bādarāyaṇa)
ChU	*Chāndogya Upaniṣad*
JMV	*Jīvanmuktiviveka*
LYV	*Laghu Yogavāsiṣṭha*
PD	*Pañcadaśī*
PPV	*Pañcapādikāvivaraṇa*
ŚB	*Śrī Bhāṣya*
SK	*Sāṃkhyakārikās*
SS	*Saṃkṣepa-śārīraka*
US	*Upadeśasāhasrī*
VPS	*Vivaraṇaprameya-saṃgraha*
YS	*Yogasūtras*
YV	*Yogavāsiṣṭha*

Introduction: What Kind of Liberation Is Liberation While Living?

The nature of liberation (*mukti, mokṣa*) is a central concern of Indian thought. The group of related systems of thought within "Hinduism"[1] called "Vedanta," which is based on the Vedic corpus culminating in the *Upaniṣads*, in particular investigated the character of liberation at length, without any unified conclusion. When considering liberation, one common question was whether liberation is possible in life, that is, while embodied. The answer to this question also varied in Hindu thought, in part because the idea that one can reach the supreme goal while still living is quite audacious, and many thinkers, within and outside of Vedanta, recoiled at such an idea. Others felt living liberation, often called *jīvanmukti*, was certainly possible.[2]

This book will look at the views of the widely known and influential nondualist Advaita Vedanta tradition on this matter. There has been vigorous debate and analysis of the existence and nature of *jīvanmukti* within Advaita, and the general conclusion seems to be that one can be liberated while living. However, members of the Advaita tradition also regularly express reservations about or describe limitations in full liberation while embodied. The chapters that follow explore in greater depth the kind of liberation that Advaitins say liberation while living is.

The first section of this book will consider the development of the idea of *jīvanmukti* in what I will call traditional Advaita, that is, the classical scholastic tradition of Śaṅkara. I range from the *Upaniṣads* and Gauḍapāda to Maṇḍana Miśra and Śaṅkara, then turn to disciples and commentators like Sureśvara, Sarvajñātman, Vimuktātman, Prakāśātman, and Citsukha, and end this section considering late scholastic Advaitins like Madhusūdana Sarasvatī,

Prakāśānanda, Sadānanda, and Dharmarāja. After briefly considering the influential views on living liberation of Rāmānuja and the *Saṃkhya* and *Yoga* schools that contest those of Advaita, I then turn to what I will call "Yogic Advaita," particularly as seen in the *Yogavāsiṣṭha* and the *Jīvanmuktiviveka*, as well as the more difficult to categorize *Pañcadaśī* and so-called minor *Upaniṣads*. "Yogic Advaita" adds emphases on *Sāṃkhya* concepts and *Yoga* practices to traditional Advaitic concerns.

The final section will look at the modern "neo-Vedanta" view of the *jīvanmukti* concept. By neo-Vedanta, I mean the confluence of traditional Advaitic ideas with modern Western concepts like global ecumenism and humanistic social concern for all. While the Advaitin scholastics claimed that they held the true and final view, they recognized themselves as a "school" or lineage; neo-Vedantic writers, however, hold that Vedanta is a universal truth transcending a mere position or "religion." I therefore use the term *neo-Vedanta* (vs. *neo-Advaita*) to better distinguish these self-understood inclusive "Vedantic" thinkers from the more dialectical traditional Advaitins. After starting the final section with some general comments on the transformation of the Vedanta tradition under the influence of the modern West, I will look at a number of continuities and changes in traditional Advaitic thought generally, and *jīvanmukti* in particular, first from the perspectives of the modern saints Ramana Maharshi and the late *Śaṅkarācārya* of Kanchipuram, Candrasekharendra Sarasvati. Finally, I consider more neo-Vedantic views, particularly of Swami Vivekananda and Sarvepalli Radhakrishnan, and how, from the impact of Western ideas, the notion of social service has been linked to Advaitic *jīvanmukti* today.

Numerous works have been written dealing with *jīvanmukti* in Advaita. The interested reader could start with Lance Nelson's excellent chapter in *Living Liberation in Hindu Thought*, and J. F. Sprockhoff's more focused studies.[3] In addition, one can turn to L. K. L. Srivastava's neo-Vedantic work *Advaitic Concept of Jīvanmukti* (which is discussed in some detail in the final chapter), A. G. Krishna Warrier's *The Concept of Mukti in Advaita Vedanta* (Madras: University of Madras,1961), S. K. Ramachandra Rao's *Jīvanmukti in Advaita* (Bangalore: IBH Prakashana, 1979), Chacko Valiaveetil's *Liberated Life* (Madurai: Dialogue Series, 1980), or by consulting Karl Potter's *The Encyclopedia of Indian Philosophies* volume on Advaita Vedanta (Delhi: Motilal Banarsidass, 1981).

I want to say a bit more about my approach, vantage point, and intended audience. This book considers the historical development of the Advaita religio-philosophical conversation on the nature of liberation while living.[4] My study is based on texts written by members of an elite scholastic tradition, and focuses on what texts the central figures have read, and who they discuss and argue with. I will give some of the cultural and ideological context as I proceed, especially with neo-Vedanta. Of course, discussion of embodied liberation was certainly not limited to the scholastic Advaita tradition, as is apparent in texts like the *Bhagavad-Gītā* and *Yogavāsiṣṭha* or in schools following yogic or neo-Vedantic experiential practices. The breadth of the aspiration for and belief in liberation while living is clear when one observes the many saints, sages, and *siddhas* who have been claimed as living liberated beings in Indian history. I aim to illumine but a small portion of this field.

I bring to this study the broadly humanistic and historical–critical values (or in less exalted terms, baggage) of most late twentieth century American academics. It is impossible to read closely the material I consider without being aware of the gulf between my worldview, that of traditional Advaita, and the modern neo-Vedantic hybrid of them. One manifestation of this gulf (and my values) is my attempt to use nonsexist language where possible, but simultaneously to respect the fact that the Advaita tradition was far from "gender inclusive." Liberation in traditional Advaita was generally meant for male Brahmin *saṃnyāsins*.[5] I am aware of, but will generally not engage directly with, postmodernism in general and the conversation about Orientalism in particular.[6] Some might see my scholarly interests as being part of a continuing neocolonialist "discourse of domination" that favors the Indian past (improperly called "classical," as this term suggests both something frozen and a superior "golden age") and the classism and sexism of Brahminical thought.[7] It is certainly the case that my work falls within a text-based Sanskritic Brahminical construction that was privileged by British and subsequently Indian interpreters, and has been used, overtly and covertly, for political purposes. I must also take seriously the responsibility of "speaking for" the Advaita tradition, as many readers will not read the original texts. This entails careful listening to the tradition's representatives, using appropriate categories, and acknowledging limits to understanding.[8] Questions about political implications of and power asymmetries in academic inquiry are important to raise. My explicit project is, however, to make clear, through careful and respectful examination, what specific Advaitic texts and thinkers in their particular contexts say about *jīvanmukti*, how they are similar, distinct, and how perspectives on living liberation transform over time. I believe that the humanist project of enlarging our horizons and understanding others more accurately on their own terms is fraught with political dimensions, but is not confined to them.

My intended audience is scholars and others (Indian or Western) interested in Indian religion and philosophy, and those curious about how modern Western thought has influenced modern Indian thinkers. Thus, I am reading these texts for purposes not intended by their authors, meaning both my goal of "disinterested" scholarly description and my selective foregrounding of certain "philosophical views" in them. The intended audience of those about whom I write is, especially in the classical tradition, quite different—the community of scholars and teachers within the Advaita tradition and those of other Indian schools of thought (*darśana*). Their quest was liberating insight and rigorously reasoned defense of truth–claims against opponents, not in self-consciously "locating themselves" as subjects or in disengaged "accurate description." Let me here note that I recognize that language like "accurate description" is contested by postmodernists and others. All readings are selective and all understandings limited, of course, and I endorse the notion of multiple readings and meanings of a text. However, I am not ready to abandon the idea (and importance) of investigating authorial intent or of claiming that some "constructions" or "imaginings" are more legitimate than others.

One sees the impact of differing approaches and audiences in the primacy traditional Advaitins give to close reading of scripture (and its commentators), as has been brilliantly analyzed by Francis X. Clooney in his *Theology after Vedanta*.[9] The Veda (meaning here particularly the *Upaniṣads)* is regarded as the key source of knowledge about the highest truth. Thus, in significant ways, the Advaita tradition looks backward, with writers attempting to clarify and elaborate on the Veda and its proper interpretation,[10] rather than displaying an interest in "breaking new ground," as is common in the West. Creative thought is imbedded within commentary; it is recovery rather than discovery. Unlike in neo-Vedanta (and much of modern Western thinking), sacred texts are more authoritative than personal experience or logic and reason.

As Clooney shows, proper textual exegesis is of fundamental importance because the texts take the skilled reader to liberating insight. And as time went on, the corpus needing mastery grew in length and sophistication. Reasoning is often rigorous, but in light of scriptural teaching; personal views need legitimation via *śruti*, for unguided reasoning is endlessly debatable. While modern scholars would say that the texts are read selectively, an Advaitin like Śaṅkara would counter that Vedic texts are coherent (not made coherent) when understood properly.[11] Further, as Clooney points out, the reader must possess the proper qualification or authority (*adhikāra*) to read these texts; he must be prepared and worthy. I should note, however briefly, that I (and all Western scholars) are not, according to the classical tradition, authorized readers, though I have been greatly assisted by modern representatives of this tradition. As stated earlier, I am using the text for, from a traditional perspective, unintended purposes. I hope, however, to prove a respectful transgressor of propriety.

What Is Jīvanmukti?

It is now time to turn directly to the fundamental question of this book: What is *jīvanmukti, living* liberation? Here I will focus on the traditional Advaitic, not the neo-Vedantic, conception. In traditional Advaita (nondual) Vedanta, liberation *(mokṣa, mukti)* is, broadly, release from bondage to the cycle of transmigratory existence (*saṃsāra*). This realm of phenomenal appearance is experienced by embodied beings due to ignorance *(avidyā)* of their true nature; this ignorance causes desire-filled action (*karma)* continually binding them to the transmigratory cycle. One gains release through immediate knowledge (*vidyā, jñāna*) of partless, pervasive, unchanging, and self-luminous reality known as *brahman. Brahman* is realized to be one's true self (*ātman*); this self is not tied to the body or intellect and is free from all limitation and sorrow. Such knowledge rises through proper understanding of sacred texts, not by devotion or works.

Jīvanmukti is knowing, while still in the body, that you are really the eternal nondual self (which is *brahman*), and knowing further that the self is never embodied, since the body (and all world appearance) is not ultimately real. Somewhat like a reflection in a mirror, the world appears and exists, but it is not finally real. One is bound to the realm of transmigratory existence by (*karma*-bearing) ignorance, not by the body, and liberation arises from knowledge, not from dropping the body.[12] Knowledge alone is the necessary and sufficient condition for liberation. Thus our problem is not the presence of a body, but identification of the qualityless self with the conditioned body. Believing you are the body, and that the body is real, is the cause of (re)embodiment.[13] Since destroying this idea that the self is embodied, not the fall of the body, brings liberation, we can conclude that knowing the self's identity with *brahman* does not contradict bodily existence—though cessation of ignorance will eventually bring eternal release from the body.[14]

If, from this perspective, the one true liberation is freedom from the bonds of ignorance, then the presence or absence of the body is (in a sense) irrelevant. However, looking more closely, a (human) body is in fact useful and even necessary, since it provides the vehicle for liberation.[15] One might underline here that Advaitins say little about about the liberation of divine beings. In his chapter in *Living Liberation in Hindu Thought*,[16] Lance Nelson makes a fascinating argument, never made within Advaita, for regarding Advaitic *īśvara* as a *jīvanmukta*, as both are free from ignorance and egoism, although the *jīvanmukta* is not a cosmic creator or controller and has a trace of *karma* remaining. In the *Bhagavad-Gītā,* the person with firm wisdom, or *sthita-prajña*, is said to act with egoless detachment, like Kṛṣṇa himself. Perhaps even more interesting is the idea that *īśvara*, like the *jīvanmukta*, is limited by being in *saṃsāra*: he is constrained by the *karma* of creatures and the necessity of conforming to name and form arising from ignorance (as mentioned in Śaṅkara's commentary on *Brahmasūtra* II. 1. 14). Thus, as Nelson writes, *īśvara* is, "like the *jīvanmukta*, liberated but somehow not yet fully liberated (44)." Both await final bodiless (*videha*) release, but the lord will actually have to wait far longer than a human. Such an unwelcome conclusion is perhaps why this idea was never explored within the tradition.

To return to the issue of human embodiment, one sees a tension in Advaitic thought between the idea that all *mukti* is necessarily originally *jīvanmukti* because one becomes liberated (i.e., gains knowledge) only when in a body, with mind and senses, and the notion, consistent with the world-denying aspect of Advaita (in which one finds empirical experience regularly compared to an illusion, a dream, or an eye defect), that full liberation is only gained after death (sometimes, generally in Yogic Advaita, called *videhamukti)*. Because Advaita's nondualism devalues empirical reality (unlike the in-the-world monism of Tantra or Kāśmīrī Śaivism), it is unsurprising to find a variety of statements in Advaita that imply that bodiless liberation must be superior to embodied *mukti,* since the body is the locus of bondage; it inevitably decays and is not the self. It is said to be just a shadow (Maṇḍana, Sarvajñātman), like a shed skin of a snake (*BāU* IV. 4. 7), or a piece of burnt cloth (Citsukha, Madhusūdana).[17]

This tension is related to the fact that the notion of liberation solely as knowledge of *brahman/ātman* identity is quite different from another important Indian conception of liberation that finds resonances in Advaita: that of *mukti* as freedom from the inevitable suffering of transmigratory existence (*saṃsāra*) or as the absence of pain (*duḥkhābhava*). This more "negative" idea of liberation generally requires some form of world renunciation that normally includes some kind of yogic practice and ends in perfect isolation (*kaivalya*) of the spirit.[18] From this perspective, the body is quite a significant limitation, since only when free from embodiment can one gain freedom from suffering (the final goal).[19] Still, until we reach what I call the "Yogic Advaita" of the *Yogavāsiṣṭha* and the *Jīvanmuktiviveka*, the relative absence of reference to yogic practices and meditation is remarkable. I will point out later that to Advaitins like Śaṅkara, meditation is a helpful support for attaining liberating *brahman* knowledge, but it is still an action of a deluded individual agent in the dualistic realm of means and ends.

The notion of liberation as absence of suffering and sorrow (and thus embodiment) raises an important question: If liberated, why is one still in a body? From the earliest *Upaniṣads* on, many strands of the Hindu tradition shared the notion that being embodied impedes release and that death brings it.[20] Despite the Advaita position that knowledge and not embodiment is the key issue, a thoughtful reader can argue that a rationale for continued embodiment is needed to satisfy both reason and experience. Experience seems to show that embodiment inevitably entails suffering, disease, and seeing illusory duality. It is reasonable to hold that none of these should exist for a truly liberated being.

Holding to embodied liberation also presents some problems for basic Advaitic doctrines. To Advaitins, the body is a result of prior activity (*karma*),[21] which is part of ignorance (*avidyā*), and thus is in some sense opposed to knowledge (*vidyā*). Gaining knowledge of nondual *brahman* is said to destroy ignorance, thus it should bring immediate liberation (*sadyomukti*), annihilating all *karma*, including the body. Since the body does not cease when knowledge rises, ignorance of some form must remain, and how can there be *avidyā* post-*vidyā*?[22] This question can be said to be the central problem in the Advaitic conception of *jīvanmukti*. It is so serious because Advaitins largely accept that there is total opposition between, rather than degrees of, knowledge and ignorance.[23] They sometimes use the analogy of the opposition of darkness and light.[24] Yet while light and darkness can be said to be opposed, one can also point to twilight, and other degrees of light and dark. This response is, of course, an argument from everyday experience (*pratyakṣa*), used to counter a theoretical problem (*tarka*).

Advaitin Rationales for Embodiment after Liberation

There are at least three answers to the problem of the continuity of embodiment post-realization, an issue that received a great deal of attention in later Advaita.[25] The first answer is that you are "bodiless" while embodied, when you know the self is not the body. As Śaṅkara states in his *BS* I. 1. 4 commentary, embodiment (*saśarīratva*) is caused by ignorance, that is, identifying body and self. Knowing that the eternal self is not and never was embodied shows one is by nature eternally bodiless (*aśarīra*), so the knower is in a sense *aśarīra* while living (or "bodiless" while embodied).[26] Bodilessness is complete detachment, not lack of a physical body. As *BāU* IV. 4. 7 states, the body is to a *brahman*-knower like a cast-off skin is to a snake. Put another way, the body "disappears" for the knower (as in sleep or swoon), although the knower's body doesn't disappear.

The second answer focuses on a more practical point: *jīvanmukti* exists so that we can learn from enlightened teachers, who compassionately remain in a body to assist ignorant humans. Śaṅkara mentions such teachers in *Chāndogya Upaniṣad bhāṣya* VI. 14. 2 (the *ācārya* who removes the blindfold of delusion that one is a body) and *BāU bhāṣya* II. 1. 20 (the young hunter [embodied being] is awakened to his true nature as a prince [supreme *brahman*] by a teacher). Vimuktātman, following Śaṅkara, adds *Gītā* IV. 34, which says that only the wise sages who realize the truth teach the highest knowledge.[27] We could not know about (or reach) liberation unless enlightened teachers exist, and they could not exist if the body falls immediately after knowledge. This would at least be the case according to the all-or-nothing view of *vidyā*. In everyday experience, we actually see many teachers without perfect knowledge helping those with even less knowledge. Also, if (as Advaitins argue) *śruti* reveals nondual *brahman*, we could learn about *mokṣa* from a nonhuman (*apauruṣeya*) source. Interestingly, both Sarvajñātman (chapter 3) and Prakāśānanda (chapter 4) argue for the idea that, from the highest perspective, the liberated teacher is only imagined yet can still bring liberation to the ignorant.

Modern neo-Vedantins make much of the role of enlightened teachers, and add another rationale for a *jīvanmukta*'s continuing existence here—to provide selfless social service to suffering humanity. Much more will be said on this subject in the final chapter. There is little discussion of the idea that the liberated being would return to teach or help when the current embodiment ends. This certainly differentiates *jīvanmukti* from the Buddhist *bodhisattva* ideal. Śaṅkara opens this possibility once, in response to *BS* III. 3. 32, which suggests a being might take birth again if there is a commission (*adhikāra*) to perform (chapter 2).

The third explanation for the body's continuation after liberation is given great attention in the later Advaita scholastic tradition. It begins with the general rule that when *brahman* is known, all ignorance (and thus *karma*) is destroyed—so how can the *karma*-based body continue? Later Advaitins assert that a remnant or trace (*leśa*) of *avidyā* can exist even after one gains release; this remnant is based on *karma* whose fruits have already commenced manifestation (*prārabdha karma*). Before one's final disembodiment, one must experience ("enjoy," *bhuj*) the fruits of those actions, which cannot be removed by knowledge. Put another way (following Śaṅkara in *ChU bhāṣya* VI. 14. 2), one can *know brahman* without quite yet *attaining brahman*. This interpretation is much elaborated on in later Advaita and requires further explanation.

Most important is that, for Advaitins, there are three kinds of *karma*, only two of which are removed by knowledge. The first is *saṃcita karma*, the accumulated mass of past *karma* that has not yet borne fruit. Knowledge burns all such *karma*.[28] The second is *āgamī karma*, *karma* to be obtained in this life that would bear fruit in the future. After *brahman* knowledge, this *karma* will not bind, since the false notion of agency has disappeared (so it seems that "backsliding" is not possible). The third type of *karma*, mentioned earlier, is currently manifesting or *prārabdha karma*. Such *karma*, which produced the current body, is not destroyed by knowledge and must bear fruit before the body falls.[29]

The idea that when one is liberated most, but not all, kinds of *karma* are destroyed was seen, both in and outside of Advaita, as a problem. How can knowledge destroy some, but not all, *karma* (and why the unexperienced rather than the partially experienced *karma*)? Further, if there is no immediate (*sadyo*) *mukti*, why would it happen eventually? If there is a little delay in liberation, why not a lot?

Śaṅkara and Maṇḍana Miśra set the pattern for the responses to this latter question, and *ChU* VI. 14. 2 becomes the key text for this issue.[30] *ChU* VI. 14. 2 states that the delay in final release is only as long as one is not free.[31] Śaṅkara asserts that this means there is delay in attaining the self as long as an ignorant embodied person enjoys the (already commenced) fruits of *karma*. Then, utilizing the *ChU* terminology, he makes a crucial distinction, mentioned earlier, between *knowing (jñā, vid) brahman,* which is immediate and happens in the body, and *attaining* (*saṃpad) brahman,* which is simultaneous with release from the body (but delayed as long as *prārabdha karma* manifests). Thus Śaṅkara argues that final release (versus "mere" liberation) happens at the time the body drops away *(dehapāta)*,[32] not when knowledge rises. Maṇḍana specifies that the delay in the body's fall is brief (or very brief, *kṣipra)*, being only the time it takes to experience already manifesting fruits.[33]

The continuance of the *mukta's* body due to *prārabdha karma* is commonly likened to the continued whirling of a potter's wheel, even after the potter has left (from *Sāṃkhya Kārikā* 67),[34] or the continued flight of an arrow after the initial impetus of the shot.[35] Body, wheel, and arrow continue for a time due to their momentum, but gradually and inevitably they will come to rest. One can find a number of problems with the analogies, the most serious of which is that the bow and arrow and the rotating potter's wheel are, in the examples, real things in a real world.[36] After knowledge, however, one realizes that the body (and arrow and wheel) are illusions and were never really connected with the Self. A real thing is not analogous to an unreal imagining.

Vimuktātman (and Citsukha) further distinguish the type of *karma* whose fruits must be experienced before bodily continuity ceases post-realization (chapter 3). There is a kind of *karma* that causes knowledge to arise, or has knowledge as its object—this (*vidyārtha*) *karma* bears fruit in a body born from *karma,* having "enjoyment" as its object (*bhogārtha)*. Citsukha claims only *vidyārtha karma* (which accounts for *living* liberation) exists after knowledge, and it neither creates a new body nor immediately destroys the existing body (chapter 4).

The most commonly voiced objection in the later Advaita tradition to the notion of the remnant of ignorance is that the embodied person's *prārabdha karma*, even if only a trace of *avidyā*, is still ignorance, and one possessing ignorance cannot be completely liberated. As Prakāśānanda asks, how can knowledge have two natures simultaneously—both destroying and not destroying ignorance? The primary response to this objection is that ignorance itself (in the form of *prārabdha karma*) does not remain, only an impression, or *saṃskāra*, of ignorance, abides.[37] The impression alone causes the body to remain, even after all *karma* is destroyed. In *BS bhāṣya* IV. 1. 15 (and *Gītā bhāṣya* 18. 48), Śaṅkara gives the example of the impression of two moons that persists in one with eye disease, although the ignorance that more than one moon exists has been destroyed. Maṇḍana holds that while *saṃskāras* outlast *karma*, the body still will drop soon (and *saṃskāras* forever cease), as a *saṃskāra* is only an effect of ignorance,[38] and the effect is not equal to the root cause (*prārabdha karma*). Prakāśātman and Madhusūdana (who also hold that impressions can continue even without ignorance) use the example of the slight smell ("trace") of a flower remaining in a vase after all the flowers, the smell's cause, have been removed, and liken the *saṃskāra*-based bodily continuity after knowledge to the slight remnant of cloth form remaining after the cloth is burnt.

The analogy most often made is that of the trembling (here equivalent to the *saṃskāra*) that continues even after the cessation of fear (equivalent to *avidyā*), generated by mistaking a rope for a snake.[39] When one knows the truth, fear (the cause of the trembling) ceases, but trembling (a mere effect) continues for a little while, inevitably but only gradually lessening over time. In the same way, when one gains the highest truth, ignorance (the cause of the body) ceases, but the body (a mere effect) continues for a little while and then inevitably falls.[40] I should note that Vimuktātman disagrees with this view, claiming that there are no *saṃskāras* without *avidyā*. While both the impressions and ignorance (their locus) form the body (i.e., essential nature) of ignorance, fear and trembling are not the body of the "snake"/rope, so the latter is not a good example. The "snake" appearance is based on ignorance itself, not a *saṃskāra*, and when ignorance ceases, the rope-based illusion of the snake never rises again.[41]

As we shall see, these ideas become even more refined (or baroque) over time: Prakāśātman differentiates *tattva* (reality) *jñāna* (which negates all ignorance) from the more specific *vyatireka-jñāna*, which negates the reality of particular objects like a snake or body (chapter 4). This suggests that one can know a specific "snake" is a rope without realizing the whole world is such a superimposition, and one can have the highest realization while still mistaking a specific rope for a snake. Citsukha and Madhusūdana discuss three forms (*ākāra*) or powers (*śakti)* of the ignorance trace, and a variety of later writers mention the role of the concealing (*āvaraṇa*) and projecting (*vikṣepa*) powers of *āvidya*, in which the former is removed by knowledge, but the latter continues due to *prārabdha karma*.[42]

Issues discussed in the preceding paragraphs, which will be fleshed out in the following chapters, show that much time and energy went into considering the problem of how *any* remnant of ignorance can continue after liberating knowledge. Despite all the attempts to clarify this issue, Advaitins are left with the following quandary: either *saṃskāras* are *avidyā* (thus the embodied one is not a perfect knower) or they are not (thus should not cause the ignorance-based body to continue).[43]

Jīvanmukti *and Worldly Activity*

Before beginning the study of specific texts and thinkers in the following chapters, I will address one more issue, about how the liberated being acts in the world. While relatively unexamined in scholastic Advaita, this topic becomes progressively more significant in later Advaita analyses of *jīvanmukti*. How does one who has reached the final goal even while living behave? First, the training on the path to liberation is highly demanding. Very briefly, Advaitins from Śaṅkara on hold that the route includes becoming eligible (*adhikṛ)* by such qualifications as discriminating the eternal (that is, *brahman)* from the noneternal, being detached from enjoying fruits of actions here or later, practicing tranquility, self-control, and so on, and intently desiring liberation (*BS bhāṣya* I. 1. 4). One must also hear, reflect on, and assimilate (e.g., perform *śravana-manana-nididhyāsana)* the Vedic scriptures. These long and difficult efforts will lead one to renunciation (*saṃnyāsa*) and detachment (*vairāgya)* from everyday activity (*vyavahāra*).[44] It is evident that for traditional Advaita, householding is not compatible with true renunciation, though following the *dharma* is certainly important preparation, and one is not free from ritual obligations until released.

However, once liberated, must the sage continue to renounce the world? Is nonaction better than action, even for the knower? The answer depends in part on how one defines action or renunciation. Does renunciation primarily indicate inaction and physical world withdrawal or simply the mental attitude of detachment?[45] After all, while physically renouncing the world may remove one from objects of desire, it still leaves one with the dualistic notion of a (limited) self opposed to a world full of temptation. World renunciation can thus reinforce a concept of liberation that takes the body to be real and the locus of suffering. Advaitins hold, however, that a liberated being knows that the body is unreal and unrelated to the true self (this knowledge brings surpassing bliss). As stated earlier, thinking you are the agent in transmigratory existence, not acting, is the problem. If one has desires and thinks oneself an agent, then both action and inaction bind, but if one is desireless and knows the self is not an agent, then neither bind. So real renunciation is that of the body-self identity and of the "I" notion, not of the world or activity.

This point is largely assumed by scholastic Advaitins, but the nature of the liberated being's renunciation is discussed at some length in the *yoga*-influenced Advaita of the *Yogavāsiṣṭha* and *Jīvanmuktiviveka*.[46] The *jīvanmukta*'s actions, according to these texts, will be considered in chapters 6 and 7. Here it suffices to say that after knowing the self is *brahman*, detached "worldly" action is still possible, as King Janaka and Yājñavalkya demonstrate. The *JMV* describes the *Gītā*'s *sthita-prajña* (one with firm wisdom) as the model of detached, desireless action.[47] The mainstream Advaita position can be summarized this way: Given the apparent necessity of long and intense renunciation before liberation, world withdrawal might be "natural" for one now liberated, but it is not necessary. Some action while embodied is inevitable, but the amount and kind of bodily activity is an issue only to the ignorant, those on the *vyāvahārika* level who see body/self linkage. While the ignorant see the embodied *mukta* acting in the world, the liberated being sees only *brahman*.

While it is clear that the liberated being acts, the question remains whether this person must act in any particular way. It is important to remember here that for traditional Advaita, "acting" seems to refer more to performing ritual duties and following the *dharma* than to a Western notion of being or doing "good." For example, Prakāśātman writes that even while still seeing duality (i.e., alive), the *jīvanmukta* does not perform rites, as no regulations or goals remain for one knowing the real (chapter 4).

Yet is the *jīvanmukta* rule bound at all? Earlier Advaitins gave limited consideration to whether the fully detached *jīvanmukta* would do "whatever he pleases (*yatheṣṭācaraṇa*)," apparently meaning ignoring dharmic duties. In comments on *BS* II. 3. 48, Śaṅkara mentions in passing that a liberated being will not do whatever he pleases, since identifying (falsely) with the body causes action and the knower identifies with the self. Sureśvara, while emphasizing nondual knowledge over action, claims in *Naiṣkarmyasiddhi* IV. 62ff. that a desireless *brahman* knower will never violate the *dharma* by doing whatever he wishes. Both Sureśvara and Prakāśātman note that all evil ceases with knowledge, yet so does the wish to do any action (implicitly even good acts). The *Pañcadaśī* author Bhāratītīrtha writes that, while unnecessary, activity in accordance with sacred texts is certainly not prohibited (VII. 268–70 [chapter 8]). Sadānanda's *Vedāntasāra* seems to represent the traditional Advaitic position well when it states, after mentioning Sureśvara's views, that only good qualities like humility and nonenmity are present in, but remain mere ornaments to, the *jīvanmukta*.[48] The consensus seems to be that although free from dharmic obligations, the desireless liberated being would never violate the *dharma*.[49]

Modern Advaitin thinkers and scholars argue both that the *jīvanmukta* is beyond "morality," so no action, even good action, is necessary, and that this being would be "naturally" good, because, knowing identity with all, he lacks the selfish desires that generate evil. Many of these neo-Vedantins also claim that the *jīvanmukta*, out of solicitude for others, will not only share his realization but also will actively "do good" and show social concern in ways that seem familiar to the modern Christian West. The traditional Advaitic commitment to following the *dharma* is certainly different from social concern as it has been understood in Western religious traditions (i.e., good works for others). As I will point out in chapter 12, if all is always nondual, one might well argue that Western-style social service is transcended. The interest in the "social ethics" of the liberated being and the entire way of speaking about "good" and "morality" is a recent and Western-influenced phenomenon.[50] The final chapter will discuss the relationship of *jīvanmukti* and social service as a case study of the neo-Vedantic transformation of the Advaita tradition.

To close, let me mention again some of the distinctive characteristics of living liberation in traditional Advaita. These characteristics include knowing that the self is not the body and that the body continues due to a remnant or an impression of ignorance in the form of currently manifesting *karma*. There is much controversy about the exact nature of the ignorance (and the time limit for the body) that remains after liberating knowledge, particularly whether it is a trace or an impression of a trace. This seems driven by the conviction that embodiedness is, after all, a limitation, which is quite consistent with Advaitic world devaluation. We have also seen that the *jīvanmukta*, after treading a long and difficult path, renounces agency, not action, and that the liberated being can teach and bring comfort while embodied (though not, at least in the traditional model, acting as a social reformer). With these ideas in mind, we turn, after notes on the terms *Hinduism* and *understanding*, to the development of the idea of liberation while living in the *Upaniṣads*.

A Note on "Hinduism"

It is quite appropriate to pay close attention to what is revealed and what is concealed in all broad categories, and certainly such problematic ones as "Hindu" and "Hinduism."[51] Reflection on these terms is important, even if one is not convinced that their usage is part of a hopelessly "Orientalist, colonialist, totalizing, and hegemonic discourse of domination." While one might find postmodern critics of Orientalism also holding to problematic totalizing discourses attempting to gain domination, they have, as mentioned earlier, properly made us more aware of issues of power and representation, who "we" are speaking for and about.

It bears repeating that the term *Hindu* was originally used by Persians to describe those who lived around the Indus River (thus, "Hindu" was first a geographical or political identification). While there have long been followers of the Veda, the *varṇāśrama-dharma*, and the notions of *karma* and rebirth, "Hinduism" was a term (and eventually an ideological and institutional reality) born in the nineteenth century, when the British- and Western-educated Bengalis like Ram Mohan Roy—began to describe or "construct" the "religion" (another originally Western notion) of most "Indians" (yet another). This Anglo–Brahmin collaboration helped reinforce the sociopolitical order, though not without resistance by groups including low- and outcastes, Muslims, and Christians. One finds this "Hinduism" in "world religions" textbooks and among some modern Indians who utilize it as part of national identity: It is seen as a single, ancient, tolerant, and inclusive *sanātana* ("eternal") *dharma*, with great classical glory (based in Sanskrit and Vedanta) and medieval decline (due in part to the Muslim "invasions") before its modern "renaissance."[52]

I will occasionally use the terms *Hindu* and *Hinduism* in the text, generally without scare quotes, despite their problematic nature. I have no intention of suggesting any concept or practice as being essential or normative to the Hindu "religion." As long as these terms are recognized as useful constructs, with traditions of their own, they can be used meaningfully. My own sympathies lie with Heinrich von Stietencron's notion that it would be useful (and accurate) to refer to Hinduism not as a religion, but as "a geographically defined group of distinct but related religions, that originated in the same region."[53] These religions coexist and mutually influence one another, and range from Veda-oriented *Smārta* traditions to anti-Brahmin *bhakti* traditions to manifold "folk religions" throughout India. Von Stietencron points out that asceticism *and* sensual indulgence, animal sacrifice *and* nonviolence, Vedic exclusion *and* devotional inclusion of women and low- or outcastes are all part of Hinduism. Thus, all "Hindu" groups are minorities in one form or another. Relevant to my later chapters is the notion that neo-Vedanta can perhaps be called a new "religion" within "Hinduism."

Von Stietencron also makes the interesting point that the degree of similarity and difference within "Hinduism" is akin to that of the "Abrahamic religions" (also founded in a single region) of Judaism, Christianity, and

Islam.[54] One could even argue the latter share more commonality than do the traditions of Hinduism. Still, von Stietencron rightly indicates that neither group has a single agreed-upon doctrine or theology, sacred text, founder or leader, teaching lineage, cosmogony, or ritual. Further, in "Hinduism," one person's supreme deity might be another's lesser manifestation, demonic force, or ignorant notion. Yet the ability of "Hindus" to coexist relatively amicably (at least until recently) does, as von Stietencron writes, present a challenge to the civilizations holding to Abrahamic traditions.

A Note on "Understanding"

When describing my goals in research and teaching, I often say that my primary commitment is to "understanding."[55] By this term, I mean the appreciative inquiry into, and sympathetic attempt to become informed about, other people(s) and their perspectives. This includes both their similarities with and differences from one's own worldview. It is an important humanistic goal to learn how an "other" thinks and speaks about himself or herself, then to communicate that thinking and speaking as accurately as possible to those in one's own culture.

Understanding demands openness, a desire to learn, careful and patient inquiry, a capacity to gather information and find appropriate categories, and a comprehension of complexity. It also requires one to recognize and overcome stereotypes, prejudices, and sheer ignorance. An important component of this process is dialogue: meeting, talking with, listening to, and asking questions of others. Another component is the close, nuanced examination of specific thinkers and texts in their particular context and historical situation. One important result is awareness of topics and issues that arise in the culture or tradition itself.

Understanding has limits—there is no "objectivity" or neutral ground. We never have complete information. We all begin with presuppositions and a (or some) perspective(s), and must bridge from the familiar to the unfamiliar. We must make generalizations (even while recognizing there is no "grand narrative") and use categories that objectify and reify. We also choose to emphasize certain themes or issues, which will to some extent distort a text's or thinker's own plan, questions, or way of knowing. These problems are practical inevitabilities, part of the process of coming to understand itself (which includes not understanding), and can be mitigated (though not overcome) by the careful process of inquiry detailed earlier.

An issue that is perhaps more difficult and raises concerns about "Orientalism" is the fact that the "other" may not want to be understood by outsiders, and a Western academic attempt to understand may, with its relentless intrusiveness, alter others by lessening their autonomy and depriving them of an earlier identity. Here, despite—or because of—"the best intentions," one becomes part of a "discourse of domination." I want to argue that this risk is in part unavoidable[56] and in part worth taking in service of enlarging human horizons. First, dialogue inevitably puts self-understanding into play—on both sides. Second, no culture is static; individual and social dialogue is always underway. Third, attempts to understand can teach—and have taught, as in the case of "Hinduism"—the investigators about the limits of their own understanding and have led to recognition of what has been "constructed" or "imagined" without sufficient collaboration with indigenous representatives or grounding in the context being examined. Such efforts, in Indology and elsewhere, can and have, for example, demonstrated political dimensions of, and power asymmetries in, the inquiry.[57] Finally, it is possible to hold to one perspective without dehumanizing or disrespecting another; in fact, recognizing and affirming difference is a form of respect.

Thus the project of understanding (anyone or anything) without diminishing or exaggerating difference from oneself is ambiguous and problematic, but it is worth the effort, especially when considering the risks of the alternatives.

Part I

Embodied Liberation in Traditional Advaita Vedanta

ONE

The Development of the Idea of Embodied Liberation before Śaṅkara: The Early Upaniṣads, *the* Brahmasūtras, *Gauḍapāda, and the* Bhagavad-Gītā

The notion of liberation while living found in Advaita Vedanta developed slowly over many centuries, and did not become a formal doctrine until after the time of Śaṅkara. Still, the basic elements of the Advaitic conception of *jīvanmukti* can be traced back to the earliest *Upaniṣads*. There we find both the idea that one (or one's essential being) gains immortality (eternal life) in a heavenly realm only after leaving the body and the rudiments of a conception of liberation (and immortality) while living by knowing *ātman/brahman* identity.[1] This liberation (*mukti*, *mokṣa*) by nondual knowledge takes one beyond both the life-and-death cycle of *saṃsāra* and any "physical" or material heavenly realm.[2]

Many scholars have noted that early Indian religious texts generally describe liberation not as knowing the self but as reaching a heavenly realm (*brahma* or *svarga loka*), that is, "going somewhere" in time and space. In some early *Upaniṣads*, two paths (*yāna*) are described that require the performance of sacrificial acts or faith and asceticism; one is the path of the fathers (*pitṛ*), which goes via the moon and leads to rebirth, the other is the path of the gods (*deva*), which is associated with the sun, heaven, and eventually knowledge.[3] Even when one attains the realm of the gods, liberation and immortality are tied to a place, albeit a heavenly and blissful place that lacks the sorrow and frustration of our human realm. This view also implies that one gains liberation and immortality only after death, since only then does one reach heavenly realms. The notion that one goes to another realm by the path of the gods is called by later Advaitins "liberation by stages" (*kramamukti*).[4]

As the ideas of *karma* and rebirth take hold, however, it becomes apparent that for most beings even a heaven is temporary, and one must eventually (and repeatedly) return to this realm of suffering and desire. *Upaniṣadic* thinking now begins to focus on the idea of liberation from all death and rebirth through desire-ending knowledge, and immortality is linked with knowing one's identity with *brahman*, rather than with going to a heavenly realm. One no longer fulfills one's desires (in heaven), one discontinues desiring (human pleasures, but not the self); this ceasing of desire and concomitant liberating knowledge can (or must) happen while living. This shift in focus takes place over an extended period, and the ideas of immortality as the attainment of a blissful eternal abode and as desire-ending knowledge of *brahman* often are found in close proximity. In some cases, one can gain liberating knowledge in a body, but one does not reach immortality or heaven before death. This position presages the extended Advaita debate about whether one can truly be fully liberated while living.

Immortality in the Early Upaniṣads

A look at the concept of immortality in the *Upaniṣads* clearly illustrates the slow and equivocal development of the idea of liberation while living. The term *immortal[ity]* (*amṛta[tva]*) appears many times in the early or "major" *Upaniṣads*.[5] Its exact meaning varies among and even within various *Upaniṣads* (illustrating their nonsystematic nature), and certain usages are ambiguous, as I shall soon show. In these texts, immortality can refer to eternal life in a heavenly realm after the body falls, but it also can mean knowing the highest truth, even while embodied. We shall see that later Advaitins did have warrant to refer back to the *Upaniṣads* for passages that indicate knowledge of *ātman /brahman* as final "immortal" liberation, yet these writers also could have found other passages describing immortality as a state a person reaches only in a heavenly realm. While there is no simple chronological development in meanings of immortality, one can perhaps discern a "direction" in *Upaniṣadic* passages mentioning *amṛta(tva)* from "going" (to a heaven) to "knowing" and "being" (*ātman/brahman*). Most *Upaniṣadic* texts referring to immortality are "in the middle" of this shift, so can seem ambiguous or "unclear," especially since "going" or "attaining" can be read figuratively or literally.

Before turning to the texts, I should point out that throughout the *Upaniṣads*, immortal(ity) is often used as one among many modifiers for our true essence or being, which is generally termed *ātman* or *brahman*. *Brahman* and *ātman* are certainly immortal,[6] and the three terms are used together in *ChU* VIII. 14. 1 and *BāU* IV. 4. 25. Two other entities found in the *Upaniṣads* that often refer to our true essence or being are regularly called immortal: the person (*puruṣa*) and the vital breath[s] (*prāṇa[s]*).[7] The vital breath is said to be immortal in *BāU* I. 5. 7, I. 6. 3, II. 3. 5, and IV. 4. 7 (where it is identified with *brahman*), as well as *Praśna* II. 5 and III. 11–2 (which says that the wise one, knowing the *prāṇa*, becomes immortal). According to *Kauṣītaki* III. 2, *prāṇa* as *prajñātma* is immortal, and with this *prāṇa*, one obtains immortality in this world.[8] The *puruṣa* is termed immortal in *ChU* IV. 15. 1, *BāU* II. 3. 5, IV. 3. 12, *Muṇḍaka* I. 2. 11, *Praśna* VI. 5, and *Taittirīya* I. 6. 1. The *Kaṭha* explicitly says the immortal *puruṣa* is *brahman* (V. 8, VI. 1) and *ātman* (VI. 17). An extensive parallelism is made in *BāU* II. 5. 1 ff., where the immortal *puruṣa* in the earth and body and so on is termed the self, *brahman*, and all.

Now we may look at specific references to immortality in the early *Upaniṣads*. First, while virtually all relevant *Upaniṣadic* passages say knowledge is central to liberation, some seem to indicate that one becomes immortal only when one reaches another realm. *Aitareya* IV. 6 states that the bodiless knower obtains all desires in heaven (*svarga*) and then becomes immortal, and *Kauṣītaki* II. 14 holds that one who knows the vital breath (*prāṇa*) leaves the body, goes to where the gods (*deva*) are, and becomes immortal like them.[9] *Kena* I. 2 says that the wise become immortal upon departure from this world.

There are a number of other passages, especially in the *Muṇḍaka Upaniṣad*, which also seem to indicate that one "goes to" immortality, but goes by knowing. For example, *Muṇḍaka* I. 2. 11 claims that knower–renouncers, practicing austerity (*tapas*) and faith (*śraddha*), depart to where the immortal *puruṣa* dwells, and II. 2. 5 states that knowing (*brahman*) as the self is the bridge (*setu*) to immortality.[10] Two other passages mention knowing the immortal (*brahman*) without indicating any "going": *Muṇḍaka* II. 2. 2 simply says the imperishable and immortal *brahman* is to be known, while II. 2. 8 states that the wise see the blissful immortal shine. The most important, and ambiguous, *Muṇḍaka* passages linking immortality and liberation (while living) by knowledge are III. 2. 6 and 9. Verse 6 states that Vedanta-knowing ascetics are immortal and liberated at the end of time among the *brahma*-worlds. Verse 9 also combines the idea of knowing *brahman* with "crossing over" (sorrow and evil) to immortality. (These texts will be looked at more closely later in this chapter.)

Other *Upaniṣads* also have passages that say that after knowing *brahman* one "goes to" (*gam*) immortality. *Kaṭha* VI. 8 states that when knowing the pure partless *puruṣa*, one is liberated and goes to immortality, and *ChU* II. 23. 1 holds that one established in *brahman* goes to immortality.

If one understands "go" in these passages to be figurative, then the texts are saying that when one knows *brahman*, one becomes immortal—indicating immortality is a state reached here rather than in a heaven reached after death.

This very view can be seen in the largest number of references to immortality in the *Upaniṣads*, which indicate that immortality arises from knowing, without any mention of "going." These passages lead us most directly to the Advaitic idea of liberation as a state of knowing *brahman* while living. The idea that one becomes immortal by knowing *ātman* or *brahman* appears as early as the *Bṛhadāraṇyaka*. In the Yājñavalkya-Maitreyī dialogues (II. 4. 2–3 and IV. 5. 3–6), one is said to become immortal by knowing the self. *BāU* IV. 4. 14 states that those who know (*ātman/brahman*) become immortal, and others go to sorrow.[11] *BāU* IV. 4. 17 holds that knowing immortal *brahman*, one is immortal. Other *Upaniṣads* make similar claims. *Kena* II. 4 states that one gains immortality by *vidyā* (of *brahman*). *Īśa* 11 says that the knower of *vidyā* and *avidyā* together gains immortality by *vidyā*. According to *Kaṭha* IV. 1–2, the wise one, desiring immortality, turned inward and saw the self; knowing immortality, the wise seek what is stable (the self). Finally, there are the important *BāU* IV. 4. 7 and *Kaṭha* VI. 14–5 passages explicitly stating that when desires cease, the mortal becomes immortal, and one attains *brahman* here (more on these soon). Before expanding on this text, let us return to passages that link "knowing" and "going" but do not mention immortality.

These linkages are made in a number of *ChU* passages that suggest that after knowing *brahman* (here), one can roam heavenly realms. *ChU* VII. 25. 2 states that one who knows the self is all this (world) has the delight and bliss of the self, and can roam all the worlds (*loka*). *ChU* VIII. 1. 6 claims that those who depart here not knowing the self do not move freely among the worlds, but those who depart knowing the self do move freely in all worlds.[12]

It remains unsaid whether the Self-knower keeps or drops the physical body before moving among other worlds. In the same way, few *Upaniṣadic* texts explicitly state the *brahman*-knower is fully liberated (or immortal) while here—though this is certainly a possible reading. For example, *BāU* I. 4. 10 claims that gods awakened to "I am *brahman*" become *brahman*—as do *ṛṣis* (such as Vāmadeva) and men (*manuṣya*), and *BāU* III. 5. 1 states that *brahman* is the self of all, and a Brahmin who knows the self (beyond illusion, old age, and death) goes beyond desires for sons, wealth, or the world. According to *BāU* III. 9. 28. 7, *brahman*, which is knowledge and bliss, is the final goal, and the knower of it is not born again. This could suggest, but does not say, that the knower may overcome ignorance while here in this birth.

Three Key Upaniṣadic *References to Liberation While Living*

We now turn to the relatively few *Upaniṣadic* passages that explicitly speak of attaining or becoming *brahman* here. These texts are, of course, central to the development of the conception of living liberation in later Advaita. The first of these passages is *BāU* IV. 4. 6–7 (and 22–3).[13] *BāU* IV. 4. 3–4 state that the self throws off this body and takes rebirth in a new one (which it creates); verse 5 claims that as one acts and desires (in earlier births), so does one become: good by good actions, evil by evil actions. *BāU* IV. 4. 6 then holds that one with *karma*-bearing desires must return to this world to perform action, but one who is free from desire, or who has satisfied the desire for the self, gains identity with *brahman*. Then one's vital breath (*prāṇa*), that is, transmigrating self, does not pass away (*utkram*) and thus one no longer suffers rebirth. This verse closes: "Being *brahman* indeed, one goes to (or merges with) *brahman*" (*brahmaiva san brahmāpyeti*).[14] This passage suggests both "knowing" and "going," that is, it seems to indicate that when one *is brahman* (by desirelessness and knowledge), one *goes to brahman* (a state or place).[15] *BāU* IV. 4. 7 then indicates that being *brahman* (by freedom from desire) is the essential, transformative aspect: "When all desires fixed in the heart are released, then a mortal becomes immortal, (and) one attains *brahman* here."[16] The *brahman*-being is immortal while the body remains, but this body is now to him like a sloughed off snake skin is to the snake. This bodiless, immortal being is indeed *brahman* (*ayam aśarīro'mṛtaḥ prāṇo brahmaiva*). This passage contains an idea absolutely central to *jīvanmukti*: one who exists, but is already dead to desire, can be said to be "bodiless" while embodied.[17] These verses put a particular emphasis on desirelessness: becoming desireless brings immortality, bodilessness, and being *brahman* itself.

This passage continues with another clear linking of "knowing" and "going:" *BāU* IV. 4. 8–10 state that wise *brahman*-knowers, being freed (*vimukta*), go to a heavenly realm (*svarga loka*) by the ancient path. While the *brahman*-knower goes by this bright path, the ignorant proceed into darkness. However, later verses continue to make evident that one can gain knowledge of the self while alive, and such knowledge is the highest goal. According to *BāU* IV. 4. 14, we can know this (self) while here (*iha*), but if we lack self-knowledge, our ignorance is great destruction: knowers become immortal, all others go to sorrow. *BāU* IV. 4. 22–3 state that after knowing the eternal and limitless self, all desires (such as those for sons and wealth) cease, and all karmic activity is overcome. The serene and self-controlled *brahman*-knower is now free from any taint of evil and can wander freely in the world.[18] Thus, *BāU* IV. 4 contains a particularly clear example of passages that use the terminology of going *from* embodiment and suffering *to* a higher, "immortal"

reference the footnote dealing with escatological states in the Ringstone of Jonah in Caner Deglis translation.

A question that arises is that of the soul (nafs), what exactly "knows" or is "liberated" must be the soul (alam al-malakūt). This higher soul must be worth something if liberation is sought for it from the lower soul.

Continued thought from previous page - This means the higher Self is sanctioned by Brahman/Atman, that it isn't simply evaporated in the Absolute upon death. (the duality is only really ever resolved by the interconnectedness of all grades of reality)

state (or place), while at the same time indicating that knowledge of *brahman* (linked with desirelessness) is the central element of liberation and that one can truly be liberated even while living (and not just after going to a heavenly world).[19] It is worth briefly mentioning here a similar mixing of "knowing" and "going" (while adding that purification by renunciation is a crucial first step) found in *Muṇḍaka* III. 2. 5–6. Verse 5 states that having attained *brahman*, seers (*ṛṣi*) are desireless, serene, full of knowledge, and yoked to the self, so they enter the all (*sarva*). As mentioned earlier, verse 6 claims that when purified by renunciation, Vedānta-knowing ascetics (*yati*) are immortal and liberated (*parimuc*) at the end of time among the *brahma*-worlds.

The second crucial early *Upaniṣadic* text is *ChU* VI. 14. 2, which contains the idea that the embodied self is "blindfolded" by ignorance and can find its way home (to liberating *brahman*-knowledge) only with the help of a teacher.[20] This passage is part of the famous instruction to Śvetaketu about his true nature as *ātman/brahman (tat tvam asi:* you are that), a nature that is omnipresent but unseen (the prior verses refer to a seed's invisible essence generating a tree and unperceived salt pervading water). *ChU* VI. 14. 1 tells of a blindfolded man who desires directions after being abandoned. In verse 2, the man is said to find his way by someone removing the blindfold and directing him home. The text claims that in just this way an ignorant ("blindfolded") person here (i.e., embodied in *saṃsāra*) who "gains direction" from a teacher (*ācārya*) comes to know, "I will remain here just as long as I am not released (*vimuc*), then I will attain (release[?])."[21]

This *śruti* text, which can be read in a number of ways, is central to the Advaitic concept of *jīvanmukti*, for it raises an issue that will continue to bedevil much later Advaitins: What is the relationship between embodiment and full, final liberation? Put another way, if, although liberated, one remains here still in a body (inevitably tied to desire and suffering), is one even more liberated (or immortal) after death?[22] The precise meaning of the last part of this passage is uncertain in part because exactly what one is released from or what one then attains is unstated. "Release" and "attainment" can indicate both "knowing" and "going," and the text leaves their referents unspecified. The passage may simply suggest that one remains embodied here until released from ignorance, and then one immediately attains the final (bodiless) end—immortality and/or identity with *brahman*. Thus, release from ignorance ("knowing") brings simultaneous release from the body ("going"). Alternatively, it can suggest that although a Self-knower, one still remains until released from a body, and only then does one attain final liberation. In this reading, the knower, since still embodied, has not yet attained the highest goal (perfect *brahman* identity), so one liberated (by knowledge) while living becomes "more" liberated at death (meaning no full knowing until after going). A related, but not identical, interpretation is to suggest that the knower remains embodied here having attained *brahman* (which is, by definition, liberation) but not the final end (heaven or immortality), that is, full knowing can precede going. In this case, one remains not due to any lack of perfected knowledge, but due merely to the workings of a remnant of *karma* that causes the body to continue for a short time. We shall see that this is the preferred answer in later Advaita.

Finally, we can look at a group of related passages in the *Kaṭha* and *Muṇḍaka Upaniṣads* that are the most suggestive of living liberation in all the early *Upaniṣads*. These passages (some of which refer back to *BāU* IV. 4. 7)[23] seem to indicate clearly the idea of liberation while living by knowledge of *brahman*, yet still contain imagery of freedom from embodiment bringing immortality (eternal life). The aforementioned *Muṇḍaka* III. 2. 6 illustrates this point; it states that Vedanta knowing ascetics, purified by *saṃnyāsa,* at their final end are immortal among *brahma*-worlds and all liberated (*parimuc*). *Kaṭha* VI. 4 seems to claim that if one knows (*brahman*) here before the body ceases, one is liberated; otherwise there is (re)embodiment among created worlds (*sarga loka*).

Yet perhaps the clearest statement of living liberation in all the "major" *Upaniṣads*, integrating language of immortality with attaining *brahman* here, lies in *Kaṭha* VI. 14–5. *Katha* VI. 14 quotes from *BāU* IV. 4. 7: "When all desires fixed in the heart are released, then a mortal becomes immortal (and) here attains *brahman*." *Katha* VI. 15 introduces the graphic, physical image of cutting knots in the heart to gain freedom; it says, "When all the knots in the heart are cut here, then a mortal becomes immortal—such is the teaching."[24] *Muṇḍaka* II. 1. 10, while echoing this, makes the central role of knowledge clearer: "One who knows this (*brahman*), hidden in the heart (*guha*), cuts the knots of ignorance here"*(etad yo veda nihitaṃ guhāyām so'vidyāgranthiṃ vikiratīha*). Finally, *Muṇḍaka* III. 2. 9 ties together a number of earlier ideas by claiming, "One who knows that supreme *brahman* becomes *brahman* itself, no one in his family lacks *brahman*-knowing; (the knower) crosses over sorrow and evil, (and) freed from knots in the heart, becomes immortal."[25] Again, we see knowing *brahman* (Advaitic liberation) mixed with body-based language (knots in the heart), and "crossing over" to immortality through freedom from knots/desires. We also see the close connection between knowing and becoming or attaining (i.e., "going to") *brahman*.

The early *Upaniṣads* go no further in developing the idea of liberation while living. The notion of liberation or immortality does seem increasingly to shift from a "going" to a blissful heaven after death to a desireless "knowing" of *ātman/brahman*. Yet while most passages focus on *brahman*-knowledge, none is completely free of the spatially oriented language of "going to" or "attaining" liberation. As *ChU* VI. 14. 2 makes especially evident, we also cannot find any clear statement about whether one must leave the body for full liberation or whether the liberated being will take rebirth to assist others (such as by teaching). Finally, nowhere is there a formal distinction made between living (*jīvan*) and bodiless (*videha*) *mukti*. These issues will appear repeatedly in later Advaita. Still, it is not difficult to understand why Śaṅkara and other later Advaitins used these *Upaniṣadic* passages as proof texts for their views on *jīvanmukti*.

Jīvanmukti *and the* Brahmasūtras

Bādarāyaṇa's *Brahmasūtras* (*BS*) are a group of brief aphorisms intended, in part by systematizing *Upaniṣadic* ideas, to illuminate the nature of reality (which is *brahman*), the ways to know it, and the fruits of that knowledge; the text takes into account both remarks by other early Vedantic thinkers and those of members of other schools of thought. Bādarāyaṇa's ideas are interesting in their own right, but have become even more important (and contested) because of the commentaries that Śaṅkara, Rāmānuja, and other Vedantins wrote on the *sūtras*. Since certain aphorisms in the *Brahmasūtras* have been interpreted as supporting the notion of *jīvanmukti*, we may pause briefly to consider them. The meaning of the relevant *sūtras*, when looked at in isolation, is not by any means clear. To the degree one can understand them independently of commentary, one seems to find that the realm of liberation (*brahma-loka*) is reached only after death.[26] Even the most likely references to the idea of *jīvanmukti* are quite ambiguous and opaque without a number of parenthetical additions. The extent of interpolation needed is exemplified by *BS* III. 4. 51; it speaks of living liberation if it is read to say "(liberation arises) even in this realm/life (*api aihika*), if there is no obstruction (*pratibandha*) in the subject discussed (i.e., liberation) due to seeing that (according to scripture)."[27] *BS* III. 4. 52 adds, "thus there is no rule concerning the fruit of liberation (i.e., that it occurs only after death) due to ascertaining that state (i.e., *jīvanmukti*)."[28]

BS IV. 1. 13ff. can also be read a number of ways, one being an argument for the continuity of a special form of *karma* after liberation. *Sūtra* 13 can be read to claim "when that (*brahman*) is realized, there is destruction of and disconnection (*aśleṣa*) from all earlier and later evil acts (*agha*)." *BS* IV. 1. 14 then adds "so also with the other (i.e., good acts), there is no connection (with *karma*) when (the body) falls."[29] For one favoring *jīvanmukti*, IV. 1. 15 then introduces a crucial distinction in types of *karma*: "But only those effects which have not commenced acting (*anārabdha kārya*) (are destroyed) due to the limit (*avadhi*, i.e., death) of that."[30] This of course suggests the notion central to later Advaita of a special (limited in duration) *karma*, called currently manifesting (*prārabdha*) *karma,* which allows for liberation while still embodied. Following this, *BS* IV. 1. 19 concludes that "finishing off the other two (currently manifesting good and evil *karma*) by experiencing (*bhoga*), one attains (*sampad*) (*brahman*)."[31] Of course, one could read the above *sūtras* very differently, perhaps as referring to sacrificial ritual (IV. 1. 16 even refers to the *agnihotra*), for most of the key words are left implicit.

BS III. 3. 32 supports *jīvanmukti* if it is read to say that (bodily) existence (*avasthiti*) (continues even after liberation) for those with a commission (*adhikāra*) as long as the commission exists.[32] *BS* IV. 2–4 focus on the nature of the self being released, the paths it goes on, and the realms it goes to. Nowhere here is *jīvanmukti* clearly asserted. *BS* IV. 4. 15–17 seem to claim that the self can enter and animate various bodies, while *sūtra* 22 states that there is no return (*anāvṛtti*)—but of what and to what is uncertain. Thus, while the *sūtras* may refer to *jīvanmukti*, they also may be far from such a notion. Again, we will revisit these texts when we look at Śaṅkara, his followers, and, for a differing view, Rāmānuja.

Gauḍapāda and Living Liberation

While considering possible early influences on later Advaitic conceptions of *jīvanmukti*, it is appropriate to look at a figure named Gauḍapāda who, according to tradition, authored a group of stanzas (*kārikā*) that ostensibly comment and elaborate upon the *Māṇḍūkya Upaniṣad.* Gauḍapāda is often held to be the teacher of Śaṅkara's teacher, and his *kārikās* (*GK*), the first writing of the Advaita school. Our examination can be brief, for Gauḍapāda never directly addresses living liberation, or uses the term *jīvanmukti*. However, he does have a number of references to a knower or advanced *yogin;* these verses implicitly suggest the existence of a being who is liberated while living. We shall look at two passages in particular, beginning with the end of the second chapter (*prakaraṇa*).[33] Although *GK* II. 32 says that there is neither seeker of liberation (*mumukṣu*) or liberated being (*mukta*), II. 34–38 speak of the (living) knower or sage. There are references to truth-knowers (*tattva-vid*) (II. 34), sages (*muni*) free from anger, fear, and passion (II. 35), the knower who has realized nonduality (II. 36), the homeless ascetic (*yati*) who does as he pleases (II. 37), and one who, having seen reality (*tattva*) inside and out, enjoys it and becomes it (II. 38).[34] All of these apparently liberated beings are of course found here while living.

The third chapter closes by describing the *yoga* of no-touch (*asparśa*) and alludes to a state of perfect mental control while living. *GK* III. 32 states that by realizing the truth of the self (*ātma-satya*), one goes to "mindlessness" (*amanastā*). The mind of the wise is controlled (*nigṛhīta*) and without fluctuation (*nirvikalpa*), unlike in sleep (III. 34). Now one achieves fearless all-knowing *brahman* (III. 35). In serene and unmoving *samādhi*, no thought arises or is grasped, and knowledge is established in the self (III. 37–38). While this *yoga* of no touch is hard for all *yogins* to realize, their awakening, peace, and cessation of sorrow depend on this mental control (III. 39–40). The following verses continue to urge controlling distractions and desires, and keeping the mind detached, tranquil, and in equilibrium. When the mind (*citta*) is neither dissolved (in sleep) nor distracted, it remains motionless and imageless, and then attains *brahman* (III. 46),[35] self-established, serene, unborn, and all-knowing (III. 47). These verses use predominantly yogic language, yet speak of the mind attaining *brahman* here, implicitly acknowledging the possibility of liberation while living.[36] While these ideas are suggestive of *jīvanmukti*, Gauḍapāda's particular terminology here is not influential in later Advaita, and he is rarely mentioned by later writers in the *jīvanmukti* context.

The Bhagavad-Gītā *and Jīvanmukti*

The *Bhagavad-Gītā*, on the other hand, is clearly important for later Advaitins, particularly those whom I will call "Yogic Advaitins," such as the authors of the *Yogavāsiṣṭha* and the *Jīvanmuktiviveka*. As is well-known, the *Gītā* describes a variety of *yogas*, and the liberated being here is generally seen as a master *yogin*, not an Advaitic *jīvanmukta*. Even when nondual knowledge is praised, one reaches such knowledge by a yogic path. Still, the status of the text made an Advaita commentary necessary, probably by Śaṅkara himself, and other, later, Advaitins refer to the *Gītā* for scriptural support on occasion. The most important description of a liberated being for our purposes (in part because of the significant role it plays in the *Jīvanmuktiviveka*) is that of the one with firm wisdom, the *sthita-prajña*, found in *Gītā* II. 54 ff.[37]

The one with firm wisdom abandons all desires and is satisfied with the Self (55), is neither distressed by sorrow nor longing for joy, is without anger, fear, or passion (56), is all ways unattached, and neither desires or hates when obtaining good or evil (57). Such detachment and renunciation of desires are shared goals of both Advaitins and followers of *yoga*. The next verses focus more on liberation through (yogic) pacification of mind and senses, however. The *sthita-prajña* withdraws senses from their objects (58) and restrains them, sitting yoked and intent on Krishna; one whose senses are controlled is established in wisdom (61). The roiling senses carry away the mind (60) and dwelling on sense objects causes attachment, desire, anger, delusion, and finally utter destruction (62–63). However, when one is self-controlled, all sorrows cease and one attains serenity and wisdom (64–65). The focus on sense control and yogic restraint (*saṃyama*) continues to the chapter's conclusion. Detachment, serenity, and renunciation of desire are compatible with Advaitic *jīvanmukti*, but the *Gītā* is clearly describing the master *yogin*, not the liberated being of Advaita.

Similar descriptions are found in later chapters. *Gītā* IV. 19–23 describe a sage who acts without desire or attachment, is satisfied with whatever is obtained, and is equipoised in success or failure, with a mind established in knowledge (*jñāna*). *Jñāna* is a central term in mainstream Advaita, where it means immediate realization of *ātman/brahman* identity. *Gītā* IV. 24 ff. describe a form of sacrifice that brings one to *brahman*, and verse 34 states "by (devotees') submission, questioning, and service, knowers (*jñānin*) seeing the truth will teach you their knowledge,"[38] and verse 37 claims that the fire of knowledge turns all *karma* to ashes.[39] All this could be consistent with Advaita, suggesting that the sage/knower above is a *jīvanmukta*, but verses 38–39 point to the necessity of *yoga*. According to 38, purifying knowledge is eventually seen in the self by perfecting *yoga*, and verse 39 asserts that one focused on knowledge *with* controlled senses obtains knowledge and soon reaches the highest peace (*parāṃ śāntim*).[40]

Gītā V. 23–24 make clear that the model of living liberation is the well-disciplined *yogin*. According to *Gītā* V. 23, the one who is able here, before liberation from the body, to withstand the agitation (*vega*) rising from anger and desire—is disciplined (*yukta*) and happy.[41] He has inner happiness, joy, and radiance; this *yogin* becomes *brahman* and reaches *brahma-nirvāṇa* (24). The following verses describe the route to achieving *brahma-nirvāṇa*,[42] again emphasizing mastering the mind and emotions, and knowing the self. With such yogic control, one is liberated forever (28). Chapter VI continues to describe the detached master *yogin* at length. It concludes by addressing the question of what happens at the death of the not-quite-liberated being (the "almost *jīvanmukta*"). Krishna teaches that no meritorious effort in this (or any) birth is wasted (40–46). The *yogin* who fails to attain liberation in this life will be reborn with strong mental discipline in a wise or wealthy family, and will, after intense effort, go to the supreme goal. This *yogin* then surpasses renunciants *(tapasvin)*, those who perform ritual action, and even knowers (*jñānin*); mainstream Advaita would of course not concur with this view. Still, this passage will resonate through the later strand of thought I call "Yogic Advaita."

The *Gītā* also provides other characterizations of living liberated beings that use terms quite similar to the master *yogin*, including descriptions of the devotee (*bhakta*) of the lord (which particularly emphasizes equanimity) (XII.

13.9), and the one beyond all qualities (*guṇātīta*), also stressing equipoise and detachment (XIV. 22–26).[43] The *Jīvanmuktiviveka* will expand on many of the aforementioned passages, an indication both of the importance of the *Gītā* and of the *JMV's* concern to integrate perspectives of both *yoga* and Advaita. On the other hand, the *Gītā*'s extensive descriptions of the apparently liberated while living *yogin* are not central to the later mainstream Advaitic conception of *jīvanmukti*. To expand on this point, let us now turn to the founder of mainstream Advaita, Śaṅkara.

A Note on Mukti *in the* Upaniṣads

References to derivatives of the verb "*muc*" are surprisingly rare in the early *Upaniṣads*. They appear mostly in the *Bṛhadāraṇyaka* and *Kaṭha*, and many of the usages that exist do not suggest Advaitic liberation. *BāU* I. 5. 17 says a son frees his father from all faults, and *BāU* III.1. 3–5 describe how a sacrificer frees himself from death, day and night, and the waxing and waning lunar fortnights, respectively. Verse 6 says the sacrificer ascends to *svarga loka* by Brahmin, mind, and moon, which is *mukti* and extreme *(ati) mukti*. In *BāU* IV. 2. 1, Yājñavalkya begins to tell Janaka where he will go when liberated (*vimukta*), and in IV. 3. 14, Janaka asks for further instruction about liberation. *BāU* IV. 3. 36 states that a person frees (*pramuc*) himself from his limbs as a fruit frees itself from a stalk (when ripe). These passages generally suggest liberation entails going to a new place or condition.

In *Kaṭha* I. 11, Yama says he will free (*pramuc*) Śvetaketu from the face (*mukha*) of death and III. 15 holds that this freeing comes from knowing the self. *Kaṭha* V. 1 claims that by ruling oneself, having been freed (*vimukta*), one is freed (perhaps following *BāU* IV. 4. 6) and V. 4 asks what remains when the self is released (*vimuc*) from the body (the answer is *ātman/brahman*). *Kaṭha* VI. 8 states that one knowing the supreme person (*puruṣa*) is liberated (*muc*) and goes to immortality. *Muṇḍaka* III. 2. 8 claims the knower reaches the supreme *puruṣa* when freed (*vimuc*) from name and form. These passages emphasize that knowing brings liberation more than do those of the *BāU*. (Incidentally, the later theistic *Śvetāśvatara* I. 8 claims that by knowing the lord, one is liberated from all bonds, and VI. 16 says the lord rules *saṃsāra* and *mokṣa*.).

Forms of *muc* appear in the important (and related) *BāU* IV. 4. 7–8, *Kaṭha* VI. 14, and *Muṇḍaka* III. 2. 9 texts (which speak of releasing desires or knots in the heart), discussed at some length in the body of the chapter, as are the usages in *ChU* VI. 14. 2 (see page 24). While all of these passages are certainly significant, the relative rarity of *Upaniṣadic* usages is surprising, given how often Indian thought is claimed to be focused upon liberation.

TWO

Knowing Brahman *While Embodied: Śaṅkara on* Jīvanmukti

Śaṅkara, the great architect of Advaita, repeatedly addresses the nature of liberation in general and often focuses specifically on whether liberation is possible while embodied.[1] While Śaṅkara only once uses the term *jīvanmukta*[2] and never directly describes the state or person, he certainly holds to the possibility of liberation while living. While later Advaitins take the discussion of *jīvanmukti* much further, Śaṅkara, as we see so often in Advaita, sets many of the parameters for considering this subject.[3] One can see clearly here that Śaṅkara did not think of himself as an innovative and a solitary "philosopher," but as a part of the Vedantic tradition; his views are based on and led by insights from the authoritative sacred *Upaniṣadic* texts. In the following, I will utilize those writings generally agreed to be by Śaṅkara. The *Brahmasūtra* (*BS*) *bhāṣya* will be the most important source for his views, although he also addresses relevant issues in the *Bṛhadāraṇyaka* (*BāU*), *Chāndogya* (*ChU*), *Kaṭha, and Muṇḍaka Upaniṣad* commentaries.

In the context of living liberation, Śaṅkara seems most concerned with exploring why and how long the body continues after liberation, which raises issues about the relationships between liberation and embodiment, knowledge and action, and kinds of *karma* (with their fruits). Issues concerning the role of the teacher, and the goals of heaven and immortality also appear. (For some related comments on Śaṅkara and *Yoga,* see the note at the end of the chapter.)

Briefly, Śaṅkara argues that liberation arises from knowledge of *brahman/ātman* identity; it does not come from, and is not the same as, the fall of the body,[4] or even becoming immortal in heaven. The highest knowledge is that you are the flawless and self-luminous self, not a body/mind entity; in fact, belief in the body's reality causes (re)embodiment, and ending identification of body and self brings liberation. Since one achieves knowledge while embodied, one can (actually, must) become liberated while living, as implicitly seen in *brahman*-established teachers. Clearly then, liberation does not contradict bodily existence (although cessation of ignorance will eventually bring cessation of embodiment).

Further, knowledge of the self does not result from any embodied action (including meditation or achieving godlike powers), but some actions (like sacrifice) can assist in attaining *brahma-jñāna*. Finally, the body continues after knowledge due to the need to experience the fruits of currently manifesting actions, but there is a limit to the continuity of this body (and in a few exceptional cases, later bodies).

Some Definitions

Next we shall look at how Śaṅkara describes living liberation and the liberated being, but we must first consider how he defines certain terms crucial for understanding *jīvanmukti*: the self (*ātman*), liberation (*mukti/mokṣa*), and knowledge (*jñāna/vidyā*).[5] While these conceptions may vary slightly among later Advaitins (and we find some terminological vagueness and ambiguity in Śaṅkara himself), Śaṅkara's understanding will generally set conventional boundaries.

The self is, of course, identical with *brahman*, qualityless ultimate reality, which is the single, conscious, efficient, and substantial cause of the world. Śaṅkara defines the self most clearly in his commentary on *BS* I. 1. 4: it is the highest reality, eternally preeminent, all-pervasive like the sky, without any activity, eternally satisfied, partless, and naturally self-luminous.[6] It also is free from bondage and any limitation, such as those that condition waking, dream, or deep sleep (*BS* IV. 4. 2).[7] In his *BāU* IV. 3. 7 commentary, Śaṅkara describes at some length the *ātman*'s self-luminous and other-illuminating nature. This self-evident and ever-shining inner light makes all knowing, sensing, and acting possible. The self's light is confused with the intellect (*buddhi*) and body and sense activity (*kārya-karaṇa-vyavahāra*), which causes the superimposition (*adhyāsa*) of unreal on the real (and vice-versa), which manifests as the name and form apparent to us.[8]

Śaṅkara defines *mokṣa*[9] as the cessation of ignorance and bondage to transmigratory existence (*saṃsāra*). More positively, liberation is the nature of the self (*ātmasvabhāva*) like heat and light are the nature of fire (*BāU* IV. 4. 6). Being liberated is like regaining your natural well-being after an illness

(*BS* IV. 4. 2).[10] *Mokṣa* also is being the self of all (*BāU* III. 9. 28, *Taittirīya* III. 10. 5–6), which is the fruit of knowledge (*BS* III. 3. 32, III. 4. 52).[11] The self is *brahman,* so it is no surprise to find liberation is also called the eternally pure nature of *brahman* (*BS* I. I. 4), being *brahman* (*BS* III. 4. 52, *BāU* IV. 4. 6–7) or merging with *brahman* (as a handful of water thrown into a water tank merges there, *BāU* III. 9. 28). Śaṅkara elaborates in *BS* III. 4. 52 by saying that the liberated being's "state" (*avasthā*) is one form: simply *brahman* alone.[12] There are no degrees or distinctions in liberation, and it is not something to reach, as it is always attained.[13]

Liberation (being *brahman* and the self of all), while always attained, is not always recognized. This is related to the fact that there are two kinds of knowledge—that of the everyday world (*vyavahārika*) and the highest nondual knowing (*paramārthika*). Everyday "knowledge" is really ignorance (*avidyā*), false knowledge (*mithya-jñāna*) or superimposition (*adhyāsa*). From the *vyavahārika* level, we do not know who or what we are. That is, only after knowing the nonduality of self and *brahman* does one realize that *mukti* is always (i.e., already) attained (*siddha*).[14] The highest knowledge is unqualified (*nirguṇa*), and since it has no distinctions, its fruit (liberation) is also without difference.[15]

To introduce a point I will return to later, Śaṅkara's understanding of *mokṣa* and *jñāna*, while making plausible liberation while living, also make him uncomfortable with much *Upaniṣadic* language describing the highest end of existence. In *BāU* IV. 4. 6, for example, he describes liberation in terms different from the more traditional *Upaniṣadic* notion of the highest end as physical immortality in heaven (as discussed in chapter 1). Since liberation is the eternal nature of the self, *mokṣa* is not really another state, reached only after death.[16] Were this so, the *Upaniṣadic* teaching of the oneness of the self would be contradicted and *karma* (not *jñāna*) would cause liberation. Thus, any distinction between "*mukta*" and "*amukta*" is ultimately a delusion.[17]

Given these definitions, let us consider how Śaṅkara describes liberation while living. Living liberation arises from knowledge of the self while embodied. As he writes in *BS* III. 3. 32: Liberation is simultaneous with right insight (*saṃyag-darśana*, which is simultaneous with the destruction of ignorance), and is directly and indubitably experienced here,[18] as is said in *BāU* III. 4. 1 ("*brahman* is direct and immediate") and the famous "*tattvamasi*" of *ChU* VI. 8. 7: "you (*ātman*) *are* that (*brahman*)," not "you will become that after death." *BāU* IV. 4. 6 puts it succinctly: "Being *brahman,* one attains (or merges with) *brahman* (*brahmaiva san brahmapyeti*)," and Śaṅkara adds this occurs here and not when the body falls.

Śaṅkara addresses living liberation perhaps most clearly in his *Kaṭha Upanisad* commentary. In *Kaṭha* V. 1, he writes that one can be free from ignorance and desires here while living and as *śruti* says, "having been liberated (from *avidyā*), he is indeed liberated (*vimuc*)," that is, he will not take on another body. *Kaṭha* VI. 4 says that if one is able to awaken here before the body falls (*visrasa*) (one is liberated, and if not) one becomes embodied in the world of creatures. Śaṅkara adds that therefore one should reach for self-realization before dropping the body, for here alone (i.e., while living *and* liberated) one sees the self as clearly as in a mirror.

The Living Liberated Being

What is the character and conduct of the liberated yet still embodied being? Śaṅkara never directly addresses this question.[19] One should probably assume success in achieving the qualifications set out in *BS* I. 1. 1: discriminating eternal from noneternal things; detachment from enjoying fruits here or later; tranquility, self-control, and so on; and the desire for liberation. One should certainly have performed *śravana-manana-nididhyāsana*, that is, have heard, reflected on, and assimilated Vedic scriptures on *brahman*.

The closest Śaṅkara comes to full descriptions of the liberated being are probably the *Upadeśasāhasrī*'s characterizations of the student desirous of liberation and the teacher (*ācārya*), and the *Bhagavad-Gītā*'s account of the one with firm wisdom (*sthita-prajña*). *Upadeśasāhasrī* (*US*) Prose I. 2 characterizes one desirous of liberating knowledge as: indifferent to all noneternal things, without desire for son, wealth, or world, in the highest state of mendicancy (*paramahaṃsa parivrājya*), endowed with equanimity, self-control, compassion, and so on.[20] According to *US* I. 6, the teacher comprehends diverse points of view, shows concern for others, and is versed in scripture.[21] He also is detached from visible and invisible enjoyments, beyond all works and means, and knowing and established in *brahman*. He has faultless conduct, being free from flaws like selfishness, lying, jealousy, trickery, evildoing, and so on, and having the sole aim of helping others, wanting to employ his knowledge.

These passages are interesting for many reasons, but the most important one here is the relatively succinct way they summarize Śaṅkara's view of the attributes of the liberated being. Śaṅkara generally says more about *mukti* than about the conduct of a *mukta*, and his remarks about proper conduct cover conventional ethical ground. His emphases on desirelessness, knowledge of *brahman,* equanimity, and detachment from works and enjoyments are expected and consistent with much else he says about liberation while living. One also could anticipate the lack of emphasis on yogic practice, dharmic activity, or supernatural powers. What is more unusual is the repeated emphasis here on the *jīvanmukta*'s compassion (*dayā*) and concern (*anugraha*) for others. As we shall see, neither Śaṅkara nor later Advaitins mention such concern often in the context of living liberation (which strongly differentiates them from modern neo-Vedantins).

Śaṅkara also looks at the liberated being at some length in the section on the one with firm wisdom (*sthita-prajña*) in the *Bhagavad-Gītā* (II. 54 ff). When considering the Advaitic conception of *jīvanmukti*, one must treat the *Gītā* passages and comments with some caution, since, as suggested in the prior chapter, the views of the *Gītā* are rather different from those of Śaṅkara and the *Upaniṣadic* passages on which he most heavily relies. Still, the *Gītā's* one with firm wisdom is recognizably similar to the Advaitin *jīvanmukta,* and Śaṅkara describes the *sthita-prajña* in much the same language as the aforementioned *mukta*: a *brahman*-knower or one who has become *brahman.* His comments on *Gītā* II. 55 are typical: gaining the highest insight (discriminating self and not self), this being is indifferent to all and enjoys the self.

As pointed out earlier, the *Gītā* says that the *sthita-prajña* abandons all desires, is without feelings (fear, anger, pleasure, etc.), is beyond like or dislike, and withdraws his senses from objects like a tortoise into a shell. As his senses and desires are controlled, he is detached and serene. In his commentary on this section, Śaṅkara repeatedly uses the term *saṃnyāsin* (renouncer) to describe the *sthita-prajña/jñānin.*[22] The renouncer (like a knower) abandons sons, wealth, and worldly desires. He wanders, doing only enough to keep himself alive, without a desire even to remain in the body. Having renounced as a *brahmacārin*, he rests in *brahman* (II. 55, 71–72). While it is not our purpose here to elaborate on the relationship between *brahma-jñāna* and renunciation, Śaṅkara generally affirms that they go together.[23] He also generally focuses on attaining knowledge—renouncing the I notion, not action, is the highest end.

A *jīvanmukta*-like figure also appears in *Gītā* V. 23–28, which, we have seen, refers to the well-disciplined *yogin* who has become *brahman* and attained *brahma-nirvāṇa* here before liberation from the body. Śaṅkara calls this (non)condition *mokṣa*,[24] even while living. Such a *yogin* has a controlled mind, with desire and anger gone. Śaṅkara again calls this being a *saṃnyāsin*, one having gained immediate (*sadyo*) and permanent (*sadā*) *mukti*. Śaṅkara's only explicit usage of "*jīvanmukta*" (in any work) appears when the *Gītā* describes the *yogin* with peaceful mind, who, being *brahman,* gains the highest happiness (VI. 27). Śaṅkara simply adds that such a one is liberated while living.

Liberation and Embodiment

A number of passages assert that liberation-granting knowledge burns the seed of *karma* and ends all rebirth. These assertions lead us into the central problems with the Advaita view of *jīvanmukti*. As mentioned earlier, possibly the most important issue concerning *jīvanmukti*, to Śaṅkara and in later Advaita, is why and how long the body continues after liberating knowledge. As suggested in the Introduction, one can set up the problem this way: the body is a result of prior activity (*karma*), which is part of ignorance, and it is the locus of suffering and seeing duality seemingly inherent in being embodied. Knowledge of the self brings liberation, thus apparently ending ignorance and destroying *karma* (including the body). How then does embodiment continue?

Śaṅkara answers this question in a number of ways. One important response appears when he describes the relationship between liberation and embodiment in *BS* I. 1. 4, and involves an unusual understanding of bodilessness. He writes that liberation itself is called bodilessness (*aśarīratva*).[25] But bodilessness does not mean being without a physical body; being liberated/bodiless means being utterly detached, untouched by dharmic activity or likes and dislikes. One now knows one is the naturally and eternally bodiless self which does not perform actions and is different from the fruits of action (including the body).[26] Since the self is not connected with the body, one does not become bodiless merely by the fall of the body.[27] Thus, you are "bodiless" while embodied when you know the self is not the body.

Embodiedness, on the other hand, is caused by the false "knowledge" (*mithyajñāna*) that identifies the body with the self. The notion of an "I" (*ahaṃpratyaya*) with a body is a false imagining. As Śaṅkara says in *BS* I. 3. 2, thinking "I am the body" is *avidyā*, and results in desire for adoring the body, hatred for its injury, and fear of losing it. He concludes in *BS* I. 1. 4 that one who knows that embodiedness is a false notion is bodiless while living (like the *Gītā*'s *sthita-prajña*).[28] In *BāU* IV. 4. 7, *śruti* and Śaṅkara emphasize the knower's abandonment of the body, using the well-known image of the skin shed by a snake. The *mukta*'s body, known not to be the self, is to him like cast-off skin is to the snake. When one thinks that the body, tied to desire and action, is the self, one is embodied and mortal, but one is truly separate from the body and immortal.[29]

Incidentally, this should help clarify Śaṅkara's references to *mokṣa* as abandonment of or complete separation from the body (*BāU* IV. 4. 6–7, III. 9. 28. 7, etc.). *Mokṣa* is not physical death, but mental detachment from the body. As he says in *BāU* IV. 4. 6, one is only "as if" with a body—it appears but is known as unreal. In *BāU* III. 3. 1, he adds that *mokṣa* is the death of transmigratory death, gained by knowledge rather than physical termination. While the *mukta*'s body and senses remain until being permanently discarded at death, they have already "disappeared" for him.

Bodily Continuity after Liberation

The explanation Śaṅkara most often uses for the continuity of the body is slightly different. It focuses on *karma* and more readily accepts the everyday understanding of embodiment.[30] The starting point for this interpretation is the general rule that when *brahman* is known, all *karma* is destroyed. *Mukti* certainly exists for the knower *after* the body falls. Yet the body (which consists of *karma*) continues after *brahma-jñāna*. Why? Śaṅkara's basic position is that all one's *karma* must bear fruit before one's body drops, and only *karma* with uncommenced (*anārabdha*) fruits is immediately destroyed by knowledge (*BS* IV. 1. 14–5, 19, *BāU* I. 4. 7, 10).

This point bears elaboration, for Śaṅkara is trying to distinguish between different kinds of *karma* and fruits, distinctions that become clearer and more formalized in later Advaita. All types of *karma* and fruits but one are destroyed immediately by knowledge, including those actions accumulated (*saṃcita*) in prior lives or in this life before *jñāna* arises and those fruits that have not yet commenced (*apravṛtta, anāgata*) manifestation.[31] The one kind of *karma* that endures post-liberation is that bearing partially experienced fruits by which this present life is begun and continues.[32] Thus, uncommenced fruits of actions accumulated in prior births or done before or after knowledge in this birth (i.e., all actions except *prārabdha karma*) are destroyed by right knowledge.[33] When enjoyment of the karmic mass (*āśaya*) requiring seeing duality (i.e., *prārabdha karma*) ends, *kaivalya*[34] inevitably arises as the body falls (*BS* III. 3. 32, IV. 1. 19).

As indicated in the Introduction, the idea that when liberated most, but not all, kinds of *karma* are destroyed was seen, both in and outside of Advaita, as a problem. How can knowledge destroy some, but not all, *karma*? Further, if there is no *sadyo* (immediate) *mukti*, why would it happen eventually? If there is a little delay in liberation, why not a lot?

Śaṅkara addresses these questions at greatest length when commenting on *ChU* VI. 14. 2 and *BS* IV. 1. 15. Final release[35] (versus "mere" liberation) happens at time of body drop (*dehapāta*), not when knowledge rises. *Jñāna* is effective for liberation, but not for the immediate fall of the body. *ChU* VI. 14. 2 states that delay in final release is as long as one is not free (from the body). Śaṅkara interprets this to mean that the delay in attaining the self is as long as the blindfold of ignorance remains in the form of an embodied person enjoying the (already commenced) fruits of action. He then makes a crucial distinction between *knowing* (*jñā, vid*) *brahman* (or *sat*), which is immediate and happens in the body as opposed to *attaining* (*saṃpad*) *brahman/sat*, which is simultaneous with release from the body (but delayed as long as *prārabdha karma* manifests).

Śaṅkara then gives the opposing *pūrvapakśin*'s view: since there is *karma* accumulated in prior births with uncommenced fruits, another body will be taken on to enjoy these fruits when this body falls. (Śaṅkara would agree so far.) And one continues to perform enjoined or forbidden actions in the body, even after knowledge rises, which then causes another embodiment and more *karma*. (Śaṅkara parts ways here.) Thus knowledge is useless relative to fruit-bearing actions. On the other hand, if knowledge destroys action, then it would cause final release (i.e., attaining *sat*/body fall) immediately. If this were so, there could be no teacher and thus no knowledge giving liberation (since liberating knowledge comes from a teacher and a teacher needs a body).

Śaṅkara rejects this reasoning by holding to the aforementioned distinction between the commenced and uncommenced fruits of *karma*. The knower does not permanently bear fruits of uncommenced *karma* (causing an endless series of embodiments); delay in body fall is only for the time it takes to experience already manifesting fruits. The body is like an arrow once launched: its momentum both necessarily continues for a time and inevitably diminishes and ceases.[36] Further, all other *karma* possibly leading to another body, both those with uncommenced fruits and those done after knowledge, is burnt by knowledge (and expiation).[37] So since the *brahman*-knower does not reach final release while living, he must be enjoying the commenced fruits of action; once a knower, no *karma* remains. For him, delay is for only so long.

BāU I. 4. 7 and 10 put most strongly that, while knowledge halts almost all effects of ignorance, *prārabdha karma* is stronger than *jñāna*.[38] Past activity causing a body must bear fruit, so bodily and mental activity necessarily continues, even after obtaining right knowledge (like the loosed arrow must finish its flight).[39] The body, arising from actions caused by faults and perverse (*viparīta*) notions, bears fruits of a sort connected with these faults and notions, and until the body falls, it throws off the faults by enjoying their fruits.[40]

Prārabdha karma can even block *jñāna* from ever arising in this embodiment. Śaṅkara writes in *BS* III. 4. 51 that *vidyā* rises in this birth if the means of knowledge is not blocked specifically by actions now bearing fruit (i.e., *prārabdha karma*); however, even if it is so blocked now, knowledge will rise in a future birth. Actions may need to bear fruit first, but once these fruits are experienced, liberation is assured eventually. The example given is that of Vāmadeva, who became *brahman* in the womb (*Aitareya* II. 5–6) showing that practice in a prior birth leads to knowledge in a later one (for a baby certainly does not practice in a womb). Śaṅkara also refers to *Gītā* IV. 40, which says that no *yoga* or right action is wasted and *Gītā* VI. 43–45, which says one gains the highest goal over many births.[41]

In *BS* IV. 1. 15, Śaṅkara again argues (in accordance with the *ChU śruti*) that knowledge does not destroy all *karma* immediately, but he here adds that the rise of knowledge is actually aided by residual actions (*karmāśaya*) whose effects have commenced. (This raises the issue of the dependence of *jñāna* on *karma*, to be dealt with soon.) This assistance also requires a waiting period for the cessation of the "momentum" (*vega*) of worldly existence, as the momentum of an abandoned whirling potter's wheel only gradually ceases.

One might mention here (as numerous others have) that both the analogies of the potter's wheel (from *Saṃkhya kārikā* 67) and the aforementioned loosed arrow are problematic. Both wheel and arrow are real, but the body with *prārabdha karma* is part of *avidyā*. Unreal imaginings are not analogous to real things. On a related issue, B. N. K. Sharma has asked the sensible question of why *karma* not yet experienced at all wouldn't be even stronger (less "burnable") than partially experienced *prārabdha karma*.[42]

The *BS* IV. 1. 15 commentary also addresses the problem of why the body lasts even (but only) a little while after knowledge, briefly giving an answer much elaborated upon by later Advaitins. While realizing the self cuts off all *karma*, a certain ignorance (*mithyajñāna*) continues awhile, due to the power of mental impressions (*saṃskāra*),[43] like the impression of two moons persists in one with eye disease despite this person having the accurate knowledge that only one moon exists. We shall see that later Advaitins debate at length how this impression, a mere effect of ignorance, is related to its cause.

Finally, after giving *śruti* quotations and reasoning explaining why the body continues after knowledge, Śaṅkara here turns to a kind of argument he rarely uses, the experience of the sages themselves. He states that the *jñānin* knows he is *brahman* even while his embodiment continues. How can any other person contradict one convinced in his heart of hearts that he knows *brahman* while retaining a body? Śaṅkara again gives as an example the *Gītā*'s one with firm wisdom, the *sthita-prajña*.

Jīvanmukti *and Rebirth*

While the body continues for a time after knowledge, it generally is assumed that the *mukta* is now at the end of the body series. This being now remains only "as if" having a body—that is, it still appears, but it is no longer thought to be real. Thus, two points are true simultaneously: immediate "merging" in *brahman* is only figurative, and yet the continual succession of bodies does now end (*BāU* IV. 4. 6–7).[44]

In *BS* III. 4. 51, however, Śaṅkara suggests release might be delayed for an embodiment or two, as some texts indicate. But if *brahman*-knowers can take on another body, *why* would they? Is there some reason beyond the power of *prārabdha karma* ? Śaṅkara responds to this question in *BS* III. 3. 32, saying that certain liberated beings can take another body while an *adhikāra* (commission) exists due to the condition of the world. As we see the sun (in accordance with its role) continue to shine for 1,000 ages, then cease, or a *brahman*-knower continue until his already commenced *karma* ceases, so one even with highest knowledge, when commissioned by the Lord (to promulgate the Veda, etc.), continues to be embodied as long as the commission (*and prārabdha karma*) remains. One should note here that this conception of commission requiring re-embodiment is specifically addressed by Bādarāyaṇa's *sūtra*. While Śaṅkara grants the idea here, he mentions it nowhere else (and adds that *prārabdha karma* must remain), which suggests that he is mostly responding to the demand of *śruti*.[45] Śaṅkara continues by saying that *brahman*-knowers move freely from one body to another to accomplish their commissions, while their residual actions (*karmāśaya*) bear fruit once and for all in due course.[46]

Śaṅkara then addresses a question arising from this point: Can some new *karma* arise and produce yet further embodiments after currently manifesting residual *karma* (in *this* round of bodies) is consumed? If so, some *karma* with unburnt seed (versus only *karma* already manifesting) would remain after knowledge, and thus knowledge would not inevitably cause liberation. Śaṅkara says this cannot be, as it is well-known from scripture (*Muṇḍaka* II. 2. 8, *ChU* VII. 26. 2) that knowledge completely burns the seed of *karma*. *Mokṣa* follows *jñāna* without exception.[47] Note that Śaṅkara always returns to the point that *prārabdha karma*, and it alone, delays liberation.

We might here briefly consider if, upon taking rebirth, the liberated being has *yoga-aiśvarya*, or godlike powers. When discussing the possibility of the re-embodiment of *brahman*-knowers in *BS* III. 3. 32, Śaṅkara says that such powers allow one to enter and superintend several bodies successively or simultaneously. The sage's power to enter many bodies (as one lamp can light many others) is also mentioned in *BS* IV. 4. 15. However, Śaṅkara is careful to point out in III. 3. 32 that sages pursuing such powers later become detached from them after noticing the powers cease (i.e., are not eternal). Only then do they gain *ātma-jñāna* and attain final release (*kaivalya*).[48] *BS* IV. 4. 16 emphasizes that attaining the state with divine powers is different from knowing *ātman/brahman* identity; the former is from the maturing (*vipāka*) of meditation (*upāsana*) on *brahman* with qualities (*saguṇa*). The latter is higher, and it alone provides right insight, which removes the possibility of return (*BS* IV. 4. 22).

Teaching and Jīvanmukti

Another reason for holding to a delay in the body's fall after knowledge is to allow for the existence of teachers who are liberated. Put in its strongest form, not only does teaching aid in bringing liberation, unless liberated beings compassionately remain here to teach, we cannot know about liberation at all. The view that *jīvanmuktas* stay to share their realization appears repeatedly in later Advaita (especially in neo-Vedanta). Śaṅkara however does not put much emphasis on this argument, and the idea that teachers are necessary in fact contradicts the notion that *śruti* by itself can bring full knowledge. Still, one can find occasional references to realized beings teaching in Śaṅkara's works. In *Gītā* IV. 34, he suggests one approach a teacher (*ācārya*) and ask about the nature of bondage and liberation, knowledge and ignorance. Śaṅkara says the knower–teacher will respond, and only knowledge taught by those with right insight will bring peace. *Muṇḍaka* I. 2. 12, with Śaṅkara's concurrence, urges the Brahmin renouncer to go to a Veda-knowing and *brahman*-established teacher for the highest knowledge, and when explicating *Kaṭha* III. 8, Śaṅkara refers to a teacher who sees nonduality and who manifests the *ātman/brahman* identity that he teaches.

Following *ChU* VI. 14. 2, he states that a teacher leads one to liberation by taking off the blindfold of delusion (that "I am a body" by indicating one is really the self). Śaṅkara waxes eloquent here, saying that the blindfold includes desires for many objects and bonds to wife, child, and friend.[49] The *brahman*-established teacher, supremely compassionate and meritorious, then shows this ignorant person that the transmigratory path is flawed, saying, "You are not a transmigrating thing, so what of being a son or possessing the *dharma*? You are that (*brahman*)!" Freed by the teacher from the blindfold of delusion, the person becomes happy, arriving at (i.e., realizing) the self, as the formerly blindfolded man quickly arrives home.

The importance of the teacher is also made apparent in Śaṅkara's famous example (in *BāU* II. 1. 20) of the prince abandoned at birth in a forest and raised by (and as) a hunter, both being ignorant of his royal lineage. Similarly, the embodied being, not knowing it is the self, follows the path of embodiment and transmigration, thinking "I am a body/sense entity, etc." with threefold desires for son, wealth, and heaven. Both the young hunter and the embodied being need awakening to their true natures (being a prince and supreme *brahman*, respectively) by a compassionate teacher. When properly instructed, the prince becomes fixed on the idea of royalty and the student on the idea of *brahman*. Perhaps the best way to look at this matter is mentioned in the *BāU* II. 5. 15 commentary: It is only those who follow the path shown by *śruti and* teachers (*ācārya*) who pass beyond ignorance.[50]

The Relationship of Knowledge and Action in Jīvanmukti

It is well-known that Śaṅkara holds to utter nonconjunction between knowledge and karmic activity. Finite activity cannot bring about an infinite, eternal result (*BS* I. 1. 4). But, as we have seen, if knowledge immediately and completely destroys all *karma*, this would disallow living liberation. One remains in the body because *prārabdha karma* is stronger than knowledge. One can go further: achieving *jñāna* also is dependent on the mass of *karma* to create a body in which to gain liberation. Śaṅkara says this explicitly in a couple of places: You need a body for knowledge to arise (*BS* IV. 1. 15, *BāU* III. 9. 28). In fact, the world is the means for experiencing the fruits of one's *karma* (so liberation can then arise), and the purpose of going from body to body is to experience these fruits.[51]

While knowledge alone causes liberation, embodied action is necessary to gain liberation for two other reasons: One must not only experience fruits of actions here, but to reach liberation one also needs to perform certain actions in this body. These actions, which remove obstacles to *brahma-jñāna*, are duties tied to caste and life stage. While Śaṅkara does not emphasize the role of caste and life stage in this context, neither does he avoid addressing the issue. For example, in *BS* III. 4. 26, he responds to the apparent contradiction that knowledge is independent of action and yet dependent on performing certain duties at different life stages (*āśrama*). He says that knowledge, once arisen, attains its result (liberation) independently, but it depends on some actions (like sacrifice) to arise. In *sūtra* 27 comments, he continues that sacrifices (*yajña*), if performed without motive, become means (albeit "external," *bāhyatara*) for a *mumukṣu* to gain knowledge.

This point is made even clearer in *BS* IV. 1. 18, where he states that rites like the *agnihotra*, performed with or without meditations (*vidyās*) in this or a prior life, cause *brahman* realization if done with liberation as the aim. Activities like rites destroy sins acquired because the realization of *brahman* is blocked—that is, certain dharmic actions can remove other actions that block knowledge, so these actions indirectly cause liberation (which arises directly only from knowledge).[52] Rites and actions like hearing, reflection, and devotion are therefore proximate (*antaraṅga*) causes bringing the same result (i.e., liberation) as *brahmavidyā*. Thus, again, the need to perform certain actions and experience the fruits of other karmic activity leads to the conclusion that one gains liberation while (and only while) living.

Liberation and the Path to Heaven

Does the liberated being aim for and reach heaven? Śaṅkara discusses the path to heavenly worlds in many places (see especially *BS* IV). However, he also repeatedly says knowing *brahman* (the aim and achievement of the *jīvanmukta*) is very different from reaching heavenly realms (*loka, svarga*) of *Brahma*, the gods, or the fathers. Such realms are reached by correct dharmic action, and as seen earlier, Śaṅkara is generally committed to the nonconnection between knowledge and karmic activity (*jñāna-karma-asamuccaya*). The differing routes of actions leading to heaven and knowledge bringing liberation are addressed in *BāU* III. 5. 1, which mentions two types of mendicancy (*parivrājya*). One type uproots all desires and is a limb of *ātma-jñāna*; the other leads to the world of *Brahma*. This lower type of mendicancy is for the ignorant, for whom regulations like the sacred thread matter. The Self-knower, renouncing desires and abandoning all karmic activity, is the highest (*paramahaṃsa*) mendicant.[53]

Only the highest mendicant could be a *jīvanmukta,* since no knowledge but that of nondual *brahman* can bring liberation. All other *vidyā* is a "meditation" on *brahman* with qualities (*saguṇa*) that will bring fruits like heavenly life. As the *BS* III. 4. 52 commentary puts it, only the highest ("surpassing,"*utkṛṣṭa*) *vidyā* is "really" knowledge, other inferior (*nikṛṣṭa*) or qualified (*saguṇa*) *vidyās* arise from activities like meditation. Since different qualities exist, *saguṇa vidyās* and their results can be different. These various means to the highest knowledge might have degrees and be faster or slower, but the highest knowledge, and its fruit liberation, cannot have difference. Śaṅkara adds in *BS* I. 1. 12 that meditations (*vidyās*, *upasāna*) cause attainment only of lower *saguṇa brahman* (i.e., heaven) in stages (*kramamukti*) versus the immediate (i.e., living) liberation (*sadyomukti*) caused by *ātma-jñāna*. In *Kaṭha* VI. 15, he says that middling (*manda*) *brahman*-knowers practicing the lower *vidyās* are fit only for transmigration or the world of *Brahma*, and thus *śruti* describes another path (cutting the knots of the heart by self-realization) in order to praise the highest (*brahman*) *vidyā*. Finally, as said earlier, one can attain godlike powers (*aiśvarya*) from the maturing (*vipāka*) of meditations, but not liberation (*BS* IV. 4. 16).[54]

Śaṅkara's main aim here seems to be to define following the lower *vidyās* as a form of activity leading to heaven (vs. knowing nondual *brahman*), whereas the earlier, more approving, reference to performance of and even dependence on certain actions (especially sacrifice) is related to their ability to remove obstacles to gaining highest *brahman* (the goal of *jīvanmukti*).

Living Liberation and Immortality

The relationship of liberation and heaven is associated with the question of the immortality of the liberated being. As discussed earlier, Śaṅkara must deal with numerous *Upaniṣadic* references to gaining immortality when desires cease (*BāU* IV. 4. 7, *Kaṭha* VI. 14–15, *Muṇḍaka* III. 2. 6). Because he wants to move beyond the notion of heaven as the highest end, and to separate all karmic activity from the highest knowledge, Śaṅkara repeatedly deemphasizes the *Upaniṣadic* conception of physical imperishability and frames immortality as becoming one with *brahman*, that is, knowing rather than going. For example, when *BāU* IV. 4. 14 states "the ignorant suffer and are destroyed, and the knowers are immortal," Śaṅkara writes that we are immortal when we know *ātman* is *brahman* (but the ignorant get death unceasingly). Most significantly for us, this recasting of the notion of immortality allows for *living* liberation, since one gains knowledge (i.e., immortality) while embodied.

The clearest example of Śaṅkara's effort to adapt concrete or corporeal *Upaniṣadic* terminology to his aims occurs when *Kaṭha* VI. 14–15, *Muṇḍaka* II. 2. 8, and III. 2. 9 refer to cutting the knots in the heart,[55] which makes one immortal and one then gains *brahman* here.[56] Śaṅkara interprets "immortality" to mean the attainment of knowledge and mortality as action, desire, and ignorance, rather than as a bodily state. In *Kaṭha* VI. 15, Śaṅkara writes that the heart's knots, cut here even while living, are notions of ignorance (which are the roots of desire). These notions are indicated by statements like "I am this body," "this wealth is mine," or "I am happy/sad." The knots/notions (and the desires rooted in them) are destroyed by knowing *brahman/ātman* identity opposed to the aforementioned. This knowledge manifests in the thought, "I am indeed *brahman* and not a transmigrating being." Thus, Śaṅkara concludes, one becomes *brahman* even while living by the complete severing of the knots of ignorance through realizing the pervasive, distinctionless self.[57]

Muṇḍaka III. 2. 5 describes *brahman*-knowers established in the self as entering all (when the body drops, Śaṅkara adds). Muṇḍaka III. 2. 6 says such Vedanta-knowing ascetics, purified by *saṃnyāsa,* at their final end are immortal among *brahma*-worlds and all liberated. Śaṅkara once again takes the *Upaniṣadic* language indicating physical state change to mean becoming one with *brahman.* He says *saṃnyāsa* here means being established in *brahman* alone[58] and immortality is becoming *brahman* even while living. Pervasive and partless *brahman* has no spatial limits like going (to heaven), which is the object of *saṃsāra*. In addition to mentioning the immortality derived from cutting the knots in the heart, *Muṇḍaka* III. 2. 9 again says that whoever knows the supreme *brahman* becomes *brahman,* crossing over grief and evil (and Śaṅkara again adds "even while living").[59] Thus to Śaṅkara, going to heaven is a lower, *karma*-bound path and true immortality is knowing *brahman.*

To conclude, and to set the stage for the discussions of *jīvanmukti* in later Advaita, let us summarize Śaṅkara's main points concerning liberation while living. As said earlier, his characterization of a liberated being is only implicit, although the *Gītā*'s *sthita-prajña* or the *Upadeśasāhasrī*'s *ācārya* seem close approximations. Here and elsewhere Śaṅkara stresses that liberation arises from knowledge of nonduality or *brahman/ātman* identity.[60] A key part of this knowledge is the realization that the real you is not the body (including mind and senses) but the eternal, unchanging self. Śaṅkara rejects the notions that liberation is inherently related to the end of physical embodiment or gaining physical immortality in heaven. In fact, believing you are embodied causes embodiment. You become bodiless and immortal when you know only the self and not your body is immortal.

Further, liberation (and therefore bodilessness) is not a result of karmic activity. Actions like meditation bring lower, qualified *brahman* and attainment of heavenly worlds. Still, one needs a body, both to gain liberation and to perform certain actions that help clear the way for the highest knowledge. Once one gains liberation, all past uncommenced *karma* is burnt, and no new karmic activity will bind. Yet one still remains in the body awhile due to the only gradually but inevitably decreasing momentum of *karma* currently bearing fruit, and when these fruits finish manifestation, the body drops. The *jīvanmukta* might (but does not have to) teach and, in rare and extraordinary cases, a liberated being might return to perform a commission.[61] Thus, as Śaṅkara writes in *ChU* VI. 14. 2, one knows *brahman* in the body and attains it upon release from the body. Therefore, his views certainly support the idea that one gains liberation while (in fact *only* while) living.

A Note on Śaṅkara and Yoga

Many writers have explored Śaṅkara's views on *Yoga*; some, most prominently Paul Hacker, have held that Śaṅkara was a follower of *Yoga* before an Advaitin.[62] Śaṅkara does seem more hostile to *Sāṃkhya* philosophy (particularly the idea that *pradhāna* or *prakṛti* is the cause of the world) than yogic practice, but there is no question that for Śaṅkara (and, he claims, *śruti*), only knowledge (*jñāna*, *vidyā*) of *brahman* brings liberation. As Michael Comans has pointed out,[63] Śaṅkara rarely discusses the highest yogic state, *samādhi,* and nowhere says that unconditioned or *nirvikalpa samādhi* is the Advaitin's goal. In fact, Śaṅkara explicitly says in *BS* II. 1. 9 that one in *samādhi* (like one in sleep) does not see any difference (*vibhāga*), but since false knowledge (*mithyā-jñāna*) is not removed, duality will necessarily reappear.

Still, Śaṅkara holds that ritual activity and meditation (*upāsana*) can purify one,[64] and thus prepare the way for knowledge. He writes in the *BS* II. 3. 39 commentary that the aim (*prayojana*) of *samādhi* is ascertaining (*pratipatti*) the self known in the *Upaniṣads*, and in *BS* III. 4. 26–27 he says ritual action and self-control are means (*sādhana*) to knowledge, although knowledge's result (release) is dependent only on *vidyā*. Again, in *BS* II. 1.

3, he writes: While *Sāṃkhya* and *Yoga* are recognized as means to the highest human goal (*parama-puruṣārtha*), one cannot attain the highest end (*niḥśreyas*) by the *Yoga* path (*mārga*) or *Sāṃkhya* knowledge, but only by knowing the oneness of the self from the Veda.[65] Throughout his writings, Śaṅkara repeatedly makes the point that all activity, even yogic practice, remains part of a dualistic world of means and ends, act and result, in which one identifies oneself as the agent.[66]

Perhaps Śaṅkara's most significant statement about yogic practice appears in his commentary on *Bṛhadāraṇyaka Upaniṣad* I. 4. 7. He states that meditation (*upāsana*) does not generate a special knowledge (*viśiṣtha-vijñāna*) whose object is the self. He refers to the stream of recollection (*smṛti-saṃtati*) of Self-knowledge, which arises from hearing *śruti*, and asserts that this knowledge causes the cessation of all other notions. This thought stream is apparently unwavering, leading to a steady, clear mental flow. Further, the cessation of mental impressions (*citta-vṛtti-nirodha*) is not a means to liberation (*mokṣa-sādhana*). According to the *Upaniṣads,* knowing that the self is *brahman* is the only means to the highest human end (*puruṣārtha*). The sole means for ceasing mental impressions is through the stream of recollection of Self-knowledge, which arises from hearing *śruti*.[67] As mentioned earlier, Śaṅkara here goes on to add that *brahman* knowledge is not a goal to be reached by mental or physical action (i.e., meditation or ritual); the self is attained by removing the obstructions that veil one's original, eternal nature. Renunciation and detachment can here play a role by regulating the stream of recollection of Self-knowledge in the face of *prārabdha karma*.

Yoga is rarely mentioned in discussions of *jīvanmukti* among the later Advaita schoolmen; the most significant references are in Madhusūdana Sarasvatī's commentary on the *Gītā* (see chapter 8). I will briefly discuss *jīvanmukti* in *Sāṃkhya* and *Yoga* before the section on what I will call "Yogic Advaita," in which the importance of *yoga* increases in part because *yoga*-oriented Advaitins are more interested in syncretism than are Advaitin school men like Śaṅkara. In the neo-Vedanta of Swami Vivekananda, yogic practice actually becomes a necessity for liberation, as Anantanand Rambachan points out in *The Limits of Scripture.*[68] He shows that Vivekananda holds that scriptural reports from the *Upaniṣads* and other texts must be "directly experienced" or "personally verified" by one of the *yogas* (*jñāna, karma, bhakti*, or especially *rāja*).[69] Such experience-based language is remarkably rare in earlier Advaita. According to Vivekananda, Patañjali's teaching, called *rāja yoga,* culminates in *samādhi*, which is the authoritative source of *brahma-jñāna* (rather than the Veda, as is the case for Śaṅkara).[70] Still, most neo-Vedantic teachers and scholars discussed here do not say much about the role of *yoga* in *living* liberation.

THREE

Maṇḍana Miśra and Śaṅkara's Disciples on Jīvanmukti: *Sureśvara, Sarvajñātman, and Vimuktātman*

The task of looking at *jīvanmukti* in the Advaita tradition becomes a bit easier after Śaṅkara, as various thinkers address this topic directly and generally in one place. The next chapters will examine the development of this concept among the well-known "schoolmen" of mainstream or "classical" Advaita. None of Śaṅkara's immediate pupils deal with *jīvanmukti* at great length,[1] although Sureśvara's views are important and will be described shortly. Śaṅkara's contemporary and purported one-time adversary Maṇḍana Miśra does look closely at *jīvanmukti,* however, and his well-nuanced understanding introduces issues that remain oft discussed throughout later Advaita, particularly concerning the role of certain attenuated impressions of ignorance called *saṃskāras* in the continuance of the liberated being's body. After describing Maṇḍana's and Sureśvara's views, this chapter concludes with a consideration of Sureśvara's disciple Sarvajñātman and the slightly later Advaitin Vimuktātman,[2] who both argue that living liberation arises due to a trace or remnant of ignorance (*avidyā-leśa*). These writers also express concern with explaining the nature of the delay in body fall, referred to in *ChU* VI. 14. 2, and the role of the teacher in bringing liberation.

Maṇḍana Miśra on Jīvanmukti

Maṇḍana, probably an elder contemporary of Śaṅkara,[3] wrote an Advaitic (if not Śaṅkaran) work called *Brahma-siddhi* (*On Ascertaining Brahman*).[4]

This text attempts, as the title indicates, to establish clearly the nature of nondual *brahman*, and how it is obscured by ignorance. Maṇḍana sets a pattern for later Advaita by discussing *jīvanmukti* late in the text, and his analysis is remarkably sophisticated for such an early consideration of living liberation in Advaita. He addresses the questions of delay in the body's fall after *mukti*, how long the delay is, the nature and role of the impressions (*saṃskāra*) of *prārabdha karma*, and the relationship between *saṃskāras*, *karma*, and embodiment.

He begins by showing the apparent contrast between two views in *śruti*: *Muṇḍaka* II. 2. 8 says that when *brahman* is seen, the knots in the heart are cut, all doubts cease, and all *karma* (which of course includes the body) is destroyed—so *mukti* is immediate, with no waiting for eventual body fall. On the other hand, *ChU* VI. 14. 2 and *BS* IV. 1. 15 and 19 suggest that not all *karma* (i.e., the body) ceases immediately with *mukti*. Thus, all ripening of *karma* is not cut off when *avidyā* is cut off. The *mukta*'s body continues for a while (but only briefly), waiting for *prārabdha karma* to cease by enjoyment (*bhoga*).[5] Maṇḍana mentions the analogy of the launched arrow's momentum here. So far, Śaṅkara and Maṇḍana are in accord, but Maṇḍana goes on to clarify this issue further.

What then is the limit (*avadhi*) of the time delay between knowledge and body drop? Maṇḍana uses the word *kṣipra*, meaning "very brief or immediate." What then counts as "immediate?" Maṇḍana says that the limit is the time it takes to enjoy the currently manifesting *karma*, and he emphasizes the speed, rather than the delay, in reaching liberation. The *ChU* VI. 14. 2 text states, "there is a delay (in body fall) only as long as I am not free (from ignorance)."[6] Here "only as long as" (*tāvad eva*) conveys speediness not delay, like "having bathed and eaten, I will come" suggests haste and not delay. So, in Maṇḍana's analysis, the above "contradictory" *śrutis* (*ChU* VI. 14. 2 vs. *Muṇḍaka* II. 2. 8) really differ little.

Maṇḍana then introduces the objection of a *pūrvapakṣin* who (like Śaṅkara) takes the *Gītā*'s one with firm wisdom (*sthita-prajña*) to be a *jīvanmukta*. The objector suggests either no *living* liberated being exists because knowledge and body fall are simultaneous, or knowledge and body drop are not simultaneous (so *jīvanmukti* is possible) but one cannot specify a limit at which the body will fall, as there should be no waiting at all when all *karma* is destroyed. This latter possibility calls into question whether knowledge quickly and necessarily leads to liberation.

Maṇḍana responds first that the *sthita-prajña* is not a *siddha* ("accomplished being," or *jīvanmukta*) with completely pure knowing but is an advanced student (*sādhaka*), having almost attained release. While this seems opposed to Śaṅkara's view that there is only one kind of *mukti* and the *sthita-prajña* has it, one can take this to mean that, like Śaṅkara says in *ChU* VI.

14. 2, one can *know brahman* without quite yet *attaining brahman*. Thus, there can be *living* liberation, since he does not say that the (immediate and embodied) knowing of *brahman* is simultaneous with separation from the body (delayed as long as *prārabdha karma* manifest). However, to respond to the objector's second point, the delay in body fall does have a specified limit—the time it takes for one to enjoy the fruits of *prārabdha karma*. And Maṇḍana has tried to show above that the delay will not be long.

Maṇḍana then expands on the amount of time post-realization it will take the body to drop. He compares the delay to the time it takes one to stop the fear-based trembling arising from imagining a rope to be a snake.[7] Both trembling and embodiment continue awhile after the truth is realized, due to the continued ripening of mental impressions (*saṃskāra*) of ignorance (*avidyā*). This notion of *saṃskāra* continuity is critical in later Advaita (especially to Prakāśātman and Madhusūdana) to account for bodily continuity despite karmic cessation.[8] Maṇḍana and some later Advaitins hold that *saṃskāras*—"weak" remnants of action—cause the body to remain, although all *karma* is destroyed, often using as an example the image of the continuing but inevitably diminishing momentum of the potter's wheel after the potter's departure.[9]

Maṇḍana then fields a natural objection in the context of the extent of delay in bodily cessation: if *brahman* knowers continue to experience ignorance-based duality until the body falls, what guarantee is there that final liberation (*kaivalya*) will come even then? Maṇḍana responds that liberation will then arise since the *saṃskāra* is a fruit not equal to (i.e., weaker than) its root cause, *prārabdha karma* rising from *avidyā*. There are many examples of an effect (trembling, potter's wheel whirling, *saṃskāra*, body) remaining but gradually (*krameṇa*) and inevitably ceasing after the cause (fear, potter, *prārabdha karma*, ignorance) disappears.[10] Maṇḍana writes that although ignorance ceases after all karmic effects (commenced or uncommenced) cease, the self continues as if an embodied enjoyer, but without attachment (*abhiniveśa*), due to the *saṃskāras* arising from *prārabdha*. Maṇḍana is here going a step beyond Śaṅkara: The body continues due to *saṃskāras,* which remain even *after* commenced karmic fruits cease. *Saṃskāras* alone cause bodily continuity. Thus, Maṇḍana cannot be criticized for distinguishing out one form of *karma* different from all others, though he can be and was (especially by Vimuktātman) taken to task for saying the effect (*saṃskāra*) is not equal to its cause (*karma*).

The detached—but still embodied—enjoyer of the self is the *sthitaprajña* (apparently equivalent to a *jīvanmukta*). This desireless knower sees that objects and the forms of sorrow (or joy) are mere shadows (*chāya*), existing only due to the slight *saṃskāra* of ignorance. To this being, the body is like the shed skin of a snake (*BāU* IV. 4. 7). The ignorant, agitated by attachments, see mere shadows as real (like taking a clay form to be a real tiger). Maṇḍana then reiterates that the body will not long continue, since the *saṃskāra* of *prārabdha karma* continues only a short time before exhaustion, and this (briefly existing) state is called *jīvanmukti*.[11]

At this point, Maṇḍana addresses some objections that arise from the problematic relationship among *karma*, *saṃskāras*, and embodiment, focusing on differentiating the power of *karma* and *saṃskāras*. *Saṃskāras* do not continue once the body falls, since the body's continuity (post-liberation) itself is solely due to the *saṃskāras* themselves remaining from *karma*, which began this body. No uncommenced effects, old or new, will arise, so once the *saṃskāras* of *prārabdha karma* cease, the body falls and final release (*kaivalya*) is obtained by the knower.[12]

The objector then argues that *avidyā* remains in *saṃskāras* (thus showing that ignorance does not completely cease while embodied). Maṇḍana responds that no bondage or suffering whatever remains after knowledge because of the utter insignificance (*akiṃcitkāratva*) of the *saṃskāras*.[13] Their ripening does not touch the pure self. Interestingly, Maṇḍana focuses on the absence of suffering and bondage caused by ignorance, but he does not explicitly say all ignorance disappears.

He gives two analogies with the end of the self's bondage when only *saṃskāras* remain: After experiencing the reality of a picture (either knowing its mere "pictureness" or seeing "the thing itself" outside the picture), one does not desire mere forms appearing in the picture;[14] or when you know that a flaw in your appearance is from a defect (like a smudge) in a mirror, you are not upset. Similarly, the Self-knower does not suffer from impurities (*malinatva*) or enjoy attractiveness, since these are known as mere appearances, and not part of the self.[15] Thus, as while using a defective mirror, flaws still appear as if on the face but one is unmoved; in the same way, while *saṃskāras* manifest, the "flaw" of embodiment continues (i.e., appears "on" the self), but there is no suffering or bondage (i.e., ignorance).

The final objection returns to whether there is any difference between bodily continuity due to *karma* and that due, as Maṇḍana argues, merely to *saṃskāras* (the "insignificant" effect of *karma*). The objector points out that *BS* IV. 1. 19 says that one attains liberation (and the body ceases) by enjoyment of already commenced fruits of *karma* (not mere *saṃskāras*). Maṇḍana responds that for the ignorant who possess sorrow and joy, *karma* keeps ripening which (at least the ignorant believe) "touches" (*saṃspṛś*) the self (and thus there is bodily continuity), but for the wise the self remains untouched, having only the continued appearance of the body due to *saṃskāras*.[16] Further, there is no ripening of *karma* since one experiences no loving or hating of anything, as *Gītā* II. 57 indicates by stating that the *sthita-prajña* neither loves nor hates in good or ill fortune. So, for Maṇḍana, there is a difference between *karma*- and *saṃskāra*-based bodily continuity; only the latter is free from bondage. One then knows the body as mere appearance—ultimately the same as not being seen at all since the self remains untouched.

Although Maṇḍana attempts to clearly distinguish *saṃskāras* from *karma* (and *avidyā* itself), mental impressions are still a problem. As S. Suryanarayana Sastri points out,[17] no matter how "insignificant" *saṃskāras* are, either they *are avidyā* (and thus one is not liberated) or they are not (and thus the *sthita-prajña* is not a mere *sādhaka*). Sastri tries to resolve this problem by saying "[T]he *saṃskāra* of *avidyā* does exist, but for the body, not for the released spirit (p. xlvi)." But *avidyā* of *any* sort or intensity *never* exists for the ever-released spirit. There is no way to resolve the continuity of the ignorance-based body post-realization if knowledge is *completely* opposed to ignorance and all its derivatives.

To sum up Maṇḍana's views, some delay of body fall after liberation exists, but such delay is brief and due only to the need to experience *saṃskāras* of *prārabdha karma*. *Saṃskāras* are the effect of, and weaker than, their cause (*karma*)—but they still have the power to cause the body to continue for a short time (as trembling is an effect of fear but continues after fear ceases). The *mukta*, although *saṃskāra*-laden, still knows the body is a mere appearance, and all bondage is unreal.

Sureśvara on Jīvanmukti

Some have claimed that Sureśvara and Maṇḍana were one person, Maṇḍana the Mīmāṃsaka becoming Sureśvara the Advaitin after conversion by Śaṅkara in debate. I will not enter this controversy, but will simply concur with the generally prevailing view that they are different people (and that Maṇḍana precedes Sureśvara).[18] In the context of *jīvanmukti*, Sureśvara (unlike Maṇḍana) does not discuss *avidyā-saṃskāras* and stresses the difference between works (which include meditation, or *prasaṃkhyāna*) and knowledge. He also treats the *ChU śruti* a bit differently than does Maṇḍana.

On liberation while living, as with many other topics, Sureśvara largely follows Śaṅkara. In his summary of Advaita thought, called *Naiṣkarmyasiddhi* (*On Ascertaining the Actionless*),[19] Sureśvara (like Śaṅkara) says that once ignorance is removed by knowledge, no action remains to be done, and no desires remain.[20] However, verses IV. 60–61 indicate that the body continues for a time, since the effect of a delusion (the body) can continue awhile after the delusion itself (ignorance of *brahman*) ceases—like trembling continues awhile after fear (from mistaking a rope for a snake) ceases.[21] As an uprooted tree withers only gradually, so does the body of the knower wither as *prārabdha karma* manifests.

In his *Bṛhadāraṇyaka Upaniṣad Bhāṣya Vārtika* I. 4. 1528 ff.,[22] Sureśvara addresses in greater detail the problem of embodiment post-realization. He, like the earlier writers, argues that the body, although based on karmic activity, ignorance, and desire, remains after knowledge solely due to the manifestation of *prārabdha karma*'s fruits, and likens continued existence to the momentum of a launched arrow or whirling wheel. An opponent objects that knowing the self should destroy all *karma* (including commenced *karma*) and its fruits immediately. If any *karma* remains, *saṃsāric* action and attendant desires will cause continued activity and repeated rebirth; without cessation of action, liberation will not arise. The opponent also suggests that a mass of mental conceptions ("imaginations," *bhāvanā*) cannot be removed without regular, intense practice. Sureśvara replies in verses 1539–41 that *brahman* knowledge rises from understanding sacred texts, and with this knowledge, all desires cease and one attains final liberation. He refers here to *Muṇḍaka* III. 2. 9: If one knows *brahman,* one becomes *brahman,* and this being the case, how could one have any desire? Right knowledge destroys the intellect (*dhī*), the world, and all objects.

In verses 1546–54, Sureśvara addresses the problem of the delay mentioned in the *ChU* VI. 14. 2 text. After hearing various *śruti* and *smṛti* quotations stating that when knowledge arises, the body immediately falls and all *karma* is destroyed,[23] how can one hold to any delay, no matter how brief, in body fall? Sureśvara argues that the *Chāndogya* text is an *apavāda*—a special exception to a general rule. The delay here is only so that a teacher can guide the seeker blindfolded by ignorance "home"; the knower/teacher will delay (i.e., remain embodied) just as long as the veil of ignorance is not removed. Sureśvara is of course following reliable guides himself here—*śruti* and Śaṅkara.[24]

In *Naiṣkarmyasiddhi* IV. 62–64, Sureśvara also addresses the issue of how "free" the *mukta* is to go beyond dharmic regulations. Verse 62 asks, "If one awakened to the truth of nonduality would do as he pleases (*yatheṣṭācaraṇa*), what is the difference between truth-seers (*tattva-dṛś*) and dogs in eating what is impure?" He argues that the liberated being will not do whatever he pleases, despite being free from dharmic duties.[25] Doing whatever one wishes arises from ignorance and improper action, and thus could not be a result of dharmic activity. He points to the *Gītā*'s rejection of the idea that the desireless sage does as one wishes (IV. 19, XIV. 22), and continues by arguing that not even one desirous of liberation (much less a *jīvanmukta*) would do as he pleases.[26] It is reasonable to imagine that since it is a long, hard path to liberation, if one followed the *dharma* and did no evil on the way, it is absurd to argue that having reached the goal, one will do ill. Desirelessness and freedom do not lead to violating *dharma*.

Sarvajñātman on Jīvanmukti

We next turn to Sarvajñātman, by tradition one of Sureśvara's students (c. eighth-ninth century C.E.) and successor to Śaṅkara and Sureśvara at the Kanchi Kāmakoṭi Pīṭha. His major work, the *Saṃkṣepa-śārīraka* (*SS*),[27] is a verse summary of Śaṅkara's *Brahmasūtra-bhāṣya*, and follows Sureśvara's emphases on qualityless (*nirguṇa*) *brahman* and *śruti* as the key to gaining *brahma-jñāna*.

In the context of living liberation, Sarvajñātman shows allegiance, but not obsequious adherence, to Śaṅkara. He stresses the importance of *saṃnyāsa* as a preliminary to *mokṣa,* the difference between knowledge and karmic activity (and the futility of such activity to bring liberation), and the significance of experience in establishing the existence of the trace (*leśa*) of ignorance. He also makes interesting remarks about the imagining (*kḷrp*) of the teacher, the possibility of liberation in various classes and life stages, and the nature of the remnant of ignorance (*avidyā-leśa*).

Sarvajñātman considers living liberation at some length in two places: *SS* III. 346 ff. and IV. 38 ff. The former emphasizes that one gains knowledge in this life by a combination of following the right path (which includes sacrifice and renunciation) and right comprehension of *śruti*. Hearing, reflecting, and assimilating remove ignorance, which allows Upaniṣadic statements like *tat tvam asi* to directly reveal the nondual self. Thus, while the two work together, only the latter (the *mahāvākyas*) gives final release or *apavarga* (346–9).

SS III. 349–50 (following Śaṅkara's *BS* III. 4. 51 commentary) introduce the idea that liberating knowledge may come only in a future birth due to an impeding cause (i.e., *prārabdha karma*), but also add that following the proper path (*sādhana*) in an earlier life will bring on *vidyā* later. He gives the example of Vāmadeva, who gained knowledge in the womb due to practice in a prior life.[28]

Sarvajñātman then discusses proximate versus direct means to liberation. Means such as Vedic ritual action, devotion, and especially self-control (*śamadamādi*) remove defects and purify one, thus are helpers (*upakāraka*) to knowing the self. In fact, a supreme ascetic's (*paramahaṃsa*) experience of the highest truth is based on these means. However, while these actions purify, they do not end all bondage. One must abandon all notion of "agentness" (*kartṛtva*) for the full ripening of knowledge (351–8).

It is crucial to renounce on the way to self-knowledge.[29] Only the pure *paramahaṃsa* ascetic attains liberation here (after employing means mentioned in *śruti* and *smṛti* like hearing, reflecting on, and assimilating the truth). For those in other classes (*varṇa*) and life stages (*āśrama*), knowledge only ripens in a later birth (359–60). *Śūdras* are excluded here due to *śāstric* prohibition against their hearing *śruti.*[30] However, Sarvajñātman goes on to say knowledge *will* ripen at some point if one practices right means like hearing, and so on, and *saṃnyāsa* in prior births, and may even ripen when one is not a renouncer (perhaps accounting for non-Brahmin or otherwise "impure" *jīvanmuktas*). He then quotes as support the *Muṇḍaka* III. 2. 6 passage, which says Vedanta knowing ascetics, purified by *saṃnyāsa,* at the end of time are immortal among *brahma*-worlds and all liberated (361–2),[31] and he ends this chapter by praising renouncing, and ceasing all activity (which brings *mokṣa*) (363–6).

The other passage in which living liberation is prominent focuses on the presence of *jīvanmukti,* whether liberation is immediate or if a remnant or trace (*leśa*) of ignorance remains post-*mukti.* The section (*SS* IV. 4 ff.) begins by stating that only knowing the self (not ritual action) removes ignorance,[32] and that knowing the self only removes ignorance (not a body). Verses 8–11 and 49–50 argue against any connection (*samuccaya*) between *jñāna* and *karma* in bringing liberation, and 29–37 state that *mukti*, the fruit of knowledge, is eternal, and is unlike, and unreachable by, karmic activity.[33] He is here clearly Śaṅkara's (and Sureśvara's) pupil.

SS IV. 38–39 seem to hold to *sadyomukti,* in which knowledge destroys all ignorance completely and immediately. If this is so, as we have seen, the body should drop at once, so there could be no *"jīvan" mukti*. Sarvajñātman seems to argue here that the scriptural notions of "*jīvanmukti*" or the "*jīvanmukta*" are to be utilized and are meaningful, but only as long as these things are imagined (*kḷp*) to exist. *SS* II. 225–7 help make sense of this statement. The ignorance-bound mind (*citta*) is said to imagine (or "create") everything, including the *guru* who teaches the truth of nonduality. This presents the problem of something unreal revealing the real. The teacher, though like all else merely imagined, still can bring full knowledge, since he is imagined to be omniscient. As long as imagined to be real, the teacher is useful and actually leads the ignorant to *vidyā.*[34]

Thus, from the *sadyomukti* perspective, Sarvajñātman accepts *jīvanmukti* as a useful imagining. The next verses state that *jīvanmukti* also makes sense if one accepts the existence of a remnant of ignorance (*avidyā-leśa*) even after knowledge. As was the case with *avidyā-saṃskāras* for Maṇḍana, Sarvajñātman says the remnant or trace of ignorance, which causes the liberated being to act, is not the same as ignorance itself—otherwise final liberation (*vimukti*) would not be attainable (IV. 40–41).

Sarvajñātman then introduces an important new element to this position by emphasizing "experience" (*pratīti*) as evidence for a trace of ignorance

(IV. 42–44). He states that according to Śaṅkara (particularly in *BS bhāṣya* IV. 1. 15),[35] *avidyā-leśa*[36] is the experience (or "persisting knowledge") of ignorance. Sarvajñātman reiterates that we know by experience (*pratīti, svānubhūti*) that *jīvanmukti* and the "shadow of duality" brought about by the *avidyā* trace coexist. Awakening (*bodha*) does destroy the delusion obstructing knowledge of nonduality, but one should still accept the trace of this delusion (the *avidyā-leśa*), since one has the experience (*pratyakṣa*) of duality continuing even after knowledge.[37]

SS IV. 45–46 indicate, in terminology reminiscent of Śaṅkara, that the *jīvanmukta* continues to experience the fruits of commenced *karma* born from the *avidyā* remnant, and when the fruits are completely consumed, one goes to *kaivalya* (final liberation). Sarvajñātman quotes *Śvetāśvatara* I. 10, which closes by saying, "again, at the end, all *māyā* ceases" from repeated attention to, meditation on, and knowledge of, reality.[38] This text seems to be meant to support both the ideas that a remnant of ignorance continues until "the end" (i.e., until the body falls) and that continual practice of meditation, and so on, is central.

Sarvajñātman then turns to the difference between the path of the gods and *brahma-vidyā*, and how karmic activity is only an indirect means to liberation. Section IV concludes by emphasizing that the student should come to know the nondual self as real and the world and body as unreal from the teachings of the *guru* and *śruti*. The teacher is given gratitude and praise here, and throughout the *SS*, but is not explicitly called a *jīvanmukta*.[39] We also saw Sarvajñātman say that the teacher, while omniscient, is also imaginary. While a teacher and a *jīvanmukta* might be identical, it is significant that traditional Advaitins do not automatically argue this (and that modern neo-Vedantins do).[40]

So Sarvajñātman, in this and other contexts, is part of the Śaṅkara tradition, with particular emphases on the imaginary teacher, *saṃnyāsa* as the preliminary path to liberation, and the importance of experience in showing the existence of the *avidyā-leśa*. The discussion of the teacher and of the trace of ignorance continues with a slightly later Advaitin, Vimuktātman, and his text, the *Iṣṭasiddhi.*

Vimuktātman on Jīvanmukti

The *Iṣṭasiddhi* (*Ascertaining What is Desired*) of Vimuktātman (c. 850–1050?)[41] is primarily concerned with the nature of *māyā* and *avidyā* in Advaita; Vimuktātman argues that ignorance is not describable (*anirvacanīya*). He takes up *jīvanmukti* in the first chapter of the text,[42] and has clearly read Maṇḍana and Śaṇkara on this topic. Vimuktātman claims that liberation does come while living, that a teacher is necessary for gaining knowledge, that the trace of ignorance causes this body to continue but brings no further births, and that (contra Maṇḍana) the body remains due to the ignorance trace itself, not mere *saṃskāras*.

Vimuktātman begins the relevant section (I. 9) by stating that a remnant of ignorance (*ajñāna-śeṣa*) exists, since we see bodily continuity for a knower,[43] but this remnant will not cause the knower another birth. Further, if the knower's body fell simultaneously with *vidyā,* then the *ChU* VI. 14. 2 *śruti* about a delay would be wrong. The delay is in the moment of the knower's body fall and not in realization, since the latter cannot occur after the body drops. So, death is not simultaneous with knowledge.[44]

The existence of the living liberated teacher also points to knowledge while embodied. The idea that one gains knowledge from a teacher (*ācārya*) who is both living and released is quite significant to Vimuktātman. He says, following *Gītā* IV. 34, that the wise teacher realizes the truth and truth-knowers (*tattva-darśin*) alone teach the highest knowledge. If the body fell immediately after knowledge, there could be no teacher, thus no reaching *vidyā,* thus no liberation—which again shows that the knower's body remains for awhile.[45] Incidentally, Vimuktātman, the Advaitin who emphasizes the teacher's role the most, never suggests the teacher is imagined.

Vimuktātman introduces a new focus for why the body continues post-realization. A knower must, he says, enjoy (*bhuj*) the fruits of all *prārabdha karma* before death, *including* those actions that cause knowledge to arise. Even the karmic activity that brings knowledge itself can bear fruit only in the body, which arises from and is the locus of enjoyment of fruits begun by other *karma.* Thus, there can be no conflict between gaining *vidyā* and living out the effects of *prārabdha karma.* And while the embodied knower remains until all karmic activity is enjoyed, the actions that have knowledge as their fruit will not bring on another body.[46]

Further, *karma* having knowledge as its fruit "protects" the knower's body for awhile, that is, until he meets a teacher (without whom one cannot gain *vidyā*), as the *ChU śruti* says.[47] Again, Vimuktātman stresses that one needs an *ācārya*; actions alone cannot bring knowledge. He concludes that by accepting that the knower's body continues for a time, one accepts the trace of ignorance.

Vimuktātman then begins to look at the nature of *avidyā-saṃskāras*. A *pūrvapakṣin* (holding to Maṇḍana's view) argues that the knower's body can continue due to *saṃskāras* without *avidyā* itself, like fear and trembling, caused by the snake illusion, continue even after the "snake" is realized to be a rope. Vimuktātman responds that there are no *saṃskāras* without *avidyā.*

While both *saṃskāras* and *avidyā* (their locus) form the body (i.e., essential nature) of ignorance, fear and trembling are not the body of the "snake"/rope, so the latter is not a good example. The snake illusion based on the rope never rises again in the absence of *avidyā,* and when the "snake" rises it is based on *avidyā* itself, not a *saṃskāra.*[48] Thus the knower's body remains due to *avidyā-leśa* (based on *prārabdha karma*), not a "mere" *saṃskāra.*[49]

Still, no ignorance that would produce another birth remains in the knower—the fire of Self-knowledge has burnt off *avidyā,* the seed of *saṃsāra*/rebirth. No evidence exists for the knower's rebirth,[50] nor for the knower enjoying the fruits of any not yet commenced body (vs. the enjoyment of the fruits that produced this body). Thus, the knower attains liberation at the rise of *jñāna*, but a trace (seemingly similar to Maṇḍana's *saṃskāra*) remains just strong enough to cause the (body-sustaining) appearance of fruits from *prārabdha karma.* When the body falls, these "enjoyments" cease forever; the ignorance trace cannot cause transmigration to another body.

Vimuktātman proceeds to quote various scriptural texts, which support *jīvanmukti* with the *avidyā-leśa* and reject additional rebirths. The *śrutis* are familiar from Śaṅkara, "having been liberated [from *avidyā*], one is liberated (released)" (*Kaṭha* V. 1), "being *brahman*, one merges with *brahman* (*BāU* IV. 4. 6), "the knower becomes immortal here" (*Kaṭha* VI. 14–5), and so on. Further, the *Gītā* passages refering to the *sthita-prajña* (II. 54 ff.) and the one beyond all qualities (*guṇātīta*, XIV. 20 ff.) also are said to illustrate living liberation. Finally, *BS* IV. 1. 15 and 19 (presumably including Śaṅkara's *bhāṣya* thereon)[51] are mentioned as favoring liberation while living.

He closes this section by arguing that these sacred texts do not conflict with those referring to going (*gati*) to liberation by the path of light, and so on. Such *śrutis* refer to the lower, or *kārya*, *brahman*. The highest *brahman* has no going or place to go—it is one, pervasive, and always attained.[52] For all of the aforementioned reasons, *jīvanmukti* is established.

To sum up, in affirming living liberation, Vimuktātman focuses on the importance of the teacher, the role of *karma* that has knowledge as its fruit, and the nature of the ignorance trace. He distinguishes between *avidyā* (which causes *saṃsāra*/rebirth), *avidyā-leśa* (based on *prārabdha karma* causing the present body to continue a short time), and *avidyā-saṃskāras* (powerless alone to sustain the body—opposing Maṇḍana's view). Like earlier Advaitins, he also takes care to give scriptural support to his position. Next we shall leap a number of centuries and consider living liberation in later scholastic Advaita.

FOUR

Jīvanmukti *in Later Scholastic Advaita: Prakāśātman, Citsukha, Madhusūdana Sarasvatī, Prakāśānanda, Sadānanda, and Dharmarāja*

In this chapter, we shall look at later scholastic Advaitins, beginning with Prakāśātman, a thirteenth-century proponent of the Vivaraṇa school in Advaita, who wrote an influential commentary on Padmapāda's *Pañcapādikā,* called *Pañcapādikā-vivaraṇa* (*PPV*, *Explanation of the Five Verses*).[1] Prakāśātman is a central figure in the elaboration of Advaita epistemology, and like his fellow dialectician Citsukha, engages in anti-*Nyāyā* polemics. Prakāśātman's work contains much more on living liberation than does Padmapāda's, and Prakāśātman has clearly read earlier writers on this topic, particularly Sureśvara. I also will consider here a commentary on the *Pañcapādikā-vivaraṇa* called the *Vivaraṇa-prameya-saṃgraha* (*VPS*, *Summary of What Is to be Known in the Explanation*), authored by Bhāratītīrtha-Vidyāraṇya in the fourteenth century.[2] The *VPS* usually follows the *PPV* quite closely, but unlike the *PPV*, mentions *jīvanmukti* explicitly a number of times. This pattern of subcommentaries elucidating and clarifying commentaries on other textual exegeses is typical of the scholastic Advaita tradition.

The *Pañcapādikā-vivaraṇa* elaborates on basic issues concerning *jīvanmukti* in two places (pp. 105–6, 283–4). Prakāśātman focuses on bodily continuity after liberation. He considers how embodiment, seeing duality, and *karma* (their basis) can remain after *avidyā* is destroyed. Like earlier writers, he speaks of the special nature of *prārabdha karma*. He argues that the *mukta* does not perform rites and/or do whatever he pleases (last mentioned by Sureśvara). Finally, he claims that *avidyā* creates *saṃskāras*, that *saṃskāras* can produce the appearance of duality (due to their being a flaw of pure consciousness, or *caitanya*), and that both *saṃskāras* and ignorance are based on the self.

The two sections on living liberation appear in the form of a series of brief *pūrvapakṣin-siddhāntin* exchanges. The second passage (p. 283 ff.) takes us to the heart of Prakāśātman's concerns (which, we shall see, are often similar to Citsukha's), particularly the relation between *karma* and ignorance. The opponent begins by asking: If immediate (*aparokṣa*) knowledge ends false (*mithyā*) knowledge, whence comes (still) seeing duality, and how can seeing duality, caused by *karma*, continue after *karma* (an effect of *mithyā-jñāna*) ceases? Prakāśātman answers that seeing duality rises from another limitation different from *jñāna* (i.e., *prārabdha karma*), as mentioned in *ChU* VI. 14. 2. One imagines (*klṛp*)[3] that the body and senses remain for a little while since (*prārabdha*) *karma,* their cause, remains.

The previously discussed issue of the *samanvaya* (agreement in meaning) of *śruti* appears here. The opponent asks whether *śruti* really speaks with one voice about the destruction of all *karma*, to which Prakāśātman responds affirmatively, for imminent destruction is the implied meaning (*arthāpatti*) of even the *ChU* passage. As Sureśvara earlier suggested, the *ChU* text gives a specification (*viśeṣa*) of a general (*sāmānya*) rule: *Karma* is burnt by *jñāna*, with the specific exception of the continuity of *prārabdha karma*. The *VPS* adds that *Muṇḍaka* II. 2. 8 ("all *karma* are destroyed when *brahman* is seen") refers to uncommenced (*anārabdha*) *karma*, and that the *śrutis* are similar in that both refer to the removal of *karma*. While knowing the real (*tattva-jñāna*) removes ignorance, the basis of all *karma*, it does not touch already commenced *karma,* which is merely a fruit (*phala*) of ignorance.

The *pūrvapakṣin* seems unpersuaded by the *śruti* quotations and returns to his question: If immediate knowledge completely destroys ignorance, how can *karma* remain? Prakāśātman responds by focusing on the power of *prārabdha karma*. The appearance of duality is dependent on *prārabdha karma,* and *tattva-jñāna* does not have the ability to remove this appearance. Thus, *prārabdha karma* obstructs knowledge, though *jñāna* removes all other ignorance, desire, and action.

Still, Prakāśātman says there is no relationship between the *jīvanmukta*'s experience of *brahman/ātman* identity and seeing duality; the latter is caused by a flaw (*doṣa*) based on already commenced *karma*. Thus one in a body can have immediate knowledge (i.e., *jīvanmukti*), since *jñāna* arises after other *karma* (*saṃcita* and *āgamī*) different from *prārabdha* is destroyed. Put another way, direct (*aparokṣa*) seeing does not destroy all *karma*, so such insight is possible in a (*prārabdha*-formed) body as in the case of Vyāsa.

Prakāśātman then addresses how a liberated being acts in the world. First, even when seeing duality, he does not perform rites (*anuṣṭhāna*).[4] Ritual performances are based on rules (*niyama*) of time, place, eligibility, and so on. These (and other) actions, caused by *prārabdha karma*, gradually cease, since no specific time and place and so on rules remain for one knowing reality. This is reminiscent of Maṇḍana's comments on *ChU* VI. 14. 2, which assert that karmic activity continues but lessens over time. For Prakāśātman, activity ceases since for knowers ritual action has no goal.[5]

However, even if beyond *śāstric* regulation, knowers will not do whatever they please (*yatheṣṭācaraṇa*). Prakāśātman points out that knowers have no desire to obtain good or avoid evil.[6] Without the desire to accomplish any human goal (*puruṣārtha*) due to their direct experience of the self, any activity or wish to act ceases; all that remains is surpassing bliss in the self (of the *jīvanmukta*, adds Bhāratītīrtha).

Prakāśātman sums up here that the body remains due to the power of *prārabdha karma*, but after knowledge there is no chance of increase in non-manifesting (i.e., other than *prārabdha*) *karma* caused by ignorance, desire and others. Commenced *karma* causes only its own fruit. So the (embodied) truth-knower sees only the duality appearance caused by *prārabdha karma* (and both appearance and this *karma* will imminently cease).

The same issue of bodily continuity is addressed earlier,[7] focussing here on the nature of the *saṃskāras* remaining post-knowledge. (Incidently, at the end of the passage, Prakāśātman says the term "*saṃskāra*" also indicates the trace of ignorance (*avidyā-leśa*), thus collapsing a distinction important to Maṇḍana, Citsukha, and others.) Prakāśātman first introduces a useful distinction in types of knowledge. A *pūrvapakṣin* here argues (as have earlier ones) that *brahma-jñāna* should cause the immediate fall of the body and senses (since without ignorance [the cause], the body [the effect] cannot exist), yet activity in *saṃsāra* continues even after immediate knowledge. The opponent here points to (a purportedly inappropriate) plurality of knowledges: *tattva-jñāna* (which negates all ignorance) and more specific *vyatireka-jñāna*, which negates the reality of particular objects like a snake or body.

Prakāśātman (seconded at some length by the *VPS*) responds by affirming this distinction, but further argues that *tattva-jñāna* removes the root (*mūla*) *avidyā*, and not the (*vyatireka*) knowledge that negates the body's reality. Thus, bodily appearance continues due to the remaining *saṃskāra* (an effect of *avidyā*, like footprints remaining after the foot is gone). Put another way, one can come to know a specific "snake" is a rope without realizing the whole world is such a superimposition, and one can have the highest realization while still on occasion mistaking a specific rope for a snake.

The rest of this section looks more deeply into the nature of the *saṃskāra*, advancing beyond Maṇḍana's or others' understanding (and preparing the way for Madhusūdana Sarasvatī). Prakāśātman gives a number of reasons why ignorance and its effects (rather than action or knowledge) generate the *saṃskāra*. First, *saṃskāras* are the residue of ignorance, like the flower smell that remains in a pot after the flowers are removed. Second, a *saṃskāra* of everything remains in destruction (*pralaya*), so we can infer that there is a *saṃskāra* of ignorance in ignorance's destruction. Third, ignorance and its effects are illusory (*mithyā*, not "real") knowledge. Finally, *saṃskāras* arise from ignorance, since they are merely an appearance (*abhāsa*) of knowledge based on the witness consciousness (*sākṣi-caitanya*). The *VPS* adds that the witness consciousness abides eternally within *avidyā* (and thus reveals both knowledge and ignorance simultaneously).

The opponent then asks how a *saṃskāra* can produce the appearance of duality in immediate (i.e., present dualistic) experience.[8] Prakāśātman responds that it is possible because a *saṃskāra*, like *avidyā*, is a flaw (*doṣa*) based on pure consciousness (*caitanya*). The *VPS* adds that this is like a dust speck on the (pure seeing of the) eye. The *doṣa*, a flaw but still based on *caitanya*, is the cause of the illusory appearance (of *prapañca*) in immediate experience. Similarly, the dust speck is adventitious, but causes something to appear to the eye.

Finally, the *pūrvapakṣin* states that only ignorance, not the *saṃskāra,* is based on the self (*saṃskāras* are said to be based on *avidyā*). Prakāśātman retorts that both are based on the self, which is why *saṃskāras* can continue even without the presence of *avidyā*. The *VPS* agrees that pure consciousness is the locus of both, and adds that *saṃskāras* need no material cause, since such a cause is necessary only for existent things (not mere traces of ignorance). Prakāśātman concludes that for the aforementioned reasons, the continuity of *saṃskāras* does not refute (imminent) bodiless liberation. *Saṃskāra* cessation (and consequent body dropping) happens gradually but inevitably due to the remembrance (*anusaṃdhāna*) of knowledge of the real (*tattva-jñāna*). Bhāratītīrtha adds that after such knowledge, living liberation with a remnant of ignorance continues until *prārabdha karma* is destroyed.[9]

To sum up, Prakāśātman is concerned with giving a clear rationale for karmic and bodily continuity post-realization, with explaining the relationship of ignorance and *saṃskāras*, and with indicating the way a *jīvanmukta* acts in the world. Later Advaitins, particularly Madhusūdana Sarasvatī, will also take up these concerns.

Citsukha on Jīvanmukti

Citsukha (fl. thirteenth century) is another important Advaita thinker who follows Śrīharṣa's dialectical (and anti-*Nyāyā*) approach. He is best known as the author of *Tattvapradīpikā* (*Illumining the Real*),[10] (or *Citsukhī*) a comprehensive defense of Advaita doctrines;[11] *jīvanmukti* is discussed at the very end of the text. He focuses on the nature of the trace of ignorance (*avidyā-leśa*), introducing the notion of three forms (*ākāra*) of ignorance, as well as the power of (*prārabdha*) *karma* to cause bodily continuity post-*vidyā,* and the relation of *parokṣa* (indirect) and *aparokṣa* (immediate) knowledge (also mentioned in *Pañcadaśī* VI. 15). He has certainly read earlier Advaitins, especially Vimuktātman and Maṇḍana.

Citsukha's discussion of *jīvanmukti* is in the form of a long *pūrvapakṣa*, then response; I will break the passage into its component parts. The opponent first argues that if knowing the self removes ignorance, then the body (part of ignorance) would drop when knowledge rises. Even the trace of ignorance ceases when knowledge rises. *Karma* (including *prārabdha*, the cause of the body), the effect of ignorance, ceases when *avidyā* ceases. The opponent also holds that *śruti* (like *Muṇḍaka* II. 2. 8 and even *ChU* VI. 14. 2) points out that all *karma* without remainder (e.g., not excluding *prārabdha*) is destroyed by knowledge.

Citsukha's response to the issue of bodily continuity post-*vidyā* due to the trace of ignorance[12] is as follows: knowledge, he says, is obstructed by strong *prārabdha karma*. *Jīvan mukti* exists since when the *avidyā-leśa* continues, *karma* (like the body) born from it also persists, despite the rise of self-knowledge. Citsukha accounts for this persistance in a new and subtle way. While asserting ignorance is ultimately one, he distinguishes three forms (*ākāra*) of *avidyā*, following the *Nyāyā-sudhā* (by a Jñānottama claimed as teacher by Citsukha).[13]

The first form of ignorance causes the illusion that *prapañca* (phenomenal manifestation) is the highest truth, the second form produces the notion that things in empirical reality have practical utility (*arthakriyā*), and the third produces the notion that objective forms really appear in perception.[14] Each form ceases in a different way. The first (imagining duality as truly real) ceases by recognizing ("theoretically") the truth of nonduality; the second (imagining—for reasons of practical utility—that *māyā* is the basis of the world) ceases by the direct experience (*sākṣātkāra*) of reality. It seems that when these two forms of ignorance cease, the *jivanmukta* sees the world as unreal and has no attachments to it.[15]

However, the third form or trace of ignorance remains for the *jīvanmukta*, producing objects that seem actually to appear in perception.[16] This form may temporarily disappear in meditative enstasis (*samādhi*), but otherwise it continues, causing the appearance of the body and the world. This appearance, while known by the *jīvanmukta* as unreal, thus allows mediate or *parokṣa jñāna* despite having the highest knowledge, which answers another objection of the opponent.[17] This form ceases only after the fruits of *prārabdha karma* are enjoyed (and then the body falls). To close, Citsukha adds a *śruti* text (*BāU* II. 5. 19), which confirms that *māyā* takes manifold forms.[18]

Citsukha also rejects the argument that the trace of ignorance ceases when *tattva-jñāna* rises, repeating that knowledge is obstructed by strong already commenced *karma*. He makes the important distinction (following Vimuktātman),[19] between *karma* having knowledge as its object (*vidyārtha*) and *karma* having "enjoyment" as its object (*bhogārtha*). The former bears fruit in a body born from the latter. Put another way, *vidyārtha karma* is based on *bhogārtha karma*, which causes the body's rise (one cannot get knowledge without a body), so these two kinds of *karma* are not opposed. It appears that only *vidyārtha karma* (which accounts for *living* liberation) exists post-knowledge, and it neither creates a new body nor immediately destroys the existing body.

The opponent then makes a second argument, based on the *Gītā* IV. 34 passage about the wise (*jñānin*) who realize the truth (*tattva-darśin*) teaching the highest knowledge.[20] The question arises whether the *jñānin* has *parokṣa* (mediate) or *aparokṣa* (immediate) knowledge, an important distinction for Citsukha. The *pūrvapakṣin* holds that these embodied knowers have only mediate knowledge,[21] in part because one cannot have the highest *aparokṣa jñāna* "within" *parokṣa.*

Citsukha responds by affirming that both *śruti* and teaching aim for immediate knowledge, not lower mediate *jñāna.* This is seen in the expression of amazement which indicates highest knowledge as in the *śruti* text "when he understood [*tattvamasi*], he went 'Ha' " (*ChU* VI. 16. 3). Such an indication is not necessary for mere *parokṣa jñāna.* Nor in the *Gītā* passage describing the knowers' teaching is the knower (like Maṇḍana's mere *sādhaka*) doing repeated practice that produces merely mediate knowledge. *Darśana* indicates immediate insight, and it is an illusion that only mediate knowledge exists in the immediately known self. Further, since illusions appear in *parokṣa jñāna*, if it was the goal there would be the flaw of variability in the highest knowledge.

The opponent continues by examining the nature of the trace of ignorance (*avidyā-leśa*). He argues it is neither a portion of ignorance, since *avidyā* has no parts like a pot, nor another form (*ākāra*) of ignorance, since no form can remain when its substratum disappears. Maṇḍana's view is then proposed: duality appearance continues due to a *saṃskāra* alone, like fear and trembling continue even after the snake illusion ceases (or the body remains awhile like the unattended potter's wheel continues to spin for a time). This view is denied: a *saṃskāra,* effect of *avidyā*, ceases when ignorance ceases (as Vimuktātman writes in chapter 3). All duality is unreal, so how can a *saṃskāra* be real? And a false *saṃskāra* cannot have reality as basis. Finally, the self cannot be the basis of the *saṃskāra,* since the self has no connection with ignorance. Thus, neither the self nor the *saṃskāra* can be a real basis for duality. (The *pūrvapakṣin* here seems to be ruling out all of the alternatives for some mediation between *vidyā* and *avidyā*, including the *saṃskāra*. If all alternatives are impossible, so is *jīvanmukti.*)

Citsukha then adds another explanation for the continuity of *karma* post-realization, due to the *avidyā-leśa*, again focusing on the third form of ignorance. His argument comes in response to the objection that the *avidyā-leśa* and *karma* are mutually dependent, that is, each continues due to the existence of the other. Citsukha denies this, refering to the important *Śvetāśvatara* I. 10 text, "again (*bhūyas*) at the end, all *māyā* ceases."[22] He explains that while the two forms (*ākāra*) of *avidyā* (or *māyā*), mentioned earlier, cease immediately after *vidyā,* the third continues while one is alive. *Karma* continues simultaneously with ignorance because precisely *karma* itself (in commenced form) is the form of the *avidyā-leśa*. All *avidyā*, without remnant, ceases when the opposer of *vidyā* (the remnant specifically characterized by *karma* with commenced fruits) ceases. He concludes (in agreement with earlier Advaitins) that despite the general statements of *śruti,* that "all *karmas* cease" with knowledge, it is proper to say *karmas* other than *prārabdha* cease, and, as indicated by *ChU* VI. 14. 2 ("it remains for just so long"), there is the (temporary) abiding both of *prārabdha karma* and its effect (the body).

Finally, Citsukha rejects the *pūrvapakṣin*'s denial that the *sthita-prajña* or the *guṇātīta* references in the *Gītā* characterize living liberation. Following Maṇḍana, the opponent calls these the state (*avasthā*) of being a *sādhaka*, not a *jīvanmukta* (who is *siddha*). Citsukha argues that the *sthita-prajña* and the *guṇātīta* are not just *sādhakas*, since the *Gītā* says they have fully abandoned desires. Cessation of all desire is only proper for the direct experience (*sākṣātkāra*) of the highest self, that is, *jīvanmukti.* He quotes *Gītā* II. 59 ("desire [*rasa*] itself ceases when one has seen the highest") and *Kaṭha* VI. 14 ("when all desires fixed in the heart cease, then a mortal becomes immortal and attains *brahman* here"). Citsukha concludes therefore that *jīvanmukti* (not just advanced studenthood) is proclaimed in sacred texts and cannot be denied merely because of personal distaste.

Thus, with Citsukha (as with Prakāśātman), we see a well-developed tradition of discourse on the nature of *jīvanmukti* (following Maṇḍana, Śaṅkara, Vimuktātman, and others). He makes his own contributions, of course, especially his refinements on the forms of ignorance and types of *karma* in the *avidyā-leśa* and on *a/parokṣa jñāna.*

Madhusūdana Sarasvatī on Jīvanmukti

Madhusūdana Sarasvatī (sixteenth century), by general agreement one of the preeminent post-Śaṅkara Advaita thinkers, is a particularly interesting figure in later Advaita reflection on *jīvanmukti.* With living liberation (as many other topics), Madhusūdana clearly writes for different audiences in different texts, which shows his fascinating but problematic attempt to integrate devotion to Kṛṣṇa with traditional Advaitic views on nonduality and renunciation.[23] *Jīvanmukti* is discussed in the fourth chapter (on liberation) of his *magnum opus*, *Advaitasiddhi* (*Establishing Nonduality*),[24] and he expands on many of the points addressed by earlier Advaita schoolmen, particularly Citsukha and Prakāśātman.[25] His commentary on the *Bhagavad-Gītā*, the *Gūḍārthadīpikā* (*Illumining the Deepest Meaning*),[26] however, shows much more devotional and yogic influence, following the *Yogavāsiṣṭha* and the *Gītā* itself. For these reasons, I will discuss his perspective on *jīvanmukti* in the *Gūḍārthadīpikā* in the section on "Yogic Advaita."

In the *Advaitasiddhi,* Madhusūdana emphasizes the following points: the body continues due to the *avidyā* trace, that is, a *saṃskāra* (an effect of *prārabdha karma*) which arises from, but is not based on, ignorance. The trace of ignorance rises from one of *avidyā*'s powers—that of producing objects capable of immediate perception. *Jīvanmukti* exists while the *avidyā-leśa* state continues, then one reaches final liberation. Following Madhusūdana's arguments is particularly challenging, given the intricate web he weaves of *pūrvapakṣin* positions and counterpositions before introducing the *siddhāntin* view.[27]

Madhusūdana begins by stating that *jīvanmukti* is established primarily by the self-experience (*svānubhava*) of *jīvanmuktas* themselves. This statement, interesting in itself, is unfortunately an isolated remark; nothing more is said here about the experience of liberated beings. Madhusūdana continues with a standard definition of *jīvanmukti*: it is the appearance (*pratibhāsa*) of bodily continuity despite ignorance's cessation by knowledge of the truth *(tattva-jñāna)*.[28] Although *avidyā* is destroyed by *tattva-jñāna,* the body does not fall immediately.[29] It continues due to a *saṃskāra* (mental impression), like the potter's wheel continues spinning without a stick or like fear and trembling continue, although the illusion of the snake ceases.

Madhusūdana concurs with Prakāśātman that *saṃskāras* (traces of ignorance) arise from ignorance (and not from action and knowledge), as the smell ("trace") of a flower remains in a container after the flowers are thrown out. All destruction, including the destruction of knowledge, is pervaded by *saṃskāras*—except the destruction of *saṃskāras* themselves. Madhusūdana continues that *saṃskāras*, although an effect of ignorance, have the pure self, not ignorance, as their locus; thus they are like *avidyā* and do not depend on *avidyā.* He likens the *saṃskāra*-based bodily continuity post-*jñāna* to the slight remnant of cloth form remaining after the cloth is burnt. Effects of commenced *karma* like *saṃskāras* (and embodiment) do not continue due to the continuance of ignorance itself, since even a thing in destroyed (*vinaś*) condition (burnt cloth or liberated being) can be seen to continue without a material cause (cloth or body).

The opponent then grants that the burnt cloth or body of the *jīvanmukta* might last a few moments, but no longer. Madhusūdana argues that if you grant any continuity, the exact length of time a thing remains is pointless to consider. But he goes on to say that unlike a fast dissipating burnt cloth, the *jīvanmukta*'s body continues for a time (e.g., until death), because only at death is there the added assistance of the absence of any obstacle to the body dropping—that is, only then has *prārabdha karma* disappeared. Madhusūdana is concerned to indicate here that currently manifesting *karma,* and not knowledge, is responsible for the body's rise and fall. He says that the body does not cease due to any final increase in knowledge (which might indicate some difference in the knowledge of *jīvan-* and *videha-mukti*) but due to the help of the absence of any obstacle like *prārabdha karma.*

The opponent then says that unalloyed bliss should manifest in the *jīvanmukti* state, yet even after the truth is known, there is continuity of contradictory delusions, as in the case (mentioned by Śaṅkara in *BS bhāṣya* IV. 1. 15) of seeing two moons even after realizing only one is real. Madhusūdana counters that the two moons example does not fit the case of living liberation, since with the latter all flaws (*doṣa*) are removable by knowledge. The flaw (of embodiment) may not be removable as long as the obstacle of *prārabdha karma* exists, but eventually knowledge removes even this flaw. He here offers a *śruti* text saying that no flaw is eternal (e.g., what rises must cease).

Madhusūdana then continues to point to the *avidyā-leśa,* not ignorance itself, as the cause of bodily continuity. The *pūrvapakṣin* says that the ignorance trace is not apart from *avidyā,* since ignorance has no parts (*avayava*), so *avidyā* itself remains as long as the body exists, again like a form of cloth remains after burning, although the cloth's "material basis" is gone. Madhusūdana, however, holds that although ignorance has no parts, still only its trace continues after *jñāna.* Like Citsukha, Madhusūdana argues that "*leśa*" here means "*ākāra*" or form, and it is accepted that *avidyā* has many forms as in the *śruti* "Indra goes about in many forms by (his) magic powers" (*BāU* II. 5. 19). While the form's basis (*avidyā*) ceases, the form continues. He gives as an example the continuity of the class (*jāti*) of pots despite the cessation of an individual pot (the "basis" of the class).

The opponent immediately asks for more detail on the nature of the form of ignorance. Is it in fact a class, or is it a quality (*dharma*) like power (*śakti*), or a particular state (*avasthā*) of a thing like gold in form of a ring?

Madhusūdana says it is not the first two, since if they are the basis of the illusion of the body, they would be *avidyā* itself (and not a *leśa*), and if they are not the basis of the body illusion, this illusion would arise without a basis. Further, they are different from the self (being removable by *jñāna*) and thus, being necessarily part of ignorance themselves, they cannot exist when ignorance ceases.

Madhusūdana argues for the third alternative, despite the apparent problem that no state like *avidyā-leśa* can exist without something (*avidyā*) "possessing" the state. The trace state can exist because of *avidyā*'s many powers (first seen in Citsukha's writing, although Madhusūdana here substitutes the word *śakti,* or power for Citsukha's term *ākāra,* or form). The first two powers of *avidyā* cease by direct experience (*sākṣātkāra*) of the truth; they are the power causing the illusion that phenomenal manifestation (*prapañca*) is the highest truth and the power producing the capacity for practical efficiency (*arthakriyā*) in *prapañca*. The third power continues after knowledge (which exists simultaneously with *prārabdha karma*); it is the power producing object semblances (*ābhāsa*)—such as the body—capable of immediate perception (*aparokṣa-pratibhāsa*). Put in other words, we can say that the projecting power of ignorance remains due to *prārabdha karma,* even though the concealing power has disappeared.[30]

Although Madhusūdana allows that such a kind of ignorance remains, it is not admitted as "full" ignorance, for that would disallow living liberation. He argues that the *mukta* remains in *avidyā,* only waiting for this third power to end. This power, like all of ignorance's powers, is destroyed by knowledge, but only when knowledge is not obstructed by *prārabdha karma* at life's end.

Madhusūdana next refers back to Citsukha's views on the *avidyā-leśa* in two ways. First, he mentions the *Śvetāśvatara* I. 10 text, which concludes "again (*bhūyas*) at the end, all *māyā* ceases," which seems to mean that only when the *prārabdha karma* sustained body drops ("the end") do all forms of illusion (including the ignorance trace) cease.[31] Second, he disputes the notion that *karma* and the *avidyā-leśa* are mutually dependent. When properly understood with the help of the aforementioned *śruti,* one realizes both that they exist simultaneously (not "dependently") and that ultimately the ignorance trace continuity is the cause of *karma* (and bodily) continuity.

Madhusūdana closes by again arguing that the *leśa* is a subtle state (*sūkṣma-avasthā*) of ignorance. He points out that a Mīmāṃsāka opponent accepts that even after a sacrifice is finished, *apūrva,* the subtle state of sacrifice, continues and accomplishes a result (like attaining heaven); in the same way, Madhusūdana holds that after ignorance is finished, the *leśa,* the subtle state of *avidyā,* continues and allows one to "accomplish" understanding the body (as unreal appearance).[32] Both *apūrva* and *leśa* remain after their bases, sacrifice and *avidyā,* are gone. The Mīmāṃsāka accepts the interval between cause and result (heaven) in sacrifice as Advaitins accept an interval between knowledge (cause) and body fall (result). Madhusūdana thus concludes that *jīvanmukti* is well-established by the continuity of the trace of *avidyā.*

Prakāśānanda on Jīvanmukti

Another important Advaitin writer of this era is Prakāśānanda (late 1500s). He is the author of *Vedānta-siddhānta-muktāvalī* (loosely, *Pearls of Wisdom from the Vedanta*),[33] a work largely concerned with the natures of awareness and ignorance according to the "*dṛṣṭi-sṛṣṭi*" or "objects exist only in perception" viewpoint.[34] Prakāśānanda gives an elaborate *pūrvapakṣa* against *jīvanmukti*, making the case against earlier Advaita (especially Madhusūdana's) arguments for *jīvanmukti* in a clear and effective manner, particularly concerning the problematic nature of ignorance and its effects. While the final arguments are in fact *for jīvanmukti*, one wonders if Prakāśānanda himself was fully persuaded by his responses to these criticisms.[35]

The section on liberation while living begins at a familiar point: If knowledge by its very nature destroys ignorance (and its effects, like embodiment), the fall of the body should be simultaneous with knowledge. And if ignorance and all its effects immediately cease after *vidyā* (and one then reaches bodiless isolation, *videha-kaivalya*) the whole lineage (of teachers) would be cut off (thus liberation, which must be taught by *brahman*-knowers, would become impossible).[36]

The opponent continues that the body cannot be said to remain, due to the power of *prārabdha karma,* since such *karma* is an effect of ignorance and thus cannot remain in *avidyā*'s absence—like cloth cannot remain in the absence of thread.[37] Nor (contra Maṇḍana, etc.) can one say that ignorance continues for a short time sufficient for enjoying *prārabdha karma*'s fruits, since knowledge would then lose its nature as the destroyer of ignorance. And destroying ignorance cannot become its nature only at a later time, because a single thing cannot have two natures.

Prakāśānanda's *pūrvapakṣin* also denies Madhusūdana's view that the concealing (*āvaraṇa*) power of ignorance ceases while its projecting (*vikṣepa*) power continues (due to the support of *prārabdha karma*). There are not, as implied here, two ignorances, and if ignorance is one, it should not have two powers, differently present or absent, for it is contradictory for one thing to cease and exist simultaneously. Nor can one argue that the power alone ceases, since the power and its possessor (ignorance) are not different; if different, ignorance does not cease when the power does.[38]

The opponent continues that ignorance does not cease by the cessation of *prārabdha karma,* since *prārabdha* cessation is not a means of knowledge (*pramāṇa*), which alone ends ignorance. Further, neither knowledge obstructed (*pratibaddha*) or unobstructed by currently manifesting *karma* ends ignorance: obstructed knowledge could not destroy ignorance because of *prārabdha*'s interference, and knowledge unobstructed by *prārabdha* cannot end ignorance because knowledge is itself absent after the body falls (i.e., when *prārabdha* is destroyed). Nor can one argue (like Maṇḍana and others do) that an impression (*saṃskāra*) or trace (*leśa*) of ignorance continues after knowledge, because any such remnant is an effect of ignorance (and thus must cease with its basis). Also, it is absurd to use the term *saṃskāra* when it is really just ignorance itself.

The *pūrvapakṣa* then addresses issues concerning scripture. One cannot claim the knower's body continues based on the authority of *śruti* and *smṛti,* which teach living liberation, since such teaching is not the aim of scripture. When the *śāstras* urge those desirous of liberation to listen to scripture, those passages are ancillary explanations (*arthavāda*) for injunctions (*vidhi*) to hear scripture. Thus, both worldly reasoning (indicated in the preceding paragraphs) and Vedic texts contradict the continued existence of the body of a knower. One might note here that the *śruti* passages quoted by earlier writers, from *BāU* IV. 4. 6–7 through *Kaṭha* VI. 14–5, make the latter point questionable.

The opponent continues that the loosed arrow example (i.e., the arrow, once shot, continues for a time at a slowly diminishing rate of speed) does not establish the existence of (bodily prolonging) *prārabdha karma,* since in the arrow example the basis of action (the arrow) is not destroyed, while ignorance, the basis of *karma* (and thus the body), *is* destroyed. Nor is the common agreement (*prasiddhi*) among people about the existence of *jīvanmukti* unchallengeable, for common agreement without proper proof (*pramāṇa*) is merely blind tradition.[39] Although *jīvanmukti* is unproven, the *śāstra* authors have a purpose in teaching it, that is, they want to destroy the ignorant student's distrust of the teacher (and this distrust can be removed by suggesting the teacher is liberated here and now).[40]

The opponent now concludes (as argued earlier) that since knowledge by nature completely destroys ignorance, knowledge cannot arise because any knower is immediately liberated, and thus no teacher who has knowledge ever exists. The existence of the *brahman*-knowing teacher is vital since, as *śruti* says, gaining knowledge is dependent on the teacher: "one having a teacher knows" (*ChU* VI. 14. 2), "this view is not achieved by reason, (but when) taught by another, it is well understood" (*Kaṭha* II. 9), "the teacher will tell you the way" (*ChU* IV. 14. 1), and "there is no way there unless taught by another" (*Kaṭha* II. 8), and so on. Thus, while agreeing with

Vimuktātman and others that a *brahman*-knowing teacher is crucial, the *pūrvapakṣin* argues that such a teacher cannot exist.

After all of these arguments, Prakāśānanda now responds, focusing on the idea that a teacher is necessary but never exists. He states that there is a teacher, albeit imagined (*kalpita*), the teacher instructs, and this accords with the *śāstras*. Further, there is no flaw of uncertainty in this conclusion (*avinigama*) due to the (wrong) conclusions of those who are ignorant. Although (as Sarvajñātman wrote)[41] no teacher exists from the highest perspective, since the knower is immediately liberated, still no impropriety exists because knowledge can arise from an imagined teacher. The imagined teacher can bear true knowledge (*satya-jñāna*), as shown in the aforementioned Vedic texts, and by the illustration of mirror reflection (the "false image" gives a "true reflection"). Further, there is no uncertainty as to who is the imaginer, teacher or student. The imaginer is the one who is ignorant (thus the student), and such a state is improper for the knower-teacher who lacks any seed of imagining.

An intellect such as Prakāśānanda's could certainly see weaknesses in the arguments for an "imagined teacher," and he does not even address the problematic nature of ignorance and its effects/traces/powers, including *prārabdha karma,* nor does he sufficiently answer the objection about the aim of scripture. It is difficult to know why he ignores all of the objections above. Perhaps he wants to hold that there is a point at which reason ends, for he concludes this section by asserting (sounding like Śaṅkara's *Upadeśasāhasrī*) that by the direct experience arising from Vedic texts like "you are that" reached by the grace of teacher and scripture, and by the simultaneous disappearance of ignorance and its effects that obstruct the appearance of liberation, he (the student) thinks, "I am eternal, pure, awakened, free, (and) by nature nondual bliss," and then all is accomplished.

Late Scholastic Advaitins on Jīvanmukti

The latest scholastic Advaitins are a heterogeneous group. We will begin here by considering Appayya Dīkṣita (sixteenth century), who wrote one of the best-known compilations of Advaitin thought, called the *(Śāstra) Siddhāntaleśa-saṃgraha.*[42] He discusses Advaita views of *jīvanmukti* briefly at the beginning of the text's fourth section. He begins with the standard Advaita view that the *jīvanmukta* retains the appearance (*pratibhāsa*) of the body after the direct experience (*sākṣātkāra*) of the truth (*brahman*), due to the binding of *prārabdha karma,* which has the remnant of ignorance as its basis. This view raises the customary problem that direct *brahman*-experience is impossible if *prārabdha karma* as *avidyā-leśa* remains. So what is the *avidyā-leśa* (which allows for *jīvanmukti*)?

Appayya gives various views: some say it is a bit (*aṃśa*) of projective power (*vikṣepa-śakti*) remaining from root (*mūla*) ignorance, which leads to bodily continuance due to *prārabdha karma*. Others (such as Madhusūdana and Prakāśātman) say it is an impression (*saṃskāra*) of ignorance, imagined like the smell of garlic remaining in an emptied pot of garlic, or it is root ignorance following the example of the burnt cloth (i.e., the form lingers after the substance is gone). Still others (here Sarvajñātman) say texts on *jīvanmukti* are only explanations (*arthavāda*) of injunctions (*vidhi*) such as "hear, reflect, assimilate," since ignorance continuity is impossible after the rise of direct experience opposing the remaining *avidyā* trace, and since it is not the aim of scripture to cause *jīvanmukti* attainment. Ignorance with pleasurable impressions (*vilāsavāsanā*) ceases only by the rise of *brahman* experience from assimilating (*nididhyāsana*) the scriptural truth. Appayya does not here argue for any particular alternative; instead, he goes on to describe views on the cessation of ignorance itself, without discussing *jīvanmukti* further.

Sadānanda's *Vedāntasāra* (*The Essence of the Vedanta*)[43] (sixteenth to seventeenth century) is a popular and syncretic summary of Advaitin thought and practice, with a particular emphasis on establishing the competency of the student. Concerning *jīvanmukti*, Sadānanda stresses the liberated being's freedom from bondage, detachment from the body, and constant goodness, although being beyond virtue. The liberated being is said to live out his *prārabdha karma*, then merge in *brahman*.

As in numerous other texts, *jīvanmukti* is the last topic addressed in the *Vedāntasāra*. Sadānanda states that when partless *brahman* is immediately realized as one's own essence by the removal of ignorance and its effects (misapprehension, doubt, and accumulated *karma*), then the *jīvanmukta* is said to be grounded in *brahman* and free from all bondage. Sadānanda also refers to the earlier cited *Muṇḍaka* II. 2. 8 text: "The knot of the heart is split, all doubts is cut off, and all his *karma* is destroyed when it (*brahman*) is seen, both higher and lower."

Sadānanda emphasizes the *jīvanmukta*'s awareness of the unreality of the body and actions. After rising (from meditation), the liberated being sees actions undertaken due to prior dispositions (*vāsanā*) and experiences their commenced fruits with: 1) a body that is the seat of flesh, blood, urine, and feces, 2) senses that are the seat of blindness, dullness, and so on, and 3) an internal organ (*antaḥkaraṇa*) that is the seat of hunger, thirst, sorrow, and delusion; still, he does not regard these things as truly real. Sadānanda gives the example of one who sees a magic trick (*indra-jāla*) and, knowing it to be magic, does not regard it as truly real (also *PD* VII. 175–80). He also cites *Upadeśasāhasrī* verse X. 13: "the one who, although seeing, does not, due to his nonduality, see duality in waking state, like one in deep sleep, and who, although acting, is actionless—he, and no other, is a knower of the self."

Sadānanda then addresses a concern formulated by Sureśvara (and addressed by Prakāśātman and the *Pañcadaśī*) about the propriety of the liberated being's behavior. He claims that while the *jīvanmukta* continues practices like eating or wandering that precede knowledge, he now either follows only virtuous dispositions or is indifferent to virtue and vice (*śubhāśubha*). He quotes Sureśvara's *Naiṣkarmyasiddhi* IV. 62, which asks, "If one awakened to the truth of nonduality would do as he pleases, what is the difference between truth–seers and dogs in eating what is impure?" Sadānanda, like Sureśvara, does not directly answer this question, but does point to an important difference: only the liberated Self-knower realizes *brahman*. He also writes that means to knowledge like humility and good qualities like non-emnity now serve merely as ornaments (*alaṃkāra*) of the *jīvanmukta*. He again turns to the *Naiṣkarmyasiddhi* (IV. 69) for support: "For one whose Self-knowledge has arisen, qualities like nonemnity occur effortlessly; they are no longer means for him."[44]

Sadānanda then sums up his view. While formulaic, it represents well the mainstream Advaita view of living liberation. The *jīvanmukta*, only to continue his bodily journey, experiences the fruits of commenced *karma* marked by joy and sorrow, obtained by his own desire, or without desire, or by the desire of others, and illumines the appearances (*abhāsa*) in his internal organ. When the fruits are exhausted and the vital breath merges into the highest *brahman*, which is innermost bliss, then due to the destruction of mental impressions and ignorance with its effects, he abides as partless *brahman*, free from the appearance of any difference, the unitary essence of bliss, and absolute isolation. He closes with well-known supporting texts: "his breaths do not depart (and being *brahman* indeed, one merges with *brahman*," *BāU* IV. 4. 6), "(the breaths) unite here (*BāU* III. 2. 11)," and "having been liberated [from *avidyā*], he is released [from the body]," *Kaṭha* V. 1).

Dharmarāja's seventeenth-century *Vedāntaparibhāṣa* (*Explanation of Vedanta*)[45] is a classic introduction to and systemization of later Advaita epistemology (largely following Prakāśātman's *Vivaraṇa* school). Once again we find the text's conclusion analyzing *jīvanmukti*. Dharmarāja is particularly concerned with the role of *prārabdha karma*, and argues that while one gains liberation by *brahman* knowledge here, final release (*videha-kaivalya*) arises only after the working out of *prārabdha karma*.

Dharmarāja, like Śaṅkara, claims that liberation is the attaining of *brahman*, consisting of bliss and the removal of sorrow, and it is not attaining some other realm (*loka*) or an objective bliss (which would be a noneternal effect) (IX. 6–7). In IX. 46–56, he elaborates on living liberation, writing that one with the direct experience (*sākṣātkāra*) of qualityless *brahman* does not go to another realm (following the *BāU* IV. 4. 6 text: "his breaths do not depart"); instead, one experiences joy and sorrow until *prārabdha karma* is destroyed, and then one is released (*apavṛj*).

Dharmarāja then addresses the familiar (and central) problem for Advaitins of some form of ignorance coexisting with the direct experience of nondual *brahman*.[46] He states that although all *karma* is burnt by knowledge (following *Muṇḍaka* II. 2. 8 and *Gītā* IV. 37), *prārabdha karma* can remain, following *ChU* VI. 14. 2, since knowledge destroys only accumulated (*saṃcita*) *karma,* which is different from activated (*kārya*) *karma* (IX. 47–48). Further, a knower can still have a body despite *brahman* knowledge's removal of root (*mūla*) ignorance. Only unobstructed (*apratibaddha*) knowledge removes (all forms of) ignorance—but contra Prakāśānanda, it does; the cessation of ignorance is not accepted when there is an obstruction in the form of (body-sustaining) *prārabdha karma* (IX. 49–50).

The text continues by addressing the issue of the number of ignorances (*avidyā*), and whether when one being is released, all are released (*sarvamukti*). Dharmarāja rejects the view implied in the *BāU* II. 5. 19 text: "Indra (goes about in many forms) by (his) *māyās* [plural]." He holds (like Madhusūdana) that ignorance is unitary, but there are different veiling powers (*āvaraṇa-śakti*) on *brahman* in different individual beings (*jīva*), and these veilings of *brahman* in the *jīvas* are destroyed at different times (so no *sarvamukti*) (IX. 51–54). Dharmarāja concludes that, as *Brahmasūtra* III. 3. 32 holds, the knower's body continues as long as there is some commission (*adhikāra*), so one like Indra could remain embodied even after the rise of knowledge. The final view, which concurs with Śaṅkara, is that bodiless release (*videha-kaivalya*) comes (only) after commenced *karma* causing the commission is finished (IX. 55).[47] Dharmarāja ends by returning to the definition of *mokṣa* proposed in IX. 6–7: Liberation is from knowing *brahman*, and is the removal of evil and attainment of the unsurpassed bliss of *brahman*. Still, it seems the embodiment of the liberated being continues as long as there is *prārabdha karma.*

As a final reflection, before turning to ideas about *jīvanmukti* beyond the traditional Advaita fold, I would like to consider a point about the nature of *jīvanmukti* using different, more Western, language, following an article by G. R. Malkani in *Philosophy East and West.*[48] The question can be asked whether, and in what way, the *jīvanmukta* can "know" or "be" *brahman*.[49] First, as Malkani points out, from the highest view, the idea of an "I" (even a *jīvanmukta*'s "I") knowing *brahman* is an illusion. In everyday usage, knowing is always dualistic, with a subject and an object, and such dualism is delusive. All conceptual knowledge of "I" knowing "something" is flawed, even "I know *brahman*." In this sense, to have awareness of oneness is contradictory. Ultimately, you do not merely "know" *brahman,* the real you, the self, *is brahman*.

However, from an everyday understanding, one does need to come to know *brahman,* even if one already is *brahman*. From our deluded dualistic way of thinking, we hold the wrong notion that *brahman*-hood is to be, rather than already being, achieved. We think identity with *brahman* is a goal, rather than realizing we are eternally *brahman*. Ultimately, then, the *jīvanmukta* is different from us by the realization that s/he is not (ontologically) different from us. Only s/he knows who s/he (already) is.

Again, from everyday understanding, our separateness while living is real enough: when embodied, we have a unique mind and personality, different from others, both in our own self-understanding and in the view of an observer. In this sense, one can rightly say "I am *brahman*" only after realizing nonduality. You are *brahman* (only) when you know that the individuated you is not really you.

Moreover, our separate bodies must be cared for and our individual minds inevitably have ever-changing states (even *nirvikalpa samādhi* is a temporary state in one mind). Therefore, in an important, if ultimately delusive, sense, embodiment does not allow one to "be *brahman*" constantly.[50] A person is thus inherently limited while living, so one might say that the remnant of ignorance after realization is the human condition, that is, having bodily needs such as hunger, thirst, and rest, as well as experiencing emotions and desires. Thus, one might put the particular nature of *jīvanmukti* this way: The living liberated being may have immediate knowledge of nondual *brahman*, but one cannot simply "be *brahman*" (or be *brahman* simply) while still in a body.

We now widen our field of vision, first to look at Rāmānuja's and some *Sāṃkhya* and *Yoga* views on the possibility and nature of liberation while living, and then consider the "Yogic Advaita" perspective of the *Yogavāsiṣṭha* and the *Jīvanmuktiviveka*.

Part 2

Jīvanmukti *in "Yogic Advaita"*

FIVE

Rāmānuja and Sāṃkhya/Yoga *on Liberation While Living*

Before turning to "Yogic Advaita" perspectives on *jīvanmukti*, I want to briefly consider an important and very different view of the possibility of embodied liberation from within Vedanta, that of Śaṅkara's influential critic Rāmānuja (fl. twelfth century), the founder of the Viśiṣṭādvaita (qualified nondualist) Vedanta tradition.[1] I will then more directly prepare the way for "Yogic Advaita" by introducing some *Sāṃkhya* and *Yoga* views on liberation while living. Rāmānuja's discussion of living liberation is interesting in its own right, but is especially relevant here because it occurs mostly in the context of his rejection of Advaita views.[2] I will focus here on the relevant comments in Rāmānuja's *Brahmasūtra* commentary, called the *Śrī bhāṣya* (*ŚB*), particularly I. 1. 4.

There are, of course, a number of fundamental differences between Rāmānuja and Śaṅkara that underlie their divergent understandings of the possibility of living liberation. Rāmānuja, unlike Śaṅkara, holds that the individual self is real and an active agent. This self is truly bound in a real world (*ŚB* I. 1. 1). Full liberation from bondage is not realization of nondual *brahman,*[3] but communion of the soul with Lord Viṣṇu in heaven, and thus requires the cessation of embodiment. The supreme bliss of experiencing the Lord's full presence is inconceivable to the being who, since embodied, is inevitably bound by *karma* and ignorance. To Rāmānuja, mere awareness of the self's bondage as ultimately unreal is insufficient for liberation. To remove one's real bondage, one must both take refuge in the Lord and perform proper ritual actions.[4] In his writings on *jīvanmukti,* Rāmānuja particularly emphasizes performance of ritual action to bring about and sustain release.

Rāmānuja's most thorough statement on this topic, found in his comments on *Śrī bhāṣya* I. 1. 4, explicitly attempts to counter the Advaita position favoring living liberation. His discussion of *jīvanmukti* directly follows his argument that injunctions to meditate (*dhyāna*) are necessary, for ignorance does not cease just by understanding sacred texts. He begins by writing that asserting liberation *with* a body exists is as absurd as saying "my mother is childless." He points out that Advaitins themselves use sacred texts that indicate that liberation entails freedom from embodiment (more on this shortly). Rāmānuja then allows the Advaitin to define the realization of the unreality of the body's appearance as the cessation of embodiment. Rāmānuja responds that if for an Advaitin this realization means the end of embodiment, *jīvanmukti* would thus be just like bodiless liberation, which is also the cessation of the body's false appearance (thus conflating realization of the body's unreality with the cessation of that unreality).

Rāmānuja then offers the "Advaita position" that the *jīvanmukta*'s embodied appearance persists, even though this illusory appearance is annulled, just like the appearance of two moons to one with an eye disease persists even after the illusion of the moon's dualness is recognized. Rāmānuja's retort to this view is that knowledge annulling appearance cannot have nondual *brahman* itself as its object; here, the appearance of embodiment, an illusion caused by ignorance, is annulled by knowledge, so the annulled appearance cannot persist. In the case of the two moons, the defect causing the appearance (eye disease) is not the object of the annulling knowledge (i.e., that one moon alone exists), so the annulled appearance (two moons) can here persist. Put another way, in the first case, the cause of illusion (ignorance) is destroyed (by knowledge of *brahman*), so the illusion—embodiment—is destroyed; in the second case, the cause of illusion (eye disease, a physical defect) is understood (not destroyed), so the illusion—two moons—persists, even after understanding.[5]

When Rāmānuja returns to *śruti*, his first example is *ChU* VI. 14. 2, which he reads to say that one attains release only after disembodiment, not just after knowing the real (which, for Śaṅkara, is liberation, if not the final end).[6] Rāmānuja then refers to *Āpastamba Dharmasūtra* II. 9. 13–17, which also states that release is not from knowing the self alone, for after release one should not (but inevitably does) experience suffering here. He then concludes that the cessation of all plurality (i.e., liberation) is impossible while one is living. He continues that bondage ceases only by employing meditation (*dhyāna-niyoga*), which brings direct *brahman* knowledge. Release rises not from the (noneternal) meditations themselves, but from their destruction of all obstacles to direct *brahman* knowledge. The mind is cleared (and kept clear) by meditation, then knowledge arises.

The fundamental problem with Rāmānuja's arguments here is that he misrepresents the Advaita position, which does not identify realization of an illusion with its immediate "objective" cessation. It is not the case that Śaṅkara, for example, holds that all appearance (including the body) is simply "unreal," and later Advaitins are careful to describe appearance as neither real nor unreal, and indescribable (*anirvacanīya*). Further, Rāmānuja does not here take into account *prārabdha*, or currently manifesting, *karma,* the entity that Advaitins claim causes embodiment to persist, even after liberating insight.

Rāmānuja does address the nature of continuing *karma* in *ŚB* IV. 1. 15–19. He holds that after *brahman* knowledge, fruits of uncommenced (*anārabdha*) *karma* perish (whether good or evil), but others continue. He again here refers to *ChU* VI. 14. 2, which, he claims in IV. 1. 19, refers not to release at the termination of embodiment, but to release from *karma* following the experience of its fruits. He rejects the Advaita idea that the liberated being's body continues for a time merely due to ongoing impetus, like a potter's wheel abandoned while spinning. Instead, he specifies that the body continues due to the Lord's pleasure or displeasure, which is caused by good or evil deeds. He also states, in *ŚB* IV. 1. 16, that performance of ritual actions like the *agnihotra* must continue even after knowing *brahman*; these actions are means causing knowledge to arise and repetition of them further perfects knowledge by clarifying the mind (*antaḥkaraṇa*). This seems to suggest, contra Śaṅkara, that degrees of knowledge are possible, and that one might "fall back" from knowledge without the constant support of ritual activity.

Rāmānuja explicitly addresses the question of what happens to *karma* currently bearing fruit after *brahman* knowledge in *ŚB* IV. 1. 9, specifically whether such *karma* ends when the current body (in which liberation arose) ceases, or whether it can cause future births. We have seen he does not read the *ChU* VI passage to claim that all *karma* ceases with liberation from current embodiment. He asserts that one must first experience *all* results of earlier good and evil actions before one becomes one with *brahman* (which occurs when the results cease). This cessation may happen at the end of this birth, or such experiencing may require a number of births. As he states in *ŚB* III. 4. 51, release is due to knowledge rising from meritorious works, but its time is not fixed, since obstruction from other works must also cease. Even a *brahman*-knower may have powerful evil deeds to overcome. Still, Rāmānuja agrees with Śaṅkara that all action performed *before brahman* knowledge whose results have not begun to bear fruit is immediately destroyed by this knowledge, and later works do not attach to the self.

Advaitins also wrestle with the question of whether the liberated being will return or not. The key text on this topic is *BS* III. 3. 32, which speaks of a commission (*adhikāra*) causing some to return. Rāmānuja holds that some (like Vasiṣṭha) who have gained the highest knowledge still retain good or evil works at death, since they have obtained some commission from prior action. They must complete their commission before the effects of the *karma* causing the commission cease, and only then do they obtain heaven's path. Again, commenced *karma* can only be destroyed by experiencing its fruits.

Jīvanmukti *in* Sāṃkhya *and* Yoga

Unlike Rāmānuja, *Sāṃkhya* and *Yoga* do not contest the possibility of liberation while living. They share the Advaitic assumption that ignorance of the true nature of reality ends by discriminating knowledge that brings release. However, the key *Sāṃkhya/Yoga* concepts of *prakṛti*, *puruṣa,* and *kaivalya* are certainly not identical with Advaita's *māyā*, *ātman*, and *mokṣa.* Similarly, the notion of freedom from attachment while living exists in both *Sāṃkhya* and *Yoga,* but this concept is not a central one, nor does the term *jīvanmukti* appear in the earliest texts of these schools. Īśvarakṛṣṇa's *Sāṃkhya Kārikā* (*SK*) describes liberation as the realization (which happens while embodied) that the pure, inactive but conscious witness (*puruṣa*) is not related to unconscious manifest nature (*prakṛti*). Further, *SK* 67 uses the image, important in the *prārabdha karma* debate, of bodily existence continuing like a potter's wheel continuing to spin from prior momentum. Patañjali's *Yogasūtras* (*YS*) state that all afflicted action ceases for the master *yogin*, who then lives on without impurity in a "cloud of *dharma*" (IV. 29–30). Next, I will briefly examine ideas related to living liberation in these foundational texts (and some later Advaita-influenced *Sāṃkhya/Yoga* writings), and some similarities and differences with *jīvanmukti* in Advaita.

The *SK* extolls discriminating knowledge that brings utter detachment and claims that activity ceases due to loss of desire and motive to act when the *puruṣa*'s difference from personal mental activity is recognized. One now attains the final state in *Sāṃkhya* and *Yoga,* often designated *kaivalya,* or perfect isolation (a term Śaṅkara uses on occasion as well). In *kaivalya,* the pure witness, *puruṣa,* rests serenely without attachment (*SK* 68, *YS* 2.25, 3. 55, 4.34); such isolation does not seem possible while living, though the *YS* states that the pure seer observes that which is seen (II. 20).

The key passage relevant in this context is *Sāṃkhya Kārikā* 64–68. It first states that after the knowledge that the "I" (*aham*) does not truly exist, the disinterested *puruṣa* sees *prakṛti,* and all *prakṛti*'s activity ceases, although the two are still conjoined (*SK* 64–66). Virtue (*dharma*) and all other causes now cease to function, due to the attainment of perfect knowledge, but *puruṣa* remains embodied due to the power of past impressions (*saṃskāra*), like the potter's wheel continues whirling after its cause (the potter's activity) has ceased (*SK* 67). In his commentary, Gauḍapāda adds that knowledge burns away all (not yet germinating) seeds of evil or good action, as well as precluding all future *karma,* concluding that liberation (*mokṣa*) rises when the body falls, due to the destruction of the *saṃskāras.* All of this, of course, is consistent with the Advaitic doctrine of *prārabdha karma. SK* 68 then states that when *puruṣa* separates from the body and now inactive *prakṛti* ceases, final complete isolation (*kaivalya*) is attained.

Little more that is relevant to living liberation is said in the *SK.* It does not discuss the path to freedom or proper activity after liberating knowledge, nor does it claim the destruction of all impurity before death, saying merely that karmic impressions (*saṃskāra*) persist until death, as in the potter's wheel analogy. As Christopher Chapple points out in an essay on living liberation in *Sāṃkhya* and *Yoga,* this might be in part due to the kind of text the *SK* is, a sort of abstract philosophical poem, without the practical "manual of methods for purification" aspect seen in the *YS.*[7]

Some much later *Sāṃkhya* thinkers, clearly influenced by Advaita, do explicitly mention *jīvanmukti.* The *Sāṃkhyasūtras* with Aniruddha's commentary (c. 1500s?) discuss living liberation in III. 77-84, in part referring back to the aforementioned *SK* verses.[8] The important synthesizer of Advaita and *Sāṃkhya/Yoga* thought Vijñānabhikṣu (c. late 1500s?) basically follows this view in his *Sāṃkhyasūtras* subcommentary (*bhāṣya*), but he uses more unambiguously Advaitic terminology, such as *jīvanmukti, prārabdha karma,* and *ātma-jñāna.* These *sūtras* introduce the notion of different degrees of discrimination (*viveka*), the highest of which brings no further experiencing (*upabhoga*). The *jīvanmukta* is said to have middle-level discrimination (*madhya-viveka*),[9] in which prior impressions (*saṃskāra*) force the desireless knower to continue experiencing for a time (77–78). Evidence for the continuing existence of the liberated being is shown by the master-disciple relation (i.e., the teacher, though liberated, remains embodied to assist the student), and by mention in scripture (*śruti*), as in *BāU* IV. 4. 6's "being *brahman,* one goes to *brahman.*" Otherwise, the text points out, there would be blind tradition (*andha-paramparā*), that is, an ignorant teacher unable to awaken the student. As Vijñānabhikṣu states, the ignorant/blind would (mis)lead the ignorant/blind (79–81).

The potter's wheel analogy is mentioned in III. 82, and Aniruddha adds that release is delayed due to the karmic impressions (*saṃskāra*) which create and support the body and can be exhausted only by experience. *Sūtra* III. 83 refers to the *jīvanmukta*'s continued existence arising from a trace (*leśa*) of the *saṃskāra.* Vijñānabhikṣu shows his familiarity with the Advaita controversy over how the body, or any trace of ignorance, can remain after knowledge. He claims that the body remains due to the trace of an impression of an object, not an impression of ignorance, as the latter would entail production of *karma*. Ignorance is not necessary for experiencing *prārabdha karma*; *jīvanmuktas* just have the "semblance" of experience. The chapter ends with the statement that one attains release when all suffering ceases by discrimination (III.84).

In his *Sāṃkhyasāra*, Vijñānabhikṣu devotes a brief section (II, 7) to the characteristics of the *jīvanmukta*, which in part refers back to the *Gītā*'s formulation of the *sthita-prajña*, one with firm wisdom: the living liberated being is said to be even-minded, without desire or aversion, undeluded, and experiencing the bliss of the self. This being is said to attain final liberation when the mind is destroyed, due to the attentuation of *saṃskāras*. When the intellect ceases, final isolation (*kaivalya*) arises and the self abides alone. The interpenetration of *Sāṃkhya* and Advaita ideas is also clear here.[10]

Yoga practice attempts to purify the body and free the mind from all attachments, conscious and unconscious, by a variety of techniques; these practices culminate in meditative enstasis or *samādhi* (while living, of course). One overcomes karmic propensities (*saṃskāra*) and afflictions (*kleśa*) such as ignorance and passion by these techniques, perhaps best known in Patañjali's eight-limbed *Yoga* formula (*YS* II. 29 ff.). According to Patañjali, after proper moral discipline and body and breath control, one progressively withdraws the mind from sense objects and concentrates on achieving increasingly subtle meditative states climaxing in seedless (*nirbīja*) *samādhi*. One now attains discriminating knowledge (*viveka-khyāti*) since all seeds of attachment and residual impure impressions are "burnt," and none can sprout again.

While one finds much discussion of the means to and nature of liberation in the *Yoga* school, little is explicitly said about liberation while living.[11] The most significant verses for our purposes are *YS* IV. 29–30. *Sūtra* 29 states that when liberated, discriminating knowledge and from that *dharma-megha* (cloud of virtue) *samādhi* arise (IV. 29), and IV. 30 claims that all affliction and action (*kleśa-karma*) then cease, though presumably some *purified* action continues until death. Vyāsa's commentary on IV. 30 adds that afflictions from ignorance and stores of good and bad action are utterly destroyed by knowledge, and "when affliction and action cease, the knower is liberated, even while living."[12] Since delusion (*viparyaya*) causes existence, its destruction ends rebirth. This seems to be the first reference in the classical *Yoga* tradition to *"jīvanmukti,"* a serene, detached liberation while still living.

One does not find much relevant to the Advaita concept of *jīvanmukti* in later *Yoga* writings until Vijñānabhikṣu's *YS* commentary, and even here *jīvanmukti* is generally mentioned briefly.[13] Vijñānabhikṣu emphasizes that the *jīvanmukta* (one who directly experiences discriminating knowledge, *viveka-sākṣātkārin*) has no afflictions (*kleśa*), or even seeds (*bīja*) or impressions (*saṃskāra*) of them (II. 4). Nor do afflictions cause *karma* or fruits; remaining commenced fruits cease by action. Only the ignorant (including some then current Advaitins, according to Vijñānabhikṣu) hold that a trace of ignorance remains for *jīvanmuktas*, either as a mental modification (*vṛtti*, II. 11) or to enjoy fruits (II. 13).[14] Vijñānabhikṣu argues that *jīvanmuktas* experience joy and sorrow from commenced fruits of *karma* but not from egoism (*ābhimānika*), since no *kleśa* exists that causes egocentricity (II. 14). The *jīvanmukta* has only the appearance of enjoyment (*bhogābhāsa*); enjoyment is secondary (*gauna*) for him, and he only experiences joy (*sukhādi*) (II. 6, 18). His wish (*icchā*) is not actual (attached) desire (*rāga*) (II. 7). Vijñānabhikṣu seems to be trying, as many Advaitins before him, to explain why the *jīvanmukta* is still embodied, despite apparent liberation.[15]

In his commentary on *YS* IV. 30, Vijñānabhikṣu opens with an objection to Vyāsa's reference to one being liberated while living when *kleśa* and *karma* cease. The objector points out that liberation is supposed to be the total cessation of suffering (*duḥkha*) and suffering is certain while living (as *ChU* VIII. 12. 1 states). Vijñānabhikṣu replies that even the lesser (*gauna*) *mukti* is the total uprooting of the cause of suffering; one knows this through the means of knowledge (*pramāṇa*) called noncognition (*anupalabdhi*) (that is, no sorrow is experienced then). Since the *jīvanmukta*'s afflictions and attendant impressions (*vāsanā*) are totally burnt, accepting that any afflictions remain (as some contemporary Vedantins asserted) is, Vijñānabhikṣu maintains, based on ignorance. In commenting on *YS* IV. 31, which holds to the endlessness (*anantya*) of knowledge from which all covering (*āvaraṇa*) is removed, Vijñānabhikṣu asserts one is then in the *jīvanmukti* state, since all affliction and *karma,* flaws covering knowledge, are removed by the endless light of knowledge.

Next we look at a number of texts that also integrate Yoga and Advaita concepts, beginning with the *Yogavāsiṣṭha*.

SIX

Yogic Advaita I: Jīvanmukti *in the* Yogavāsiṣṭha

One who stands firm while doing everyday activity,
Abiding like the empty sky: he is called liberated while living.
One who does everyday activity having achieved perfect awakening,
In waking (seeming) like one asleep: he is called liberated while living.
His luminous countenance does not rise in joy or fall in sorrow,
Having attained his proper place: he is called liberated while living.
One who is awake while seeming asleep, for him waking does not exist.[1]
Fully awakened without mental impressions: he is called liberated while living.
Although acting according to passion, hatred, and fear, etc.
One who remains (internally) transparent as the sky: he is called liberated while living.
One whose nature is not ego-centered, whose intellect is untainted
While acting or not acting: he is called liberated while living.
One who comprehends (cosmic) creation and destruction in the blink of an eye,
He sees the three worlds as his own self: he is called liberated while living.
One who fears no one and no one fears,

Free from fear, anger, and joy: he is called liberated while living.
Tranquil amid roiling phenomenal existence, partless though having parts (limbs),
The one who, though conscious, is without (fluctuating) mind: he is called liberated while living.
One who is cool while dealing with all things,
Filled with the self while among material objects: he is called liberated while living.[2]

This passage introduces *jīvanmukti* in the *Yogavāsiṣṭha*,[3] an eleventh-century eclectic mix of myth, poetry, philosophy, and moral exhortation, containing approximately 30,000 stanzas in six sections (*khaṇḍa*).[4] The *Yogavāsiṣṭha* seems to have played a role in popularizing the notion of liberation while living, and to have been important in the development of what I call "Yogic Advaita," also seen in the *Jīvanmuktiviveka* and many later *Upaniṣads*. Briefly, Yogic Advaita holds to Śaṅkara's view that knowledge of the nondual self brings liberation, yet adds emphases on *Sāṃkhya* ideas[5] and *Yoga* practices, exerting control of mental states (and even urging "destroying the mind"), and the contrast between *jīvan-* and *videha-mukti*, as well as much less interest in *prārabdha karma* than mainstream Advaita. Along with this Yogic Advaita perspective, the *YV* also contains more Buddhist (particularly *vijñānavāda*) and Puranic ideas[6] (but less *Upaniṣadic* material) than any other work considered here.

Throughout the text, the liberated sage Vasiṣṭha exhorts his student Rāma (and the reader) to be detached, destroy the ego, lose the mind, know the world to be illusory and to differentiate the transient body from the self. While in the world, one should do one's duty, follow the sacred texts (*śāstra*), and associate with the wise. According to the *Yogavāsiṣṭha,* liberation while living is possible. Like Śaṅkara, the *YV* holds that *mukti* arises from knowledge of the nondual self, not from austerity or right (dharmic) action. The *jīvanmukta* can act in the world or renounce all action with complete detachment. The *YV* (and later the *JMV*) do not say much about the body's continuity after liberation, due to *prārabdha karma*; instead, they emphasize the control of the *jīvanmukta*'s mind and destruction of mental impressions, which brings one to a nondual "state" beyond all consciousness states.

References to *jīvanmukti* and the *jīvanmukta* appear throughout the text,[7] and as with most topics in the *Yogavāsiṣṭha*, living liberation is not considered systematically. Still, the *Upaśama khaṇḍa* (chapter on Cessation) contains many of the most important passages, and various (largely congruent) themes appear repeatedly. These will be discussed next.

The World and Human Bondage

To begin, we will look at the *Yogavāsiṣṭha*'s view of the nature of the world and human bondage in it. The most common perspective is the Advaita view that the world is an illusion, appearing as it does due to ignorance and delusion; all visible objects are utterly unreal, empty like a rainbow or mirage.[8] While without reality, the manifest world is as if existent; birth and destruction appear but are not real.[9] Perhaps most eloquent is the Buddhist-sounding Up 77. 35–37: in this world containing the endless rise and fall of beings, life is like a froth bubble, people arise and scatter perpetually, and the sights of the world vanish in a moment.

Numerous passages detail the characteristics of bondage and those who are bound. First, it is, as Śaṅkara writes, bondage to think the self is a body or otherwise limited. Second, it is bondage to have an uncontrolled mind; such a person is like one drunk or stupid, or like a child, grabbing at everything without knowing its proper application (Up 77. 24–25). Sunk in the muck of everyday enjoyments, those with uncontrolled minds are attracted to useless, sorrow-producing wealth or to beautiful but empty women who lead them to burn in hell.[10]

These attachments bind one to impure *vāsanās* (mental impressions); one now enjoys what one desires, but also suffers from its loss. When addicted to external objects, the presence or absence of desired things gives constantly changing sorrow or joy.[11] Thus, foolish-minded non-*jīvanmuktas* are never at peace;[12] their minds, attached to *saṃsāra,* buzz with joy and sorrow like flies; the fool is like a worm or a dog, undeserving of liberation.[13]

Knowledge Leads to Liberation

The *Yogavāsiṣṭha* and Advaitins like Śaṅkara concur on the way out of bondage to illusion and sorrow; the route is knowledge (*jñāna*) or right discrimination (*viveka, vicāra*)—specifically knowledge of the self. The defining characteristic of one liberated while living is knowledge (while embodied) of the nondual, unfettered self.[14] The text repeatedly states that those solely intent on *ātma-jñāna* reach liberation while living, and one obtains liberation only by right discrimination; *jīvanmuktas* are termed *ātma-jñānins*, *tattva-jñas*, and *tattva-vids*.[15] Seeing the self in the not self or reality in unreality arises from nondiscrimination and is destroyed by discrimination (Up 86. 17). King Janaka is the model of unvarying flawless insight (Up 12. 4–5),[16] but anyone, outcast (*mleccha*) or animal, who attains the highest knowledge is liberated (U 118. 22). While obtainable only by the few (Up 74. 56), once obtained, *jīvanmukti* is never destroyed (Ut 125. 56).[17]

Interestingly, the *Yogavāsiṣṭha* says *it* is the crucial text that leads to right knowledge and liberation while living. *Utpatti* 8. 15–16 states that one gains *jīvanmukti* upon hearing this text,[18] and Ut 95. 25 asserts that only by studying this "*mahārāmāyaṇa śāstra*" does one obtain *jīvanmukti. Utpatti* 8 continues by claiming that one attains liberation by knowledge alone: *jīvanmukti* is not gained by almsgiving, austerity (*tapas*), or thousands of Vedic performances. *Upaśama* 12. 17 adds that *jīvanmukti* can not be gained by virtue, *guru*, sacred text, or associating with the wise, but only by clear discrimination. Further, the highest sage (*sādhu*) is awakened *from* heaven, future rewards, and the fruits of austerity (*tapas*) or charity (*dāna*); *tapas*, and so on, destroy suffering only for a short time, but equanimity (*samatā*) brings indestructible happiness (P 101. 36–37). While not forbidding performance of dharmic actions, it is clear in these passages that such duties are not the route to *mokṣa.*

The Utter Detachment of the Jīvanmukta

The *YV*, like traditional Advaita, also emphasizes that the living liberated being is detached (*asaṅga, asamsakti*) and indifferent (*sama*).[19] *Sama* also suggests being always the same, constant, equable, impartial, and even-minded. The *jīvanmukta* is calm and *sama* in all states of awareness.[20] Amid whatever happens, the liberated sage always remains the same, as motionless water and shifting waves, or still air and gusting wind, are the same (*Mumukṣu* 4. 1, 5).

Detachment is even more commonly mentioned; entire chapters are devoted to the nature of detachment and behavior of the detached *jīvanmukta* (see *Upaśama* 77). Detachment brings the highest end and is the essential cause of crossing *saṃsāra*.[21] The detached sage is unchanging in joy and despair, thinks "the partless self is all," and has lost all desire and anger.[22] *Jīvanmuktas* wander the world with detached minds whether rulers (like Janaka) or renouncers.[23]

Throughout the *Yogavāsiṣṭha,* the detached *jīvanmukta* is said to be always even-minded and indifferent to the dualities of sorrow *and* joy, dislikes *and* (pleasant) desires.[24] He does not give or take praise or blame, joy or grief; he is not ashamed or shameless, elated or sad.[25] The liberated being may laugh or cry on the outside, but truly remains unmoved,[26] desiring neither what most people wish for nor avoiding what people detest.[27] A real sage is to be sorrowless whether god or ruler, failure or worm (Up 93. 98–99). The *Yogavāsiṣṭha* mentions, but does not emphasize, that the *jīvanmukta* ultimately realizes that there is not even any bondage or liberation. The nondual self cannot be bound, and if it is not bound, how can there be release? For one not even considering bondage or liberation, the world is one.[28]

The Jīvanmukta *and Action in the World*

More than any other Advaita text discussing *jīvanmukti*, the *YV* emphasizes the *jīvanmukta*'s detached action in worldly or everyday activity (*vyavahāra*).[29] The text asserts that many men (and gods) abide in *saṃsāra* while liberated, doing various activities in everyday life with a "cool mind" (Up 75. 25–26).[30] The *jīvanmukta* goes in the world, not abandoning or striving after anything, being in accord with all beings (S 46. 26). The *JMV* will make similar points, but puts more emphasis on renunciation (*saṃnyāsa*).

Instead of rigorous world renunciation, then, the *Yogavāsiṣṭha* emphasizes that one should do whatever course of action falls to one (P 56. 3). A *jīvanmukta* performs everyday activities according to his circumstances (*yathāsthita*) and does whatever is proper to his place without attachment. Internally renounced, the *mukta* does actions according to customary or family duties and his own *karma*.[31] Content with whatever is obtained, the *jīvanmukta* takes whatever comes with equanimity.[32] This peacefulness allows the sage to understand human behavior and the world as they are, without delusion (Up 18. 10).

The contrast between external activity (like following customary duties) and inward detachment is a constant theme. We saw earlier that due to internal indifference, the sage is not really joined to any aim and reaps no fruits. That is, the truly detached person never "acts" in the karmic sense (and is certainly never said to do "evil" acts). Outwardly, this being *seems* active and hoping for good, but inwardly grasps no hope and does not act.[33] While acting and enjoying, the liberated being has abandoned the illusion of being the doer; only fools think "this act will I shun, this act will I choose."[34] The *jīvanmukta* is, in a sense, "sleepwalking"; with a one-pointed "sleep mind," he is not a doer even while acting. When "asleep while awake," one who does all does nothing (that is, nothing that brings fruits).[35] Because of apparent worldliness, the *jīvanmukta* is not recognized as liberated by unliberated folk, despite having destroyed all mental impressions and possessing an unmoving mind.[36]

The *Yogavāsiṣṭha* clearly takes the position that, according to the highest truth, there is no gain by doing or not doing anything (Ut 125. 49). Some *jīvanmuktas* have abandoned action and duties, and some have not (we shall see that the *JMV* generally takes a "harder line" on the importance of *saṃnyāsa*). This point is made most clearly in *Utpatti khaṇḍa* 199, which describes the diversity of behavior among detached and liberated beings, and begins with the question, "What is the point of abandoning *or* desiring any action?" The wise know there is nothing to be striven for or abandoned, so, as said earlier, they do whatever is appropriate to their station. Some with detached minds are kings or householders, and others wander,[37] having abandoned all duties. Some follow actions prescribed in the Veda, adhering to the *agnihotra*, and so on, and those within the four *varṇas* ("castes") perform various actions such as meditation, worshipping gods (*devārcana*), and so on (199. 9–12).

On the other hand, some abandon everything and remain beyond all (dharmic) acts eternally. They devote themselves to meditation in empty forests, or practice conduct to gain peace, promote virtue, and be loved by the wise and good. Some leave their native places to avoid desire and hatred, and they settle elsewhere. Others wander from place to place, whether woods, city, mountain, shore, or cave. Visits to Banaras, Prayāga, Badari, and Mathurā, among other holy cities and mountains, are mentioned with approval (199. 13–24).

Still, the text continues, many sages are settled "in the world," and the cause of liberation is not forest dwelling or practicing austerity. In fact, those who are proud of their knowledge and who abandon all action are only half awakened. The chapter concludes that neither abandoning nor resorting to action is the essential cause of crossing *saṃsāra;* as stated elsewhere, a detached mind is what brings liberation and nonreturn (199. 28–33).

The Variety of Liberated Beings

The *jīvanmukta* is generally seen as a human being, though there also are a number of references to gods as *jīvanmuktas*.[38] King Janaka is the most often cited *jīvanmukta* in the *Yogavāsiṣṭha.* Desireless, cool, and even-minded, Janaka rules and acts without delusion and with flawless insight; he does whatever comes without attachment and knows the self of all beings.[39] *Upaśama* 75 mentions Janaka, along with a long list of other humans and gods, who are *jīvanmuktas*, acting in the world while detached. This chapter, more than any other in the *YV* and unlike any other Advaita text when considering *jīvanmukti,* shows the wide variety of beings who are liberated while living. It begins by referring to Janaka, who governs his kingdom while detached, as do Buddha (!) and Manu, who is eternally the form (*ākṛti*) of *jīvanmukti.* Māndhātā also obtained the highest goal, though constantly active in battle.[40] Bali, a renouncer doing good in hell, and Prahlāda, protector of hell, are both detached *jīvanmuktas*. While possessing desire, they act without desire (Ut 125. 62).[41] Namuci and Vṛtra have inner control and cool minds while fighting; other gods, drinking *soma*, are detached. Even the sacrificial fire, which eats all, is free while enjoying.

Lord Hari, always free, moves and plays in the sea of duality.[42] Liberated Śiva is joined in body with Gaurī, and Skandha makes war while *mukta*. Sage Nārada, liberated by nature, wanders with cool actions, and the *jīvanmukta* Viśvamitra presides over Vedic sacrifices. Śeṣa bears the earth, Sūrya makes the day, and Yama causes death, all while *jīvanmukta.* Many other *yakṣas, asuras*, and men abide in this realm of rebirth while actually liberated. Acting in everyday life with an inner coolness, they are unmoving, like stones.

This passage indicates clearly that dharmic behavior and a liberated mind can be linked. Mental detachment and world renunciation are not identical. Further, as we saw in the previous section, these gods and humans need not reside in any particular place. Some (Bhṛgu, Viśvamitra), having attained the highest knowledge, go to the forest, and some (Janaka) remain as rulers. Some abide in the sky, some in the sphere of the gods, and some (like Bali and Prahlāda) in a cavelike hell. Even some animals are said to be wise, and some gods are foolish. All of this indicates that knowledge, not bodily form or location, leads to *jīvanmukti.*

Bodiless Liberation (Videhamukti)

The notion that embodiment is not central to defining who is liberated is an important theme in the *Yogavāsiṣṭha.* The point is made explicitly in a number of places: the liberated sage is the same with or without a body, like still water and rolling waves or gusting wind and motionless air are the same. With or without form, one does not experience objects or enjoyments; in both conditions, the *jīvanmukta* sees oneness of the self (M 4. 1–6). A peaceful mind, untouched by joy, sorrow, or their objects, is possible with or without a body.[43]

Upon first reflection, it seems implausible to speak of the irrelevance of the body's presence or absence. However, like Śaṅkara and Vidyāraṇya's *Jīvanmuktiviveka,* the *Yogavāsiṣṭha* asserts that one can be "disembodied" while in the body. This notion is put most clearly in Up 60. 2–7: When all-knowing, you are free from life and death in the body. Although embodied, when detached you are *adeha* (not embodied) like the wind in the sky. The body is irrelevant to those at peace and knowing the real. Since you are always one pure consciousness, why should you grasp or reject the body? Echoing Śaṅkara, the *YV* states that "I am embodied" is a false notion,[44] and emphasizes detachment and right knowledge. *Uttaranirvāṇa* 125. 31–32, 38 adds that once liberated, the mind of the embodied *jīvanmukta* is not bound and never again bindable, like a fruit fallen from its stalk. The *jīvanmukta*'s essence does not die at (body) death. Thus, one's fundamental identity is not tied to one's body.

Despite this line of reasoning, there are numerous passages distinguishing those liberated in the body (*jīvanmukta*) and those liberated without a body (*a-* or *videha-mukta*). In fact, the "Yogic Advaita" texts introduce the category "*videhamukti*," not used in scholastic Advaita (though some later schoolmen refer to *videha-kaivalya*). According to Up 42. 11–13, two types of liberation are possible, with and without a body. The *jīvanmukta* is detached and desireless, while the bodiless *videhamukta* is free from rebirth and does not enter the visible (*dṛśyatā*). *Utpatti* 9, which begins by saying that those who reflect and are solely intent on knowledge of the self reach both forms of *mukti*, later describes *videhamukti* as like motionless wind, not rising or setting, existing or not existing, without I or other.[45] Interestingly, this kind of liberation is here termed *nirvāṇa,* literally, of course, "extinction."

In this context, it is often implicit or explicit that while *jīvanmukti* is truly liberation, *videhamukti* is a little "higher" kind of liberation—a notion that also appears in the *JMV*. *Upaśama* 16. 14–17 say that complete abandoning of *jñeya* ("thinkable") *vāsanās* leads to cessation and the *videhamukta*'s bodiless freedom in all-encompassing *brahman*. Merely abandoning *dhyeya* ("fit for meditation") *vāsanās* leaves one with a (moving) body although the body is unafflicted and one is indifferent and "gone to *brahman*hood." *Upaśama* 90. 4 says there is extinction of mind (*citta-nāśa*) with form (*sarūpa, jīvanmukti*) and without form (*arūpa, dehamukti*).[46] The latter is the highest: pure, flawless, beyond *sattva*-bearing good qualities (*guṇa*), and beyond joy and sorrow; nothing at all is seen there (90. 23–27).

Finally, *Upaśama* 71. 2–3 asserts that *jīvanmukti* is the mysterious and final "fourth" (*turīya*), but *adehamukti* is beyond the fourth. Only *videhamuktas* reach the distant way of peace, like only birds reach the way of the sky.[47] Thus, although the main stream of the *Yogavāsiṣṭha* suggests that liberation is one, whether in a body or not, nonembodiment here, as elsewhere in the tradition, sometimes seems a higher (non) condition than embodiment.

The Nature of the Jīvanmukta*'s Mind*

The nature of the liberated being's mind (*cetas, citta, dhi, manas*)[48] is another oft-discussed aspect of *jīvanmukti* in "Yogic Advaita." In many passages of the *YV*, the mind (the locus of desire and ignorance) is seen as our greatest problem and its destruction (or at least control) the way to liberation. We shall later see that mental impressions (*vāsanā*) and their presence (or absence) are a particular focus when the mind is discussed. This terminology is largely foreign to the Advaita schoolmen, though we will find some more systematic reflections on the nature of the mind in the *Jīvanmuktiviveka*.

Many passages devalue the mind: the mind pervaded by *tāmasic* (dull, ignorant) impressions is the cause of birth and is the root and seed of the forest of sorrows (Up 90. 6–9). The mind is a *vāsanā* mass causing rebirth, and the ignorant *(mūḍha, aprabuddha)* mind is bound and born repeatedly (P 101. 28, 31–32). Further, *jīvanmuktas* and those knowing reality (*tattva-jña*) have no minds (or destroyed minds); awakened beings are not "mind-based" (*citta-bhū*). Pure and clear minds are called *sattva;* in such minds, burnt by the fire of knowledge, delusion does not sprout again—as burnt seeds sprout no flowers.[49] Other passages point to the *jīvanmukta*'s controlled (vs. destroyed) mind: it rests unmoving, with senses controlled and passions gone, without pride, lust, or envy, having doubts burnt by knowledge.[50]

Using more traditional Advaitic language, the *YV* says one should in particular abandon the aspect of the mind called the "I" notion (*ahaṃkāra, ahaṃbhāva*). The attachment to separate "individuality" causes great sorrow. One is a detached and clear-minded *jīvanmukta* when without the "I" in action or rest and when the "me" and "mine" are utterly destroyed.[51] The "I" notion is treated in more detail twice, when it is said that the *jīvanmukta* attains the highest viewpoint. *Sthiti* 33. 49–53 describes three types of *ahaṃkāra*: the first (worldly, or *laukika*) imagines the body with hand and foot; this body-based conception must be forsaken, as it causes desire and attachment. The second type, linked to *jīvanmukti*, imagines the "I" as a minuscule hair and pure consciousness different from all. The highest liberating conception is of the self as all this (*"ahaṃ sarvam idaṃ viśvam"*).

Upaśama 17.13–20 is roughly similar, but adds a fourth kind of "I" notion. The first conception, tied to bondage, sees the "I" and body as made by mother and father; the second, bound for liberation, sees the "I" as finer than a hair and beyond all beings. The third "I" notion is the indestructible self, the essence of world appearance that never experiences sorrow. The fourth "I" concept is held by *śūnyavādins* (adherents of emptiness); to them, the "I" and world are completely empty, like the sky.[52] Each of the latter three are said to shine as *jīvanmukti.*

Both of these descriptions hold to an Advaitic understanding: the first concept is dualistic and tied to bondage, the second "almost there" but still contains some separation, and the third recognizes the nondual self. Given that the latter conceptions are "higher," one wonders why the emptiness view is put last; unified fullness should transcend "mere" emptiness.

*Mental Impressions (*Vāsanā*) and the* Jīvanmukta

The existence and destruction of latent impressions (*vāsanā*) in the mind are a particular focus of the *Yogavāsiṣṭha,* and of Yogic Advaita generally.[53] *Vāsanās* are said to be the cause of bondage and their absence the cause of liberation (*Uttaranirvāṇa* 125. 61). As stated earlier, the mind at root is a mass of mental impressions causing rebirth.[54] Attachments are evil (*malina*) *vāsanās* and only fools are bound to them. The impure and unreal embodied self (*jīva*) has the form (*ākāra*) of *vāsanās*, and the *jīva* ceases when *vāsanās* cease. Even those devoted to the *dharma,* if not free from impressions, are bound like a bird in a cage. There is no permanent satisfaction, even in pleasant *vāsanās*: one bound to impressions enjoys what is desired but also suffers from their loss. *Vāsanās* constantly change to joy or sorrow in the presence or absence of desired objects.[55]

Pure (*śuddha*) *vāsanās* are free from joy and sorrow, and cause no further birth. When fully awakened, one gains no pleasure from objects nor suffers when they are destroyed—so one should try to minimize or remove *vāsanās*.[56] As *mokṣa* is free from *vāsanās,* the *jīvanmukta* is free from the snare of mental impressions; in fact, *vāsanā* destruction is a defining characteristic of one liberated while living (as it is in the *JMV*). Such absence of *vāsanās* also brings inner coolness.[57]

As mentioned earlier, *Upaśama* 16. 9–14 describes two kinds of *vāsanās,* those fit for meditation (*dhyeya*) and those to be known (*jñeya*). The former seems to refer to a more limited set of impressions than the latter. One destroys *dhyeya vāsanās* by acting with a cool intellect (*antaḥśītala-buddhi*) and abandoning the notion of an "I-maker." One devoted to destroying such impressions is a *jīvanmukta* (like King Janaka).[58] The destruction of *jñeya vāsanās* brings indifference, peace, and renunciation of the body, eventuating in attainment of *videhamukti.* The two types of *vāsanās* are unfortunately not described further here, but they do affirm the aforementioned notion that *videhamukti* is a bit "higher" than *jīvanmukti.*

When the *jīvanmukta's vāsanās* (or lack thereof) are discussed, the term *sattva* (sometimes spelled *satva*), untainted wisdom, regularly appears. The *jīvanmukta* is said to possess pure *sattva-vāsanās,* which lead to freedom from rebirth. Noble Prahlāda rested 1,000 years turned within to his own *sattva-vāsanās*.[59] More commonly, we hear that the *jīvanmukta*'s mind *is sattva* when without *vāsanās*. The awakened mind or intellect with clear discrimination is called *sattva.* The *jīvanmukta*'s "*vāsanā*" is not really a *vāsanā,* but pure wisdom (*śuddha-sattva*). Worldly *vāsanās* are called mind, but the *jīvanmukta* has gone to the *sattva* realm.[60]

Further, the *sattva*-established mind of the *jīvanmukta* is variously called controlled, abandoned, and destroyed. When the mind is destroyed but with form (i.e., *jīvanmukti*), it is explicitly called *sattva;* when one's (destroyed) mind attains formlessness, his pure wisdom, bearing a mass of good qualities (*guṇa*) also disappears.[61] *Sattva* absence, like body absence, is the highest state.

The references above to *sattva*, the *guṇas*, and mental processes generally bring to mind *Sāṃkhya/Yoga* conceptions. By far the most interesting passage relevant in this context is *Upaśama* 89. 9–21, which looks at why *jīvanmuktas* do not exhibit yogic *siddhis* (supernatural powers) like flying.[62] Following the Advaita view, it is said that knowing the nondual self is different from, and superior to, supernatural powers. Self-knowers are not attached to such powers, unlike the unliberated who try to master *mantras* or *yoga.* Self-knowers enjoy the self and do not sink into the ignorance of bondage to worldly things (including powers like flying). Knowers could fly if they wanted to, but they are beyond such things, content in the self, doing and desiring nothing.[63]

The Jīvanmukta's *"State of Consciousness"*

A related topic in the *YV's* "Yogic Advaita" discussion of *jīvanmukti* is the liberated being's elevated "state of consciousness," particularly when compared to everyday states such as dream and sleep. These ideas also are mentioned in the *JMV,* but most *JMV* references to the topics discussed next are borrowed from the *YV.* Even though awake, the *mukta*'s *vāsanās* and *vṛttis* are at rest. Thus, the liberated being is often described as "asleep while awake": detached and desireless, doing all while doing nothing, having perfect equanimity in activity. When acting with a one-pointed "sleep mind," this being is not a doer and acts without bondage.[64]

The *jīvanmukta*'s "state of consciousness" also is frequently discussed in the context of the fourfold *catuṣpād* doctrine (waking, dream, deep sleep, and the unifying "fourth," *turīya*).[65] Waking and dream mislead us into accepting illusory duality.[66] Deep sleep (*suṣupta*) is valued more highly because one then experiences no duality or suffering. In the *vāsanā*-less deep sleep state, the knower has equanimity and coolness within. When detached and possessing the self after "awakening" as a *jīvanmukta*, one sees like one asleep, that is, always fixed on the formless.[67]

Sleep, when *vāsanās* are destroyed, leads to the nondual fourth, *turīya,* which is also *jīvanmukti* (U 22. 7).[68] Blissful *turīya* is further described as the single object of *jīvanmukti* and of *vāk* (i.e., *śruti*), beyond fear, sorrow, and the illusion of *saṃsāra,* and without the bondage of rebirth or the darkness of egoism.[69] There is even a stage beyond the fourth, called *turīyātīta*, which is a nondual "state" beyond great (and no) bliss. *Turīyātīta*, unsurprisingly, is associated with bodiless (*videha*) liberation.[70]

Jīvanmukti also appears in a seven-stage (*bhūmi*) meditation model linked in the *Yogavāsiṣṭha* with the four states doctrine.[71] One version (P 120.

3–9) says *jīvanmukti* begins in the fifth stage (*ānandarūpa* or *śuddha saṃvid*), which is called "deep sleep" (*suṣupta*), since (like sleep) it is a mass of bliss. *Jīvanmukti* also exists in the sixth ("massed sleep," *suṣupta ghana*) and seventh (equanimous and peaceful *turīya*) stages. The utterly full (*paripraudha*) seventh stage is beyond the fourth (*turīyātīta*), the highest *nirvāṇa*, ungraspable by mind or words, and not the object of the living (i.e., *videhamukti*).

A second version (P 126. 64–71) says the sixth stage, beyond eternally restful "massed sleep," manifests *jīvanmukti*. This stage unites opposites: it is neither I or not I, being or not being, without duality or oneness, full and empty within and without, like a water-filled pot in the ocean (or an air-filled pot in air). The seventh stage is again called "bodiless liberation," which is peaceful and unreachable by words. While these models are not completely congruent (in this and many other respects), they do indicate the high status accorded to *jīvanmukti*, as well as its "junior" relationship to *videhamukti*.[72]

Conclusion

Let us review the main points the *Yogavāsiṣṭha* makes about liberation while living. Like mainstream Advaita, the *Yogavāsiṣṭha* holds that *jīvanmukti* arises from knowledge of the nondual self, not from austerity, powers, or karmic acts. The apparently manifold world with its pleasures and sorrows is an illusion (as bondage itself is ultimately an illusion). More in line with "Yogic Advaita" is the idea that utter detachment allows the *jīvanmukta* to act freely in the world according to *dharma*, or to renounce the world and all action. Gods and humans are liberated when detached, not due to any form of action—or inaction. Instead, the notion of being an "actor" disappears. Even embodiment itself can be seen as irrelevant to liberation, though there also is a recurrent theme that bodiless liberation is a little "higher" than *jīvanmukti*.

While mainstream Advaita emphasizes the self-body difference, the Yogic Advaita of the *YV* stresses the cessation of mind and its impressions. The *jīvanmukta*'s mind (and especially the individuating "I" notion) must be controlled or destroyed; all mental impressions (*vāsanā*), good or bad, must be removed—ultimately including the highest impression, *sattva*. The mind is fundamentally just a mass of mental impressions causing rebirth. The liberated being also must go beyond the illusions of waking, dreaming, and even undifferentiated deep sleep. The *jīvanmukta* rests in nondual *turīya*, the "state" beyond states of consciousness.

While Śaṅkara's Advaita and the *Yogavāsiṣṭha* emphasize different things, there are no irreconcilable contradictions. The *Yogavāsiṣṭha* spends more time on detached action in the world and the nature of the *jīvanmukta*'s mind (and mental states) than does Śaṅkara. There also is less concern with bodily continuity due to *prārabdha karma*, criticizing other *darśanas* or with rejecting dharmic action in the *Yogavāsiṣṭha.* Many aspects of this Yogic Advaita perspective also can be seen in the text to which we now turn, Vidyāraṇya's *Jīvanmuktiviveka*.

SEVEN

Yogic Advaita II: Liberation While Living in the Jīvanmuktiviveka[1]

The *Jīvanmuktiviveka* (*JMV*) (*Discerning Liberation while Living*)[2] is a syncretic fourteenth-century work by Vidyāraṇya,[3] which outlines the nature of living liberation and teaches the path to liberation via a combination of knowledge, yogic practice, and renunciation.[4] This text is especially interesting because of the author's attempt to weave a number of strands of Indian thought together into what I have called "Yogic Advaita." While primarily an adherent of Advaita (nondual) Vedanta, Vidyāraṇya also emphatically enjoins following the ascetic path, and refers far more often and more favorably than does Śaṅkara to the yogic practices of Patañjali and the *Bhagavad-Gītā*. In a way rarely seen in Śaṅkara's "mainstream" Advaita, Vidyāraṇya claims that *yoga* and ascetic renunciation (*saṃnyāsa*) together both lead to and express the liberating knowledge (*jñāna, vidyā*) of *brahman*. In fact, the text uses the terms *yogin, saṃnyāsin,* and *mukta* (with appropriate qualifiers) to identify the same person—one with full knowledge of nondual *brahman*.

Another indication of Vidyāraṇya's Yogic Advaita is his repeated citation of the *Laghu* (short or abridged) *Yogavāsiṣṭha* (*LYV*);[5] at times, the *JMV* virtually becomes a commentary on the *LYV*. While deeply influenced by the *LYV*, the *JMV* is more respectful of Vedic and *saṃnyāsa* traditions linked with mainstream Advaita, while the *LYV* has a much greater complement of *Sāṃkhya*, Puranic, and Buddhist ideas.

The significant differences in emphasis and focus between Vidyāraṇya's (and the *LYV*'s) Yogic Advaita and Śaṅkara's mainstream "Vedantic" Advaita rarely lead to direct opposition or contradiction—thus it is still Advaita. For example, Vidyāraṇya does not dispute Śaṅkara's (and most later Advaitins') views on the importance of ending identification of self and body, and on bodily continuity, due to currently manifesting (*prārabdha*) *karma,* but he does not focus on them. He spends much more time than does Śaṅkara on yogic issues relating to the mind and its manifestations (*citta-vṛtti*) and the importance of renunciation to make suffering cease. While Vidyāraṇya talks of *ātman/brahman* more than of *puruṣa/prakṛti,* he describes the *Sāṃkhya* evolutes at some length and makes far more use of *Sāṃkhya* and *Yoga* terminology and analysis than does Śaṅkara. The *JMV* cites Śaṅkara, and other Advaitins like Sureśvara,[6] but references to the *Sāṃkhya-Yoga* influenced *LYV* and *Bhagavad-Gītā* are far more extensive.

Unlike Śaṅkara, who takes a dialectical approach (stressing reasoning and debate), Vidyāraṇya seems to be a syncretist. Where Śaṅkara excludes or disputes *Yoga* concepts of mental activity or *Sāṃkhya* ideas of world evolution, Vidyāraṇya wants to be inclusive, or at least omit opposition. Yogic Advaita agrees with the Advaita schoolmen that knowledge of nondual *brahman* is the *sine qua non* of *jīvanmukti.* However, while Śaṅkara holds that yogic practice is at best merely a preparatory form of action, Vidyāraṇya claims it is central in attaining and safeguarding *brahman* knowledge. We shall see that this perspective further shapes Vidyāraṇya's views on the relationships between embodiment and liberation, and renunciation and living in the world.

The Nature of Jīvanmukti

As stated previously, Vidyāraṇya holds that knowledge of nonduality is the fundamental cause of liberation while living, but yogic practice is necessary to gain and safeguard this knowledge. Both aspects can be seen in his definition of liberation while living. He writes, "Bondage exists for a living being since the nature of affliction [is] having mental notions consisting of joy and sorrow, being enjoyer and doer, and so on. Living liberation is the cessation of this."[7] When such dualistic notions as "I am doer/enjoyer" cease due to knowledge of *brahman,* one is liberated while living. Vidyāraṇya then immediately adds a yogic component to this Advaita claim; he writes that ultimately all mental modifications (*citta-vṛtti*) that cause this bondage can be overcome by repeated yogic practice (*yogābhyāsa*) (10, 195). Here and throughout the text, Vidyāraṇya's view seems to be that the *jīvanmukta* must, first and foremost, realize nondual *brahman* and thereby gain Advaitic serenity; but he must also concomitantly work to end suffering by destroying the mind and its impressions (*vāsanā*) by means of renunciation (*saṃnyāsa*) and yogic enstasis (*samādhi*). According to Vidyāraṇya, then, attaining living liberation requires personal renunciation and yogic body mastery as necessary complements to nondual knowledge.

One of Vidyāraṇya's main reasons for emphasizing yogic practice for the *jīvanmukta* is related to *yoga*'s role in removing *karma* currently bearing fruit (*prārabdha karma*) (10, 195). Vidyāraṇya follows mainstream Advaita in holding that the fruits of currently manifesting *karma* obstruct ignorance-destroying knowledge and cause the body and senses to continue. However, he parts company with the Śaṅkaran tradition by claiming that one can overcome the necessity of experiencing the fruits of actions by making personal effort—specifically repeated yogic practice. Vidyāraṇya here argues (unlike Śaṅkara) that even though *prārabdha karma* is stronger than ignorance-destroying knowledge, yogic practice is stronger even than *prārabdha karma* (11,196). He repeatedly declares the necessity of human effort to overcome being controlled by mental modifications and preexisting *karma*. These efforts include Advaitic means such as following the sacred texts (*śāstra*) and associating with the wise (although he does not here mention the fourfold *sādhana* Śaṅkara discusses in *Brahmasūtra bhāṣya* 1. 1. 1) as well as yogic efforts such as resisting desires and controlling the mind. He cites approvingly the *LYV* claim that all results—hell, heaven, or liberation—derive from human effort, and only right effort can bring the highest goal (12, 197–8). He also endorses the *LYV* claim that strong and repeated personal effort will allow one to guide the everflowing stream of mental impressions (*vāsanā*) into the right channel, creating waves of good (*śubha*) impressions that wash over impure ones (13, 199).[8] Śaṅkara, on the other hand, carefully separates the effort of yogic practice from knowledge, which alone brings liberation.[9] Thus, in Vidyāraṇya's Yogic Advaita, unlike mainstream Advaita, yogic effort is necessary to both foster and sustain knowledge of nondual *brahman*.

However, Vidyāraṇya curiously changes course at this point (15, 201). He agrees with the *LYV* statement that after accumulating enough good impressions, one then gives up *all* impressions and desires, including the desire to follow a sacred text and a master. When the highest goal is realized, the effort to give up all desires is abandoned. Put another way, the supreme effort takes one to a state beyond any effort. Vidyāraṇya concludes that *jīvanmukti* is indisputably due to the disappearance of all desire by yogic practice.

Vidyāraṇya could be clearer here. He is perhaps suggesting that efforts and practices, even yogic ones, indicate that one still sees the world dualistically, as if there is something left to do or someplace to get. Ultimately, however, the *jīvanmukta* is content with whatever comes his way—and "whatever" comes, of course, only from currently manifesting (*prārabdha*) *karma,* since the *jīvanmukta* no longer initiates any efforts of his own. We will return to this point when we discuss the highest renunciant (*paramahaṃsa*) *yogin.*

The Jīvanmukta *as* Sthita-prajña

We can also find yogic Advaita in Vidyāraṇya's interpretation of the *Bhagavad-Gītā*, particularly in his consideration of the *jīvanmukta* as one having firm wisdom (*sthita-prajña*) (20, 211 ff.). It is significant that the *Gītā*, with its extensive use of *Sāṃkhya* and *Yoga* categories like qualities (*guṇa*) and mental manifestations (*citta-vṛtti*), is second only to the *LYV* in number of references throughout the *JMV*. This suggests not only the authority of the *Gītā* to Vidyāraṇya and his audience, but also its congeniality with his views. Vidyāraṇya wants to show that the existence of living liberation is established through the many scriptural references, not only to the *jīvanmukta* per se, but also to one having firm wisdom, one who is devoted to the Lord (*bhagavad-bhakta*), to one gone beyond the three qualities (*guṇātītā*), to one who is a true Brahmin, and to one who has transcended caste and life stage (*ativarṇāśramin*). According to Vidyāraṇya, all of these persons are (at least potentially) liberated while living.

Vidyāraṇya spends considerable time elaborating on the *Gītā*'s description (II. 54-72) of the *sthita-prajña.* He explains that firm wisdom gives knowledge of the real (*tattva-jñāna,* the highest end of *jīvanmukti*), and one with firm wisdom, abandoning all desires, attains the highest renunciation by repeated yogic practice. The *sthita-prajña*'s mind never budges from the truth, and (in an image surprising given the text's misogyny) the sage focused on truth is compared to a woman whose mind is constantly on her lover, forgetting even her household duties (20, 211). Vidyāraṇya holds to the mainstream Advaita position that knowing the self brings supreme satisfaction and a bliss higher than any bliss from mental manifestations, including those in concentrated (*saṃprajñāta*) *samādhi.* The *sthita-prajña* is detached from joy and sorrow, attraction and repulsion, craving, anxiety, and anger. These attachments arise from actions currently bearing fruit, and especially from dull, ignorance-filled (*tāmasic*) mental impressions (*vāsanā*). Such impressions are impossible for a sage (22, 214).

While the *sthita-prajña* is also an exemplar of the liberated being to Śaṅkara, we saw that his description emphasizes the *sthita-prajña*'s knowledge of *brahman* and desireless renunciation. Vidyāraṇya again adds a strong yogic component: by the repeated practice of meditative enstasis (*samādhi*), the *sthita-prajña*'s senses are restrained and mastered and *brahman* is "seen" (23, 216). Before knowledge arises, pursuing it by means like *samādhi* takes effort, but such means become natural for one with firm knowledge. Put another way, efforts (like *samādhi*) bring and safeguard knowledge; after the rising of firm wisdom, *samādhi* is natural. Knowing the self by unbroken self-illumination is in fact called *jīvanmukti* (25, 217).[10] Again, we see Vidyāraṇya's ambivalence about the necessity of unceasing yogic efforts for a *jīvanmukta.* He seems to want to hold both that unceasing efforts are necessary and that the one who reaches the highest goal is beyond any effort.

The Threefold Means to Obtain Jīvanmukti

So far we have seen how Vidyāraṇya describes the nature of living liberation; we next consider his views on how to reach this *mukti.* The largest portion of the *Jivanmuktiviveka* (37, 232 ff.) is devoted to describing and analyzing the threefold means for obtaining liberation while living: knowing the truth (*tattva-jñāna*), extinguishing the mind (*mano-nāśa*), and destroying mental impressions (*vāsanā-kṣaya*). While Vidyāraṇya holds that priority must be given to knowing the truth (the highest end in Advaita), he also claims that without practicing all three means, liberation while living is impossible. These means are mutually reinforcing and should be worked on together. Both the focus on the mind and its impressions and the model of threefold means are central to Vidyāraṇya's Yogic Advaita, and references to the *LYV* and the *Gītā* abound in this section. On the other hand, the threefold means to liberation does not appear in Śaṅkara's Advaita, which holds that yogic practices of any sort are a form of action, and thus are ultimately part of the lower, dualistic realm.

Vidyāraṇya analyzes the relationship of these three means by discussing the continuity and discontinuity among them (this is formally called "positive and negative concomitance" or *anvaya-vyatireka*). Throughout this section he seems to be both descriptive and normative. For example, he claims that destroying impressions and extinguishing the mind must take place simultaneously (40, 237). Impure impressions (*vāsanā*) generate anger and other mental forms (*ākāra*); destroying such impressions prevents anger from arising (even with just cause), since it implants pure impressions like self-restraint and equanimity born of right discrimination (another way of saying *tattva-jñāna*). When mental manifestations (*vṛtti*) cease (*mano-nāśa*), new, impure impressions will not arise, and when impure impressions are destroyed, mental transformations will cease.

Mental manifestations also cease by the first means, knowing the truth (*tattva-jñāna*), that is, knowing that apparent diversity is illusory and the self alone is real. Until nonduality is known, mental forms continue as a fire constantly fed with fuel continues. These ever-arising forms then reaffirm the experience of apparent diversity, creating a never-ending cycle. Thus, knowing the truth of nonduality destroys mental impressions like anger, whose destruction, with the concomitant rise of equanimity, reveals nondual *brahman.* Vidyāraṇya is suggesting that practicing any one means reinforces the others. His emphasis on the importance of repeated human effort, particularly to counter impure mental impressions by developing pure impressions, shows the influence of *yoga.* Impressions are not destroyed all at once, nor is liberation gained with one insight. Knowledge and yogic practice are linked, for discerning nonduality breeds the cessation of mental activity, and ceasing mental activity by *yoga* assists seeing nonduality.

Vidyāraṇya also points out that these three means stand in different relationship for renouncers desiring and those already possessing knowledge—though in all cases these means should be pursued simultaneously. In seeking to clarify the proper relationship of these means, Vidyāraṇya is perhaps settling a then-current dispute on primacy of means to liberation (within Vedanta or between "Vedantins" and "*yogins*"). For the renouncer seeking knowledge (*vividiṣā-saṃnyāsin*), coming to know the truth (*tattva-jñāna*) is primary; but for the renouncer already having knowledge (the *jīvanmukta*), extinguishing the mind and destroying impressions is primary. While *vāsanās* and mental manifestations continue after knowledge (thus necessitating continued yogic practice), becoming a *jivanmukta* is not possible without gaining knowledge (45, 244).[11]

Destroying the Mind to Gain Living Liberation

Vidyāraṇya's entire chapter on extinguishing the mind (*mano-nāśa*) indicates his Yogic Advaita; the chapter's theme is controlling and restraining the mind by yogic discipline, particularly Patañjali's eight-limbed *yoga.*[12] He claims that while the mind is extinguished when mental impressions are destroyed, only repeated practice of *mano-nāśa* secures permanent destruction of mental impressions. In fact, Vidyāraṇya begins the chapter by calling extinguishing the mind *the* means to living liberation (*atha jīvanmukti-sādhanam manonāśam*), for only extinction of the mind keeps destroyed impressions from ever rising again (86, 303).

This *yoga*-oriented emphasis on extinguishing the mind is not found in Śaṅkara or later mainstream Advaitins, yet Vidyāraṇya's exegesis of *mano-nāśa* still affirms the centrality of knowledge of *brahman.* Yogic practices, while crucial on the path to *jīvanmukti,* must still be informed by knowledge of the nondual self. For example, Vidyāraṇya notes that some *yogins* attain supernatural powers (*siddhi*) like flying, which are not seen in *jīvanmuktas.* However, even one ignorant of the self can get powers like flying, and such powers are not the object of self-knowledge. The pursuit of powers only indicates one's ignorance and does not help one attain the highest end. All desires must cease, so desiring powers is ultimately an obstacle. Further, since such wonderful powers come from the self, any one who knows the self could achieve them (103, 327).[13] This passage echoes a common Indian refrain that *brahman*-knowers can certainly gain and use supernatural powers, but they are too wise and detached to do so. Such claims affirm the ultimacy of the path of knowledge over yogic mastery.

Throughout the chapter on extinguishing the mind, Vidyāraṇya examines types of meditative enstasis (*samādhi*) that aim to still the mind, and urges the cessation of the activity of *Sāṃkhyan* evolutes through yogic practice. However, he says, even the highest (*nirodha* or *asaṃprajñāta*) yogic *samādhi* is not the final goal; it leads to knowledge of the self (114, 344). Vidyāraṇya here indicates clearly a limitation in *yoga* alone: texts of the *Yoga* school focus only on stilling the mind by *samādhi,* so they do not explicitly mention the Advaitic realization of the self (*ātma-darśana*), and seeing the self is the ultimate goal. He claims that even after one attains the highest *samādhi,* another mental manifestation (*vṛtti*) called knowledge of *brahman* (*brahma-vidyā*) must arise in order to reach identity with *brahman.* This *vṛtti* appears by hearing the *Upaniṣadic* great statements (*mahāvākya*), like "you are that" (*tat-tvam-asi*). Thus, one can realize one's self, the "basis of you" (*tvaṃpadārtha*), by either the highest meditative enstasis (*yoga*) *or* by *Sāṃkhyan* discrimination of consciousness (*cit*) and gross matter (*jaḍa*), but one only realizes the highest (Advaita) teaching that the self (the "basis of you") is *brahman* by the *Upaniṣadic* great sayings (115, 345). Once again we see Vidyāraṇya's "Yogic Advaita" holds both that meditation is vital *and* that the path of knowledge is higher.[14]

Another passage that makes this point appears when Vidyāraṇya directly addresses the relative status of a *yogin* and a knower (147, 391). He considers whether the *yogin* concentrated (*samāhita*) in meditation is better than the truth-knower involved in the world (*loka-vyavahāra*). He quotes *Laghu Yogavāsiṣṭha* 25. 5–9 which states that they are equally good, if both keep their "inner cool" (*antaḥśītalatā*). This inner cool takes form as both destruction of impressions and extinction of the mind. For Vidyāraṇya, the key to liberation is mental quiescence, not action (or lack thereof) in the world.

He continues by arguing that at one level the *yogin* concentrated in meditation is better than a person involved in the world, although ultimately knowing the truth is the highest goal. Generally, *samādhi* is better than worldly involvement. If one lacks knowledge and still has mental impressions, *samādhi* practice is better because it leads to heaven (*uttama loka*). However, worldly involvement without mental impressions is better than *samādhi* with them—and such a *samādhi* is not really the highest *samādhi* anyway. Once knowledge is fully established and impressions are absent, *samādhi* is then also superior to worldly involvement, for it preserves liberation while living (148,

392–3). Again, in Vidyāraṇya's Yogic Advaita, liberation is beyond mere yogic practice but is at risk without it.

Jīvanmukti *and* Videhamukti *in the* JMV

We also see the Yogic Advaita of the *JMV* in its discussion of the relationship between liberation while living (*jīvanmukti*) and bodiless liberation (*videhamukti*).[15] While Vidyāraṇya argues that one certainly gains liberation here (in life), he sometimes suggests that embodied liberation is not quite equal to liberation without a body. His reservation appears in two not completely congruent claims, to be documented more fully soon. Apparently influenced by the yogic notion that embodiment (with its inevitable suffering) is a limitation, he seems at times to claim that *videhamukti* is a greater achievement than *jīvanmukti*, precisely because one then has no body. In other places, he follows mainstream Advaita, asserting that liberation while living and after death are essentially similar, as both lack any notion of duality and in both only pure self-luminous consciousness remains. From this view, merely dropping the body, without the liberating knowledge of the unconditioned self, will inevitably bring reembodiment. One is fully liberated even while living, since the body and senses are merely adventitious adjuncts of the self.

Both of these claims can be seen in his very first reference to living versus bodiless *mukti* (15, 202 ff.). He here interprets *Kaṭha* V. 1, which says "having been liberated, he is released," to mean that one liberated from present bondage (like desire) while living is further liberated from future bondage at the fall of the body (*deha-pāta*).[16] This implies that *videhamukti* is beyond *jīvanmukti*, because one then has no body and this state lasts forever. However, he goes on here to say one *is* liberated when all mental manifestations (*dhi-vṛtti*) cease after knowledge, citing the *Bṛhadāraṇyaka Upaniṣad* IV. 4. 7 claim that the desireless sage realizes *brahman* even here. He explains (following Śaṅkara) that one should not aim merely to drop the body, since without liberation one will soon again be embodied in another birth. Only knowledge of the unconditioned self brings permanent liberation (16, 203). In the most important way, says Vidyāraṇya, liberation while living and after death are similar, as neither contain any notion of dualism. They are differentiated "merely" by the presence or absence of the body and senses, both adventitious adjuncts of the self (16, 204).

In the most interesting passage on this topic (45, 245 ff.), Vidyāraṇya introduces a new solution to this difficult issue of the relationship between full liberation and embodiment. He begins by saying that knowledge alone brings release or perfect isolation (*kaivalya*), and release means being bodiless (*videha*). Destroying impressions and extinguishing the mind without studying the knowledge texts (*jñāna-śāstra*) will not bring release, since only knowledge destroys the subtle body (*liṅga-deha*) and all bondage (46, 246).[17] Bodiless liberation is therefore simultaneous with the rise of knowledge. However, as seen earlier, he repeatedly claims that one can have knowledge while living (i.e., embodied). An implicit but obvious question then arises: How can this be so if bodilessness is simultaneous with the rise of knowledge?[18] Vidyāraṇya clarifies this point here with an interesting definitional maneuver. He claims one can have bodiless liberation while living. This view does not contradict mainstream Advaita, but he gives a novel articulation of it. He points out (accurately) that the term *deha* (body) has been understood in many ways (47, 247).[19] Here, *deha* refers just to *future* (*bhāvi*) bodies; the present body is a *prior* acquisition, so it can not cease even with knowledge. Bodiless liberation is thus freedom from future (not present) embodiment, and knowledge is simultaneous with *this* freedom. Dropping the present body is no mark of knowledge, for death will be reached eventually by even the most ignorant person.

Here, Vidyāraṇya, like other Advaitins, holds that knowledge removes only uncommenced (*anārabdha*) *karma,* not actions bearing fruit now (*prārabdha*) (47, 248). Knowledge is thus the necessary but not sufficient cause of bodilessness. Only when *prārabdha karma* ceases will the body/sense world cease. A fire must burn out its current fuel, and knowledge is not water, but absence of fuel. So knowledge and embodiment this time around are not related, allowing Vidyāraṇya to state "bodiless" liberation and knowledge arise simultaneously. Thus the *jīvanmukta*—who will take no future body—is also a *videhamukta*.[20]

However, Vidyāraṇya elsewhere seems to suggest that *videhamukti* is actual bodilessness, not living liberation with no future births (128, 365). He cites *LYV* 28. 15–27, which says that the extinguished mind has two modes: with form (*sarūpa*), belonging to the *jīvanmukta,* and without form (*arūpa*), belonging to the *videhamukta.*[21] The *jīvanmukta*'s "formed" mind (*sarūpa citta*) contains the quality of purity (*sattva guṇa*), full of attributes like friendliness. The extinguished mind of the *videhamukta* is beyond even this, however; it is formless, for even purity (*sattva*) is dissolved there. This apparently "bodiless mind" is pure bliss, taking all space itself (*ākāśa*) as its body. Thus, Vidyāraṇya seems to argue that while *jīvanmukti* is full liberation, bodiless (or space-embodied) *videhamukti* is a little fuller.

The Purposes of Attaining Liberation While Living

Vidyāraṇya's *yoga*-influenced Advaita is also evident in his description of the five "purposes" (*prayojana*) of attaining living liberation: guarding knowledge (*jñāna-rakṣa*), austerity (*tapas*), nondisputation (*visaṃvādābhāva*), destroying suffering (*duḥkha-nāśa*), and manifesting serenity (*sukhāvirbhāva*) (130, 367 ff.). One should note that Vidyāraṇya's usage of *prayojana*—translated by Sastri and Ayyangar as "purpose" or "aim"—can be taken a number of ways. *Jīvanmukti* would not seem to have any purpose beyond itself, for realizing nondual *brahman* while living is itself the ultimate aim of existence. Neither are the five "purposes" simply causes or benefits of living liberation. The difficulty can be partly clarified by the lack of distinction in the text between means and end. Vidyāraṇya seems to regard these "purposes" both as the practices of one who wants to reach liberation and the identifying marks of one who has already achieved it. Put another way, one practices these means to attain the highest end, and the achiever of the highest end is recognized by his constant practice of these means. Further, Vidyāraṇya is here describing the prescription for liberation (or better, prescribing his description).

Both the yogic and Advaita influences on Vidyāraṇya are apparent in his exposition of the five aims. Consistent with his claim that knowledge is the central, but not sole, characteristic of *jīvanmukti,* Vidyāraṇya makes clear that guarding (or preserving) knowledge is the primary purpose and mark of attaining liberation while living. However, he adds that unless the *jīvanmukta* guards his knowledge by practicing yogic pacification of mind, doubt (*saṃśaya*) and error (*viparyaya*) may arise, even after the truth is known (130, 367).[22]

Vidyāraṇya then differentiates knowers (*jñānin*) and *jīvanmuktas*, a distinction foreign to Śaṅkara but significant for *yoga*-influenced Advaita, for it suggests that "merely" knowing the truth is somehow less than the fullest liberation—which is brought by yogic practice. He describes types of *brahman*-knowers (*brahmavid*) based on the stage of knowledge each has achieved (134, 373). This categorization of *brahman*-knowers is based on passages from the *Laghu Yogavāsiṣṭha* (13. 113–23). As J. F. Sprockhoff points out (1970, p. 137 ff.), Vidyāraṇya combines the model of seven stages of knowledge (*jñānabhūmi*), seen in chapter 118 of the *Yogavāsiṣṭha*'s *Utpatti khaṇḍa*, with a similar model in *Pūrvanirvāṇa khaṇḍa* 126, which includes talk of states of consciousness.[23] One becomes a knower of *brahman,* but not yet a *jīvanmukta,* in the stage (fourth of seven), which brings the direct realization of *brahman/ātman* unity from the Vedantic great sayings.

The next three stages, Vidyāraṇya writes, are subdivisions (*avantārabheda*) of *jīvanmukti;* they derive from differing degrees of repose (*viśrānti*), which arise from repeated practice of unconditioned (or nonconceptual, *nirvikalpa*) *samādhi* (136, 375).[24] Thus, Vidyāraṇya holds that there are even degrees of *jīvanmukti,* and these degrees arise from yogic practice. Unlike Śaṅkara, who makes no distinction between a *brahman*-knower and a liberated being, Vidyāraṇya finds knowledge of *brahman* a necessary, but not sufficient, cause for *jīvanmukti.* How can one be a *brahman*-knower, but not a *jīvanmukta*?

According to Vidyāraṇya, only in the *jīvanmukti* stages does no doubt or error arise, since all appearance of duality has vanished. Only after one gains the repose from the highest *samādhi* is knowledge completely safeguarded (so *jīvanmukti* attained) (137, 377).

Vidyāraṇya also discusses how it is possible for a *brahman*-knower to have attachments, such as pride in learning, if the knowledge that ends in *jīvanmukti* supposedly allows for no pride (73, 285). Vidyāraṇya first claims the knower has only the semblance (*ābhāsa*) of attachment, and he recognizes its mere seeming, like recognizing the rope's appearance as a "snake." But what then of the sage Yājñavalkya, proud, greedy for cows, and even cursing Śakalya to death (*Bṛhadāraṇyaka Upaniṣad* 3. 1)?[25] Vidyāraṇya says Yājñavalkya is not a *jīvanmukta* with peaceful mind, even though he is a knower of *brahman* (74, 287). *Brahman*-knowers (unlike *jīvanmuktas*) have impure impressions like jealousy and anger. This point reinforces Vidyāraṇya's emphasis on continuing to extinguish the mind and mental impressions even after knowledge of the real. Further evidence is his distinction between 1) a knower (*jñānin*) or seeker (*vividiṣā*) renunciant and 2) a *jīvanmukta* or realized (*vidvat*) renunciant (51, 254).[26] The "mere" knower must renew his efforts of destroying impressions and extinguishing the mind to become fully realized. Due to currently manifesting (*prārabdha*) *karma,* even one with knowledge cannot permanently remove impressions and mental manifestations without practicing *yoga* steadily. Doubt, error, and other attachments fully disappear only when (by *yoga*) the mind is pacified (51, 255).

The four latter purposes or marks of attaining liberation while living reinforce and reflect the first, guarding knowledge. Austerity (*tapas*) focuses on gaining a one-pointed mind from yogic practice and detachment from works, not on bodily mortification (137, 377 ff.). The most interesting aspect of this section is Vidyāraṇya's suggestion that austerity provides for the welfare of the world (*loka-saṃgraha*). Here we may glimpse what a *jīvanmukta* does for others, his "social ethics" and role in society (which will be discussed at some length in the final chapter). Austerity here has a transpersonal, or even cosmic, potency.

Vidyāraṇya suggests that the "austere" *yogin* performs a most important activity or service by allowing others to follow, serve, and worship him. His presence is a great favor. For example, those who take the *yogin* as teacher (*guru*) attain knowledge rapidly. Devotees who provide his food and shelter are doing the equivalent of austerity by such service. Believers (*āstika*) merely observing him begin to follow the right path (*san-mārga*), and even unbelievers are freed from evil when seen by him. Thus, the opportunity to serve or even see the *yogin/jīvanmukta* arises from his grace (*upakāritva*).[27]

According to Vidyāraṇya, the third aim, nondisputation (*visaṃvādābhava*), arises because the sage has no concern with the world, so no reason for argument or censure rises. As he is without anger and talks only of the self, how could anyone dispute with him (143, 385)?[28] The last two aims of *jīvanmukti*, destroying suffering (*duḥkha-nāśa*) and manifesting serenity (*sukhāvirbhāva*) combine knowledge, following dharmic regulation, and renunciation (145, 388 ff.). Serenity, described in terms also used by Śaṅkara, manifests in three ways: obtaining all desires, completing all duties, and attaining all that is attainable (146, 389). Also like Śaṅkara, Vidyāraṇya here affirms that the *jīvanmukta* realizes he is *brahman,* and not a body. Thus, in Vidyāraṇya's Yogic Advaita, these aims and practices taken together both point to and demonstrate having reached and safeguarded the highest end, *jīvanmukti.*

Saṃnyāsa *and* Jīvanmukti

Throughout the text, Vidyāraṇya closely connects liberation while living with renunciation (*saṃnyāsa*). As suggested earlier, he distinguishes two kinds of renunciation: the renunciation of one who possesses knowledge (*vidvat*), which is the cause of liberation while living, and the renunciation of one who merely desires knowledge (*vividiṣā*), which causes liberation only after death (1, 177). (How exactly they "cause" liberation and how any liberation can happen after death go unexplained.)

While knowledge of nondual *ātman/brahman* is the defining feature of liberation, renunciation (which includes yogic practice) both leads to and follows knowledge. Vidyāraṇya's description of the practice (*sādhana*) of the renunciant (*saṃnyāsin*) is in line with mainstream Advaita. The *saṃnyāsin,* he says, renounces the worlds of the not self to experience the self alone, abandons desire-impelled actions, and studies the Veda (3, 181). The realized renunciant (*vidvat-saṃnyāsin*) specifically has attained the truth by having renounced worldly desires for offspring and wealth, and by having performed hearing, reflection on, and assimilation of (*śravana-manana-nididhyāsana*) the Veda (4, 183).

While virtually all Advaitins endorse *saṃnyāsa,* few emphasize it as much as Vidyāraṇya. He repeatedly prescribes rejecting the world's temptations. Attachment to wife and children is bad: women's bodies are tempting but disgusting, and parenting is a misery (77, 291 ff.). Isolation and indifference, on the other hand, bring many benefits. For example, the renunciant should not greet or bless others, because such acknowledgment demands the mental agitation of attending to proper word choice for salutation (29, 223). Following Śaṅkara (in *Upadeśasāhasrī* 17. 64), Vidyāraṇya here asks: When established in the nonduality beyond names, who would one greet (30, 224)? The *saṃnyāsin* should remain alone, focused on meditation; three mendicants together are a village, and more are a city. Solitude allows uninterrupted meditation, but a place full of people hinders realizing the bliss of the self (33, 228).

Again we see Vidyāraṇya's close intertwining of knowledge of nondual *brahman* with renunciation and yogic practices like solitary meditation. This emphasis on renunciation diverges from the *Yogavāsiṣṭha*'s stress on detached action in the world, seen in the prior chapter. The *JMV* repeatedly speaks of isolation and abnegation, while the *Yogavāsiṣṭha* puts more emphasis on the nondifference between bondage and liberation and the ease of completely detached action in the world. For the *YV*, abandonment of any activity is virtually optional.

The Way of Liberation: The Renunciation of the Paramahaṃsa Yogin

Vidyāraṇya recounts the *jīvanmukta*'s way of life most clearly in the final chapter of the *Jīvanmuktiviveka,* which forms a commentary on the *Paramahaṃsa Upaniṣad.* The chapter, devoted to describing the supremely ascetic (*paramahaṃsa*) *yogin* or realized renunciant (*vidvat-saṃnyāsin*), interweaves renunciation, yogic practice, and knowing nonduality. We here find the terms *yogin, saṃnyāsin,* and *mukta,* with their respective qualifiers (*paramahaṃsa*, *vidvat*, and *jīvan*) all identifying the same being. This discussion illustrates both the path to, and "lifestyle" in, living liberation. While Vidyāraṇya's understanding is undergirded by Advaitin metaphysics and ethics, it is certainly not narrowly Śaṅkaran, for it includes notions of yogic practice and transcending dharmic duties unexpressed by Śaṅkara.

To Vidyāraṇya, a *paramahaṃsa yogin* (i.e., *jīvanmukta*) combines the best qualities of the knower and the *yogin*: a mere *yogin* does not have knowledge of the real and desires supernatural powers like flying; a mere *paramahaṃsa,* while knowing reality (*brahman*), spurns Vedic injunctions and prohibitions (*vidhi-niṣedha*). A *paramahaṃsa yogin,* however, neither desires powers nor disregards injunctions (150, 395). Thus, this *yogin* still follows both the Vedantic and yogic paths. He removes ignorance (of nonduality) by realizing the meaning of the great sayings (*mahāvākya*) and removes impressions (*vāsanās*) arising from ignorance by repeated yogic practice (159, 412). Only together can these paths bring eternal awakening (*nitya-bodha*).

What then, Vidyāraṇya asks, is the worldly manner (dress, speech, etc.) of this rare bird of a *yogin*? And what is his internal condition (*sthiti*)?

Sometimes Vidyāraṇya simply argues that the *paramahaṃsa yogin* treads the path of total renunciation, including the abandonment of "dharmic" regulations: he departs from family and friends, and ignores even Vedic study and ritual action. He gives up all that brings worldly *or* heavenly rewards (155, 405). All rules and injunctions are abandoned since such everyday conventions breed attachment (27, 221).[29] Clothed or unclothed, he roams anywhere and eats anything, recognizing neither good nor bad—for separating these two (or seeing *any* opposites) is itself a flaw.[30]

Vidyāraṇya goes on, however, to claim that the renunciation of the knower (*vidvat-saṃnyāsa*) has another dimension: while ultimately unconcerned with actions and injunctions, the *brahman*-knower also continues to perform them. Performing duties is necessary, since even after the self is known, adventitious adjuncts (*upādhi*) remain in the *yogin's* "mind" (*antaḥkaraṇa*). Although knowing the truth, he still has not achieved the satisfaction (*tṛpti*) and mental repose that comes from completing every duty (154, 402–3).[31]

Vidyāraṇya's inclination toward synthesis and perhaps purposeful ambiguity are apparent here. He could certainly say more about the need to perform duties after knowledge (which is not the same as continuing yogic practice so often emphasized elsewhere), but he nowhere explicitly explains why the *dharma*-transcending *jīvanmukta* will live in accord with the *dharma,* a topic briefly discussed by Sureśvara and other later Advaitins.[32] One possible reason is that since the *dharma* is the cosmic structure and law, a detached *jīvanmukta* (despite being beyond the *dharma*) will "instinctively" follow the nature of things.[33]

Still, while renunciation and knowledge go together for Vidyāraṇya, knowing the nondual self ultimately takes one beyond conventional *saṃnyāsa.* Ordinary renunciation affects the body, not the ever-detached self. For the *paramahaṃsa yogin,* body-based injunctions such as wearing a loincloth and using a bamboo walking stick (*daṇḍa*) are not essential, for thinking about them could perturb his one-pointed mind (156, 407–8). Renunciants in the lower stage of merely desiring knowledge (*vividiṣā*) hold on to the bamboo stick and the performance of Vedic injunctions, while the *paramahaṃsa yogin* carries no stick—or, rather, carries only the "stick" of knowledge. The true ascetic (*tridaṇḍin*) does not hold a triple staff, but shows threefold control of speech, mind, and action (163, 419). He needs no blanket, as he is beyond feeling any heat or cold. And he is certainly beyond slander, pride, greed, anger, and so on. He disputes with no one, knowing no other truly exists. Clearly then, the highest knowledge takes one beyond mechanical adherence to Vedic ritual and the ascetic path. Still, how can anyone, even the *paramahaṃsa yogin,* give up all material goods and worldly feelings while embodied? Vidyāraṇya, citing the *Paramahaṃsa Upaniṣad,* states that the *yogin*'s body is now merely like a corpse (*kuṇapa*), since it is known as other than the self that is pure consciousness (*caitanya*). Feelings like slander and pride can be abandoned while living when the body (different from consciousness) is seen as a corpse (158, 411).[34] Thus, detachment from the body ultimately comes from knowledge, not renunciation.

The text concludes by reaffirming Yogic Advaita, that is, maintaining the importance of yogic practice and renunciation in both leading to *and* expressing knowledge of nondual *brahman*. The liberated being (*jīvanmukta*, *vidvat-saṃnyāsin*, or *paramahaṃsa yogin*), with sense activity at rest and unobstructed meditative enstasis, abides in the self. Blissfully realizing "I am *brahman*," he has completed all duties (172, 431). Thus, in Yogic Advaita, repeated human effort (via yogic practice) and renunciation are necessary to end all desires and gain *brahman* knowledge. The liberated being also is recognized by his yogic practice and renunciation. However, the true *jīvanmukta* is no longer bound even to *samādhi* or a ritually pure life (which presuppose duality). His effortless nondual bliss both results from and perfects *samādhi* and purity.

Conclusion

I will close by reviewing Vidyāraṇya's key arguments. First and most important is his claim that to be liberated while living one must have the knowledge (*jñāna*) that *brahman* and *ātman* are one. Such knowledge, which comes from hearing and studying the Vedanta texts, is the necessary basis for *jīvanmukti*. However, one who knows (i.e., the *jñānin*) is not automatically a *jīvanmukta*. Vidyāraṇya points out that even a sage like Yājñavalkya was jealous and proud, and that even a *brahman*-knower can have doubt and error. Due to currently manifesting (*prārabdha*) *karma*, one must also practice *yoga* repeatedly to destroy the mind and mental impressions (which produce doubt and error). *Karma* currently bearing fruit is stronger than knowledge, but yogic practice can overcome even the necessity of experiencing *prārabdha karma*.

Vidyāraṇya repeatedly stresses the importance of yogic techniques in destroying mental impressions (*vāsanā-kṣaya*) and extinguishing the mind (*mano-nāśa*) while seeking knowledge of the truth and even after finding it; this is a key reason for calling his view "Yogic Advaita." Yogic influence also appears in his concern about the "mental state" and *samādhi* level of the *jīvanmukta*. However, Vidyāraṇya makes it clear that *yoga* alone cannot make one a *jīvanmukta*. To be liberated while living, one needs both discernment (*viveka*, or *brahma-jñāna*) and sense-restraining "unconditioned" *(asaṃprajñāta* or *nirvikalpa*) *samādhi.* A concentrated *yogin* without knowledge may have supernatural powers and may go to heaven, but is not liberated, nor better than a knower acting in the world. This *yogin* reaches the insight of the "basis of you" (*tvaṃpadārtha*), but not of the unity of *ātman* and *brahman.* Again, we see Vidyāraṇya's central claim that both Vedantic knowledge and yogic enstasis are necessary to gain and sustain full liberation. Further, Vidyāraṇya's discussion of both the threefold means to liberation and the five marks or purposes of *jīvanmukti* indicates that the means to reach liberation are also the way of life after liberation. They not only lead to and safeguard liberation, they are the expressions of the achievement of *mokṣa.*

Vidyāraṇya also holds that one can be fully liberated while embodied—if liberation means knowing the nondual self, extinguishing the mind and its impressions, and never taking another birth. The embodied knower of *brahman* is already dead to the world, a corpse, so in a sense "without a body" (*videha*). However, he also suggests that *videhamukti* only exists when one is literally without a body, and this *mukti* is the fuller liberation. Thus, for Vidyāraṇya, liberation does occur while embodied, but he also considers bodilessness to be a sign (or reward?) of the highest release.

Finally, Vidyāraṇya points out that renunciation is critical to *jīvanmukti,* both as a path to and as an indicator of liberation. However, he suggests that the path to *jīvanmukti* goes beyond conventional *saṃnyāsa,* which calls for living in solitude and renouncing desires and all that consists of worldly "householding"—gaining wealth or offspring, or even performing Vedic ritual actions. Knowledge of nondual *brahman* leads ultimately to a renunciation higher than conventional world renunciation. In a sense, "dharmic" renunciation affirms the existence of the world of duality by rejecting it. The realized (*vidvat*) renouncer (and *paramahaṃsa yogin*) goes beyond (but does not transgress) all Vedic prohibitions and "good" or "evil": he is both a Brahmin and beyond any caste or life stage. As the *Bhagavad-Gītā* says, mental detachment is more important than worldly action (or nonaction). The highest *yogin* is not one with a loincloth and staff, but one who keeps his "inner cool" (*antaḥśītala*), destroying the mind and its impressions. He thus lives "in the world" completing karmic duties, and as a truly free being, passes beyond disgust for, and rejection of, everyday human existence. At this highest level of detachment, he can allow others to follow and serve him, freeing them and purifying the world by his injunction-transcending austerity.[35]

To conclude, let us again briefly contrast Vidyāraṇya's Yogic Advaita with Śaṅkara's mainstream Advaita. While their views are rarely directly opposed, their emphases and interests are often dramatically different. Vidyāraṇya's Yogic Advaita is linked, both by philosophical commitment and by extent of textual references, more to the views of the *Laghu Yogavāsiṣṭha* and the *Gītā* with their *Sāṃkhya* and *Yoga* emphases than to Śaṅkara and the scholastic tradition—though, as mentioned earlier, the *JMV* is not as free from concerns with performing dharmic duties and following the path of *saṃnyāsa* as are both forms of the *Yogavāsiṣṭha.* Both Vidyāraṇya and Śaṅkara hold that the primary mark of a *jīvanmukta* is knowing nondual *brahman,* but only Vidyāraṇya claims that such knowledge cannot be gained or sustained without repeated yogic practice. With such practice, liberation can be achieved while embodied; and with the highest knowledge, the *jīvanmukta* can live in the world while detached from it. Vidyāraṇya's emphases on yogic practice, cessation of mental activity, and the distinction between the *jīvanmukta* and *brahman*-knower are not shared by Śaṅkara. On the other hand, Vidyāraṇya rarely explores some of Śaṅkara's central concerns, such as discriminating between body and self or the utter separation of knowledge and activity. Also unlike scholastic Advaitins, who focus on the role of *prārabdha karma* (or any remnant of ignorance) in the continuity of embodiment, Vidyāraṇya instead emphasizes the importance of yogic practice now to remove remaining *karma.* Vidyāraṇya and Śaṅkara do not disagree on "bodiless" liberation, but Vidyāraṇya's understanding is more refined and clearly articulated. Śaṅkara does argue that one is bodiless while embodied when one knows that the self is not the body and that embodiedness itself is a false notion (*BS* I. 1. 4). However, he never uses the term *videhamukti,* much less employs Vidyāraṇya's specification of *videhamukti* as freedom from future (versus present) embodiment, nor does he discuss the relationship between *jīvan-* and *videha-mukti* (or Vidyāraṇya's occasional suggestion that the latter is "more" free). Vidyāraṇya's examination of the purposes or marks of attaining *jīvanmukti,* which describes a nondisputatious and actively world-purifying liberated being, is also expanded far beyond any of Śaṅkara's descriptions. Finally, both argue that renunciation is central to liberation, but Vidyāraṇya's intense focus on *saṃnyāsa* and his claim that the renouncer passes beyond all dharmic duties would be disputed by Śaṅkara. Thus, Vidyāraṇya, while Advaitin, is his own kind of Advaitin—a yogic Advaitin.

EIGHT

Yogic Advaita III: Jīvanmukti *in the* Pañcadaśī, *the "Minor"* Upaniṣads, *and Madhusūdana's* Gūḍārthadīpikā

While the *Yogavāsiṣṭha* and *Jīvanmuktiviveka* are the central texts for "Yogic Advaita," there are some other works that should be mentioned in this context. We will first look at the *Pañcadaśī* (*The Fifteen Chapters*) (*PD)*,[1] which is a widely known thirteenth to fourteenth century introduction to Vedanta. While primarily committed to Advaita views, it includes *Sāṃkhya* cosmological ideas (*prakṛti* and the *guṇas)*, and does not fit comfortably into either the "mainstream" or "Yogic" Advaita category. There is also some doubt about whether the *PD* and *Jīvanmuktiviveka* are by the same author, as is asserted within the Advaita tradition. The best discussion of this issue is still that of T. M. P. Mahadevan, though the matter is best regarded as unresolved. Mahadevan argues that there is a Bhāratītīrtha-Vidyāraṇya who was a teacher of Mādhava-Vidyāraṇya (who was also possibly the brother of Sāyaṇa).[2] Mahadevan holds that Bhāratītīrtha-Vidyāraṇya is the author of the *PD* (and the *Vivaraṇa-prameya-saṃgraha*), and Mādhava-Vidyāraṇya the author of the *JMV*.[3]

Even after taking into account the different interests of the texts, I also find it unlikely that the Vidyāraṇya of the *Pañcadaśī* (who I shall henceforth call Bhāratītīrtha) is the same Vidyāraṇya who authored the *JMV*.[4] Both in general and specifically when considering *jīvanmukti,* the *Pañcadaśī* author follows the Śaṅkara tradition of Advaita more closely than does the *JMV* author. To a degree quite different from the *JMV,* the *Pañcadaśī* emphasizes knowing the world's unreality, *cidābhasa* ("ego") versus *kūṭastha* (self), the nature of bliss (*ānanda)*, and the role of *prārabdha karma* in causing bodily continuity. On the other hand, key aspects of the *JMV*, such as types of renunciation, extinguishing the mind (*mano-nāśa)* and destroying mental impressions (*vāsanā-kṣaya)*, and the purposes of *jīvanmukti* are mentioned rarely or not at all. Further, the *Pañcadaśī* contains more references to key *Upaniṣadic* passages on *jīvanmukti* (such as *ChU* VI. 14. 2, *Kaṭha* VI. 14–15, and *Muṇḍaka* III. 2. 9) and far fewer to the *Laghu Yogavāsiṣṭha* than does the *JMV* (though both refer to the *Gītā* often). Finally, although already discussed here, the *JMV* is certainly later, as it refers to the *Brahmānanda* section of the *PD* twice (*JMV*, pp. 293, 388). Still, some similarities exist, as I shall point out in the following pages.

As with the *YV* and *JMV*, the *PD* does not address living liberation in a consistent, systematic way. Perhaps the best summary of Bhāratītīrtha's views on this topic appears in IX. 75–76. He here claims that realization (*bodha)* arises from contemplation (*vicāra)*, and burns off any belief in the reality of *saṃsāra.* Reaching liberation, one has accomplished all (*kṛta-kṛtya)*, gained eternal satisfaction (*tṛpti)*, and attained *jīvanmukti,* waiting only for the destruction of commenced *karma*. Still, Bhāratītīrtha almost never describes a *jīvanmukta* directly, and often makes his points about living liberation when referring to other texts—texts we are familiar with from earlier authors. For example, he calls the *Gītā's sthita-prajña* (here: *sthira-dhi)*, one well-established in knowing nonduality, as a *jīvanmukta* (II. 102–3).[5] He quotes *Gītā* II. 72, which says such a one has gained a "state" of *brahman* (*brahma-sthiti*, *brahma-nirvāṇa)*.

In VI. 259–60, he refers to two scriptural texts (*BāU* IV. 4. 7 and *Kaṭha* VI. 14–15) important for *jīvanmukti.* These verses state that when all knots of the heart are cut, that is, when all heart-based desires cease, then one gains immortality and *brahman* here. Bhāratītīrtha goes on to claim that when ignorant, the self (*cidātman*) and the "I"–consciousness (*ahaṃkāra*) are thought to be one; when the knower realizes their difference, desires may exist due to commenced (*prārabdha) karma* (more will be said about such *karma* later), but they do not bind, since their knots are cut (261–3).[6] Thinking the "I" is the self <u>is</u> the knot; in fact, the only difference between *mūḍha* (fool) and *buddha* (sage) is this knot (266). When the self is known and I-consciousness disappears, one is as unmoved by one's bodily condition as by the growth and death of a tree (perhaps following *NS* IV. 61) (264).

As suggested earlier, Bhāratītīrtha, like other Advaitins, often emphasizes that to know the real and to attain *jīvanmukti* one must throw off the bonds of desire. *Śruti* teaches that the path to liberation is by calmness (*śama)* and concentration (*samādhi)*, and the goal is desirelessness. Like Śaṅkara, he holds that there is ultimately no satisfaction even in a heavenly birth, only in abandoning desire (IV. 50–53). Bhāratītīrtha then makes a point based on Sureśvara's *Naiṣkarmyasiddhi*. He claims that if, after knowing the truth, one does not abandon desire, the supposed sage will do whatever he wishes (*yatheṣṭācaraṇa),* like a dog eating impure food (*NS* IV. 62). Before the purported realization, one only had internal faults (*doṣa)*, but now (since he falsely claims desirelessness) the whole world censures him—what a "knowledge." So the knower should not be a desire-filled pig (or dog), and must abandon all mental faults to be worthy of worship as a god by the people (IV. 54–57).

Bhāratītīrtha also holds to the utility of constant contemplative practice over time (IX. 33 ff.) to assist liberation. He claims that no practice is wasted, even if one is not liberated in the present birth. His starting point is Śaṅkara's commentary on *BS* III. 4. 51. He states that if the self is not obtained here before death, despite repeated contemplation (*vicāra)*, one will gain it later (*amutra)*, presumably in another birth, when all obstacles (*pratibandha*) are destroyed. As *Kaṭha* II. 7 indicates, many who hear the truth here still do not know. As evidence for future (living) liberation from present practice, he also refers to Vāmadeva's realization while still in the womb, due to prior repeated contemplation (33–35). Further obstacles are destroyed by proper calming (*śama)*, hearing (*śravana)* sacred texts, and so on, and then one attains *brahman,* as Vāmadeva did in a single additional birth (44–45). Again following Śaṅkara on *BS* III. 4. 51, Bhāratītīrtha refers to the *Gītā* passage that affirms this point (VI. 40–45): the *yogin* may take many births to destroy impediments, but no contemplation is useless. From knowing the reality of the self, one obtains a realm of virtue (*puṇya)*, and even one having desires is born in a pure and rich family. If desireless, one comes to a family of pure-minded *yogins*, there controls the mind as in prior births, advances by following earlier practice, and, ultimately over many births attains the highest goal (46–50).

While often following Śaṅkara, the *PD*'s discussion of living liberation has clear echoes of the *JMV*'s "Yogic Advaita" in two places. In IV. 59–61, Bhāratītīrtha writes, following *Gītā* II. 62, that dwelling on any object causes desire, anger, and delusion; these can be overcome by *samādhi.* Verse 62 says *manorājya* (the realm of delusion) is overcome by realizing the truth, the absence of mental faults, and one-pointed *vāsanā*, reminding us of the threefold practice mentioned in the *JMV.*[7] After overcoming delusion, the pure mind rests empty of any modification and *nirvāṇa* is gained, as Vasiṣṭha teaches Rāma in the *YV* (*Sthiti* 57. 28) (63–64). *PD* VI. 276 mentions another interrelated threefold means to achieve liberation: realizing the truth (*tattva-*

bodha), renunciation (*vairāgya)*, and cessation of activity (*uparama*). While the latter two are not identical with (and less yogic than) the *JMV*'s *mano-nāśa* and *vāsanā-kṣaya*, the former is said in both to be the main and most direct means to liberation (281). Like the *JMV*, verses 283–4 say detachment *(vairāgya)* and cessation (*uparati)*, without *bodha,* bring a heavenly world (*puṇyaloka)*, not *mokṣa,* but realization, even without the other two, gives full awakening now (though visible sorrow is not destroyed). Perhaps the later *JMV* formalizes and expands on these suggestions of a threefold model of means to liberation.

Also similar to the *JMV* (10, 195) is Bhāratītīrtha's claim in IV. 66–69 that the mind is distracted by enjoying *karma* and concentrated by repeated yogic practice *(abhyāsa)*. Without dualistic projection (*vikṣepa)*, one is not merely a *brahman*-knower, but is *brahman* itself. The *jīvanmukta*'s final stage is freedom from the duality of the *jīva*.[8] Similarly, in XIII. 82, he writes that by repeated practice (*abhyāsa)*, one becomes well established in knowledge *(vidyā)* and then free from the body even while living.

Much is written in the *Pañcadaśī* about the relationship of *prārabdha* ("commenced," or already manifesting) *karma* and liberation. According to VII. 175–80, knowledge and commenced *karma* are not opposed, since they have different objects. The aim of knowing the real is recognizing the world as illusory, while the aim of commenced *karma* is the enjoyment of pleasure and pain by the individual self *(jīva)*. As one enjoys seeing magic although knowing it is an illusion, so one's enjoyment (or experience) of commenced *karma* does not require imagining the world to be real. Neither does knowledge destroy the world (annihilating commenced *karma*), it awakens us to the world's illusoriness. Thus, as knowing a magic show to be unreal destroys neither the show nor people's enjoyment, so knowing the world's illusory nature does not destroy the illusion or one's experience of it.

Bhāratītīrtha, like virtually all other Advaitins, uses the existence of *prārabdha karma* to explain why embodiment continues post-liberation. He argues that embodiment continues because *karma* only gradually ceases, using analogies both old (trembling from fear of a "snake") and new (the healing of a head wound) (VII. 241–50). He begins here by referring to the oft-used *Muṇḍaka* III. 2. 9 *śruti,* which states that the one who knows *brahman* (which occurs while living) becomes *brahman* (241). Yet as long as the body exists (due to the enjoyment of commenced *karma*'s fruits), there is no (immediate) freedom from appearance—as even after the "snake" is known as a rope, trembling ceases only gradually. Still, even if, while enjoying fruits, one sometimes thinks "I am mortal" (as when seeing the rope in the darkness, one might be frightened again), this mistake does not destroy knowledge of the truth, since *jīvanmukti* is a natural condition (*vastu-sthiti)*, and not a vow or practice (*vrata*) (243–46).[9]

Bhāratītīrtha then introduces a variation of the "tenth man" example. A person searching for a "missing" tenth person in a group suddenly realizes "I am the tenth." The person then stops crying and beating his head (out of sorrow for the "lost" tenth person). Happy now, the sorrower forgets the aching head, and, with the help of medicine, the wound gradually heals. Similarly, obtaining *mukti* (with the help of repeated contemplation) causes one to forget the sorrow (or "heal the wound") of commenced *karma*, but such *karma* must still be enjoyed before final liberation (VII. 247–50).

Bhāratītīrtha, like Madhusūdana, also says embodiment continues due to the projecting (*vikṣepa)* rather than the concealing (*āvaraṇa)* aspect of ignorance (VI. 53–56). Knowledge destroys the concealment of self, but projection is removed only by experiencing *prārabdha karma*. Like Maṇḍana, Bhāratītīrtha argues that an effect (like a body) can continue for a moment, even after its basis (ignorance) is destroyed, as illustrated by *śruti* (*ChU* VI. 14. 2), reason, and experience (potter's wheel).

Bhāratītīrtha states a number of times that the conduct (*vartana*) of awakened beings varies according to differences in (*prārabdha) karma,* although realization itself is always the same (VI. 287–8)—a point also made in the *YV* and *JMV*. For example, one can be both a knower and a ruler (like Janaka, VII. 130). Verse IX. 114 states that knowing the truth is not affected by any means (*sādhana)*, so the knower can rule (rightly). The mind and senses do not disappear when one is a knower, so one can (and must) act (IX. 90). Further, while desireless since knowing the world is unreal, one may meditate *or* act in various ways according to one's *prārabdha karma* (IX. 115). In fact, *karma*'s destruction proceeds by awakened and unpolluted beings living according to their *karma*. Bhāratītīrtha states that from following this *karma*, even these beings are not beyond any flaw, for who is able to prevent manifestation of *karma*? While commenced *karma* is the same for the knower and the ignorant, the knower alone has no affliction (*kleśa*), due to patience (*dhairya)* (VII. 131–3). Again we see it argued that *karma* must manifest, but the knower is untouched by its working.

Bhāratītīrtha holds that support for this view comes from the *Gītā* as well. *PD* VII. 152–61 point out that no one can avoid experiencing one's *karma*, even if one does not want to, like Arjuna (in *Gītā* III. 36–37). But how can the knower have desires? While desires (like *karma*) are not absent, they are annulled (*bādha)* like the (im)potency of a burnt seed (VII. 163). As a roasted seed cannot germinate, a wise man's desires, known to be unreal, cannot produce an effect. Yet as a roasted seed can still be used as a bit of food, so the sage's desires yield a little (*alpa*) enjoyment (but not evil habits) by the fructifying of *prārabdha karma*. Full-fledged evil habits (*vyāsana*) arise only by the illusion that one is an enjoyer (VII. 164–6). Bhāratītīrtha here shows his sensitivity to the central Advaita problem of a form of ignorance (desire, *karma*) remaining after knowledge.

Finally, *PD* VII. 252 ff.[10] describe the nature of the satisfaction (*tṛpti*) of the *jīvanmukta* at some length. Sounding unlike most mainstream *or* yogic Advaitins, he claims satisfaction is limitless (*niraṅkusa*) and constant, requiring no further vow or duty. After liberation, one has accomplished all and obtained all obtainable (252–4).[11] Bhāratītīrtha then expounds on his joy in the first person.[12] He states that unlike the ignorant with worldly desires, he is full of the highest bliss. The supreme bliss of liberation takes him beyond ritual duty, competence/commission (*adhikāra*), or meditation: "Let those wanting another realm (*paraloka*) perform ritual activity; pervading all realms, how and why should I act? Let those with competence explain scripture or teach Veda; I have no commission since without activity. I do not wish to sleep or beg, I do not bathe or purify myself; if observers imagine so, what are other's imaginings to me?" (256–8) He even goes so far as to reject the threefold means of hearing, reflecting, and assimilating: only those not knowing the truth need to listen to *śruti*, and only those with doubts need to reflect (260).

Bhāratītīrtha then specifically rejects the efficacy of meditation (*dhyāna*, *samādhi*) to remove *karma* (which distinguishes this text from the *JMV*).[13] Since he has no wrong notions (*viparyāsa*), the sage has no need to meditate. Although undeluded, he still thinks "I am human (*manuṣya*)," a notion imagined due to propensities (*vāsanā*) developed over a long time (*cira*).[14] When commenced *karma* is destroyed, worldly activity (*vyavahāra*) ceases, but as long as such *karma* continues even thousands of meditations will not end this activity. Knowing this, why should the liberated being meditate? Both projection (*vikṣepa*) and meditative enstasis (*samādhi*) are merely transformations of the mind, and being the essence of experience (*anubhava-rūpa*) itself, the *mukta* has (as said earlier, verse 252) accomplished and obtained all (261–66). Yet, in a distinct change of tone, Bhāratītīrtha then presents a more "dharmic" approach—although its optional status is emphasized. He states that, although all is accomplished, there is no harm (*kṣati*) in following the *śāstric* path, rising from a desire to benefit the world (*lokānugraha*).[15] While not necessary, various actions are not prohibited. From this perspective, one may beg, bathe, chant, or worship god. Still, when a witness (*sākṣin*), one truly does nothing and causes no action, whether meditating on Viṣṇu or merging in *brahman* bliss (268–70).

Thus, as suggested earlier, the *Pañcadaśī* is an Advaita text, but without the consistent, dialectically oriented argumentation of scholastic Advaita, nor with the degree of yogic orientation of the *JMV* and *Yogavāsiṣṭha*. Bhāratītīrtha's primary emphases concerning *jīvanmukti* seem to be the importance of desirelessness and contemplation (*vicāra*), which will allow one to accomplish all and to attain living liberation, and (like mainstream Advaita) the role of *prārabdha karma* in delaying final liberation. And while the text acknowledges that yogic practice has value, unlike in the *JMV*, it is not central to liberation.

Jīvanmukti *in the Minor* Upaniṣads

Most references to living liberation in the large corpus of works known as "minor" *Upaniṣads* are congruent with the "Yogic Advaita" seen in the *Yogavāsiṣṭha* and the *Jīvanmuktiviveka*. J. F. Sprockhoff has examined the concept of *jīvanmukti* in these *Upaniṣads* in great detail, including an extensive listing of parallel references in the minor *Upaniṣads* and the *YV* and *JMV*.[16] The *Upaniṣads* that mention *jīvanmukti* are found primarily in the grouping called "*Sāmānya-Vedānta*" *Upaniṣads*.[17] Like the rest of the minor *Upaniṣads*, these texts do not follow or argue for any formal philosophical school. Instead, they focus more on descriptions of the path to liberation by knowledge, renunciation *(saṃnyāsa)*, or yogic meditation, or on the nature of the liberated being, and often seem conducive to use in chanting or other ritual contexts. They often refer to the ideas of extinguishing the mind (*mano-nāśa)* and destroying mental impressions (*vāsanā-kṣaya*), seen in the *JMV*.

The *Mahā, Tejobindu, and Varāha* (the latter two "*Yoga*" *Upaniṣads) Upaniṣads* are typical. *Mahā* II. 42–62 verses, which duplicate those in the *Yogavāsiṣṭha*,[18] end with the refrain "he is called liberated while living" (*sa jīvanmukta ucyate)*, and list the many qualities of the *jīvanmukta,* stressing peace, mindlessness (*amanastā)*, and being beyond opposites like joy and sorrow. The same refrain is used in *Varāha* IV. 2. 21–30, which follows *YV Utpatti khaṇḍa* 9. 4–13 and emphasizes realizing the unreality of the world and obtaining pure, objectless consciousness. Here, as in the minor *Upaniṣads* mentioned below, there is great emphasis on elevated consciousness states and mind control, as well as on the serenity and bliss of liberation, making *jīvanmukti* a bit more "positive" than in Śaṅkara's Advaita. *Tejobindu* IV. 1–32 also includes the "*sa jīvanmukta ucyate*" refrain, and the virtues of living liberation are clearly intended to be chanted here. Bodiless liberation is praised in verses 33–81.

In the context of living liberation, perhaps most interesting among the "minor" *Upaniṣads* are the *Annapūrṇa* and *Muktika.* The *Annapūrṇa Upaniṣad* mentions *jīvanmukti* in a number of places, first stressing being detached (*asaṅga*, II. 3–6), reaching the blissful fourth (*turīya*) state of consciousness (II. 18), and destroying the mind (II. 24). *Annapūrṇa* III begins by describing the living liberated sage Māṇḍavya, emphasizing his firmly controlled mind. The yogic language and focus on consciousness states seen here is clearly representative of Yogic Advaita. *Annapūrṇa* IV. 14–20 describe the distinction between the extinguished mind *(citta-nāśa)* "with form" (*sarūpa*) of the *jīvanmukta* and that without form (*arūpa*) of the *videhamukta* seen in the *JMV* (128, 365) and *Muktika* II. 32–35. As in these other texts, "formless" bodiless *mukti* here seems a little more liberated than "mere" living liberation.[19] Various verses in *Annapūrṇa* V clearly refer to ideas also found in the *YV* and *JMV*: detachment (4), forms of *vāsanās* or mental impressions (6, 16), the importance of effort or *prayatna* (68), and the seven-stage (*bhūmi)* consciousness state model (83). The concluding verse (V. 120) asserts that one who studies this *Upaniṣad* with a *guru* attains liberation while living and becomes *brahman* itself.

Muktika Upaniṣad II bears close resemblance to the *JMV* in places and mentions most of the ideas referred to earlier. Sprockhoff finds the *Muktika* II passage the most important among all minor *Upaniṣads*, suggesting it influenced the *JMV*.[20] *Muktika* II begins by virtually duplicating the *JMV* passage that asks about the aims, characteristics, and means of attaining *jīvanmukti,* as well as its definition of living liberation, which states that "bondage exists for a person since the nature of affliction [is] having mental notions consisting of joy and sorrow, being enjoyer and doer, and so on. Living liberation is the cessation of this."[21] The one significant change in the *Muktika* is the direct reference there to bodiless (*videha*) *mukti.* Following the definition of living liberation, it next says, "bodiless liberation is due to the destruction of commenced (*karma*), (and is) like the space in a pot free from any limitation."[22] (The final verse—II. 76—also mentions reaching bodiless liberation after leaving *jīvanmukti).* The *Muktika,* unlike the *JMV*, then adds that the means of knowing (*pramāṇa*) both forms of liberation is studying the 108 *Upaniṣads*. Both texts go on to emphasize obtaining living liberation by human efforts, including yogic practice and hearing the Vedanta, which destroy all *vāsanās*.

The *Muktika* continues by describing various forms of *vāsanās*, and how to extinguish them and the mind (II. 1–31). The talk about the interplay of mind, its impressions, and bodily extinction is again quite typical of "Yogic Advaita." *Muktika* II. 32 ff. continue this theme, but use language emphasizing destroying the mind (*citta/mano-nāśa*); this section begins with the "formed" (*sarūpa*, *jīvanmukti*) and "formless" (*arūpa*, *videhamukti)* types of mental destruction seen in the *JMV* (and *Annapūrṇa* IV. 14–18 mentioned earlier). While *jīvanmukti* goes virtually unmentioned in the rest of the chapter, the remaining portion continues to describe the path to liberation and to praise achieving it. Like the *YV* and *JMV*, the remaining text includes traditional Advaita language about knowing the self and yogic ideas of breath (*prāṇa*) control and stilling the mind, along with its primary focus on types of *vāsanā* that need extinguishing for liberation.

Incidentally, although renunciation (*saṃnyāsa*) is often an important part of the path to liberation (as we saw in the *JMV)*, the specific language of *jīvanmukti* is not commonly linked with *saṃnyāsa* in the minor *Upaniṣads*. Patrick Olivelle, in his translation and analysis of the branch of minor *Upaniṣads* called "*Saṃnyāsa*" *Upaniṣads*, writes that "[t]hroughout these documents there are eulogies of the renouncer who has liberated himself in this very life."[23] However, direct references to *jīvanmukti* are relatively infrequent and often are derived from other texts. For example, the *Bṛhatsaṃnyāsa* includes a series of verses from the *YV Upaśama khaṇḍa*,[24] and the *Bṛhad-Avadhūta* takes verses from *Pañcadaśī* VII. 253–70 and 291–97.[25] The *Paramahaṃsa*, a "*Saṃnyāsa*" *Upaniṣad*, was, we have seen, interpreted by Vidyāraṇya in the *JMV*. Its references to *jīvanmukti,* as those of *Jābāla Upaniṣad* VI, are largely indirect. *Maitreya Upaniṣad* III is a song of praise about being released, but does not explicitly speak of living liberation. Thus, while the minor *Upaniṣads* do mention living liberation and continue the "Yogic Advaita" emphases on renunciation and yogic practice, along with Self-knowledge, they break little new ground.

Madhusūdana on Jīvanmukti *in the* Gūḍārthadīpikā

As mentioned earlier, Madhusūdana wrote a commentary on the *Bhagavad-Gītā* called *Gūḍārthadīpikā.* He discusses aspects of *jīvanmukti* in a number of places in the commentary, and he offers a much more "Yogic Advaita" interpretation here than in the *Advaitasiddhi.*

The first reference to *jīvanmukti* occurs in the introduction and uses terminology familiar to the *JMV*. In verses 20–22, Madhusūdana writes that all *karma* is destroyed by knowledge, but mental impressions (*vāsanā)* rising from the projection (*vikṣepa)* of already commenced (*prārabdha) karma* persist. These impressions cease through the yogic practice of *saṃyama (dhāraṇa, dhyāna,* and *samādhi* of the *Yogasūtras). Samādhi* is said to be attained quickly by fixed attention on the Lord (*īśvara-praṇidhāna*), which brings extinction of the mind *(mano-nāśa)* and destruction of mental impressions (*vāsanā-kṣaya)* (23). With repeated practice of these two, along with knowing the real (*tattva-jñāna), jīvanmukti* is firmly established (24). Madhusūdana states that sacred texts (here unreferenced) call this threefold means to liberation the renunciation of the knower (*vidvat-saṃnyāsa*) (25).

He continues that one having achieved the highest nonconceptual (*nirvikalpa*) *samādhi* is called (in various places in the *Gītā*) a Brahmin, the best of *brahman*-knowers, one beyond qualities (*guṇātīta*), one with firm wisdom (*sthita-prajña*), a devotee of Viṣṇu, one beyond caste and life stage (*ativarṇāśramin*), and a *jīvanmukta;* since all is accomplished, even the sacred texts cease for this being (26–29). Unlike in the *Advaitasiddhi*, Madhusūdana here says devotion to the Lord (*bhagavad-bhakti)* must be employed in all stages of the pursuit of liberation, and worshipping Kṛṣṇa is natural even for the detached Self-knower who attains living liberation (31–37).[26]

The notion of liberation while living next appears in Madhusūdana's discussion of the one with firm wisdom, the *sthita-prajña,* in *Gītā* II. 54 ff. He writes that the *samādhi*-established *sthita-prajña* is thoroughly detached, but continues to experience good and bad fruits from *prārabdha karma* (II. 54–57). The one with firm wisdom has senses disciplined (*indriya-saṃyama*) and the direct experience (*sākṣātkāra*) of being *brahman* from hearing the key sayings of the Vedanta (68–69). All ignorance and karmic activity now cease, and, attaining the renunciation of the knower (*vidvat-saṃnyāsa*), one is now a *jīvanmukta* (70). The body continues and experiences fruits from the power of commenced *karma,* but one is peaceful, desireless, and without samsaric sorrows. The knower exists in the "condition" of *brahman* (*brahma-sthiti, brahma-nirvāṇa)* as long as life continues (71–72).[27]

The Yogic Advaita of the *JMV* and *YV* is seen most clearly in commentaries on two passages in the *Gītā,* III. 18 and VI. 43 ff. *Gītā* III. 17–18 assert that one knowing and content in the self needs neither to do nor avoid doing works. Madhusūdana affirms that one cannot attain the highest goal (*nihśreyasa)* by action, for the self is eternally attained. The Self-knower established in *brahman* has no aims (*prayojana*), whether acting or not. Madhusūdana then turns to the *LYV's* description of the seven stages of knowledge (*jñāna-bhūmi)*.[28] This model, also appearing in the *JMV*, suggests that there are degrees of *jīvanmukti* and that these degrees are related to yogic practices. These ideas are not found among other Advaita schoolmen, nor in the *Advaitasiddhi.*

Madhusūdana here writes that in the first three stages one begins by desiring liberation, preceded by pursuit of the fourfold means for gaining release (meaning those stated by Śaṅkara in *BS* I. 1. 1), then one hears and reflects on the sayings of the Vedanta after approaching the *guru*, and finally one has the capacity to grasp subtle matters (*sūkṣma-vastu*) by a one-pointed (*ekāgrata*) mind through the repeated practice of assimilation (*nididhyāsana*) of sacred texts.[29] The fourth stage (called *sattvāpatti*, obtaining the real) is the direct experience (*sākṣātkāra*) of unchanging *brahman/ātman* identity, and the *yogin* attaining this stage is called a *brahman*-knower (*brahma-vid)*.[30] Following Vidyāraṇya (*JMV* 136, 375), Madhusūdana says that *bhūmis* 5–7 are three stages of *jīvanmukti,* differing in degree (*avantārabheda*). He repeats Vidyāraṇya's point about the achievement of ever higher degrees of *brahman*-knowing[31] through the progressive deepening of mental restraint by practice of nonconceptual meditative enstasis (*nirvikalpa samādhi),* and his homologization of these stages with deep sleep and the highest fourth "state," *turīya.*[32] The highest liberated being can never be roused from *samādhi*, sees no difference whatever, and constantly abides in a perfect mass of bliss. His body is taken care of by others and vital breath (*prāṇa*) directed by (and to) the supreme Lord. Among other texts, Madhusūdana here quotes the *BāU* IV. 4. 7 passage about the similarity of this *brahman*-knower's body to a discarded snake skin on an anthill, and he concludes that the living liberated knower has no commission (*adhikāra*) to act.

Gītā VI. 43 ff. describe how wisdom and yogic attainment carry over from prior births.[33] Madhusūdana, after affirming that no prior effort (such as renouncing all action and following the *guru)* is wasted on the way to gaining highest knowledge, again refers to the *LYV's* seven stages of knowledge model, found in the *JMV.*[34] Using language quite similar to the preceding passage, Madhusūdana says that after following the fourfold *sādhana* for gaining release (indicated by Śaṅkara in *BS* I. 1. 1), renouncing all action, and hearing, reflecting on, and finally assimilating the sayings of the Vedanta (done in stages 1–3), one gains direct experience of the real (*tattva-sākṣātkāra*) in stage 4. Madhusūdana again says here that *bhūmis* 5–7 are three stages of *jīvanmukti,* differing in degree. Once having obtained the fourth stage, one will, if not actually be liberated while living, certainly gain bodiless isolation (*videha-kaivalya*) upon death.[35]

Following VI. 46, which describes the preeminence of the *yogin* over an ascetic, ritualist or knower, Madhusūdana states that the *yogin* with immediate (*aparokṣa*) knowledge is better than the knower with mere everyday (*parokṣa*) knowledge, and the *yogin* who is a *jīvanmukta* by having extinguished mind (*mano-nāśa)* and destroyed mental impressions (*vāsanā-kṣaya)* is greater than one with immediate knowledge who is not liberated while living, due to lack of such mental cessation. Like Vidyāraṇya, Madhusūdana asserts that the highest, living liberated, *yogin* simultaneously brings about mental cessation, impression destruction, and knowledge of the real (*tattva-jñāna).* Again, the talk about yogic practice, mental discipline, stages of *jīvanmukti,* and the threefold means to liberation are all typical of Yogic Advaita, and range far afield from topics considered by Advaita schoolmen, including Madhusūdana's own *Advaitasiddhi.*

A Note on the Sthita-prajña *as "Yogic* Jīvanmukta*"*

In some texts mentioned earlier, the *Gītā's sthita-prajña,* one with firm wisdom, could be called a "yogic *jīvanmukta.*" Like Advaita's *jīvanmukta,* the *sthita-prajña* is a detached renouncer, but this being gains liberation primarily through yogic practices of controlling the senses and pacifying the mind, rather than by knowing *brahman*.[36] We saw Śaṅkara's relevant *Gītā* comments (chapter 2) give the *sthita-prajña* a largely Advaitic cast, however, calling him a *brahman*-knower and emphasizing his desireless renunciation (*saṃnyāsa*).[37]

Yet we have also seen that the *JMV*'s elaboration on the *Gītā*'s description of the *sthita-prajña* (chapter 7) adds back a significant yogic element to Śaṅkara's emphasis on this being's *brahma-jñāna* and desire-free renunciation (though in the *jīvanmukti* context, the *sthita-prajña* goes unmentioned in other "Yogic Advaita" texts). Vidyāraṇya speaks of the importance of repeated practice of *vāsanā*-removing and sense-controlling *samādhi*, which becomes "natural" when wisdom is firm (and one is liberated while living). In his aforementioned *Gītā* commentary, Madhusūdana Sarasvatī also combines *yoga* and Advaita, saying the *sthita-prajña/jīvanmukta* has both sense-disciplining *samādhi*, and the direct experience of being *brahman*. Both also say the *jīvanmukta* is a desireless *vidvat-saṃnyāsin*.

Finally, we observed the Advaita-influenced *Sāṃkhya/Yoga* commentator Vijñānabhikṣu refer to the *Gītā*'s formulation of the *sthita-prajña* when describing the characteristics of the *jīvanmukta* in his *Sāṃkhyasāra* (chapter 5); here, the living liberated being is called an even-minded, undeluded, and detached Self-knower. He is said to reach liberation when the mind is destroyed and *saṃskāras* attentuated. When the intellect ceases, there is perfect isolation (*kaivalya*) and the self abides alone. Thus, as with the others mentioned here, it is fair to call Vijñānabhikṣu's liberated being a "yogic *jīvanmukta*."

Part 3

Embodied Liberation in Neo-Vedanta: Adaptation and Innovation

NINE

Neo-Vedanta and the Transformation of Advaitic Jīvanmukti

In the Introduction, I indicated that Western categories and ways of thinking have had a profound influence on many modern Indian thinkers.[1] In the last section of this book, I want to look at this matter more closely. My views here have been particularly informed by Wilhelm Halbfass' *India and Europe: An Essay in Understanding*,[2] which demonstrates brilliantly (from a European perspective) how the "Europeanization of the earth" has affected these thinkers.[3] The book argues that the modern encounter of India and Europe was initiated and sustained by the West, and that India had no choice but to respond to this unprecedented, pervasive penetration. Western thought has become so influential in India that even when challenged, it is often presupposed. However, I agree with Halbfass that the modern West's "overcoming" of India does not mean the superseding of Indian thought. "Modernity," purportedly neutral, open, and self-questioning, is, like every perspective, a parochial horizon, and the "Europeanization of the earth" is not necessarily good or humanity's end point.[4]

Those who write about and see themselves as part of Śaṅkara's Advaita tradition have certainly felt the impact of the West. As mentioned earlier, I call these thinkers and/or scholars "neo-Vedantins" to suggest both that they are part of a tradition based on the *Upaniṣads* and Śaṅkara's nondualist interpretation thereof,[5] and that these figures are participating in and contributing to a new understanding of this Vedanta tradition, one influenced by

Western premises and categories (imposed *and* chosen), which include humanistic globalism, the importance of egalitarian social ethics, and a focus on psychological experience.[6] Such influence is not surprising, as most neo-Vedantins, including such well-known figures as Swami Vivekananda and Sarvepalli Radhakrishnan, were schooled in educational institutions (often missionary-founded) that follow Western models in administration, curriculum, and language of instruction. Thus, to varying degrees, the connection of neo-Vedantins to the Hindu tradition came after a Western, Christian-influenced and English-language-based intellectual formation.[7] We shall see that even the relatively more traditional teachings of certain modern figures who themselves are regarded as *jīvanmuktas*, such as Ramana Maharshi and the recently deceased *Śaṅkaracārya* of Kanchipuram, Candrasekharendra Sarasvati, show the impact of their early Christian mission school training.

Neo-Vedanta has become the primary interpretive model in modern Indian scholarship on Advaita. In this model, one finds both new terms like *philosophy* and *religion* (versus *darśana* or *saṃpradāya*) and old terms like *dharma* and *yoga* that carry new meaning. Discussing the modern reinterpretation of long-established Hindu ideas is beyond our scope, though I might mention in passing that the traditional view of *dharma* as a birth-determined moral and social law unique to Aryans, maintained by Vedic rituals and hereditary duties, undergoes a dramatic change in neo-Vedanta, becoming a global, ahistorical, ethical norm related to a person's dispositions and talents. This "*dharma*" is found in, though it transcends, all religions. Fortunately, however, the Advaitic concept of *jīvanmukti* itself offers a vivid illustration of how a traditional Hindu idea has been and is being transformed by Western ways of thinking.[8]

There is not just one neo-Vedanta view, of course. In the following section of this book, I want to look first at more traditional figures, especially Ramana Maharshi and Candrasekharendra Sarasvati, then some more highly Westernized thinkers, such as Vivekananda and Radhakrishnan. The discerning reader will find as the Vedantins become more "neo," my remarks become somewhat more critical. I want here to express some ambivalence about faulting neo-Vedantins for their sometimes tradition-distorting reinterpretation of classical Advaita and occasionally insufficiently self-conscious appropriation of Western ideas. This ambivalence has a number of sources. First is the fact of my own "Westernness," which appears both in my participation in the Western scholarly model and in my personal sympathy for neo-Vedanta tolerance, globalism, and humanism, and its jettisoning of various aspects of the tradition like casteism and world devaluation long part of foreign critiques.[9] Humility and respect are important in any analysis that comes from a tradition that has a history of political domination and "categorical imperialism."

Second, enduring traditions build over time a body of writings that later thinkers reflect on and refine. Unlike neo-Vedanta, Śaṅkara's Advaita school has a long history of scriptural learning and exegesis and of rigorous critical thinking (and both the attraction and difficulty of being genuinely "other" to a modern Western worldview). This lack of a tradition of disciplined reflection and critique has contributed to the at times muddled and insufficiently self-aware thought found in neo-Vedanta. I concur with Anantanand Rambachan's view that while scholastic Advaita's reasoning and critical analysis (all under guidance of the Veda, of course) led to good arguments for and against key doctrines, Swami Vivekananda and later neo-Vedantins too often emphasize "experience" while downgrading "mere theory."[10] While sympathetic to some of the neo-Vedantins' agendas, I find their reasoning often easier to criticize than the clear, if hard to digest, arguments of traditional Advaitins.

Third, I am utilizing these authors' (or their interpreters') English writings in which they inevitably use Western terminology and categories and which clearly indicate that the intended audience is Western (including Indians educated in Western-style schools). Of course, a Western education or writing in English does not necessarily indicate complete enclosure in Western thought. In fact, deep knowledge of two traditions can assist in comprehending each one, as Halbfass and J. L. Mehta illustrate.

Perhaps most important is the recognition that all religious traditions—whether broad groupings like "Christian" and "Hindu" or narrower ones like "Episcopalian" and "Advaita"—are products of a never-ending process of assimilation and integration of concepts (and practices) deriving from a variety of sources. All thinkers, when attempting to formulate a coherent and plausible worldview, select and interpret from the cultural materials available to them. All people also respond to current personal and social issues before them and look to discover how past traditions may address (or serve) present concerns and interests. Neo-Vedantins struggle, to differing degrees, with the tension between understanding and responding to the Sanskrit- and *paṇḍit*-dominated commentatorial tradition of scholastic Advaita and the increasingly privileged science-influenced historical-critical tradition of Western scholarship. One sees the impact of the latter in a pattern common to many neo-Vedanta scholars of Advaita, who defer to or claim validation from primarily Western scholarly "authorities." It is sometimes forgotten that this tradition's "objectivity" and self-questioning skepticism is itself Eurocentric and historically conditioned.

Still, one can credit both more traditional thinkers like the *Śaṅkarācāryas* and the "neo" Vedantins like Vivekananda or Radhakrishnan with being at the forefront of creative religio-cultural assimilation, syncretizing and harmonizing past and present. During a time of rapid cultural change (not to say breakdown and unrest), they are undertaking two difficult and important tasks: that of self-definition and identity forging and that of mediating between and trying to integrate two (at least) very different cultures. One could fairly say that reinterpreting and finding new meaning in one's tradition is not only a right, but a duty. In this respect, an outsider should listen carefully to neo-Vedantins and honor their ability to speak for and challenge themselves—which in turn can bring Western self-understandings into question. For example, a number of neo-Vedantins claim that Hindu thought generally, and Advaita in particular, is superior to that of the West, as it goes beyond "mere" philosophical theorizing and analysis or the "dogmatic faith" of religion. Instead, it emphasizes transforming intuitive "experience" and the achievement of fully liberating insight. Documenting and contesting these claims goes beyond our purposes here, but does indicate an attempt to challenge Western "hegemony" of thought. Particularly relevant here is the plausible claim that the very idea of *living* liberation (vs. mere post-mortem salvation) shows the superiority of Advaitic thought. This assertion has perhaps been inhibited by the constraints, thoroughly discussed earlier, of *prārabdha karma* on *jīvanmukti*, and by the tradition's limiting of liberation largely to Veda-knowing male Brahmin renouncers.[11] Still, one can argue that making the case for the value of living liberation today is a legitimate task, not only for traditional Advaitins, but also for all modern seekers of wisdom from the Hindu tradition.

The criticisms that I make will focus not on the ultimate truth or value of neo-Vedantic claims, but on a distortion of traditional Advaitic understandings and ways of knowing and a related lack of self-awareness about certain fundamental premises, goals, and conversation partners among neo-Vedantins (both scholars and advocates) writing on traditional Advaita in general and on *jīvanmukti* in particular. Within most understandings of Western *and* Advaitin scholarship, we need to, and indeed it is in our interest to, understand and make explicit our assumptions and represent accurately both our allies and opponents. The limitations mentioned earlier make neo-Vedantic claims less persuasive than they might be otherwise.

An important part of the problem is the degree to which Western thought and values have affected modern neo-Vedantic thinkers. This influence has made them, like most in the West, "other" to the classical Advaita tradition. For example, as mentioned earlier, neo-Vedantins do not hold textual exegesis (Vedic or otherwise) in the same esteem as does scholastic Advaita, and they privilege experience more. Their otherness can be seen as part of the ongoing "Europeanization of the earth" (or at least India) mentioned so prominently—and ambivalently—by Halbfass (and Hacker and Heidegger). Yet neither are neo-Vedanta thinkers and scholars fully imbedded in the Western tradition of "critical inquiry," though they often use categories and research methods of Western scholarship. As I will show in the case of *jīvanmukti* and social service, one often finds neo-Vedantins advocating Vedantic truths rather than analyzing Vedanta as a perspective or an ideology, or examining specific thinkers and texts in their particular historical context. Not being fully in either tradition, and a lack of self-consciousness about this fact, hinders the neo-Vedantic scholar's ability to contribute to either. While some may find these judgments presumptuous, they are intended to increase awareness of our assumptions and bring an even greater understanding of and respect for traditional Advaita thought. As mentioned earlier, I also acknowledge that neo-Vedantins may have good reasons to "update" Advaitic thought, yet still want to argue that accurate representation is one form of respect due to important thinkers, and neo-Vedantins sometimes fall short of honoring Śaṅkara and classical Advaita in that way.[12]

As stated previously, there are degrees of enclosure within the neo-Vedantic perspective. I want to begin with two well-known figures who are commonly regarded as modern Hindu saints, Ramana Maharshi and Candrasekharendra Sarasvati. I start with them for two important reasons: they are less Westernized than many neo-Vedantins, though they are similarly mission educated and hold some similar views on religious ecumenism and social service. Their primarily Hindu focus is reflected in their relative lack of concern with Western audiences and English writings. Second, they are religious models of *jīvanmukti* more than scholars writing about *jīvanmukti*. They are therefore the best indicators of what counts as living liberation today.

TEN

A Liberated Being Being Liberated: The Case of Ramana Maharshi

The South Indian nondualist Ramana Maharshi is generally regarded as one of the great religious figures in modern Indian history. Most contemporary advocates of Advaita consider Ramana our century's best example of a *jīvanmukta*. His followers even refer to him as *Bhagavan*, or "God." Perhaps the next most revered modern figure among contemporary Advaitins is the recently deceased senior *Śaṅkarācārya* of Kanchipuram, Candrasekharendra Sarasvati. Such major religious personages are worth discussing for many reasons, but it is particularly interesting for us to observe how these two figures, thought to be *jīvanmuktas* themselves, viewed various means to liberation (such as renunciation and devotion), what they understood living liberation to be, and how their followers understood them to represent living liberation.

As part of our consideration of neo-Vedantic ideas, and to prepare for the final chapter, it will also be valuable to look at how these reputedly liberated beings view other religions, and to consider their positions about the relationship of liberation to the social order and social service in everyday existence (*vyavahāra*). We will observe the extent to which their understandings are consistent with the classical Advaita tradition, and when not, ways in which they have altered it. Both are traditionally Advaitin in a number of ways: they are philosophically nondualist (though terming Ramana an Advaitin is in some ways problematic), are committed to the renouncer ideal, and hold knowing the Self to be more important than practicing *yoga* or devotion. Both are also committed more to Self-realization than social reform, and Candrasekharendra is a defender of the traditional order of caste and life stage (*varṇāśrama-dharma)*.

However, I will also argue that both Ramana and Candrasekharendra, in different ways, are examples of figures who creatively adapt the Advaita tradition to modernity. In Ramana's case, this alteration of the tradition can be seen in his advocacy of the primacy of personal experience over scripture and tradition, and in a relatively broad-minded approach to other religions. With Candrasekharendra Sarasvati, we find active promotion of Hindu ecumenism and to some extent concern with social welfare. This advocacy of religious inclusivism, personal experience, and social service is, I have argued, typical of neo-Vedanta.

Neo-Vedantin scholars, who generally hold (or have held) posts in Western-style universities in India and often write (in English) for a Western or Western-educated audience, are some of the leading proponents of the teachings of both Ramana and the *Śaṅkarācārya*. In the next two chapters, I will refer regularly to a prime example of such proponents, the highly influential neo-Vedanta scholar T. M. P. Mahadevan, who was widely read in both Western and scholastic Advaita philosophy, and also was the first director of the Center for the Advanced Study of Philosophy at the University of Madras. Throughout the following chapters, we shall see that while neo-Vedantins like Mahadevan argue that Advaita views are superior to any Western doctrine, they are also comfortable discussing Advaitic thought using Western categories like "philosophy" and "religion" (and Christian ones like "grace" and "love"), and hold that traditional Advaita provides great resources for the modern Western interests in "experience" and social service. Neo-Vedantins are also, like Ramana, religiously ecumenical (and socially liberal about caste) in ways unlike any traditional Advaitin thinker. In Mahadevan's book on Ramana,[1] for example, we find the claim that in order to understand the similarity of Ramana's and Śaṅkara's views, one must recognize that Advaita "is the culmination of all religious sects and philosophical schools [and] the common end of all philosophical endeavour and religious practice (123)." Mahadevan goes on to explain that "[w]hen Sankara points out the defects and inconsistencies in the various schools and cults, he does so not in the spirit of a partisan, but with a view to making them whole (126)." Such an argument is a clear indicator of Mahadevan's neo-Vedantic perspective, for Śaṅkara himself was unreservedly a partisan. In what follows, then, we shall keep in mind the relationship of Ramana, Candrasekharendra Sarasvati, and their interpreters to both traditional Advaita and neo-Vedanta.

This chapter will look specifically at aspects of the life and thought of Ramana Maharshi, himself a reputedly liberated being. We will consider Ramana's—or followers' reports of Ramana's—understanding of liberation, how he viewed various means to liberation (such as devotion and *yoga*) and other religions, and his position about the role of social service when pursuing liberation. Finally, we will explore what Ramana understood *living* liberation to be, and how his followers understood him to represent *jīvanmukti*.

The Life of Ramana Maharshi

While many are familiar with the outline of Ramana's life,[2] it is appropriate to mention a few key events again here. Ramana, born near Madurai in South India in 1879, was a seventeen-year-old student in a mission high school when he had his famous transformative "death experience," realizing that while the body dies, one is not the body.

> I was sitting alone in a room on the first floor of my uncle's house. I seldom had any sickness, and on that day there was nothing wrong with my health, but a sudden violent fear of death overtook me . . . I just felt "I am going to die" and began thinking what to do about it. . . . The shock of the fear of death drove my mind inwards and I said to myself mentally, without actually framing the words, "Now death has come; what does it mean? What is it that is dying? The body dies." And at once I dramatized the occurence of death. I lay with my limbs stretched out stiff as though *rigor mortis* had set in and imitated a corpse so as to give greater reality to the enquiry. I held my breath and kept my lips tightly closed so that no sound could escape, so that neither the word "I" nor any other word could be uttered. "Well then," I said to myself, "this body is dead. It will be carried stiff to the burning ground and there burnt and reduced to ashes. But with the death of this body am I dead? Is the body I? It is silent and inert but I feel the full force of my personality and even the voice of the 'I' within me, apart from it. So I am Spirit transcending the body. The body dies but the Spirit that transcends it cannot be touched by death. That means I am the deathless Spirit." All this was [seen] as living truth which I perceived directly, almost without thought-process.[3]

While this passage largely speaks for itself, note particularly the importance of his realization that his essence was not a body and the very fact of the report being firsthand. Traditional Advaitins like Śaṅkara emphasize that one's self is not the body, but they rarely speak of their own experience. It is also interesting to note that Ramana compares death to his body's temporary silence and inertness during which he still feels his personality and "I" voice.

After this realization, Ramana became an ardent meditator and Śiva devotee and journeyed (from Madurai) to the well-known Śaiva center of Tiruvannamalai at the foot of Arunacala hill in north central Tamil Nadu. He never again left the city. He quickly became famous for his rigorous austerities, sitting in airless temple corners in deep trance and fasting until forced to eat. According to his biographers, he only now began to read traditional Advaita texts, generally in Tamil. The texts he read and commented upon were not Śaṅkara's classic *Upaniṣad* or *Brahma-sūtra* commentaries, but were works like the *Vivekacūḍāmaṇi* and *Ātmabodha*, which modern Western scholarship regards as unlikely to be by Śaṅkara. The work considered here to which he refers most often is the "Yogic Advaita" *Yogavāsiṣṭha* (as will be seen later). During this period, Ramana lived a renouncer's life, at first in a cave halfway up the hill. As he steadily gained followers, including his mother and brother, he moved to an ashram at the base of Arunacala hill, and this modest retreat eventually grew to include a temple, school, offices, dispensary, library, bookstore, and lodgings for his followers.

As time went on, Ramana became more willing to live "in the world"; he ate regularly, read papers and books, did daily chores, and gave audience (*darshan*) daily. He began to gain Western followers, the best-known being Paul Brunton,[4] who was sent to Ramana by Candrasekharendra Sarasvati. All reports indicate that he remained simple, humble, and kindly to all, and much is made of his fondness for animals. There are numerous accounts of the peace and security people felt in his presence, of the serenity his followers gained by his touch or look, and of the profound teaching by his example of perfected living. Ramana's health began to fail in 1948, yet he remained detached to the end, saying the body itself was a disease. He died of cancer in 1950.

The ashram, currently thriving,[5] is well-managed by the third generation of Ramana's brother's family and is an oasis of quiet surrounded by the bustling city. Both visitors and resident devotees are generally silent, calm, and often withdrawn. During both of my visits, over 100 were living in or staying at the ashram, including approximately thirty Western devotees; Indian visitors seemed to be mostly middle-class Tamils. A respectful place (and permanent housing) is given to senior devotees, who continue to embody and communicate Ramana's message.

Dozens take part in the daily round of worship, chanting in Sanskrit and Tamil, and meditation. Ramana's "samadhi hall," where these activities primarily take place, is rather spare; most of its decor is large pictures of the sage. The adjoining shrine to Ramana's mother is more traditionally Śaiva and includes a number of Gaṇeśa images. During worship, many people circumambulate the central *pūjā* shrine within the hall.[6] Ramana's sitting room has become a meditation space, which, on my visits, had an average of twenty-five attendees in late afternoon. His retiring room, still as he left it at death, has become a memorial site, and there are burial shrines to his mother, leading devotees, and favored animals. Fittingly, given Ramana's love of animals, monkeys, dogs, and peacocks freely wander the grounds (though cows are tethered in the *gośāla)*. The lodging rooms are spartan, but clean and comfortable (donations are accepted, but not directly requested). Free vegetarian meals are available to all in residence. These meals, like all activities, are well-organized and begin right on schedule. The ashram also offers a well-attended feeding of *sādhus* at 11 A.M. daily, as well as a free dispensary. The ashram library has a good selection of Hindu religious magazines and Ramana's works, both in Tamil and English, and it is often crowded. Many visitors also take a daily twenty to thirty minute hike to Skandashrama, Ramana's early retreat halfway up Arunacala hill, which has an excellent view of the Tiruvannamalai temple, city, and environs.

Ramana's Writings

Ramana wrote very little, so most of his thoughts come to us filtered through the understandings of his devotees. To discover his views on *jīvanmukti* and the other topics discussed here, an English speaker's major sources must be two books edited by a Western follower, Arthur Osborne: the already mentioned *The Teachings of Bhagavan Sri Ramana Maharshi in His Own Words* (henceforth *Teach)* and *The Collected Works of Ramana Maharshi* (henceforth *CW)*.[7] Both are published by the ashram itself and are in their fifth editions. These texts present a variety of hermeneutical problems. Both books consist of translations (from Tamil), often of oral dialogues, and Osborne writes that some translations by others have been "improved" by him. *The Teachings* are Osborne's selection, intended "to build up a general exposition of the Maharshi's teachings by selecting and fitting together passages from these dialogues and from his writings." Osborne adds "(n)o distinction is made between the periods at which the Maharshi made any statement (1)." Nor are particular questioners always identified. A final hermeneutical problem is Osborne's self-conscious attempt to avoid using Sanskrit terms "to avoid giving the false impression that the quest of Self-Realization is some intricate science which can be understood only with a knowledge of Sanskrit terminology (*Teach*, 5)." One can hardly imagine what earlier Advaitins would have made of such a claim!

It is certainly the case that Ramana was never concerned with writing down a systematic body of doctrine. As Osborne states, "The Maharsi wrote very little" and "(n)early everything that he wrote was in response to some request, to meet the specific needs of some devotee" (*CW,* ix). He and his followers claim that his silent presence spoke loudest. While Ramana's respect for and knowledge of the classical Advaita tradition is made clear by his reported composition of hymns to Śaṅkara, the founder of Advaita, and his free translations of various *stotras* and other works (such as the *Ātmabodha* and *Dṛk-dṛśya-viveka)* purportedly by Śaṅkara, he did not feel bound to scriptural commentary as did Śaṅkara and many other Advaitins. Unlike earlier Advaitins, Ramana claimed that his reading of texts came after his experience of liberation. He reportedly said that the "strength of experience" is decisive for liberating knowledge, not "the strength of the scriptures (*CW*, 74)." As mentioned earlier, only after arriving at Tiruvannamalai did he study any Advaita literature, and then he claimed that "the books were analysing and naming what I had felt intuitively without analysis or name (*Teach*, 4)." In fact, when asked if his teaching was the same as Śaṅkara's, Ramana is said to have replied that his teaching "is an expression of [my] own experience and realization. Others find it tallies with Sri Shankara's (*Teach,* 9)." The experience-based language here raises both questions of how traditionally "Advaitin" Ramana is and to what extent his ideas have been altered when written down and translated.[8]

Thus, the Ramana discussed here will be to some degree Osborne's Ramana, although it will be informed by other understandings (such as that of T. M. P. Mahadevan) and my visits to his ashram and conversations with some living devotees. The two most authoritative followers I interviewed, the senior devotee Kunju Swami (now deceased) and the librarian J. Jayaraman, gave views of Ramana consistent with the one found in Osborne's translations. Additional indications of Osborne's reliability as a witness are the fact that he was a favorite devotee and his works are endorsed by the ashram community as a whole. So, given the limitations mentioned earlier, let us proceed to briefly outline Ramana's thought and then look more closely at his views on various means to liberation, social service, and *jīvanmukti*.

Ramana and the Path to Liberation

Ramana's views are certainly profoundly nondualist and in line (though not identical) with classical Advaita, which holds that all this (*idam sarvam*) is *brahman*, and *brahman* is the Self (*ātman)*. As seen earlier, his greatest emphasis is on Self-inquiry, particularly into the question, "Who am I?" He claims that this inquiry takes one beyond the "I" thought (which identifies itself with the body and is really just the false "I" of the mind or ego) to realize the true "I," the Self. To Ramana, bondage is thinking "I am the body," and liberation arises when the origin of this false "I" (the Self) is seen. From the highest view, Ramana claims, you are really already the Self, eternally liberated: "If you consider yourself as the body, the world appears to be external; if you are the Self, the world appears as Brahman manifested (*Teach*, 41)." There is really no bondage (or liberation), no "doer" or *karma,* and no body (thus, as we shall see, he denies the distinction between living and bodiless [*videha*] *mukti).* In a passage reminiscent of Śaṅkara, Ramana is reported to have said "[r]ealization consists only in getting rid of the false idea that one is not realized. It is not anything new to be acquired. It must already exist or it would not be eternal (*Teach*, 19)." Further, "[t]here is no goal to be reached. There is nothing to be attained. You are the Self (148)." Ramana often uses the analogy of a cinema show, where the Self is both the lamp and the screen on which the illusory show (whose appearance we take to be real) is projected.[9]

Ramana always advocates Self-Enquiry as the highest path, but he makes a place for other practices and routes to gain liberation, both within Hinduism and among other religions. This point is worth emphasizing, for Ramana takes an interesting middle position between the sometimes polemical assertiveness of traditional Advaitins (from Śaṅkara even to later Advaitin harmonizers like Appayya Dīkṣita) and the expansive ecumenism of modern Western-influenced neo-Vedanta. Osborne provides a good example of neo-Vedanta when he introduces the section on Ramana's views of other religions. Osborne asserts that Ramana "was not opposed to any religion" and "[s]trictly speaking, [Ramana] was not exclusively a Hindu . . . since Hinduism recognises that one who is established in constant conscious identity with the Self is above all religions; he is the mountain peak towards which the various paths converge (*Teach*, 62)."[10] This statement sounds more like Swami Vivekananda than Ramana.

Ramana himself is reported to have said that the utilization of various paths or religions depends "on the temperament of the individual (*Teach*, 168)."[11] He continues, "I approve of all schools. The same truth has to be expressed in different ways to suit the capacity of the hearer (169)." However, "[a]ll these viewpoints are only to suit the capacity of the learner. The absolute can only be one (170)." Further, while Ramana is quoted as holding that "[a]ll methods and religions are the same (*Teach*, 65)" and that "the highest state is the same" for all (67), whenever pressed, he indicates that all methods lead to, and the "same" highest state is, Advaitic Self-realization. Interpretations may be different due to "upbringing" or "circumstances," but ultimately the (nondual) "experience is the same (67)." Ramana's statements indicate a lack of interest or even impatience with discussions of religious differences; he seems to be more concerned with experientially bridging those divergences. This certainly differs from traditional Advaita's reliance on *śruti* and dialectic. If doctrines and sacred texts speak of differences, one must look beyond them: "People will not understand the bare and simple truth—the truth of their everyday, ever-present and eternal experience. That is the truth of the Self. . . . Because [people] love mystery and not the plain truth, religions pamper them—only to bring them around to the Self in the end (*Teach*, 69)."

Ramana explicitly ranks various methods of liberation in his "Essence of Instruction" (*Teach*, 209). While inquiry into the "I" leads to dispassion and knowing the Self, "if the aspirant is temperamentally unsuited for Self-enquiry, he must develop devotion," whether to God or *guru* or some other ideal. Attachment to the object of devotion breeds detachment from all else. "If neither enquiry nor devotion appeals to him, he can gain tranquility by breath control," and if none of these suit the aspirant, "he must try karma marga, the path of good deeds and social service," which develops his "nobler instincts" and prepares him for one of the other paths (209–10). As mentioned earlier, one can observe the pursuit of all of these paths at Ramana's ashram today. Along with meditative Self-inquiry, there is regular offering of *pūjā,* Vedic chanting, yogic practice, and social service in the form of feeding and basic medical care. Ramana's ranking and discussion of these various methods illumines both his close relation to traditional Advaita and the influence of neo-Vedanta.

First let us consider Ramana's understanding of the role of devotion. Although he always emphasizes the primacy of knowing the Self, he (like Candrasekharendra Sarasvati) seems to speak freely of a God who is infinite, and in a sense "personal," and he quotes statements from the Bible like, "I am that I am (*Teach*, 57)." He advocates surrender to and trust of God, not so much to gain a Lord's grace, but to burn out other attachments. To Ramana, no God or liberation external to oneself truly exists; the surrender is that of the ego to the Self within (*Teach*, 57, 195, 201). God is really seen "only in the devotees' mind (65)." Still, one should not object to a person "having a separate God to worship so long as he needs one (199)." Moreover, he is largely unconcerned with any debate between dualism and monism; one must realize the "I," and only then can one know "whether the 'I' will get merged in the Supreme Being or stand apart from Him (*Teach*, 52)." Complete surrender is the goal; "[d]o that first and then see for yourself whether the one Self alone exists or whether there are two or more (199)." His own worship of a deity is also ultimately nondual. While he says "Śiva is eternal," Śiva is held to be better known as "Consciousness" and "BE-ing (*Teach*, 202–3)." When asked about his composition of a number of hymns to Śiva and to the sacred hill Arunacala, Ramana is recorded as saying, "[t]he devotee, God, and the hymns are all the Self (54)" and "[t]he Self is Arunacala (55)." Candrasekharendra Sarasvati is not so unambiguous.

Ramana also claims, particularly in his earlier writings,[12] that *haṭha yoga, āsanas*, and breath control are useful, but he never argues that they are more than auxiliaries: "Breath control is only an aid for diving inwards. . . . On the mind being controlled, the breath is automatically controlled (*Teach*, 175)." In contrast to the deep trance of yogic *samādhi,* the *samādhi* that Ramana advocates allows one to remain aware: "In this state, you remain calm and composed during activity. You realize that you are moved by the deeper Real Self within and are unaffected by what you do or say or think (*Teach*, 227)." He also states that a mild, vegetarian diet is best, and fasting unnecessary (192). He is unimpressed by *kuṇḍalinī yoga* (186–8), and, like earlier Advaitins, downplays the significance of supernatural powers (*siddhi).* He is reported to have said, "Enlightened enquiry alone leads to Liberation. Supernatural powers are all illusory appearances created by the power of *maya*. . . . They come unsought to some persons through their *karma*. Know that union with Brahman is the real aim of all accomplishments (*CW*, 73)." Further, "[t]he spiritual force of Realization is far more powerful than the use of all occult powers (*Teach*, 220)."[13]

Ramana, rather surprisingly given his own ascetic background, also rejects traditional renunciation, claiming that one can be in the world *and* detached. Passages on this topic provide clues to his views on *jīvanmukti*. He states that even after realization, the knower can act in the world. "Some withdraw to solitary places and abstain from all activity . . . [while others] carry on trade or business or rule a kingdom. . . . We cannot make any general rule about it (*Teach*, 228)." To Ramana, the key to renunciation is knowing you are not the doer. "Knowledge and activity are never mutually antagonistic," and the householder, when detached, is rendering "selfless service" to his family (*Teach*, 93). Ramana is reported to have said that *saṃnyāsa* is "renouncing one's individuality, not shaving one's head and putting on ochre robes (91)," and real *brahmacārya* is living in *brahman*, not being celibate (90). This position differs dramatically from traditional Advaita (and Candrasekharendra's views as well).

Consistent with his other views, but also differentiating him from earlier Advaitins, is the extent of his indifference to intellectual training and textbook study: he is quoted as holding that "[m]ere book learning is not of any great use" to gain liberation (*Teach*, 7). Followers should attain realization first and ask questions (about even such basics as the truth of rebirth) later (24). After all, the intellect cannot understand its source (*Teach*, 52). This view was supported by J. Jayaraman, who was identified to me as the ashram "intellectual" by two devotees. Jayaraman said that cultivating the intellect is useful to a point, but experiencing the Self is the highest goal.

Ramana and Social Service

Ramana's views on social service are especially worth considering because he is said to exemplify how a liberated being acts in this life. His emphasis on being detached and knowing the Self rather than doing "good works" is more consistent with classical Advaitic ideas than with modern Indian neo-Vedanta scholars who hold that Advaita has always had a large measure of social concern. Ramana felt that self-reform should precede social reform and that concern about the world's suffering stemmed from the misidentification of body and self.[14] He consistently devalues the "external world" and its social reality. To mention an obvious example, while Ramana himself was apparently not caste conscious, he certainly did not take a strong position against the this-worldly inequities of the *varṇāśramadharma* system. On the other hand, he does not endorse it to the degree Candrasekharendra Sarasvati does.

Moreover, it is clear from *The Teachings* that many visitors were interested in, and even troubled about, Ramana's views on "social ethics." When asked about the cause of famine, pestilence, and other miseries, Ramana is said to have responded "[t]o whom does this all appear?" The questioner retorts sharply, "[t]hat won't do. I see misery all around." Ramana's response is uncompromising: "Turn inwards and seek the Self and there will be an end both of the world and of its miseries." When told such an answer is "selfishness," Ramana is said to add, "Because you wrongly identify yourself with the body, you see the world outside you and its suffering becomes apparent to you; but the world and its sufferings are not real. Seek the reality and get rid of this unreal feeling (*Teach*, 38–39)." Here Ramana is certainly consistent with traditional Advaita in devaluing the merely apparent everyday realm (*vyavahāra)*: "[t]he trouble now is due to your seeing the world outside and thinking there is pain in it. But both the world and the pain are within you (*Teach*, 40)." Even when specifically asked if a war then underway "is only in the imagination," Ramana replies that it is just a thought of the deluded questioner (41): "All suffering is due to the false notion 'I am the body.' Getting rid of this is knowledge (42)."[15]

Do sages play *any* role in ending worldly suffering? Ramana is reported to assert that "mahatmas" (great souls) help by silent centeredness: "Public speeches, outer activity, and material help are all outweighed by the silence of the Mahatmas. They accomplish more than others (*Teach*, 39)." To Ramana, silence is "the highest spiritual instruction (125)." Ramana seems suspicious that much socially oriented talk and action might really be egotism masquerading as altruistic concern for others: "[p]reaching is simple communication of knowledge and can be done in silence also. . . . Which is better: to preach loudly without effect or to sit silently sending intuitive force to act on others

(*Teach*, 105)?" It is not coincidental that many admirers of Ramana, ranging from senior follower Kunju Swami to neo-Vedanta scholar T. M. P. Mahadevan to Western seeker Paul Brunton, specifically refer to his silent presence as ending all questions and leading to serenity and liberation. Brunton is a good example. After sitting in Ramana's presence for over an hour, he writes, "I become aware of a silent, resistless change which is taking place within my mind. One by one, the questions which I prepared in the train with such meticulous accuracy drop away . . . I know only that a steady river of quietness seems to be flowing near me, that a great peace is penetrating the inner reaches of my being, and that my thought-tortured brain is beginning to arrive at some rest."[16]

According to Ramana, the real way to ameliorate the condition of the world is to "remain free from pain" by turning within (*Teach*, 40), as *mahātmas* do. "Self-reform automatically results in social reform (98)." Also, "a self-realised being cannot help benefiting the world. His very existence is the highest good (*Teach*, 108)." In response to the Tibetologist Evan-Wentz asking if the sage's "realization leads to the uplift of mankind without their being aware of it?", Ramana reportedly responds, "Yes, the help is imperceptible but it is still there. A Realized Man helps the whole of mankind, although without their knowledge (107)." The sage does not mix with others, but realizes there are no others to mix with (108). Evan-Wentz then leads Ramana into criticism of the Western notion that one must work "in the world" to be useful. Ramana is said to hold that "Europe or America" are "but in the mind," and when the self is realized "all is realised (108)." Thus, Ramana's lack of Western-style social concern is replaced by a focus on Self-realization, which, one might argue, gets nearer ignorance, the root of all evil, than does addressing any of ignorance's particular effects through social action. This response, of course, appears in a variety of Hindu (and Buddhist) schools of thought.

When reporting on Ramana's views about social reform, Mahadevan supports and elaborates on Ramana's view that self-reform must come first: "It very often happens that so-called social service is a self-gratification of the ego," which increases the ego's pride and demoralizes the one served. "It is only such service as that which contributes to the reduction of the ego that is the harbinger of good . . . so, unless one seeks to know the true Self, one cannot really serve society. . . . He who has realised the End and has become liberated while alive works—or more correctly appears to work—for the salvation of the world (*loka-sangraha*)."[17]

Ramana's de-emphasis of social service has been problematic for some neo-Vedantins. The Advaita scholar R. Balasubramanian,[18] seems to take the neo-Vedantic position that Ramana advocates social activism. He disputes critics who argue that nondualists (and *jīvanmuktas*) like Ramana "do not care for the welfare of others and that they do not actively endeavour to remove the misery of the people through social reform."[19] He writes that mystics or *jīvanmuktas* like Śaṅkara and Ramana are a "source of inspiration" and "exemplar[s] of perfect life on earth." For support of this view, Balasubramanian quotes Śaṅkara's *Gītā* commentary III. 25, calling for one who knows the Self to act on behalf of others *(parānugraha)* and Ramana's advocacy of detachment and living with "the good."[20]

Balasubramanian's references here show Ramana's (and Śaṅkara's) spiritual concern for individuals, but not "social reform." He seems to realize this at the end of his article (231). He again denies that Ramana was "indifferent to the miseries of the people," and reminds us of the "solace" Ramana's "gracious look" provided to so many. However, Balasubramanian then states that a mystic cannot "be judged exclusively in terms of moral and social activities," which are not the only ways to show concern for others. A sage like Ramana can comfort others "by his benign look and gentle touch, and also by his 'eloquent silence.' " This, of course, is all Ramana claimed to do, as Balasubramanian notes: "Ramana used to say that only those who know the Self can serve others; moral activity, social reform, and community service undertaken by the rest will be much propaganda and little service." Thus we see here Balasubramanian's attempt to deny Ramana's lack of Western-style social ethics, ethics that Ramana never advocates, ends up by granting its absence. One can certainly argue that Ramana's spiritual service of spreading peace and calm is a sufficient "moral" contribution, unless one (perhaps under the influence of a Western value system) feels that this individualistic effort is insufficient and Western social reform more valuable.

Ramana himself comes closest to supporting Western-style social service in responding to the following question: "But we see pain in the world. A man is hungry. It is a physical reality. It is very real to him. Are we to call it a dream and remain unmoved by his suffering (*Teach*, 39–40)?" After reiterating that the world of suffering *is* a dream, he is reported to have answered

> But all this is not to say that while you are in the dream you can act as if the suffering you feel in it is not real. The hunger in the dream has to be appeased by dream food. The fellow beings you find hungry in the dream have to be provided with dream food. . . . Similarly, till you attain the state of Realization and thus wake out of this illusory, phenomenal world, you must do social service by relieving suffering whenever you see it. But even so you must do it without ahankara, that is without the sense of: "It-is-I-who-am-doing-it." Instead you should feel: "I am the Lord's instrument." Similarly you must not be conceited and think: "I am helping a man who is below me. He needs help and I am

in a position to give it. I am superior and he is inferior." You must help him as a means of worshipping God in him. All such service is serving the Self, not anybody else. You are not helping anybody else, but only yourself (*Teach*, 102–3).

Thus, Ramana here can be found to accept a subsidiary role for social action. Still, even this, his clearest statement on social service, is hedged by saying such service is part of a "dream," and recognition of it as Self-service is stressed. Also interesting is his (or Osborne's version of his?) reference to being the Lord's instrument. While not completely inconsistent with other passages, this idea is certainly not one Ramana emphasizes.

Ramana on Jīvanmukti

Ramana's views on living liberation are particularly interesting because he has been seen by many people as the preeminent twentieth-century *jīvanmukta*. Articles or books about Ramana referring to him as liberated while living have been written by the important neo-Vedanta scholars T. M. P. Mahadevan, N. Veezhinathan, and R. Balasubramanian. Mahadevan, who knew Ramana and Candrasekharendra Sarasvati personally, wrote a biography and summaries of Ramana's works in his *Ramana Maharshi: The Sage of Arunacala*.[21] Mahadevan assumes, rather than argues for, Ramana's status as a *jīvanmukta*. He often compares Ramana with Śaṅkara,[22] and regards Ramana's views on liberation and other topics as authoritative, precisely because he is a *jīvanmukta*. N. Veezhinathan's "Bhagavan Ramana—A *Jīvanmukta*,"[23] gives thanks to Mahadevan as teacher, and like him, calls both Ramana and Śaṅkara *jīvanmuktas*. Veezhinathan's paper largely describes living liberation according to the *Yogavāsiṣṭha* and *Bhagavad-Gītā*, and he argues that Ramana exemplifies the *jīvanmukta*'s characteristics of impression (*vāsanā)* free devotion and detachment. Such characteristics "were clearly discernable in the Bhagavan [Ramana] whose life and teachings vindicate the ancient truth imparted in the Upaniṣad-s (17)." Like Veezhinathan, R. Balasubramanian's aforementioned article refers to Ramana's status in the title "Ramana Maharshi, The Liberated-in-Life," and in it he calls Ramana, like Śaṅkara, an "exemplar of perfect life on earth (230)," the "embodiment of freedom (228)" and the "personification of love (229)."[24] Finally, it is worth mentioning that the currently reigning *Śaṅkarācārya* of Kanchi, Jayendra Sarasvati, also, when asked, called Ramana a *jīvanmukta*, although the Sringeri *Śaṅkarācārya* Bharati Tirtha termed him a *mahant*, but not a *jīvanmukta*.

While Ramana mentions *jīvanmukti* in various places and he certainly accepts its existence, remarks about living liberation are usually brief and only in response to queries. For example, when asked a series of questions about *jīvanmukti* (whether it was possible, the role of *karma*, etc.), Ramana is reported to have answered, "Why worry about all these things? Does Liberation consist in knowing the answer to these questions? So I tell [questioners], 'Never mind about Liberation. First find out whether there is such a thing as bondage. Examine yourself first (*Teach*, 213).' " Perhaps his longest statement on *jīvanmukti* appears in his first work, called "Self-Enquiry," which was compiled from responses to disciple's questions when Ramana was just twenty-two and living in a cave on Arunacala hill. When asked about the characteristics of both the *jīvan* (living) *mukta,* and the *videha* (bodiless) *mukta*, Ramana is said to have responded that the *jīvanmukta* is one who realizes "I am not the body; I am Brahman which is manifest as the self." Further, a *jīvanmukta* is one "endowed with a mind that has become subtle [through prolonged meditation], and who has the experience of the Self (*CW*, 34)." The state of living liberation is also called attributeless *brahman* and *Turiya* (the fourth state beyond limited consciousness).[25]

Ramana then makes a remark about currently manifesting (*prārabdha) karma*, a central focus of traditional Advaita when *jīvanmukti* is discussed. He states that until liberated, one may experience misery due to currently manifesting *karma.* In accordance with the tradition, Ramana holds that everyone's "course of conduct in this life is determined by *prarabdha* (*Teach,* 97)," that one remains embodied here due to *prārabdha karma* despite being a knower, and that "*karma* alone is responsible for the activity or inactivity of the sages (*CW*, 72)."[26] He elsewhere adds that the *jīvanmukta* may appear to lapse into ignorance due to *prārabdha*, but really he "revels" in the Self alone, and "[a] jivanmukta is one who does not see anything separate from the Self."[27] With *jīvanmukti,* as elsewhere, Ramana wanted to focus the seeker's attention on detachment from the body. He is quoted as saying, "So long as one identifies oneself with the body, all this is hard to understand. That is why it is sometimes said . . . that the body of the Realised Man continues to exist until his destiny [*karma]* has worked itself out, and then it falls away." He uses the traditional Advaitic analogy of bodily continuity being like an arrow loosened from its bow, continuing until it hits its mark.[28] "But the truth is that the Realised Man has transcended all destiny and is bound neither by the body nor by its destiny (*Teach*, 231)."

On bodiless liberation (*videhamukti)*, Ramana is reported to have said, "[W]hen even the subtle mind gets resolved, and experience of self ceases, and when one is immersed in the ocean of bliss and has become one with it without any differentiated existence, one is called a videha-mukta (*CW*, 35)." This passage generally accords with traditional Advaita, though the nature of "subtle mind" remains obscure. Ramana seems uninterested in, and in fact disputed, differences between embodied and bodiless liberation. One report has him responding to a question about the difference between these *muktis* by denying *any* true distinction: "A *jnani* with a body is a *Jivanmukta* and he attains *Videhamukti* when he sheds the body. But this difference exists only for the onlooker, not for the *jnani*. His state is the same before and after the body is dropped (*Teach*, 126)." Both Kunju Swami and J. Jayaraman endorsed this view. He is also reported to have said that "[t]here are no stages in Realization or *Mukti*. There are no degrees of Liberation. So there cannot be one stage of Liberation with the body and another when the body has been shed (*Teach*, 236)." In the final verse of "Reality in Forty Verses," Ramana is quoted as claiming, "If it is said that Liberation is of three kinds, with form, without form and with and without form, we say Liberation is the destruction of the ego which discusses whether it is with form, without form and with and without form (*CW*, 119)."[29] Ramana recognized that there are different views on this matter; he is reported to say that "Jivanmukti and Videhamukti are differently described by different authorities; Videhamukti is sometimes said to occur even when the man is seen with a body (*Talks*, 213)."[30] However, although "[b]ooks speak of different kinds of Liberation" (that is, *jīvan-* and *videha-mukti)*, "[t]here may be different stages on the path but there are no degrees of Liberation (*Teach*, 200)."

In a later dialogue, which, after rearrangement and expansion by devotees, was designated "Spiritual Instruction," Ramana addresses the nature of the knower or *jñānī* (*CW,* chapter 4). The *jñānī* is said to belong to the fourth of seven stages of knowledge (*jñānabhūmis,* as mentioned in the *Yogavāsiṣṭha* and *Jīvanmuktiviveka)*, and stages 4-7 are said to be based on experiences of the *jīvanmukta* or "realized person (*CW*, 70-1)." Although seven stages are mentioned, Ramana again states that there is no distinction in stages of knowledge once released; the ego of the *jñānī* dies in the fourth stage (71).[31] In "Self-Enquiry," he is said to have held that categories of *brahman*-knowers are used "[b]ecause of the grades in misery and happiness," but the distinctions are only from the standpoint of the observer, really "there are no distinctions in release gained through jnana (35)."

While Ramana's aforementioned views are certainly comfortably within Advaitic orthodoxy, he does not appear to have read the scholastic writers on this topic. Still, *jīvanmukti is* mentioned at the end of his introduction to his paraphrase of the probably pseudo-Śaṅkaran *Vivekacūḍāmaṇi.* He says that attaining the "state of freedom from duality is the real purpose of life, and only he who has done so is a *jīvanmukta*." According to Ramana, Śaṅkara declares the *jīvanmukta* "to be free from the bonds of threefold *karma (sanchita, agami,* and *prarabdha)*. The disciple attains this state and then relates his personal experience. He who is liberated is indeed free to act as he pleases, and when he leaves the body, he abides in Liberation and never returns to this birth (*CW,* 198)." Actually, Śaṅkara never specifically writes of threefold *karma*, nor does he endorse "relating one's own experience." As with most subjects, Ramana's views here show both continuity with and change from traditional Advaita.

Finally, one should note that Ramana, like Śaṅkara (and unlike many modern neo-Vedantins), makes few references to the ethical actions of the *jīvanmukta*. He reportedly said, "[i]f a man is Self-realized, he cannot tell a lie or commit a sin or do anything wrong," though even here Ramana adds, "Self-enquiry is quite enough for acquiring all the divine qualities; [one] need not do anything else (*Teach*, 162)." In a different context, Ramana is said to claim that the *jīvanmukta*'s "actions should be taken to be only divine manifestations on the plane of humanity. . . . He lives only for the good of the world (*Talks*, 423)." This statement is in line with the neo-Vedantic view, and one may wonder here about the exact terms Ramana himself used.

In the preceding pages, I have attempted to show how a reputedly liberated being talks about liberation and goes about being liberated. Ramana primarily preached *and* practiced meditative Self-inquiry, leading to knowledge of nondual *brahman*. I have also tried to show that while some consider Ramana Maharshi an uncontroversial representative of traditional Advaita, it would be more accurate to say that Ramana's ideas are generally consistent with Advaitin thought, but he did not feel bound to the tradition of Śaṅkara. Ramana, unlike classical Advaitins, shows little interest in making distinctions among religious paths and faiths, and he emphasizes personal experience over scriptural tradition. Yet on the issue of Western-style social service, Ramana appears quite traditional; instead of social reform, he emphasizes the primacy of knowing the Self and the grace of the silent presence of the teacher. And to the degree he says anything about living liberation, his views would be unobjectionable to earlier Advaitins. Thus, Ramana Maharshi, while not a completely traditional Advaitin, can be seen in part to bridge the gap between Śaṅkara's Advaita and modern neo-Vedanta.

After a brief look at Sri Aurobindo's views on *jīvanmukti*, we turn to another figure who bridges this gap, and who is also the main competitor for Ramana's preeminent status as a contemporary *jīvanmukta*, Candrasekharendra Sarasvati, about whom all the earlier named neo-Vedantins have also written.

A Note on Sri Aurobindo on Jīvanmukti

Sri Aurobindo Ghose, the nationalist turned mystic and founder of Integral Yoga, is another not-quite-Advaitin who mentions *jīvanmukti* occasionally. In this (and many other) context(s), his perspective is similar to, but more world-affirming than, the Advaita of Śaṅkara (or Ramana). Most interesting here is Aurobindo's consideration of how one can remain in *māyā* while a *jīvanmukta*. It seems that liberation while still living, in a body with a personality, makes more sense from Aurobindo's viewpoint than from Śaṅkara's. Since Aurobindo holds that existence, from grossest Matter to highest Spirit, is an integral unity, the deluded individuated self *(jīva)* is real and can evolve back to its Spirit-ual basis (Supermind). Put another way, for Aurobindo *brahman* includes *māyā*, and *māyā* is dynamic (*śakti)*, including its derivations of mind and body. True (integral) liberation is not separation from *saṃsāra*, but realization of the Divine (*brahman*) in the Divine. Thus, while traditional Advaita must resort to a logically suspect notion of a trace of ignorance remaining after knowledge, Aurobindo does not need to reject lower levels of truth or hold that the body is inevitably bound by *karma*. To Aurobindo, activity assists you to liberation, whereas to Śaṅkara, actions can not bring you to liberation because they are part of the realm of *saṃsāra*.[32]

Still, Aurobindo's viewpoint on *jīvanmukti* is in many ways Advaitic. When writing about various states of Self/*brahman*, Aurobindo states that a *jīvanmukta* is "one who lives and is yet released in his inner self from the bondage of phenomenal existence." He continues that "*brahman*, as realized by the *jivanmukta* . . . is that which we usually term Parabrahman, the Supreme Eternal and the subject of the most exalted descriptions of the Vedanta (XII, 15)."[33] He makes a number of remarks on *jīvanmukti* in his commentary on the *Ishavasya Upaniṣad*, focusing on detached action or *niṣkāma karma*. He defines *mukti* as release from ignorance (thinking that you are bound) and the knowledge that all is and always will be *brahman*, so one cannot be bound. One then acts without fear, knowing "once free, always free. Even if he is reborn he will be reborn with full knowledge of what he really is, of his past lives and of the whole future and will act as a Jivanmukta (XII, 463)." A *jīvanmukta* is ready to live even 100 years, but is utterly detached from his body (464).[34] Desireless (*niṣkāma) karma* is beyond bondage, so one can be liberated even while acting. "Both the teaching and practice of the greatest Jivanmuktas and of Bhagavan [Krishna] himself have combined Jnana and Niskama karma as one single path to mukti (461)." In accordance with Śaṅkara, he holds that "no one who possesses a body can be free from karma," and without *mukti*, "this karma will forever bind him." Further, "even if he is Mukta, his body and mind are not free from karma until his body is dropped off, but go on under the impulse of prarabdha until the prarabdha and its fruits are complete (461–2)."

When asked about the central Advaitic problem of how one can be both *mukta* and bound, Aurobindo responds (as Guru in the text)

> The Jivanmukta is not indeed bound, for he is one with God and God is the master of His *prakrti*, not its slave; but the Prakrti attached to this Jivatman has created causes while in the illusion of bondage and must be allowed to work out its effects, otherwise the chain of causation is snapped and the whole economy of nature is disturbed. . . . In order to maintain the worlds therefore, the Jivanmukta remains working like a prisoner on parole,[35] not bound indeed by others, but detained by himself until the period previously appointed for his captivity shall have elapsed (XII, 462).

He later adds, "When we know the Self and experience our true Self, then we are masters of our Prakrti and not bound by her creations (XII, 465)." Aurobindo's interpretation here recasts the problem in terms of *Sāṃkhya-Yoga* notions of *prakṛti* and God (*īśvara)*, which allows him to say that the *jīvanmukta* controls his actions and remaining embodiment.

Aurobindo wrote a poem called *Jivanmukta*, which stresses silence, timelessness, and the ecstasy of liberation. His language here is far more world affirming than is typical of traditional Advaita. As he says when commenting on the poem, "[t]he subject is the Vedanta ideal of the living liberated man—Jivanmukta—though perhaps I have given a pull towards my own ideal which the strict Vedantin would consider illegitimate (V, 581)." He writes that the poem is "a transcript of a spiritual condition" and expresses "the essential spiritual emotion of the state." It is a "feeling of possession by the Ananda rapture . . . the tremendous and beautiful experience of being ravished, thoughtless and wordless, into the 'breast' of the Eternal who is the All-Beautiful, All-Beloved (IX, 436)." The poem indicates that, "Although consenting here to a mortal body,/He [the *jīvanmukta]* is the undying; limit and bond he knows not." His soul enjoys "Infinity and the sempiternal All is his guide and beloved and refuge (V, 576)." We have come a long way from Śaṅkara here.

ELEVEN

Candrasekharendra Sarasvati: Śaṅkarācārya *and* Jīvanmukta?

Unlike absolute renunciates like Ramana Maharshi, *Śaṅkarācāryas*, while celibate ascetics, have duties traditionally associated with being leaders of Brahminical or *Smārta* Hinduism. The model is obviously Advaita's founder, "Ādi" Śaṅkara. Like the first Śaṅkara, *Śaṅkarācāryas* today play a variety of roles, including teacher/scholar, administrator, and spiritual leader.[1] In addition to effectively representing and transmitting this tradition, Candrasekharendra Sarasvati, the recently deceased *Śaṅkarācārya* of Kanchipuram, is also widely regarded (by Advaitins and others) as the foremost contemporary example of a *jīvanmukta*. His stature is indicated in William Cenkner's statement that "[h]e, Sri Ramana Maharshi, and Sri Aurobindo Ghose have dominated South India as religious personalities in modern times, but the *Śaṅkarācārya* has the broadest appeal and effectiveness among the people."[2] T. M. P. Mahadevan, a particularly ardent devotee of Candrasekharendra, writes that the *Śaṅkarācārya* is "[c]ast in the image of Ādi Śaṅkara, the immaculate Sage is divine and yet human; his saving grace is universal in its sweep; his concern is for all—even for the lowliest and the last."[3] Shortly before his death in January 1994, the popular journal *Hinduism Today* praised Candrasekharendra's almost century-long "distilled piety and unremitting selfless service in the cause of Sanatana Dharma," and refered to government plans to issue a commemorative stamp and coin honoring him.[4]

In the following chapter, in addition to the *Śaṅkarācārya*'s statements about *jīvanmukti* and the methods to attain liberation, I will consider his views on other religions and social service, which are an interesting mix of traditional Advaita, in which he emphasizes Self-knowledge, Vedic study, and performing *dharmic* duties, and neo-Vedanta, in which he concurs with its emphases on religious ecumenism and social service. Both aspects are of course significantly influenced by his role as *Śaṅkarācārya*, especially in a time of great cultural change. In fact, his successor Jayendra Sarasvati has expanded the emphasis on social reform and the opening to new, non-caste groups. It is worth observing how any *Śaṅkarācārya* works to conserve *and* update the Hindu tradition, and the interest is only enhanced when this project is undertaken by a reputedly liberated being.[5]

One of the most intriguing points of tension between traditional and modern views in Candrasekharendra's thought is his expansive notion of Hinduism as "religion" versus his far more restrictive view of Hinduism as "social system" (i.e., the *varṇāśrama-dharma*). Put another way, he is far more concerned about Hindu orthopraxy than orthodoxy. We shall see that the *Śaṅkarācārya* shows great ecumenical inclusivism for different views within Hinduism and toward other religions; for example, he long allowed Indian Muslims and Westerners of all types to visit and talk with him.[6] On the other hand, he fully endorses some of the most conservative social practices of Brahminical Hinduism, such as supporting Brahmin and *saṃnyāsin* privilege as well as wives' submission to their husbands. On this and other issues, Candrasekharendra embodies in a most interesting way the puzzle of how to be "modern" while still representing traditional *Smārta* Hinduism.

Many contemporary (Brahmin) Advaita scholars who represent neo-Vedanta also wrestle with this issue, and it is no coincidence that a number of them have close relationships with the Kanchi *Śaṅkarācāryas*.[7] Many of these scholars have taught at the University of Madras (thus near Kanchi) and count Candrasekharendra as their *paramaguru*, as do the more traditional scholars at the Madras Sanskrit College and Kuppuswami Sastri Research Institute (KSRI) in Mylapore. In fact, when in Madras, the *Śaṅkarācārya* stayed and gave talks at the latter's grounds. Further, the KSRI library is housed in Candrasekharendra Sarasvati Hall, and *paṇḍits* affiliated with the Sanskrit College helped train both the reigning and future *Śaṅkarācāryas*.[8] It would be fascinating, but beyond my goals here, to examine the relationships and influences of these figures on one another. Instead, we shall begin with a review of the *Śaṅkarācārya*'s life, noting particularly aspects relevant to his views on "society" and "religion," and how he integrates tradition and modernity.

The Life of Candrasekharendra Sarasvati

Candrasekharendra Sarasvati was born in central Tamil Nadu (Villupuram) in 1894 and began his education at an American mission school.[9] Unlike Ramana, however, he was an outstanding student, excelling at languages. He was chosen to become the sixty-eighth Kanchi *Śaṅkarācārya* at age thirteen. He spent most of the next decade studying classical Advaita texts (in Sanskrit), learning the branches of Vedic knowledge, and otherwise preparing himself for his life's work. He lived in Kumbakonam, not setting foot in Kanchi until 1931. He began the first of many walking tours (*yātra*) of India in 1919. On his tour, Candrasekharendra both lectured in Sanskrit to other *paṇḍits* and gave eloquent popular discourses. In these talks, he attempted to revitalize the traditional teachings and customs of the Hindu *dharma*, while still being aware of cultural changes. From the start, he met with *harijans* ("untouchables"), Muslims, and Christians, which certainly was a major innovation for a *Śaṅkarācārya*, traditionally the locus of Brahminical purity.[10] His popular following was greater than that of any prior *Śaṅkarācārya*. He traveled throughout South India over the next decade, speaking, performing *pūjās*, and consecrating temples. According to Mahadevan, the *Śaṅkarācārya*'s presentations included "[t]he essentials of Hindu *dharma*, the obligatory duties, the supreme duty of being devoted to God, the harmony of the Hindu cults, the significance of the Hindu festivals and institutions, the cultivation of virtues, and the grandeur of Advaita ("Sage," 37)." Robert Slater adds that Candrasekharendra's tours allowed him to gain "intimate acquaintance with the life of the people and shape his teaching to their changing needs [which showed] his concern not only for their spiritual but also their physical welfare,"[11] such as his interest in cooperative projects for village improvement. Spiritual welfare came first, however; as the *Śaṅkarācārya* also said (to Paul Brunton), "[n]othing but spiritual understanding between [nations and peoples] will produce goodwill and thus bring real peace and prosperity."[12] We shall look more closely at the relative emphases on the aforementioned themes in the following pages.

While not playing any overtly political role during the Indian struggle for statehood, Candrasekharendra endorsed nationalist activity in a way Ramana never did. In the 1920s and 1930s, he met with a number of nationalists, including a cordial meeting with Gandhi in 1927 (though they disagreed on the merits of the caste system and whether or not *harijans* could enter temples).[13] When India achieved independence, the *Śaṅkarācārya* lamented communalism and issued a statement which says in part, "For a long time our country has striven for freedom; by the Grace of God, by the blessings of sages, and by the unparalleled sacrifices of the people, freedom has came (*sic*) to us. Let us pray to the all-pervading God that he may shower his Grace so that our country will become prosperous, being freed from famine conditions, and the people will live unitedly and amicably without any communal strife ("Sage," 52)." This statement clearly indicates the *Śaṅkarācārya*'s ecumenism and this worldly social concern, which differ significantly from that of world devaluation and philosophical disputation prevalent in traditional Advaita.

He also differs here from Ramana Maharshi. Candrasekharendra visited Tiruvannamalai in both 1929 and 1944 for a month during a festival, decades after Ramana settled there, but the two never met. Ramana of course never left his ashram, and it would have been unseemly for the *Śaṅkarācārya* to go to Ramana, but, given Candrasekharendra's interest in Hindu ecumenicity, one wonders if attempts to arrange such a meeting were made. It certainly would have been fascinating to hear the conversation of the two most prominent modern Advaitin "*jīvanmuktas*." The fact that neither considered it imperative to meet is another indication of Ramana's unconcern with adhering to the classical Advaita tradition. In this context, it is also interesting that two years later, in response to Paul Brunton's request for a *guru* (including possibly the *Śaṅkarācārya* himself), Candrasekharendra said he was too busy for personal pupils and sent Brunton to Ramana with his endorsement ("Sage," 33–34).

After a lengthy *yātra* in northern India,[14] Candrasekharendra spent the next three decades performing a wide variety of duties. He continued to promote the study and teaching of Sanskrit and Vedic literature; he also favored mass education, especially if it included moral instruction. Candrasekharendra regularly met with leaders of other religious institutions to promote unity, teaching of *dharma*, and otherwise supporting Vedic traditions. He had a great concern for temple renovation and the popular observation of appropriate *dharmic* duties and Vedic ceremonies. He also organized assemblies of *paṇḍits*, conferences for scholars, and publications about Advaita. Finally, he advocated social service for the needy. He initiated charitable giving by his followers to feed the poor and low caste and to pay for cremations, medical services, and talks on *dharma* to prisoners. His work in each of these dimensions has borne fruit: today there are trusts set up to support schools and conferences and to establish a university at Kanchi (called Candrasekharendra Sarasvati Vidyalaya, which I saw under construction outside Kanchi in 1997) to teach both traditional Vedic and modern Western subjects, funds to provide income for temple renovation and for worshippers (*arcaka*) who memorize and recite hymns, and a social service foundation to provide for the needy. Given all of these activities, it is no surprise that Kanchi is the wealthiest *Śaṅkarācārya pīṭha* in India.

In 1954, when he was sixty, Candrasekharendra selected and began to train his successor Jayendra Sarasvati, who was then nineteen. In 1957, he celebrated his 50th anniversary as *Śaṅkarācārya* and spent two years in Madras performing *pūjās* and temple consecrations and giving talks that often had the themes of Advaita's all-inclusive nature and the goal of interreligious understanding. He continued his travel through Tamil Nadu and Andhra Pradesh until the early 1970s and then turned the affairs of the *maṭha* over to Jayendra Sarasvati.[15] From that time on, he generally lived in silence and seclusion. He died in January 1994 at the age of ninety-nine and tens of thousands came to Kanchi to mourn his passing.

Candrasekharendra and the Hindu "Religion"

Candrasekharendra's teachings, at least according to his popular lectures in Madras, mentioned earlier, are an interesting mix of traditional and neo-Vedanta. Unlike in Ramana's case, these discourses were formally prepared by the *Śaṅkarācārya* himself, and his command of English was reported to be quite good. The lectures range over a wide variety of topics in Hinduism and Vedanta, but often focus on the nature of the Veda and *dharma,* the all-embracing character of Hinduism, and the importance of devotion (which ultimately is identical with knowledge).[16]

Candrasekharendra both uses and brings into question problematic Western terminology like "Hinduism" and "religion." He begins one talk by saying, "The name *Hinduism* which is used now to denote our religion was unknown to our ancestors and is also unknown to the common man among us (*Aspects*, 1)." Elsewhere, he states, "It is a misnomer to call our religion as 'Hinduism.' That is the name given to it by the foreigner as the religion of the people who lived on the banks of the Sindhu. The more proper name is to call it *Vaidikamata*, the religion of the Vedas. It is also called *Sanatana-dharma*, the eternal religion [which existed] from time immemorial (*Call*, 33)." To Candrasekharendra, the beginningless Vedic "religion" preexisted all "founded" religions. As source of all religion, the Vedas originally "minister[ed] to the spiritual needs of mankind as a whole (*Aspects*, 2)." They are also "the taproot of all sects of our religion. Whatever denomination we may belong to, our common allegiance is to the Vedas (*Aspects*, 3)."

Like many neo-Vedantins, Candrasekharendra holds to the view that Vedic teaching was the original and best religion, *and* that since all religions grew from the Veda and lead to the same goal, all should be respected. Mahadevan reports him to say that a "resurgent and strong Hinduism is necessary not only for the salvation of the Hindus but also for the betterment of the world. The *Veda* . . . is not a sectarian text. Whatever truth was declared by any great prophet can be traced to the *Vedas*" ("Sage," 57)."[17]

While using the modern term *spirituality*, Candrasekharendra follows Advaita tradition by repeatedly arguing that all must follow the Veda. "[A]ll spirituality must be firmly established on a high moral code, which involves the doing of what is prescribed and the avoidance of what is prohibited (*Aspects*, 17)."[18] He adds, "the first stage in the spiritual ladder is the due performance of the obligatory duties prescribed in the sastras[19] (22)." These include wearing the sacred thread, propitiating ancestors, and so on. If the

Veda is unclear, one should follow the *smṛtis* and example of good people. Here and elsewhere, the *Śaṅkarācārya* laments modern India's secularism and falling away from Veda study and ritual performance (*Call*, 85, 125). He is quoted in *Hinduism Today* to say, "People have given up a lot of the shastric rules. If I myself were to relax them, how much more lax will the people become?" He criticizes modern subjectivist and psychologistic tendencies: "Now-a-days, however, the fashion is . . . to give the first place to what is called one's conscience relegating all the other prescribed guidances to a secondary place, or, as is often done, to condemn them as meaningless and irrational (*Aspects*, 20)." Unlike Ramana and many influenced by the modern West, Candrasekharendra does not put personal experience above Vedic revelation.

Still, as mentioned earlier, Candrasekharendra is a keen advocate of harmony among Hindus and between Hindus and other religions. His ecumenicity and humanitarianism, like his use (despite reservations) of categories like "Hindu" and "religion," is shared by well-known neo-Vedantins like Sarvepalli Radhakrishnan and Swami Vivekananda. The *Śaṅkarācārya* certainly looks beyond Hinduism in a way rare in earlier Vedantic thought. Both Mahadevan and Candrasekharendra himself seem to see his role as being a "*jagadguru*" or *world* teacher in a way that would be foreign to traditional Advaitins.[20] As Mahadevan writes, "the Sage's teachings are meant for the entire mankind. Even when they are addressed to the Hindus, they are applicable *mutatis mutandis* to the followers of other faiths ("Sage," 15)." Candrasekharendra was an advocate for the neo-Vedanta view favoring religious harmony and argues that "the teaching of the Vedas" is that there are "many paths to the same goal (*Call*, 26)." He writes that "[w]hen it is realised that all paths in religion lead to the same goal, there will be no need to change the path one is already following (*Aspects*, 46)."[21] Mahadevan further reports the *Śaṅkarācārya* to say that "[a]s the God of all religious denominations is one, there is no need to give up one religion and adopt another. This does not mean that all the religions are uniform; uniformity is not important; what is important is unity; and all our faiths are united in proclaiming the supreme reality of one God ("Sage," 56)."[22] In a statement reminiscent of Ramana, Candrasekharendra adds that, "religions are many only to cater to the different tastes of man (56)."

The neo-Vedantin Mahadevan both speaks for himself and accurately represents Candrasekharendra's views when he writes that "[t]he special contribution of Hinduism to the world's history of religions is the truth that there are as many modes of approach to Godhead as there are minds. And yet, on account of misunderstanding and narrowness, the followers of the different cults of Hinduism have indulged in quarrels sometimes ("Sage," 47)." Mahadevan states that Candrasekharendra, on the other hand, wants "to call attention to the golden thread of unity that runs through the differing sects and keep alive the idea of unity, the central theme of Hinduism (*Call*, 134)." Candrasekharendra both pleads for Hindus to become unified and argues that unity is the basis of Hinduism. He worked particularly hard for unity between Śaivas and Vaiṣṇavas in Tamil Nadu and organized a number of conferences to promote such unity. He says that a "fellow feeling between the different sects" is needed, and that it is an "article of faith" for Hindus that different religious sects are "only various phases of one Eternal Religion (*Call*, 134–5)." To Candrasekharendra, "according to all our scriptures and the teachings of all the great masters, Siva and Vishnu are one ("Sage," 56)."[23] These statements are, of course, highly debatable and are key elements of the neo-Vedanta view.

Interestingly, Candrasekharendra claims that the Hindu tendency to accommodate and reconcile other views starts from Śaṅkara's Advaita. Ignoring Śaṅkara's many polemical statements against other schools, he speaks of the "catholicity of Advaita" and asserts that Śaṅkara believed that "no school of thought is foreign to Advaita," which "comprehends every warring sect and system into its all-embracing unity." He continues that "the survival of Hinduism is itself due to this Advaitic temper (*Call*, 225)."

Like Ramana, the *Śaṅkarācārya* endorses different teachings for different levels of spiritual awareness. He urges all Hindus, who are overwhelmingly householders, to follow *dharma*, worship God by *pūjā, japa* (chanting), and prayer, and to follow the possibly universal but certainly Western ethical standards to do good, be kind, and live a simple life. Only a few (such as *paṇḍits* and students in the *maṭha*) can purify the mind through meditation, or comprehend the highest teaching, *nirguṇa brahman* of Advaita.[24] Candrasekharendra seems even more open than Ramana (or Śaṅkara) to the worship of God as a start on the path to liberation, and he refers to devotion (*bhakti*) toward a personal Lord in many discourses. He argues, "When practicing devotion, it is enough if one has knowledge *of a sort* of God. Without such knowledge there can be no devotion. Starting with devotion to God limited by name and form, if one later realizes the unlimited nature of God, the limited will then be transcended. Yet, to realise the unlimited, one must start with devotion to the limited (*Aspects*, 39)." Further, even *jñānins* enjoy "the delights of contemplating God's form and features (*Call*, 240)." Still, Candrasekharendra holds that ultimately Hindus do not have many gods; instead "we think of God in many ways and worship Him in many forms. We give a separate name to each of these forms to help us in our acts of worship and contemplation . . . [but] the One can manifest itself and be worshipped according to the tastes and the capacities of the worshippers, and according to the innumerable varieties of functions of Divinity . . . How can there be higher or lower, superior or inferior, when in reality there are not two, but it is only One God manifested differently (*Aspects*, 42–43)?" When discussing image worship, the *Śaṅkarācārya* makes a similar point:

> Our religion recognizes the psychological limitations of ordinary men. Not all of them can at one bound contemplate God in His abstraction from physical features. For directing the mind towards God and keeping it steady during contemplation of Him, a concrete image or idol is an invaluable help. The frail mind must go from the concrete to the abstract, from the forms of God in images to God without form . . . [Finally], even though in the ultimate conception He is formless, there is nothing inherently impossible in His assuming a variety of forms for the sake of His devotees (*Aspects*, 59–60).

As the aforementioned suggests, Candrasekharendra is finally an Advaitin, however. He says that devotion ultimately leads to nondual knowledge (*jñāna*), for "[t]he goal of bhakti is the annulment of duality and the attainment of oneness (*Aspects*, 26)." While one begins by choosing a particular form of god (*iṣṭadevatā*), as one "progresses in his devotion and concentration, he will be led on to the One where the differences disappear (*Aspects*, 43)."[25] He also states "[u]ltimately, being oneself is to realize one's true Self which is God. That is the consummation of bhakti (*Aspects*, 26)." The highest truth is thus Advaitic: the knower or *jñānin* is the highest being, and realizes that one is the *ātman*, not the body, and *ātman* is *brahman*. Candrasekharendra at times sounds much like Ramana: "By proper training one should learn to detach the *atman* from the body and its parts. The sense of the 'I' must be separated from the body. When this happens, the sufferings will be understood as pertaining to the body and the person will be unaffected by them (*Aspects*, 30)." He concludes that "[h]aving attained this goal of unitive consciousness with the Supreme, nothing remains to be deemed higher than that . . . One who has acquired it is a true jnani (30)." According to Mahadevan, the *Śaṅkarācārya* also states that "[t]he man of wisdom, the Sage, is the ideal of man. He has no attachment and aversion; praise and blame are equal to him . . . *Moksha* or release is not a *post-mortem* state; it is the eternal nature of the Self. The *jñānī* realizes this; and hence there is no more travail for him ("Sage," 57–58)." Thus, the *jñānin* is a *jīvanmukta*. But, according to Mahadevan's report, Candrasekharendra goes on to hold the neo-Vedantic view that such a *jñānin/jīvanmukta* is not tied to Advaita or Hinduism: "Such *jnanis* have appeared at all times and in all places. Their presence is a blessing to the world . . . There is no discord or divergence of views among the wise. The peace that passeth understanding is what they spread (58)." A reader of Vivekananda's works might again be struck here at the similarities with Candrasekharendra.

Candrasekharendra and the Social Order

Despite his favoring of Hindu (and even global) unity in worship, Candrasekharendra is far more traditional in his support of the hierarchical societal divisions in the *varṇāśrama-dharma* system and a woman's submission to her husband. Like earlier Advaitins, the *Śaṅkarācārya* sees important differences between people in everyday reality. He argues that the traditional caste and life stage divisions are proper (even if "arrogance" about them is not), and that social service, while valuable, is secondary to Self-knowledge. On these topics, his role as guarantor of the *Smārta* tradition continues. Concerning caste, he acknowledges that many foreigners and Indians criticize the caste system, and that "in the context of modern life, the rules of caste are not practiced as before," but he wants to inquire into whether caste "is so bad and injurious as it is said to be (*Aspects*, 48)." The caste system "was designed for the smooth functioning of society . . . each man doing his allotted duty and all contributing to the general welfare of the community (49)." Candrasekharendra claims that "[t]he main argument against caste is that it has led to conflicts (48)." Actually, the main arguments by foreigners and many modern Indians have been that it is discriminatory and oppressive, and thus its injustices have led to conflict. But Candrasekharendra holds that since conflict due to caste is comparatively recent, while the system has survived for thousands of years, "[t]hat it has survived all through shows it is not so bad after all. If it were really injurious to society, our ancestors would have abolished it long ago (48)." It is notable here that he uses historical continuity, not Vedic scripture, to support his position. He compares "quarrels" over caste to controversies over differing forms of government and language, and points out that no one recommends abolishing these things (though few hold that either language or government are inherently unjust). He then concludes that instead of abolishing caste, "the sane view is to retain the thing for its good and eliminate the root cause of the evil (49)."

What is the root cause of the evil in caste? It is when "one caste consider[s] itself superior to another," for which "there is no justification (49)." Such an argument certainly flies in the face of the numerous justifications of superiority, or at least hierarchy, in classical *dharma-śāstra*.[26] "We should think only of the duties of our respective castes without any consciousness of superiority or inferiority (50)." Here Candrasekharendra seems to fall somewhere between ardent defenders of the transcendentally ordained *dharma* and the modern reformers in India who find the caste structure itself, not "feelings of superiority" about one's caste, to be the root evil. On the one hand, he states that "[w]hatever be one's caste, if one has devotion to God, one can become divine in essence (50)." However, despite our inherent similarity in divine essence, he also argues that there are "certain restrictions [which] pertain to marriages and personal observances. They are restrictions which each caste imposes on itself; they are not imposed from outside (49–50)." Again, we see a human- (vs. Veda-) centered legitimation. Further, many would dispute such a benign understanding, which could fairly be called Brahmin-centered. Mahadevan and other (Brahmin) neo-Vedantins ignore the elitist implications of this outlook, and one should note that Candrasekharendra's successor, Jayendra Sarasvati, has moved some distance beyond this view.

Candrasekharendra also gives a benign interpretation of the rationale for the duties of the Brahmin caste. He states that Brahmins are obliged to take on the lifetime job of learning the Veda, and "[p]ursuit of other avocations will interfere with" this task (*Aspects*, 5)." To preserve the Veda, Brahmins "are forbidden from engaging in other pursuits [and those with other avocations] have been prohibited from learning the Vedas. This is not to be understood as discriminating against them. This has been ordained only to ensure that they discharge their own functions in society undistracted by other pursuits (5)." (He ignores here the view of Śaṅkara and later traditional Advaitins that only learning the Veda allows one to enter the path to liberation, and access to the Veda is limited to twice-born males.) Candrasekharendra shows an awareness of viewpoints that question Brahmin prerogatives: "[T]his is not to be understood as giving the Brahmin a privileged position in society, nor is he to be considered as a parasite on society (6)." The Brahmin traditionally has accepted his duty to look after the "spiritual welfare" of others with "joyous willingness," though "[u]nfortunately, in modern times, most brahmins have neglected this duty and are pursuing professions proper to others in the society (6)."

He goes on to make the tradition-altering argument that "[c]aste-consciousness can be eradicated only if one is filled with regard for dharma, is imbued with bhakti, and has acquired jnana," like holy men and sages (*Aspects,* 50). It is in one sense true that, as Candrasekharendra states, single-minded *bhaktas* and *jñānins* have "no caste consciousness," but such figures have been rare and either passively ignore or actively reject the mainstream *dharmic* order. He continues that the "[a]rrogance of caste superiority is a sin according to our sastras (50)." While one cannot ask for scholarly documentation in a public discourse, such a claim ignores much textual counterevidence and seems to indicate a modern neo-Vedantic compromise with the tradition.

One might also argue that the *Śaṅkarācārya*'s main aim is not to promote Brahmin privilege, but to restore morality and order in the chaos of modern life. He claims that when caste "was strictly observed it was an effective instrument to keep people in the path of righteousness." If one violated the rules of one's caste, one lost caste and was "degraded and ostracized from the community. This practice had a deterrent effect on the people and hence the moral tone of the community was high (*Aspects*, 51)." This beneficial effect (of social debasement) has been lost with "the loosening of restrictions," so less efficacious legal means must now be used (51). Modern education has also led to the breakdown of *dharma*. In ancient India, "education was what was in accord with *dharma*. Modern education is utilitarian; it does not aim at the cultivation of character and the development of noble virtues (*Call*, 169)." This lament for the loss of long-standing social norms in the transformation to a modern secular society is widely shared. Still, one might respond that modern education does aim to cultivate character and virtue, but ones different than the traditional model, and in fact, ones that call parts of the Vedic tradition into question.

The disparity between Candrasekharendra's and modernity's views on "noble virtues" is raised in perhaps starkest fashion in Candrasekharendra's discussion of the role of women in marriage, which may include self-immolation (*satī*). In fact, he acknowledges women's existence generally only in the marital context. For Hindus, he writes, "marriage is a *sacrament* for the elevation of the soul (*Call*, 110)." For women, marriage is "a means of spiritual attainment"; while men are to seek a religious guru, "to the woman, her husband alone is her guru. She is to look upon him as her God and in that attitude, she has to surrender herself to him, body and soul." He claims that "[t]he disciplines and restrictions regulating marital relations are willingly accepted by women," and notes in this context that "[w]hen we question why a particular religious practice should be observed, it is a sign that we are beginning to lose faith or bhakti (110)." It would be interesting to see his arguments and evidence for women's willing acceptance of the disciplines regulating marriage, and to hear further why questioning them is to him a loss of faith.

The *Śaṅkarācārya* uses *satī* as an example of wifely faithfulness in the past: "When a woman has dedicated her body completely to her husband or God, she finds no use for it after the death of her husband (*Call*, 111)." Then, in an apparent endorsement of *satī* in principle, he adds, "[I]t is good to observe a practice with faith even though we may not know the reason for it. The practice of *sati* may appear cruel if considered apart from the ideal of which it is the expression. It is not every woman who can practice it. For such widows who cannot sacrifice themselves in the funeral pyre of their husbands," such as those who have small children to care for, other codes have been prescribed (112). For Candrasekharendra, religious liberation is obviously not related to nor contradicted by social or gender equality, a position to which few Western or modern Indian admirers of the *Śaṅkarācārya* draw attention, and which might well make many of them uneasy.

Candrasekharendra also defends the *āśrama* (life stage) system, particularly that of the last stage, the renunciant or *saṃnyāsin,* one who is desirous of, and is ideally near, liberation. The *Śaṅkarācārya* endorses the traditional lifestyle of the world-devaluing renouncer more than does Ramana, who emphasizes knowing one is not the doer (vs. any specific doing or not doing). For Candrasekharendra, it seems that male Brahmin *saṃnyāsins* alone can gain liberation, though this goes unstated in his English writings. Thus, the characteristics of the renunciant illumine Candrasekharendra's views of the nature of living liberation. He makes much of the importance of the *saṃyāsin* in society, but this importance is more spiritual than social. He rejects the "wrong view that Sanyasins are parasites of society, because they do not do 'productive' work (*Aspects*, 53)." While some wanderers are mere beggars, a "real sanyasin is a spiritual stalwart spending his time in contemplation of the Supreme and in instructing others in the way of dharma." He further "is the exemplar of the highest values of life and as such is an asset to society (54)." Politics or public service are "not at all the duty of a sanyasin. It is his life mission to purify himself steadily and gradually and throw himself completely into the quest and experience of the ultimate Truth, namely God (55)." To Candrasekharendra, like Ramana, the highest service a *saṃnyāsin* can perform is serene detachment: "in truth, service to others is offered in the largest measure possible, by persons who are dedicating themselves to self-purification and complete God-consciousness more than any body else. A person who has not purified himself cannot purify others. . . . The mere *existence* in the world of a few such souls engaged in self-purification creates an aura by itself which tends to bring solace and peace to an innumerable number of troubled hearts." Echoing Ramana, the *Śaṅkarācārya* concludes that *saṃnyāsins* are "benefactors of society much more than any political or social leader (*Aspects*, 55–56)."

Candrasekharendra further holds to the primacy of detachment when he considers the connection between knowledge (*jñāna*) and social service. He states that "[t]here is an impression that service to another is for the purpose of relieving his sufferings and to help him. This may be the ostensible purpose of service. But the main thing is that such service chastens your own mind (*Call*, 130)." He continues that the true *bhakta* sees others as God, and "does to them what he would do to his God." This activity "is true *paropakaram* (service to others). A life habituated to *paropakaram* is both the means to *jnana* and the effect of it (131)." He argues that in the *Bhagavad-Gītā* Krishna teaches detachment by *jñāna* before social service: "[U]nless one is perfect oneself, one is not qualified to engage oneself in acts of public good, *lokaksema*." If one overcomes sorrow and anger, "then his very existence will contribute to public weal. He need not actively reform the world; he need not *strive* for *lokaksema*; the world will learn by his example to reform itself (*Call*, 198)." The evidence for this last assertion is certainly mixed.

Despite the aforementioned focus on individual detachment, Candrasekharendra rejects the accusation by other religions that "Hindus are mainly concerned with individual salvation and are indifferent to the collective welfare of mankind in general."[27] He states that this "indifference" (which is really serene detachment) is only true for renouncers in the fourth life stage. He points to King Janaka, who as ruler worked without attachment for the welfare of others and whose "dealings with the people of the world is love and kindness in an equal and impartial spirit."[28] The *Śaṅkarācārya* supports service by manual labor (well digging, temple or road construction, etc.), again with the goal of liberating nondual insight: "[B]y such physical labour people will shed their vanity and egoism and develop a feeling of oneness with others. Their minds will, thereby, be disciplined and cleansed of impurities, be in a proper condition to receive and enshrine the Paramatma, which is the ultimate purpose of life (*Call*, 172)."

Candrasekharendra also argues that the West can learn from Hinduism, though a question remains as to whether the teaching he offers focusing on love is influenced *by* the West or put in neo-Vedantic terms *for* the West. When asked by a visitor what message the *Śaṅkarācārya* would want to send West, Candrasekharendra is reported to have replied, "In all that you do, let love be the sole motive ("Sage," 63)." While violence, punishment, and even war may be necessary, "whatever be the nature of action, the agent must act out of love. Passions such as desire and hatred, anger and malice must be totally eschewed." According to Candrasekharendra, this understanding is "the message of the sages and saints of India (63)." His conception of "love" seems more what Westerners would call "detachment," and his views on the *dharmic* order indicate that love does not include Western notions of equality among castes or genders.

Candrasekharendra on Jīvanmukti

Candrasekharendra's views on *jīvanmukti* are particularly interesting because, like Ramana, the *Śaṅkarācārya* is himself widely considered liberated while living. Jayendra Sarasvati, Candrasekharendra's successor, is typical in linking the *Śaṅkarācārya* with two other reputed *jīvanmuktas*: Śaṅkara and Ramana.[29] The translator of his discourses, P. Sankaranarayan, writes, "[o]ur Acarya's advaitic temper coupled with his endearing *karuna* [compassion] is opposed to whatever is private or partisan and is all-comprehensive. A *Jivan-mukta* himself, he exhibits a synthesis of *karma, bhakti*, and *jnana*. . . . To us of this generation belongs the rare good fortune to be alive at this time, to have his *darshan*, to listen to his voice, and, if only we would, to abide by his precepts (*Call*, 15–16)." I have already mentioned T. M. P. Mahadevan's view. When I visited Mahadevan in 1979, a picture of the *Śaṅkarācārya* hung over the inside front doorway, and he explicitly termed Candrasekharendra a *jīvanmukta*. Mahadevan claims all of Candrasekharendra's visitors experience "an inner transformation" and "a noble revolution in their soul ("Sage," 16)," and quotes a variety of foreign seekers and scholars, including Paul Brunton, Arthur Koestler, and Syed Hussain Nasr, about the effect meeting Candrasekharendra had on them. Typical are Robert Slater's comments: the *Śaṅkarācārya* had both "saintly serenity" and "concerned interest" in the world, as well as an "ecumenical outlook."[30]

N. Veezhinathan, in his article on the *Śaṅkarācārya* and the Kanchi *pīṭha*,[31] also states that Candrasekharendra follows in the line of *jīvanmuktas* like Śaṅkara and Sarvajñātman in presiding over this *maṭha*. The bulk of Veezhinathan's essay describes *jīvanmukti* (or being a "realized soul [86]").[32] He concludes here, as he did when writing on Ramana, that Candrasekharendra achieves the characteristics of *jīvanmukti* discussed in various classical texts; he states that "temperance in speech, self-control, and a sense of detachment constitute the essential nature of the Sage of Kanchi, and He reveals them in order that his disciples may realize them to achieve perfection (90)." He ends praising the *Śaṅkarācārya,* and says, "[i]t is our good fortune that His Holiness is in our midst as a *jīvanmukta* directing us at every stage in the spiritual path (90)."

Candrasekharendra, like Ramana, does not deal with *jīvanmukti* at length, but one can glean from a few passages that his understanding accords with traditional Advaita. He holds that "[t]he source of the body is the *karmas* that we performed in previous lives. Those that we do now only serve to perpetuate the bodily state in future lives too. So to get rid of suffering, we should get rid of the body" by ceasing karma, its cause (*Call*, 56)." He also writes that "[s]ince residual karma brings the soul in conjunction with the body, all karma should be liquidated, burnt out, with the body of the present life (*Aspects*, 17)." Further, as suggested earlier, Candrasekharendra holds that the knower or *jñānī* is the highest being. According to Mahadevan, the *Śaṅkarācārya* holds that "[t]he man of wisdom, the Sage, is the ideal of man. He has no attachment and aversion; praise and blame are equal to him . . . *Moksha* or release is not a *post-mortem* state; it is the eternal nature of the Self. The *jñānī* realizes this; and hence there is no more travail for him ("Sage," 57–58)." Thus, the *jñānī* seems to be a *jīvanmukta*. But

Candrasekharendra holds (according to Mahadevan's report) that such a *jñānī/jīvanmukta* is not tied to Advaita or Hinduism: "Such *jnanis* have appeared at all times and in all places. Their presence is a blessing to the world. . . . There is no discord or divergence of views among the wise. The peace that passeth understanding is what they spread (58)."

Candrasekharendra himself explicitly mentions *jīvanmukti* only in a few places. Two will be mentioned here: the first is is a brief, rather conventional, statement; he says that the "final realization is the result of *jnana* of the Supreme Truth received from the guru and contemplated on by the pupil. In that state, one is freed from the shackles of life and is said to be liberated even while one is alive. This state is called *jivanmukti*. This is the goal of the spiritual path laid out in our religion (*Aspects*, 32)." The second appears in a discussion about the peaceful mind. Candrasekharendra states that to acquire peace (*śānti*) is to attain *mukti*. He then quotes sacred text (*śruti*): "Thus the knower becomes immortal here."[33] He continues by arguing (in accordance with Ramana and traditional Advaitins) for liberation while embodied, rather than after death:

> It [*śruti*] conveys that one attains *mukti here*, in *this life*. The Sruti speaks about *jivan-mukti* and not about *videha* [bodiless]-*mukti*. . . . If *videha-mukti* is the truth, then one would have to acquire *santi* after death and attain *mukti* by that *santi*. But how can *santi* arise after death if there was none before death? Therefore, for obtaining *mukti*, which is freedom from rebirth, one should acquire *santi* springing from *Brahma-jnana* in this life itself and that is the only means to *mukti* (*Call*, 49).

Candrasekharendra continues by refering to *Gītā* V. 23, which states that one is able here (*iha*), before liberation from the body, to withstand the agitation (*vega*) rising from anger and desire, is disciplined (*yukta*) and happy. This, he concludes, is the real peace (*Call*, 50). Such a view is in harmony with Śaṅkara's ideas. One also observes no linkage of *jīvanmukti* with social service.

In conclusion, let us explore the relationship between the traditional understandings of a *Śaṅkarācārya* and a *jīvanmukta*. This comparison is well illumined by the differences between Candrasekharendra and Ramana Maharshi. We begin by considering the *Śaṅkarācārya's* roles. As Cenkner writes, the first task of a *Śaṅkarācārya* is to be a teacher and leader of the Brahminical tradition, not a "saint" or "mystic."[34] The *Hinduism Today* article offers a similar, popular understanding of the differences between world-renouncing ascetics and *Śaṅkarācāryas,* who must "mix with the world, guide, comfort, instruct . . . [and] be more concerned with the fostering and perpetuation of the ageless Sanatana Dharma than with their individual salvation (p. 1). "This was echoed by the Sringeri *Śaṅkarācārya* Bharati Tirtha, who said that his main responsibility was "to propagate the *sanātan dharm*."

As these statements suggest, *Śaṅkarācāryas* primarily represent a social and religious institution within Hinduism that bears responsibility for continuing the traditions of Vedic education and ritual activity and for following customary *dharmic* duties. This in part accounts for the relative lack of emphasis on the philosophical subtleties of Advaita Vedanta, which is far less comprehensible to most Hindus than worship of a deity or performing Vedic duties.

Yet, as Cenkner points out, the *Śaṅkarācāryas*' traditional vision is losing influence today among the majority of urban and secular Hindus, who show diminishing interest in Vedic ritual and education, and who question caste and sect exclusivity and a lack of social concern.[35] With their calls for ecumenicity and social service, the Kanchi *Śaṅkarācāryas* (as well as various neo-Vedantic thinkers) are clearly attempting to make themselves and Hindu *dharma* relevant to the contemporary world by reaching out to modern Indians, particularly Westernized Tamil Brahmins. Ultimately, however, at least until the ascension of the most recent *Śaṅkarācārya*, Jayendra Sarasvati, the *Śaṅkarācāryas* have been far more representatives and transmitters of the *varnāśrama-dharma* tradition than social activists.

The *Śaṅkarācārya,* then, is a model of a teaching *guru* and "worldly ascetic," while the *jīvanmukta* is primarily a detached, liberated being whose principal "teaching" is his serene presence. A *jīvanmukta* like Ramana embodies oneness with *brahman*, and tasks like teaching about *dharma*, administering a *maṭha*, and consecrating temples are tangential to this. Similarities certainly exist: both Ramana and Candrasekharendra are religious models and spiritual guides, Ramana taught, and Candrasekharendra embodied wisdom and saintliness. Further, both preached global ecumenicity and both started organizations that assist the needy, yet neither felt social service to be their primary task. Still, their primary roles were different. As Jayendra said to me, caring for the welfare of the world (*loka-saṃgraha*) is necessary for a *Śaṅkarācārya,* but not for a *jīvanmukta* like Ramana. A *Śaṅkarācārya* must teach Hindu *dharma*, but *saṃsāric* activity is finished for a liberated being.[36] In this context, the Sringeri *Śaṅkarācārya* Bharati Tirtha quoted *Gītā* III. 22–23, which indicates that the liberated being (here Kṛṣṇa) need do nothing, but still engages in action to properly lead the common people.

While not identical, these traditional roles can to some degree be integrated (though it is harder to make either fit a Western-style social progressive model, as some neo-Vedantins would like). The model *Śaṅkarācārya,* and a model *jīvanmukta*, is said to be Ādi Śaṅkara. He both achieved knowledge of *brahman/ātman* identity and lived in the world as teacher, philosopher, debater, and administrator. If Ramana is justly famed for the purity of his insight into nonduality, Candrasekharendra is so significant because of the claim by his followers that he combined qualities of both *Śaṅkarācārya* and *jīvanmukta*.

As suggested earlier, the *Śaṅkarācārya* tradition remains strong, at least in South India. I have had the opportunity to speak with the reigning Kanchi and Sringeri *Śaṅkarācāryas*, Jayendra Sarasvati and Bharati Tirtha, respectively, about *jīvanmukti*. Before turning to what I see as a further stage in the transformation of traditional Advaita to Western-influenced neo-Vedanta, I include here brief remarks on these figures' view of embodied liberation.

Interview with Jayendra Sarasvati

I had the chance to have *darshan* of Candrasekharendra and an interview with Jayendra Sarasvati (attended by Vijayendra) on the morning of January 9, 1990. We conversed in a receiving area on the porch of his *maṭha*, and our talk was interrupted regularly by offerings and requests for blessings.

The *Śaṅkarācārya's* views on *jīvanmukti* were generally traditional, perhaps most closely identified with the "Yogic Advaita" of the *Jīvanmuktiviveka*. When asked what *jīvanmukti* is, Jayendra responded that normally the individualized self goes "I," "I," "I" or "my," "my," "my," and experiences joy and sorrow (*sukha-duḥkha*); cessation of this experience is liberation while living. All *saṃsāra* is destroyed (*naṣṭa*) for the *jīvanmukta;* his *ātman* is peaceful (*śānta*) and eternal (*nitya*). According to Jayendra, *jīvanmukti* exists where there is knowledge (*jñāna*) of *brahman*, and all sorrow and fear is destroyed. Following the *Bṛhadāraṇyaka Upaniṣad*, Jayendra claimed that the liberated being sees no duality, for he knows there is no other thing to see. As examples of *jīvanmuktas*, he mentioned Śaṅkara, Ramana Maharshi, and Candrasekharendra; Sri Aurobindo was termed a *karma-yogī*. He held that the *Jīvanmuktiviveka* and *Pañcadaśī*, as well as Śaṅkara's *bhāṣyas* and the *Upadeśasāhasrī*, were instructive texts (*śāstra*) about *jīvanmukti*. The *Yogavāsiṣṭha* was termed a book about means to liberation (*sādhana-grantha*). When asked, he agreed with Vidyāraṇya's view that *videhamukti* meant *jīvanmukti* with no future birth, and that Janaka was a *jñānī*, then a *mukta*.

When questioned about the relationship of renunciation (*saṃnyāsa*) to living liberation, Jayendra stated that the *jīvanmukta* is totally detached, so renunciation is then unnecessary. No desire or bond of any sort remains.[37] Still, renunciation is a means (*sādhana*) to liberation. The *jīvanmukta* is beyond (*ātīta*) Vedic regulations *(vidhi/niṣedha*), meditation (*dhyāna*), chanting (*japa*), and ritual performance (*yajña*), though all of these are means. Jayendra also held that *yoga* was a means (*sādhana*), and that *jīvanmukti* comes after *samādhi*. He continued that one first hears the sacred texts, meditates (*dhyāna*), and achieves *samādhi*, then one reaches knowledge of *brahman* and self-illumination (*ātma-prakāśa*), which bring living liberation.

Jayendra also claimed that the *jīvanmukta* was not required to act for the welfare of the world (*loka-saṃgraha*). No action of any sort is necessary for one whose *karma* is completely finished (Hindi: *khatam*), as was the case with Ramana Maharshi. He continued that the *jīvanmukta*'s *saṃcita* and *āgamī karma* are finished, and that when the remaining *prārabdha karma* is experienced (*bhoga*), one attains bodiless liberation (*videhamukti*). The *Śaṅkarācārya*, on the other hand, must act for the welfare of the world, which means he must teach (*pracāra*) Hindu *dharma*. When asked, Jayendra stated that a *jīvanmukta* does remain embodied to teach, preparing students (*śiṣya*), and giving instruction (*upadeśa*) to others. When discussing social reform in Hinduism, Jayendra became quite animated, quoting the *Bhaja Govindam* and the *Gītā* ("all forms (*viśvarūpa*) are within me [Krishna])." Seeing any difference indicates ignorance. He held that since the highest self (*paramātman*) is in all of us, we must not do evil to others.

He concluded by talking about choosing a new *Śaṅkarācārya*,[38] and claiming that the institution of *Śaṅkarācārya* rule and Hinduism in general were strongest in South India.

A Note on the Sringeri Śaṅkarācāryas

The Sringeri *pīṭha,* in the coffee- and tea-growing hills of Karnataka, was reputedly the first *maṭha* (along with a shrine to *Śrī Śāradā*) founded by Śaṅkara and has had an unbroken succession of *Śaṅkarācāryas* since his pupil Sureśvara. It attained high status during the Vijayanagara empire under the leadership of Bhāratītīrtha and Vidyāraṇya, authors of the *Pañcadaśī* and *JMV*.[39] It is a thriving pilgrimage site, which features both a renovated *Śāradā* temple and a large Vidyāśaṅkara temple.

Next to the reigning *Śaṅkarācārya*'s residence, across the river from the temples and *maṭha* offices, there is a memorial housing *samādhi* shrines honoring the last three *Śaṅkarācāryas*. Narasimha Bharati (ruled 1878–1912) revived Sringeri as a pilgrimage site, had a shrine built to Ādi Śaṅkara in his reputed birthplace Kaladi, and arranged for the publication of Śaṅkara's collected works (*granthāvalī*) by Vanivilasa Press. His successor, Candrasekhara Bharati (ruled 1912–1954), is called a *jīvanmukta* in *maṭha* literature.[40] Candrasekhara Bharati was known for his intense *tapas* and was often said to be in *samādhi*.[41] Like other *Śaṅkarācāryas*, he emphasized studying the Veda, following the *guru* and *śāstras*, performing *dharmic* duties, and held that worshipping God was good, although the highest *brahman* is beyond name and form. Interestingly, reports show he was often critical of British rule and modern secular society, and felt the West had too strong an influence on India. He saw secular tolerance as anti-Hindu, or at least against the traditional *dharmic* order. He said that women should stay at home, all Hindus should keep to the caste structure, and one could only attain happiness through following the *dharma*.[42]

The recently deceased Sringeri *Śaṅkarācārya*, Abhinava Vidyatirtha (ruled 1954–1989), was also called a *jīvanmukta* and was widely revered in southern India (though perhaps not as widely as Candrasekharendra Sarasvati). Like Candrasekharendra, he is described as being warm, approachable, and charismatic as well as a skilled administrator. He also spent years touring South (and later North) India performing *pūjās*, giving discourses, and consecrating temples. Again, like Candrasekharendra, he was an expert linguist, and while teaching that *brahma-jñāna* was the highest truth, he stressed following ritual duties and offering devotion to God. In accordance with his predecessor, he seemed less responsive to modern ecumenical trends than Candrasekharendra, emphasizing issues like cow protection and the difficulty of right action in the modern world.[43]

The current *Śaṅkarācārya*, Bharati Tirtha, like those mentioned earlier, a Telugu Brahmin and an excellent linguist, was born in 1951. He became Abhinava Vidyatirtha's disciple at age fifteen, was designated his successor at twenty-three, and was installed as *Śaṅkarācārya* in an elaborate ceremony in October 1989.[44] I had the opportunity to interview him about *jīvanmukti* on a visit to Sringeri on January 10, 1997. Bharati Tirtha defined a *jīvanmukta* as one who has attained the direct experience of *brahman* (*brahma-sākṣātkāra*); such persons include Śaṅkara, Vidyāraṇya, and Abhinava Vidyatirtha.[45] The *JMV* was said to be the most important text on liberation while living.

Bharati Tirtha stated that the *jīvanmukta* has no need to act. When asked whether this created some tension between being a *jīvanmukta* and a *Śaṅkarācārya*, Bharati Tirtha responded by quoting *Gītā* III. 22–23.[46] Kṛṣṇa here states that he has nothing he must do, nothing to attain that is not attained, yet still he engages in action. If he did not continually act properly, neither would common people. When I asked if this constituted *loka-saṃgraha*, Bharati Tirtha agreed. He added in Hindi that whatever path great people (*mahān log*) go along, others follow, and, in English, that the latter "imitate" the former. He said specifically that Śaṅkara and Abhinava Vidyatirtha (both liberated *Śaṅkarācāryas*) taught about liberation by their examples, but "for them, there is absolutely no necessity of action."

I then asked about the difference between living and bodiless (*videha*) *mukti*. Bharati Tirtha said the only difference was embodiment—*sa-* versus *a-śarīratva*. When the *jīvanmukta*'s body goes (upon completing fruits of *prārabdha karma*), then there is *videhamukti*. ("*yah hi, bas*"). I inquired if Patañjali's *aṣṭāṅga yoga* was necessary for the *jīvanmukta*. Bharati Tirtha stated that some yogic practice is necessary for settling the mind (*man*). When mental activity lessens, then knowledge is obtained, and the practice (*sādhana*) is completed. Further, he held that the *jīvanmukta* pursues no supernormal powers (*siddhi*); powers are "obstacles" to liberation. Finally, I inquired whether it was important for living liberated beings to be present today. Bharati Tirtha rapidly replied (in English), "Of course, they are always important."[47]

TWELVE

The Liberated Being and Social Service: Vivekananda, Radhakrishnan, and the Neo-Vedantic Jīvanmukta

It is now time to turn to some neo-Vedantins who (like T. M. P. Mahadevan), by the categories and medium of discourse (English) they use, often seem at least as much influenced by and in dialogue with Western ideas and writers than with the classical Advaita tradition.[1] As I have argued earlier, I believe this Western orientation interferes with a good understanding and an accurate representation of traditional Advaita.[2] An obvious example is how a number of neo-Vedantins, generally in response to Western, particularly Christian missionary, criticisms of traditional Advaita, have—to a much greater degree than Ramana or Candrasekharendra Sarasvati—downplayed or even ignored often censured Advaitic teachings about caste exclusivity and devaluation of everyday activity.[3] On the other hand, ideas seen as laudable to the West, such as this-worldly technological progress, valuing ecological harmony with nature,[4] or caring for and actively providing humanitarian social service to all persons without distinction, are claimed to be present but go without support (or even reference) in the classical texts.

We will here examine the attempt of some modern neo-Vedantic thinkers and scholars of Advaita to significantly reinterpret the traditional notion of *jīvanmukti* from a conception tied to world renunciation and a call for liberation from bondage to all desire to one that fits a Western (both humanist and Christian) ideal. This ideal includes worldly action requiring social service, that is, actively performing "good works" for the welfare of others, especially the poor. This notion of service is quite different from that of worshipful service (*sevā*) to a god or *guru,* as well as from the *guru*'s spiritual service of teaching and blessing devotees. Many neo-Vedantins then attempt to read this newer understanding back into traditional Advaitic views. As stated earlier, all traditions change, and adding social service to the classical model of *jīvanmukti* is legitimate (and one might even say good), yet it is still important to note that this idea is a reinterpretation—even a distortion—of the views of Śaṅkara and his followers. It is a greater break with the past than admitted or might first seem apparent. While it *is* traditional to claim unity and continuity in Advaitic thought, those of us in the Western academic tradition cannot so easily ignore changes from earlier ideas, particularly when unrecognized or unstated.

Traditional Advaita tells us that liberation is the cessation of ignorance about the nondual nature of reality and the end of bondage to transmigratory existence (*saṃsāra*). One who attains liberation while living realizes the identity of *ātman/brahman* and becomes utterly detached from worldly desires, knowing the self is not related to the conditions and sorrows of body and "ego." Questions about the relevance of social service in this view include: thus detached, does the Advaitin *jīvanmukta* show concern for the welfare of other, ignorant beings, and, if so, how? In particular, does the *jīvanmukta* actively do "good works" for all or perform social service in ways familiar to the modern West? Will the liberated being at least teach others about his realization? In the following pages, we shall see that neo-Vedantins (including many contemporary Indian scholars of Advaita) assert that *jīvanmukti* and social service are compatible and/or are closely related. They hold that the *jīvanmukta,* although desireless and knowing that all is ultimately nondual, stays here to teach and serve other (ignorant) beings. Social service, while not necessary for one so detached, is regarded as the "natural" outflow of the compassionate love of the liberated being. This view, I will argue, stems largely from a desire to justify *jīvanmukti,* and Indian "ethical" thought, generally, in light of Western and Christian notions that a perfected person looks after the welfare of others, particularly "the least among us." It also is meant to establish the relevance of the *jīvanmukti* ideal in contemporary life.

To begin, we should look at the central problem with which neo-Vedantins must contend when asserting their views on social service: the devaluation of everyday existence (*vyavahāra*) in Advaita thought. If the liberated being realizes the world of duality lacks ultimate reality, this being would not necessarily show any concern for (non)others in this realm, even by teaching them. R. C. Pandeya has made the case well that Advaitic views on nonduality lead to a "transcendence" of Western-style social ethics,[5] (and we have seen his view implicitly supported by many of Ramana Maharshi's teachings). He argues that while the body and the social realm persist for a *jīvanmukta,* this being knows they are not the highest truth. Thus, liberation brings a thoroughgoing detachment from everyday existence, with no mandatory duties. Looking out for the welfare of others means attending to the world of duality and the "others" there to care for. Not only is concern for others ultimately based on a delusion, but such concern can itself become an attachment. We might even grant that once one knows nonduality, the liberated being will do no evil action, given the extensive training on the path to liberation, but there still is no imperative to do Western- (or *bodhisattva-*) style good. Pandeya concludes that while some modern Indians might be uncomfortable in finding Advaita lacking social concern, they must admit that, from the traditional Advaita view, such concern is based on ignorance (*avidyā*).[6]

When turning to the actual textual record in classical Advaita, one finds no explicit call to perform social service or to do "good works" for those who suffer. In light of neo-Vedantic claims to come about tolerance and brotherhood, we might briefly mention here that Advaitin statements about the metaphysical identity of all being(s) are not linked to statements about helping others in need, or more generally to social and religious equality in *vyavahāra*. It is well known that the hierarchical *varṇāśrama-dharma* (law of caste and life stage) privileges certain people (especially Brahmin males) by birth. In current language, it is classist and androcentric. Śaṅkara clearly concurs with this privileging; in his *Brahmasūtra* I. 3. 34–38 commentary, he states that low-caste *śūdras*, even if interested and literate, are not entitled to hear or study the Veda or to perform Vedic rites (the necessary starting points to gain release), for they have not undergone investiture of sacred thread. In fact, the commentary on *sūtra* 38 refers to texts indicating a *śūdra* hearing the Veda should have his ears filled with lead and one reciting the Veda should have his tongue chopped off.[7] Women are not even mentioned in this context. Contrary to neo-Vedantins, who generally ignore this passage, traditional Advaitins find the highest nondual truth irrelevant to equality in everyday social relations, and, as Halbfass writes, they instead link identity in liberation with "an uncompromising adherence to an unequal, caste-bound access to it."[8] One might add here that while some have argued that Śaṅkara himself, through his activity as debater and teacher, embodied the social action of the *jīvanmukta*, he nowhere demonstrates or advocates the liberated being as egalitarian "social worker."

In fact, the clearest indications of a "proactive" concern for ignorant beings in traditional Advaita appear when Śaṅkara and later Advaitins occasionally refer to the knower as a teacher, that is, one who compassionately remains in a body to share his (spiritual) realization. In his commentaries, Śaṅkara writes that the *brahman*-knower will, out of great compassion, teach one blinded by *saṃsāra* about the true nondual self (*ChU* VI. 14. 2) and that the truth-seer teaches the supreme knowledge (*Gītā* IV. 34).[9] One could argue that Śaṅkara himself was an example of such a person. Śaṅkara also expresses concern for ignorant beings in *Upadeśasāhasrī* Prose I. 6, in which the teacher's compassion (*dayā*) and concern (*anugraha*) for others are mentioned, but not elaborated upon. I pointed out earlier that the traditional Advaita thinker, Vimuktātman, makes the liberated being's role as teacher a central issue. He and others claim that a teacher is necessary for liberation, but not that a knower (*jñānin*) is obliged to teach.[10] It is probably going too far to suggest, as some have, that social service is intended in Śaṅkara's comments on *BS* III. 3. 32,[11] which imply that a liberated being could take birth again to fulfill a certain commission (*adhikāra*) arising due to the condition of the world. Śaṅkara seems here to be responding to the demands of the text; he does not mention the idea of a commission elsewhere. He also indicates the commission is to promulgate the Veda, which, while keeping the world well ordered, is not what a reader might immediately think of as the neo-Vedanta version of social service.

When arguing that Śaṅkara calls for "social service," most neo-Vedantins make reference to the idea of *loka-saṃgraha,* which is often translated "welfare of the world," and suggest that this is part of the liberated being's orientation to perform service to society. However, in the most important references to *loka-saṃgraha* relevant here, found in *Bhagavad-Gītā* III. 20 and elsewhere, Krishna seems to instruct Arjuna to act for the "well-being" of the world (or people in general) by upholding or preserving dharmic order rather than general (and perhaps hierarchy challenging) human or global welfare. In his commentary on this passage, Śaṅkara certainly holds to a *dharma*-affirming understanding of *loka-saṃgraha.* Sustaining the *dharma* may bring well-being, in the cosmos and to (Aryan) people, but will not necessarily provide service or "welfare" for all, especially the downtrodden.

From this traditional view, *Gītā* III. 20 states that one attains perfection (*saṃsiddhi*) through (detached) action (*karma*), so one should act considering only *loka-saṃgraha,* that is, the world's well-being, which is brought about by selflessly upholding the dharmic order. In his commentary, Śaṅkara argues that while pursuing or after achieving right insight (*samyag-darśana*), in which one achieves perfection (i.e., *mokṣa*), one continues acting, due to currently manifesting or *prārabdha karma.* Śaṅkara seems to suggest that the wise person should be a "role model" and world order preserver; he here defines *loka-saṃgraha* as preventing the world's (or people's) activity from going astray (*lokasya-unmārga-pravṛtti-nivāraṇaṃ*). The exact nature of this activity, while unspecified, seems to mean not straying from the *dharma.* In accord with the ensuing verses (III. 21–25), Śaṅkara points out that since people follow the standard a superior person sets, such a person, despite being (like Krishna) utterly detached and needing to do nothing, should and does act only for the sake of others.[12] Here then one may see a call to attend to the well-being of the world (at least the part that includes the Aryan twice-born), but neither Śaṅkara nor the *Gītā* prescribe any Western-style "social action," nor do they describe the actions the wise perform for the world's welfare as humanistic service to all.[13] And, this is certainly not a theme in later scholastic Advaita.[14]

Swami Vivekananda on Jīvanmukti *and Social Service*

I stated earlier that the most common interpretive framework in modern Indian scholarship on Advaita is that of neo-Vedanta. All lines of interpretation have a history and, to some degree, an identifiable "lineage." Two modern thinkers who have greatly influenced all later members of the neo-Vedanta lineage on a wide range of topics are Swami Vivekananda and Sarvepalli Radhakrishnan. Like many later neo-Vedantins, both were trained in English-speaking missionary schools, read widely in Western literature and philosophy (and read many "Hindu" texts first in translation), and travelled extensively in the West. Both endorsed Western values like rationalism, tolerance, and social progress. Neither was simply "Western," of course; both were familiar with, and claimed as authoritative, Vedantic texts and Indian philosophical thought in Sanskrit. They also were critical of Western individualism and materialism, and hoped to "conquer the world" with Vedantic "spirituality." They emphatically claimed that Advaita Vedanta—not Christianity—was the most ethical, scientific, progressive, and universal religion. Their writings and lives can be seen as models for the interaction and assimilation of traditional Hinduism with Western humanistic traditions. It is certainly the case that to understand the claims of contemporary neo-Vedantic scholars of Advaita about the close relationship of *jīvanmukti* and social service, we must begin with Vivekananda and Radhakrishnan.

Swami Vivekananda, the most famous disciple of the Bengali master Ramakrishna, exemplifies the neo-Vedantic mix of Indian and Western influences mentioned earlier. In addition to a British mission education, he also participated in both sides of the traditional *guru*-student system, took the vow of *saṃnyāsa*, and worshipped the Goddess. Although his views were quite different from Ramakrishna's, he certainly felt guided by his *guru*'s spirit. He organized a Hindu monastic order, but his "practical Vedanta" stressed Christian-style charity and the performance of social service activities to uplift the masses at least as much as retreat and contemplation. In his view, renunciation and selfless service go together naturally. Vivekananda also became, following the 1893 Parliament of Religions in Chicago, by far the best-known messenger of Hinduism in the West. He is particularly important here both because of the exemplary nature of his remarks on living liberation and social service and because many present-day Indian scholars of Advaita refer to Vivekananda as a model of modern *jīvanmukti.*

Detailing Vivekananda's interpretation of Advaita and of "Hinduism" generally is beyond the scope of this inquiry; here I will merely point out that he calls Advaita "the fairest flower of philosophy and religion that any country in any age has produced."[15] For him, Vedanta was not *a* religion, but a universal truth reconciling and transcending all religions. We shall see here that, while a skillful communicator and an advocate, Vivekananda was little concerned with scholarly accuracy or systematic philosophy, and made little reference to the problems of interpreting and matching categories and concepts across cultures.[16] Certainly he was in part purposefully revising the tradition to incorporate his concerns for social service and national uplift and unity.[17]

Vivekananda often claimed that Vedanta and social service are completely compatible; spiritual and social reform should happen simultaneously. Reacting in part to criticism of Hindu caste boundedness (and general "lack of ethics") by Christian missionaries, he argued strenuously for "spiritual harmony," tolerance, and universal brotherhood, and held that such ideas were Vedantic because Vedanta teaches the "oneness of all" and that "you are your brother." For example, he claimed that when we feel oneness in human nature and with the universe, we "rush forth to express it. . . . This expression of oneness is what we call love and sympathy, and it is the basis of all our ethics and morality. This is summed up in the Vedanta philosophy by the celebrated aphorism *Tat Tvam Asi,* 'Thou Art That.'" This means your soul and body are one with all others, and "in hurting anyone you hurt yourself; in loving anyone you love yourself."[18] Serving others thus becomes a form both of spiritual training and love of self. Interestingly, however, Wilhelm Halbfass points out that when Paul Hacker surveyed ethical maxims in Sanskrit literature and their links with philosophical teachings, he found no evidence that the metaphysical identity statement "*tat tvam asi*" was ever used to justify "practical" ethical imperatives as Vivekananda attempts to do.[19] Vivekananda admits that India has actually been a nonpareil "land of privilege," but he goes on to say that "[n]one can be Vedantists and at the same time admit of privilege to anyone," and that "[t]he work of the Advaita, therefore, is to break down all these privileges." His exemplar of one holding to a "Vedantic ethics" of equality without special perogatives is the Buddha.[20] Such statements are, of course, advocacy rather than description and go far afield from traditional Advaita (and even from the views of his master, Ramakrishna). Further, he was of course speaking primarily to the privileged educated upper caste elite, and his rather paternalistic reformism did not threaten Brahmin power.

Vivekananda only rarely explicitly mentions *jīvanmukti,* and in these passages he sounds rather traditional and generally does not make extravagant claims for the social ethics of the liberated being. For example, he writes that "there are men still living for whom delusion has vanished forever." Although having the highest knowledge, their bodies will continue "until the momentum of past work is exhausted." Further, "[t]he man who has in this life attained to this state . . . is called 'free while living.' This is the goal of the Vedantist, to attain freedom in life."[21] He expands on these ideas elsewhere, comparing the body's continuation after liberation to the unattended potter's wheel temporarily continuing motion. He states that when the liberated being knows the world's unreality, and lives without bondage or pain, in "that state he is called *jīvanmukta*, 'living-free.' " *Jīvanmukti* is the "aim and end in this life for the *jnana-yogi*." He "can live in this world without being attached," like the lotus, water-borne but unwet. He is "the highest of all beings; for he has realized his identity with the Absolute" and oneness with God. Vivekananda then specifically asks, after liberation, "[W]hat good shall we do to the world?" Once we know "there is nothing else but this *ātman*, that everything else is but a dream, with no existence in reality, then this world with its poverties, its miseries, its wickedness, and its goodness will cease to disturb us. If they do not exist, for whom and for what shall we take trouble? This is what the *jñāna-yogis* teach."[22] Here Vivekananda takes seriously the world devaluation of traditional Advaita, and thus one finds no social responsibility mandated for the *jīvanmukta.*

Yet Vivekananda has a bit more to say about living liberation and action in the world. While the liberated being is utterly free and beyond all moral law, Vivekananda disputes that the *jīvanmukta* would do any evil; "good is the inner coating of the Real Man, the Self." He argues that "what is left attached to the man who has reached the Self and seen Truth is the remnant of the good impressions of his past life, the good momentum." This good manifests in a remarkably Christian-sounding way:

> Even if he lives in the body and works incessantly, he works only to do good; his lips speak only benediction to all; his hands do only good works; his mind can think only good thoughts; his presence is a blessing wherever he goes. He is himself a living blessing. Such a man will, by his very presence, change even the most wicked persons into saints. Even if he does not speak, his very presence will be a blessing to mankind. Can such men do any evil?[23]

Vivekananda concludes that the realized being does good by loving all, thus bringing peace. Here we see a neo-Vedanta mix of social and spiritual service, combining saintly presence *and* good works.

Radhakrishnan on Jīvanmukti *and Social Service*

After Vivekananda, Sarvepalli Radhakrishnan is probably the best-known champion of neo-Vedanta. Radhakrishnan, born a Telugu *Smārta* Brahmin, was, like Vivekananda, educated in English in mission schools and steeped in Western ways of thinking (valuing "rationality," religious humanism, and "progress" in history). Unlike Vivekananda, however, he saw himself as a university-based scholar/educator and studied Vedanta and Sanskrit in depth. One notes his commitment to and success in the Western model of education by his appointments to the vice chancellorship of Banaras Hindu University and the Spalding chair at Oxford.[24]

Throughout Radhakrishnan's works, one sees a tension between his desire to be an impartial scholar and his inclination to be an apologist, for a reified "Hinduism" in general, and for Śaṅkara's Advaita in particular. As Paul Hacker has written, one can understand Radhakrishnan's desire to reinterpret Vedanta for his time, while still criticizing his lack of attention to the original philological and historical context of Advaitic thought.[25] This tension is quite evident in his writings on both *jīvanmukti* and social service. As Robert Minor points out in his *Radhakrishnan: A Religious Biography*,[26] Radhakrishnan constructed his own normative "Hinduism," whose essence was not, as its critics charged, world-denying, polytheistic, caste-bound, or deficient in social concern.[27] Instead, like Vivekananda, Radhakrishnan claims that Hinduism is a progressive, activist, rational, and tolerant "religion of the spirit." The purportedly experience-based "monistic idealism" of Advaita Vedanta is the highest manifestation of this spiritual religion (which is also the essence of all religions).

Particularly relevant here is the importance that Radhakrishnan, again like Vivekananda, ascribed to social ethics and his sensitivity to Christian missionary criticisms of Advaitic "world denial." Radhakrishnan argues that Advaita's inclusive, eternal wisdom would bring world community (unlike the exclusivist "dogma" found in much of Christianity). He claims that detachment due to realization of nonduality is not necessarily world renunciation, and that in fact, Advaita is quite compatible with social service. In his more than 200-page chapter on Śaṅkara's thought in *Indian Philosophy*,[28] Radhakrishnan writes that Śaṅkara's own life "is a standing refutation of the charge that the existent world order with its institutions is a thing to be escaped from (632)," and that Śaṅkara's emphasis "is not on retirement from the world, but on renunciation of the self (633)." So far, Radhakrishnan's view has merit: according to the Advaita tradition, Śaṅkara was an active teacher and a debater. Yet Radhakrishnan goes on to link this activity with a more expansive and questionable claim of selfless world saving; he continues (and anticipates his description of the *jīvanmukta* elsewhere) that the detached person's attitude is not "world-fleeing, but world-saving. The perfect man lives and dies, not for himself, but for mankind (633)." He makes a similar claim in *Eastern Religions and Western Thought*, where he writes that "[T]he liberated individual works for the welfare of the world (1)," and quotes the *Bhagavad-Gītā* to that effect. Until their absorption into "the Absolute," he states, "freed individuals share, though in a disinterested spirit, in the work of the world (11)." While words like "freedom" and "welfare of the world" can at times appropriately be linked to the terms *mokṣa* and *loka-saṃgraha*, Radhakrishnan's usage here seems rather different than Śaṅkara's.

The alteration of meanings in shared terminology is made evident when Radhakrishnan goes on to suggest (as Vivekananda does) that *"tat-tvam-asi"* (you/*ātman* are that/*brahman*) indicates social responsibility as well as metaphysical identity. Responding to Albert Schweitzer's ideas, he claims that *tat-tvam-asi* "is bound up with an ethic of active service." His support for this assertion comes not from Śaṅkara or another Advaitin, but from Paul Deussen, the German scholar of Advaita, who draws a parallel with the Sermon on the Mount by saying "That art thou" indicates "[y]ou should love your neighbor as yourselves because you are your neighbor."[29]

Radhakrishnan's most extensive comments on *jīvanmukti* specifically are at the end of the introduction to his translation of the *Brahmasūtra*.[30] His interpretation is largely in accordance with the Advaita tradition: One can be liberated while living, for liberation is based on detachment and knowing *brahman,* not on dropping the body.[31] However, consistent with his desire to deny that Hinduism is world renouncing, he emphasizes the idea, found in the *Yogavāsiṣtha,* that the detached knower may act in the world in various ways (he mentions Kṛṣṇa, Śuka, Rāma, and Janaka). He gives a long (unreferenced) quotation from the *Yogavāsiṣṭha* on the detached action of the *jīvanmukta*, and states that "what binds us is not action but the spirit in which it is done (217)." He does not here claim that Advaitins hold that the egoless activity of the liberated being is social service. Still, he clearly presents his own Christian-influenced neo-Vedantic views by saying he favors the liberated being acting for "*sarva-mukti,*" which he calls "corporate salvation (218)" and "world redemption (22)." For Radhakrishnan, "[t]wo conditions are essential for final salvation, (i) inward perfection attained by intuition of self, (ii) outer perfection possible only with the liberation of all. The liberated souls which attain the first condition continue to work for the second (219)." While he implies that Śaṅkara agrees with this view, he explicitly writes only that "Śaṅkara's view of the *Jivan-mukti* condition makes out that inner perfection and work in the finite universe can go together (222)." Even this goes without citation, however. One can see here the tension between accurate reporting and apologetic wish.[32]

The activity of the *jīvanmukta* also is mentioned in *Indian Philosophy*: While Śaṅkara first seems to say that the nondual realization of *mokṣa* is not consistent with dualism-accepting work in the world, Radhakrishnan states that "so far as *jīvanmuktas* are concerned, activity is allowed," since they are "above the sense of egoity" and the "law of *karma* (644)." Again, no textual citation appears, although he does go on to mention the *BS* III. 3. 32 passage on the possibility of a liberated being taking rebirth to fulfill a commission (*adhikāra*), such as teaching the Veda. Further, concerning ethical behavior, Radhakrishnan also claims that Śaṅkara "holds that moral obligation has no meaning for the freed soul," yet "moral virtues are [not] abandoned by him." For the liberated being, "[e]vil action is psychologically impossible," for he has "died to sin (62)."[33] Once again, Radhakrishnan's writing about Śaṅkara's views is filtered through Christian categories of "morality" and "sin." In the next section, we shall see that, as Vivekananda and Western ways of thinking shaped Radhakrishnan, modern scholars of Advaita continue to be shaped by Radhakrishnan and the enduring impact of Western thought on India.

Modern Advaitin Scholars on Jīvanmukti *and Social Service*

Modern scholars of Advaita do not speak with one voice about living liberation and social service. Some argue that while *jīvanmuktas* do not perform or promote Western-style social action, they do assist others by being teachers and "good examples" of liberated living. For example, Chacko Valiaveetil writes that the *jīvanmukta*'s presence and teaching increase the spiritual, versus material, welfare of the world, but that no "social" activity is possible given ultimate nonduality.[34] Ramana Maharshi can be seen as such a teacher; his primary "lessons" were said to be his peace-giving presence and his comforting and healing look. In his book translating Sarvajñātman's *Saṃkṣepa-śārīraka*, N. Veezinathan also writes that "a preceptor is necessary in order to preserve and propagate the Advaitin tradition (p. 139)." The view that the *jīvanmukta* compassionately teaches can, as mentioned earlier, be grounded in the Advaita tradition. Veezhinathan's view on the necessity of a teacher echoes that of Vimuktātman, and Veezhinathan points to passages in sacred texts that hold that "one who has a teacher directly experiences *brahman-ātman* " (*ChU* VI. 14. 2) and that truth-seeing sages impart that knowledge to students (*Gītā* IV. 34).[35] These are not far from Śaṅkara's interpretations.

The Vedanta *paṇḍit* at Madras Sanskrit College, R. Krisnamurthi Sastry, gave two additional reasons why a *jīvanmukta* would remain and teach. First, he claimed that since anyone remaining embodied still has *prārabdha karma,* which includes a unique personality, it might be part of a particular *jīvanmukta*'s disposition to teach or do good. He also suggested the idea that the *jīvanmukta* stays to teach, due to the good karmic fruits of the not yet liberated. In this view, we ignorant beings cause the detached liberated one to remain.

Other contemporary neo-Vedanta scholars writing on living liberation follow traditional Advaitic thinking in part, yet also make some more original claims concerning the social ethics of the *jīvanmukta.* While accepting that the *jīvanmukta* is utterly detached from desire and has no duty to act, many of these scholars stress that the liberated being's nature is to "altruistically" love and serve others. While not contradictory to the gracious action of a traditional *guru,* these conceptions of "love" and "service" are not typical of traditional Advaita. This refashioning can be seen in N. Veezhinathan's and S. K. Ramachandran's assertions that the *jīvanmukta* has a "mission as teacher and saviour . . . to enable men to realize their true self (127)," and that the liberated being "cannot but help others to attain" liberation (128), for "pure love [is the] spontaneous expression of his very nature (127)."[36] Veezhinathan and Ramachandran also claim that the *jīvanmukta* tells followers to follow their *dharma* "out of sheer love for fellow-beings (129)." In a similar vein, A. G. Krishna Warrier, author of *The Concept of Mukti in Advaita Vedanta*, argues that liberated beings postpone "deliverance [for] missions of service to struggling humanity (58)." He elsewhere adds that such a "superman . . . invites and assists all to self-transcendence. The *mukta* rules by the power of self-effacing love and service (503)." A. K. Lad claims that the *jīvanmukta* is "Supra-moral, not immoral," and that while doing "spontaneous activity for the welfare of the world," he "overcomes the dualism of 'Is' and 'Ought.' "[37] Few, if any, classical textual references are supplied for any of the aforementioned assertions, and one can argue, as Pandeya does, that Advaitic desirelessness in practice has not and in theory will not "naturally" breed love and service.

Neo-Vedantic views combining spiritual and social service were also held by the contemporary scholars and translators of Advaita texts, P. K. Sundaram and R. Balasubramanian. We have already observed Balasubramanian's remarks on Ramana as a *jīvanmukta* (chapter 10). Balasubramanian has also written that the *jīvanmukta* is "engaged in action of his own accord for the sake of *lokasangraha*, that is, for the preservation of the world order, for social service, without the sense of 'I' or 'mine.' "[38] One notes here (and will see again soon) the explicit linkage of preservation of the world order (*loka-saṃgraha*) with social service, a tie never specifically made in traditional Advaita. In conversation, Balasubramanian added that the *jīvanmukta,* seeing others suffer in the world of duality, serves both as a model for right action and as a teacher, due to compassion for the ignorant. He added, "His attachment is not like ours. He acts without any sense of agency," and is not (like us) impelled by desire.[39] P. K. Sundaram also held the view that after knowing oneness, one would naturally altruistically help alleviate the suffering of others, since with his mental clarity, a *jīvanmukta* sees human unity. For one knowing identity with others, social service is inevitable, since, Sundaram argued, no one wants to hurt oneself (in actuality, a debatable proposition). In response to the view that the liberated being would not act since he knows suffering to be unreal, Sundaram claimed that the *jīvanmukta*'s activity is "not logical but phenomenological" because he knows the ignorant person feels the suffering as real.[40]

I have written elsewhere about the clearest recent example of linkage between *jīvanmukti* and a highly Westernized (particularly Christian) notion of social service: L. K. L. Srivastava's *Advaitic Conception of Jīvanmukti.*[41] Srivastava, who is a good example of the neo-Vedanta "lineage" of Vivekananda and Radhakrishnan, argues that the *mukta* is a "detached saint," rooted "in an all-comprehensive love;" further, "his service is rendered to all regardless of caste and class. . . . His actions tend towards the uplift of the whole human race (17)." The liberated being looks from the "viewpoint of the welfare of mankind," an ideal "based on universal brotherhood and love (24)"; he "is not fulfilled if he does not do good to others or does not strive for removing woes and sufferings from the world (25)." Srivastava concludes that liberated beings "should perform selfless activity so that others may be benefitted" and "should spotlight the dark corners of the enquirer's subconsciousness (25)."[42] One does not find such language in earlier Advaita, and this is a particularly clear opportunity to note the modern alteration of the notion of *jīvanmukti.*

Srivastava, however, claims that this view is part of the *loka-saṃgraha* notion found in the *Gītā.* Yet, as discussed earlier, detached action that sustains the world's dharmic order is not the same as social service for all.[43] When Srivastava argues that his notion of *loka-saṃgraha* "represents the true spirit of Indian culture" (25), one must respond that this statement is true only of an "India" influenced by modern Western ideas. At times, Srivastava recognizes that traditional Advaitins like Śaṅkara emphasize *karma-saṃnyāsa* and no obligations to society, including social service (28). Srivastava, showing untraditional but quite neo-Vedantic ecumenism, here and later praises Buddhist and Jain models of socially concerned liberated beings,[44] while lamenting the lack of such examples found in Śaṅkara's and Vidyāraṇya's writings (80 ff.).[45]

Srivastava then indicates that the life-affirming ethical aspect of *jīvanmukti* reappears in modern, Western-influenced figures like Ramakrishna, Gandhi, and Aurobindo, who are part of "a line of spiritual personages" who proclaim that "service to humanity is the only end of an enlightened one (29)." Unsurprisingly, here and later, he focuses in particular on Swami Vivekananda as the ideal model of *jīvanmukti.*[46] However, he does not mention the radical cultural changes in India after the British arrived, or the profoundly different influences on Vivekananda due to these changes. Srivastava accurately states that Vivekananda "gave a new pattern to the Advaitic thought of India (3)," and his views on living liberation, are, unlike the world-renouncing emphasis of Vidyāraṇya, in "conformity with the humanistic demand of the modern mind (285)."[47] Srivastava approvingly quotes Vivekananda's aforementioned claim that the liberated person "works only to do good, his lips speak only benediction to all, his hands do only good works; his mind can only think good thoughts, his presence is a blessing wherever he goes."[48] While Srivastava argues that Vivekananda is "a burning example of this ideal (284)," the ideal mentioned seems closer to a nineteenth-century image of a Christian saint than that of the *jīvanmukta* in traditional Advaita.

It seems apparent that the number and range of the arguments put forward here by modern neo-Vedantin thinkers and scholars of Advaita are in part an attempt to counter the view that Advaita is not concerned with being compassionate or doing good in the world (as opposed to the Buddhist *bodhisattva* or some Christian ideals). These scholars seem persuaded that interest in and action to increase social welfare is good, and thus the Advaitin *jīvanmukta* (at least today) must have such concern. In closing, I would argue, however, that one might better compare the traditional image of a *jīvanmukta* in Advaita to a Theravada Buddhist *arhat* than to a socially active saint or *bodhisattva*, for the *arhat* assists others primarily by "mere" presence, being a field of merit and modeling detached serenity (as well as teaching). Yet in the end, the *arhat* is not focused on world-affirming social service, but is waiting to reach *anupādhiśeṣa nirvāṇa* (which Advaitins might say occurs when *prārabdha karma* ceases).

Throughout this book, and particularly in this final section, we have observed the transformation of the Advaitic concept of *jīvanmukti* over time, watching meanings be added, expanded, and subtracted. We have noted various thinkers wrestle with why and how a remnant of ignorance remains, causing continued embodiment even after liberating knowledge. We have seen different views on the role of yogic practice in attaining *jīvanmukti,* and on the nature and extent of a *jīvanmukta*'s worldly activity. In recent times, we have especially noticed the influence and power, if not "hegemony," of

Western ideas on the *jīvanmukti* concept, resulting in new topics and issues being addressed and old ones downplayed. In this chapter, I hope to have shown that, due to the impact of new perspectives, neo-Vedantins do not always fully comprehend or accurately represent the traditional Advaitic way of thinking, in part because they do not sufficiently recognize and acknowledge its otherness to their own thinking. This is unfortunate for a number of reasons: Proper delineation is generally inherently desirable and self-consciousness of one's own position aids in giving integrity and consistency to one's views. Also, recognizing otherness inhibits the inaccurate projection of personal views and comprehending difference can widen our own viewpoint. Like Halbfass, I think that part of the importance of traditional Indian thought is precisely that it is not encompassed by Europe or modernity; it offers new understandings (one of the goals of modern Western thinking), since it is not part of the "new." One merit of the increasing historical and philosophical self-awareness of the modern West is that it illumines the limits of its own hermeneutical horizon, and its distance from traditional Indian thinking. Ironically, then, we must come to know that, at least to some degree, by understanding, we cannot understand.

Notes

Introduction

1. See "A Note on Hinduism."

2. One might begin looking at this topic with *Living Liberation in Hindu Thought,* edited by Andrew O. Fort and Patricia Y. Mumme (Albany: State University of New York Press, 1996).

3. "Die Vorbereitung der Vorstellung von der Erlösung bei Lebzeiten in den *Upaniṣads*." *Wiener Zeitschrift fur die Kunde Sudasiens* 6 (1962): 151–78, "Die Idee der *Jīvanmukti* in den Späten *Upaniṣads*." *WZKSO* 7 (1963): 190–208, and "Der Weg zur Erlösung bei Lebzeiten, Ihr Wesen and Ihr Wert nach dem *Jīvanmuktiviveka* des Vidyāraṇya." *WZKSO* 8 (1964): 224–62 and 14 (1970): 131–60.

4. While it is the case that from the highest view *(paramārtha), jīvanmukti* is ineffable, we shall see that the Advaita tradition says a great deal about embodied liberation, showing that fine philosophical distinctions and close reasoning were important to them.

5. I will not enter into the debate about who exactly is eligible for renunciation and liberation in traditional Advaita. Interested readers can turn to Śaṅkara's comments on *BāU* I. 4. 15 and IV. 4. 22 and *Muṇḍaka* I. 2. 12.

6. For a valuable and an illuminating discussion of these views, with conclusions similar to my own, see Wilhelm Halbfass's introduction to *Beyond Orientalism: The Work of Wilhelm Halbfass and Its Impact on Indian and Cross-Cultural Studies.* Edited by Eli Franco and Karin Preisendanz. Poznan Studies in the Philosophy of Sciences and Humanities No. 59. (Amsterdam/Atlanta: Editions Rodopi, 1997). Among

other things, Halbfass points out that critics of Orientalism generally use English, live and teach in the West, and write for Western academics. These critics often polemically collapse and essentialize many different thinkers and strands of thought over a long period of time, as they accuse their opponents of having done. More perniciously, they remain Western (or Westernized) authorities, still speaking for and about (and not much to) Indians.

7. This is discussed a bit more in "A Note on Hinduism."

8. For more on this subject, see "A Note on Understanding."

9. (Albany: State University of New York Press, 1993). See also *Texts in Context,* edited by Jeffrey Timm (Albany: State University of New York Press, 1992).

10. Thus, the Vedanta comes to be called "the later exegesis," or *uttara mīmāṃsā.*

11. If one takes seriously Clooney's argument, one might fault my topical or thematic approach for insufficiently recognizing various texts' and thinkers' own plans and interests, and for decontextualizing the topic of *jīvanmukti* too much from imperatives of the (particularly *Pūrva Mīmāṃsā*) tradition. I would argue that my tracing of this theme, which arises from the tradition itself, does not inappropriately distort the concerns of the tradition and, more positively, illumines aspects of it helpfully for my audience.

12. Liberation is not gaining immortality in heaven either.

13. Put in another (more Western) way, liberation is a transformation in one's perspective: the body exists, but is without value; your worldview shifts, but you do not leave the world. When *brahman* is known, no desire remains, because all (of value) is obtained.

14. I will mention only in passing that Advaitins debated vigorously about the nature of individualized selves (*jīva*) and whether ignorance (*avidyā*) is located in the *jīva*. In general, it was thought that there are many *jīvas,* each with ignorance, and thus one *jīva* is liberated at a time.

15. See chapter 2. While the example is given of Vāmadeva gaining liberation in the womb (Śaṅkara, Sarvajnātman, *JMV, Pañcadaśī),* Advaitins do not argue that gods or animals attain *jīvanmukti.*

16. Pp. 38–44.

17. For a good discussion of this point, see Nelson's essay, pp. 45–47.

18. See Christopher Chapple's chapter in *Living Liberation in Hindu Thought.* In scholastic Advaita, *(videha-) kaivalya* indicates final release "beyond" living liberation.

19. I will not here examine a third conception of liberation: that of love of and communion with a personal lord. Many Indian thinkers argue that a loving surrender beyond "mere" world withdrawal or serenity in the self is the highest liberation. For more on this, see Chacko Valiaveetil's *Liberated Life*, p. 64 ff.

20. For more on this, and for a good analysis of the development of the *jīvanmukti* concept in the *Upaniṣads*, see J. F. Sprockhoff's 1962 article, mentioned in note 3.

21. *Karma* is a difficult term to translate, as it can mean all activity, the effects of action, morally retributive action, sacrificial rites, and so on. Here, it will generally indicate those actions that bear fruits that must manifest, in accord with the moral and ritual order, before liberation is attained.

22. A different but related issue is how long the body continues after knowledge. See especially Śaṅkara and Maṇḍana (chapter 3) on this matter.

23. The problematic implications of their complete opposition was brought out most effectively by Prakāśānanda; see chapter 4.

24. See, for example, Śaṅkara's *BāU bhāṣya* III. 5. 1.

25. A fourth answer, one based upon experience, is remarkably absent. Śaṅkara only uses this argument once, and even here only after giving scriptural texts and reasoning. At the end of *BS bhāṣya* IV. 1. 15, he writes that the *jñānin* knows he is *brahman* even while embodiment continues. Śaṅkara asks: How can any other person contradict one convinced in his heart of hearts that he knows *brahman* yet retains a body? Sarvajnātman refers to this experience as evidence for the presence of the trace (*leśa*) of ignorance (chapter 3). In his *Advaitasiddhi*, Madhusūdana Sarasvatī mentions in passing that *jīvanmukti* is established primarily by the self-experience (*svānubhāva*) of *jīvanmuktas* themselves (chapter 4).

26. In *BS bhāṣya* IV. 1. 15, Śaṅkara talks of the *brahmavid* who knows he is *brahman*, yet remains in the body. He attains, but does not yet become, *brahman* (*ChU bhāṣya* VI. 14. 2). Vidyāraṇya, in his *Jīvanmuktiviveka*, takes a slightly different tack. He claims that "*jīvanmukti* " refers to liberation with no future births, so one in the last birth is a *videhamukta* while living (chapter 7).

27. Other supporting quotations from *śruti* can be found in chapter 4.

28. They also can be removed by certain ritual actions, thus indicating karmic activity can assist one in attaining *brahma-jñāna*. See Śaṅkara's *BS bhāṣya* IV. 1. 18 (chapter 2).

29. This kind of *karma* is responsible for the return of one with a commission mentioned in *BS* III. 3. 32. Such return will be brief (for no work is wasted, *Gītā* IV. 40 and *BS* III. 4. 51) says Śaṅkara and Sarvajñātman, but Vimuktātman holds forcefully that a *jīvanmukta* will never return.

Interestingly, there is no discussion of different types of *prārabdha karma*, "good" or "bad."

30. The most often-mentioned text holding the opposing view is *Muṇḍaka* II. 2. 8, which says that when *brahman* is seen, all *karma* (which of course includes the body) is destroyed—so *mukti* is immediate, with no waiting for eventual body fall (Maṇḍana, Citsukha, Prakāśātman, and Sadānanda).

31. *tasya tāvad eva ciraṃ yāvan na vimokṣye, atha saṃpatsya.*

32. I will regularly refer to "body fall" or "body drop" instead of "death," since these terms put the focus where it should be, on the body.

33. As I will show in the chapter on Maṇḍana's views, he holds that the "only as long as" *(tāvad eva)* in the statement "there is delay only as long as one is not free (from the body)" conveys speediness not delay, like "having bathed and eaten, I will come" suggests haste and not delay (chapter 3). Sureśvara calls the *ChU* text an *apavāda*—a special exception to a general rule (chapter 3). Prakāśātman agrees (chapter 4). The delay here is only so that a teacher can guide the seeker blindfolded by ignorance "home"; the knower will delay just this long.

34. A more modern example is the whirling of the ceiling fan that continues but slowly diminishes after the electricity stops.

35. To use the arrow analogy with the two other types of *karma*, one would say that after liberation, the quiver full of arrows is dropped (*saṃcita*), and no future arrows will be shot *(āgamī)*.

36. Also, they are not destroyed, while ignorance (the basis of body and *karma)* is, as Prakāśānanda's *pūrvapakṣin* points out (chapter 4).

37. See Śaṅkara's *BS bhāṣya* IV. 1. 15 and Maṇḍana Miśra, who devotes much of his writing on *jīvanmukti* to differentiating *saṃskāras* from *karma*. The later writers Vimuktātman, Citsukha, Prakāśātman, and Madhusūdana Sarasvatī also discuss this topic.

38. Maṇḍana calls the *saṃskāra* a "weak" and an "insignificant" remnant of *karma* (chapter 3).

39. Maṇḍana, Sureśvara, Vācaspati, Vimuktātman, and Bhāratītīrtha mention this.

40. Sureśvara gives the analogy of gradual body cessation being like the gradual withering of an uprooted tree (*Naiṣkarmyasiddhi* IV. 61).

41. Vimuktātman, chapter 3. See also Citsukha's *pūrvapakṣin*, chapter 3.

42. On the concealing and projecting powers, see Appayya, Madhusūdana, and Dharmarāja contra Prakāśānanda's pūrvapakṣin (all in chapter 4). See also *PD* (Chap. 8) and Lance Nelson's above-mentioned essay (pp. 33–34).

43. Their commitment to wrestling with this issue shows its importance and Advaitins' problems in connecting a real self with unreal physical manifestation. Still, I think their arguments for the linkage of *karma*, body, and realization while living are more forceful and widely shared than does Lance Nelson in *Living Liberation in Hindu Thought*.

44. It is worth noting here that Śaṅkara rarely writes about the conduct of a *mukta* at any length. Perhaps most revealing are *Upadeśasāhasrī* Prose I. 2 and 6, where he characterizes the student desirous of liberation and the teacher (*ācārya)*. See chapter 2.

45. For an illuminating discussion of this topic, see Mackenzie Brown's chapter on Śuka in the *Mahābhārata* and *Purāṇas* in *Living Liberation in Hindu Thought.*

46. One result of which is the introduction of stages of *jīvanmukti.*

47. For more on the one with firm wisdom, see chapter 1 and "A Note on the *Sthita-prajña* as "Yogic *Jīvanmukta*" after chapter 8. Among mainstream Advaitins, the *sthita-prajña* is mentioned occasionally, but is not emphasized. Śaṅkara (chapter 2) says the *sthita-prajña* is a *saṃnyāsin*, for whom renunciation and knowledge of *brahman* go together (though the latter is more important). Maṇḍana examines whether the *sthita-prajña* is an advanced seeker (*sādhaka*) or a fully liberated *siddha* (chapter 3), concluding it is the latter, with which Citsukha agrees. Vimuktātman also mentions the *sthita-prajña* in passing (chapter 3).

48. Chapter 4. For a similar modern perspective, see Ramana Maharshi's view that "[w]hen knowledge comes, ignorance goes and all the divine qualities appear automatically. If a man is Self-realised he cannot tell a lie or commit a sin or do anything wrong." *The Teachings of Bhagavan Sri Ramana Maharshi in His Own Words.* Edited by Arthur Osborne. 5th edition. (Tiruvannamalai: Sri Ramanashramam, 1988), p. 162.

49. The rationale for this is never clearly argued, but one could hold that the long, hard path to liberation burns out the possibility of doing evil and that the desireless *jīvanmukta* would, when acting, "naturally" follow the *dharma.*

50. The liberated being's concern for others is mentioned in "Yogic Advaita" texts like Vidyāraṇya's *JMV*, however. See especially his description of austerity (*tapas)* as an aim of *jīvanmukti* (chapter 7).

51. Of course, categories like "the West" or "Euro-American" also are problematic. One can always subdivide such reified geographical and cultural entities. For good introductions to the problems in using "Hindu(ism)," see John S. Hawley, "Naming Hinduism," *Wilson Quarterly*, summer 1991: 20–34, Robert Frykenberg, "Constructions of Hinduism at the Nexus of History and Religion," *Journal of Interdisciplinary History* 23: 3 (winter 1993): 523–50, and Alf Hiltebeitel, "Hinduism," *The HarperCollins Dictionary of Religion.* Edited by Jonathan Z. Smith. San Francisco: Harper San Francisco, 1995.

52. This conception of Hinduism also has become linked to the growing, highly politicized "fundamentalist" movement of Hindutva, which includes an exclusivist nationalism.

53. "Hinduism: On the Proper Use of a Deceptive Term," in *Hinduism Reconsidered.* Edited by Gunther Sontheimer and Hermann Kulke (Delhi: Manohar Munshiram, 1989), p. 20.

54. He writes that "some of the Hindu religions are closely related to each other," deriving from similar sources, using some similar concepts and techniques, and many influencing each other. "But the same close relationship, the same type of similarities derived from common origin, common stock of traditions, and common

theological and ethical concepts exist between Judaism, Christianity, and Islam, and yet they are different religions (p. 17)."

55. For a good, thought-provoking look at "understanding" in the contexts addressed in this book, see *Beyond Orientalism.*

56. When one culture or ideology confronts another, there is generally essentializing, suppression, and exclusion, whether within or between (for example) the West, India, China, or the Islamic world.

57. One example of a text demonstrating the current awareness of these issues is *Orientalism and the Postcolonial Predicament: Perspectives on South Asia.* Carol Breckenridge and Peter van der Veer, Eds. (Delhi: Oxford University Press, 1994).

Chapter 1

1. As mentioned in the Introduction, J. F. Sprockhoff has written extensively on the development of the notion of *jīvanmukti* in the *Upaniṣads* (both early and late), and is very informative on these matters. See the Introduction, note 3.

2. See the "Note on *Mukti* in the *Upaniṣads*" at the end of the chapter.

3. While the nature of these paths is an interesting topic, it is not central to this study, as it is not discussed much in the context of Advaitic living liberation. See Sprockhoff (1962), pp. 160–64 and A. G. Krishna Warrier, *The Concept of Mukti in Advaita Vedanta.* (Madras: University Madras, 1961), pp. 477–80. See also Surendranath Dasgupta, *A History of Indian Philosophy* (1922; Reprint, Delhi: Motilal Banarsidass, 1975), Vol. 1, pp. 53–58; Paul Deussen, *The Philosophy of the Upanishads*, Trans. A. S. Geden (1906; Reprint, New York: Dover Publications, 1966), pp. 334–38, 359–61; Wilhelm Halbfass, *Tradition and Reflection: Explorations in Indian Thought* (Albany: State University of New York Press, 1991), pp. 323–28; and Kim Skoog in *Living Liberation in Hindu Thought*, p. 83.

4. *Kramamukti* is contrasted with immediate (*sadyo*) and living (*jīvan*) liberation, which are attained by nondual knowledge. I would here concur with Krishna Warrier, who writes that the Advaitic notion of *kramamukti* tries to "make sense of the various statements of the *Upaniṣads* regarding the departure of certain types of knowers along the path of the gods, and their nonreturn to a state of earth life. Perhaps here we have to reckon with an article of ancient faith in a heaven beyond our present habitat, and in life there as the destiny of virtuous and wise souls" (*Concept of Mukti*, p. 480). This also seems to be Sprockhoff's view.

Again, not much is said about *kramamukti* when Advaitins discuss *jīvanmukti*; the time of body fall is tied much more to the end of the fructifying of commenced (*prārabdha*) *karma.*

5. I try to avoid the latter term, since there is no unanimity on what constitutes a "major" *Upaniṣad.* I refer to the scholarly consensus represented by Hume

et al., while acknowledging that there may be a nondualistic bias in that consensus that would contribute both to a particular (mis)reading of these *Upaniṣads* and to their ranking as "major."

6. In this context, the terms *immortal* and *fearless* (*abhaya*) often are paired, especially in the *ChU* when referring to *brahman*. See *ChU* IV. 15. 1, VIII. 3. 4, 10. 1, 11. 1, and *BāU* IV. 4. 25. See also *Muṇḍaka* II. 2. 12 on immortal *brahman*. *Ātman* is termed immortal in *ChU* VIII. 12. 1 and *BāU* III. 7. 3 ff.

7. *ChU* I. 4. 4–5 claims the *om mantra* is immortal and fearless, and upon entering it, the gods—and humans—also become immortal and fearless.

8. This seems to differ from *Kauṣītaki* II. 14, mentioned in the next paragraph.

9. As mentioned above, *Kauṣītaki* III. 2 seems to hold a different view, holding that one can be immortal here.

10. This image seems taken from *ChU* VIII. 4. 1–2 and *BāU* IV. 4. 22, which describe a bridge separating this and other worlds but do not say knowing is the bridge to *immortality*. The later, devotional *Śvetāśvatara* calls the Lord the bridge to immortality (VI. 19).

11. For similar statements, see also *Kaṭha* VI. 2 and 9, and see *Śvetāśvatara* III. 1, 10, 13, and IV. 17 and 20 on the Lord as immortal. The *Śvetāśvatara* passages are very similar in describing knowing as bringing immortality, but its knowing is theistic. Thus, it argues that by knowing the Lord, one becomes immortal (III. 10) or blessed by the Lord, the *jīva* goes to immortality (I. 6).

12. In a similar vein, *ChU* VIII. 4. 1–3 say that the self is the bridge to the flawless *brahma*-world, and only the *brahmacārin* moves freely in all worlds.

13. Sprockhoff (1962) is illuminating here; see p. 166 ff.

14. One might see a similarity in *Kaṭha* V. 1, which says that one ruling one's mind and senses does not grieve and after being freed (*vimuc*), one is indeed freed.

15. This idea seems to appear in *ChU* III. 14. 4 as well: one knowing *brahman* as the self of all reaches *brahman* upon departing from here.

16. *yadā sarve pramucyante kāmā ye'sya hṛdi sritāḥ,*
atha martyo'mṛto bhavati, atra brahma samaśnute.

Note that the verb indicating attaining (*sam-aś*) includes a prefix denoting close conjunction.

17. This text will be critical to Śaṅkara, who argues that embodiment (*saśarīratva*) is related to ignorance, not directly to a physical body—thus, one can have knowledge while embodied. See chapter 2.

18. An interesting sidelight here is the statements in IV. 4. 22, that the Self-knower is unaffected by good or evil *karma*, and in 23 that the *brahman*-knower is free from evil (*pāpman*). One can read this to mean that a liberated being can do no wrong. This issue of "liberated ethics" is not, unfortunately, explored at any length

here or in the later Advaita tradition. In this context, see also *ChU* IV. 14. 3, which says that as water does not cling to a lotus leaf, evil (*pāpman*) *karma* does not cling to one who knows. *Kauṣītaki* III. 1 also suggests a *brahman*-knower can do no wrong. All of these passages seem to refer to a *brahman*-knower still in a body, that is, a *jīvanmukta*. In later Advaita, Sureśvara briefly discusses the *brahman*-knower being free to do whatever he pleases (*yatheṣṭācaraṇa*); see chapter 3.

19. However, we are still far from the explicit distinctions between *brahman*-knower and *jīvanmukta* or *jīvanmukta* and *videhamukta*, found in later Advaita and the *YV/JMV*.

20. The issue of the necessity for a teacher to attain liberation is important to later Advaitins. For a brief summary of the pros and cons, see chapter 4.

21. *Tasya tāvad eva ciram yāvan na vimokṣye, atha saṃpatsya*. This passage closes by stating again that the self is the subtle essence of all, and "you are that, Śvetaketu."

Note that, as with *BāU* IV. 4. 7, the verb indicating attaining (here *saṃpad*) includes a prefix denoting close conjunction. Incidentally, the verbal root describing release from the blindfold is *pramuc*, and from life is *vimuc*.

22. This question leads directly to the later distinction between *jīvan*- and *videha-mukta*, and to the notion of *prārabdha karma*.

23. *Kaṭha* VI. 14–15 and *Muṇḍaka* II. 1. 10 and III. 2. 9.

24. *yadā sarve pramucyante kāmā ye'sya hṛdi sritāḥ,*
atha martyo'mṛto bhavati, atra brahma samaśnute.
yadā sarve prabhidyante hṛdayasyeha granthayaḥ
atha martyo'mṛto bhavaty etāvad anuśāsanam.

This may also in part refer back to *ChU* VII. 26. 2, which claims that one who sees that all is from the self sees and obtains all, and ultimately gains release from all knots in the heart.

25. *sa yo ha vai tat paramaṃ brahma veda brahmaiva bhavati,*
nāsyābrahmavit kule bhavati,
tarati śokam tarati pāpmānaṃ guhā-granthibhyo vimukto'mṛto bhavati.

26. Dasgupta, *History*, Vol. 1, p. 421. This is unsurprising if, as George Thibaut in his *BS bhāṣya* translation (and others) have argued, Rāmānuja's interpretation of the *BS* is closer to Bādarāyaṇa's than is that of Śaṅkara.

27. *aihikam apyaprastutapratibandhe taddarśanāt.*

28. *evaṃ mukti-phalāniyamas-tadavasthāvadhṛtes-tadavasthāvadhṛteḥ.*

29. *tadadhigama uttara-pūrvāghayor-aśleṣa-vināśau tadvyapadeśāt. Itarasyāpy-evam-asaṃśleṣaḥ pāte tu.*

30. *anārabdha-kārye eva tu pūrve tadavadheḥ.*

31. *bhogena tvitare kṣapayitvā saṃpadyate.*

32. *yāvad-adhikāram-avasthitir-ādhikārikāṇām.*

33. Thus I shall only mention in passing claims in the first *prakaraṇa* that one awakens to nonduality (*GK* I. 16), that the wise sage (*muni*) is worthy of adoration and respect (I. 22), and that the *om* knower is a sage (I. 26). All of this presumably occurs in this life.

34. *GK* II. 38: *tattvam ādhyātmikaṃ dṛṣṭvā tattvaṃ dṛṣṭvā tu bāhyataḥ,*
tattvībhūtas tadārāmas tattvād apracyuto bhavet.

35. III. 46: *yadā na līyate cittaṃ na ca vikṣipyate punaḥ,*
aniṅganam anābhāsaṃ niṣpannaṃ brahma tat tadā.

36. Various statements also implying living liberation can be found in the fourth *prakaraṇa*, which many have argued is by a different (and Buddhist) author than are the first three chapters. The statements here are as suggestive but also as inconclusive as the aforementioned references. There are allusions to one who is all-seeing (IV. 84) and to one who has attained perfect omniscience, the nondual *brāhmaṇic* goal (*sarvajñatāṃ kṛtsnāṃ brāhmaṇyaṃ padam advayam*, IV. 85). The one with great intellect (*mahādhi*) becomes omniscient everywhere (IV. 89). Great knowers are certain of the unborn and uniform (*sāmya*) (IV. 95). The last verse (100) urges that, after awakening to the profound and hard to see unborn and uniform state, homage be constantly given. Again, these suggest the existence of a liberation while living.

37. The *sthita-prajña* is mentioned by Śaṅkara, Maṇḍana, Citsukha, and Madhusūdana as well.

38. *tad viddhi praṇipātena paripraśnena sevayā/upadekṣyanti te jñānaṃ jñāninas tattva-darśinaḥ*. This passage is mentioned by Śaṅkara, Vimuktātman, and Citsukha as well.

39. *jñānāgniḥ sarva-karmāṇi bhasmasāt kurute tathā.*

40. Similarly, V. 6 claims that the sage yoked to *yoga* soon reaches *brahman*, and V. 20 states that the undeluded *brahman*-knower is one with a stable intellect.

41. *śaknotīhaiva yaḥ soḍhuṃ prāk śarīra-vimokṣaṇāt*
kāmakrodhodbhavaṃ vegaṃ sa yuktaḥ sa sukhī naraḥ.

42. This combination of terms is interesting, given that the *Gītā* is generally hostile to Buddhism. Perhaps it is both arguing that the yogic path gives the highest Buddhist goal and suggesting that those who pursue *brahman* (i.e., Advaitins) are, like the Buddhists, a bit misguided.

43. Lists of virtuous qualities of a liberated being also are found in XVI. 1–3 and XVIII. 50–54 (one who has become *brahman*).

Chapter 2

1. This chapter is a revised version of my article, "Knowing *Brahman* While Embodied: Śaṅkara on *Jīvanmukti*," *Journal of Indian Philosophy* 19 (1991): 369–89.

2. In comments on *Gītā* VI. 27, he writes "*brahma-bhūtam jīvanmuktaṃ*."

3. While I will not duplicate the form of argument adopted by Śaṅkara, I should point out that his thinking is imbedded in commentary format. He generally takes up a topic determined by the text he is commenting on, introduces a doubt and/or an opponent's view (the *pūrvapakṣa*), and then gives his counter, correcting position (*uttarapakṣa*), concluding with the proper view (*siddhānta*).

4. As mentioned earlier, I use the words "body fall" or "body drop" instead of "death" throughout, since these terms put the focus where it should be, on the body.

5. For a highly illuminating essay on some key terms in Śaṅkara's thought, refer to Paul Hacker's "Distinctive Features of the Doctrine and Terminology of Śaṅkara: *Avidyā, Nāmarūpa, Māyā, Īśvara,*" in *Philology and Confrontation*, edited and translated by Wilhelm Halbfass (Albany: State University of New York Press, 1995). Hacker makes the excellent point that Śaṅkara was not prone to tight definition and rigorous conceptual schematizing (p. 95). His followers were more "scholastic" in their systemic and polemical theorizing.

6. *Paramārthikaṃ kūṭasthanityaṃ vyomavat sarvavyāpi sarvakriyārahitaṃ nityatṛptaṃ niravayavaṃ svayaṃjyotiḥ svabhāvam.*

7. Thus, while deep sleep might suggest liberation because one is then blissful and nondual like when knowing *brahman,* still one is not aware during sleep and one always returns to waking. See Andrew O. Fort, *The Self and Its States* (Delhi: Motilal Banarsidass, 1990), pp. 17–21, 55–61.

8. For more, see *Philology and Confrontation*, chapters 4 and 9.

9. On occasion, Śaṅkara uses *kaivalya* (literally, "isolation") as a synonym for *mokṣa*, but it is significant that Advaitic liberation (knowing *ātman/brahman* identity) is more positive than mere monadistic isolation. Yogic *kaivalya* suggests that only freedom from embodiment brings freedom from suffering (the final goal); Śaṅkara's usage of *kaivalya* is not this clear.

10. Health, like knowing one's identity with *brahman*, is one's "natural state." One recovers this condition by removing the dis-ease of *avidyā*. See also the mention of *svasthā* in *Upadesasahasri* 14. 23 and 17. 74.

11. In *BS* IV. 4. 2, he adds that *mokṣa* is a "fruit" only in reference to the cessation of knowledge, not in reference to the arising of any new result, as is the case with *karma*. Śaṅkara is always careful to keep separate the results of knowledge and action.

Mokṣa also is called the death of (transmigratory) death (*BāU* III. 3. 1) and *brahman*-knowers are said to be immortal (*BāU* IV. 4. 14). More will be said later on how Śaṅkara deals with the *Upaniṣadic* language of immortality.

12. A number of well-known *Upaniṣadic* texts are quoted in support of this view: "*neti, neti*" (*BāU* III. 9. 26), "where one sees no other" (*ChU* VII. 24. 1), "all this is this self" (*BāU* II. 4. 6), and so on.

13. We shall see that "Yogic Advaita" texts like the *YV* and *JMV* do talk about degrees of *jīvanmukti*.

14. *BS* I. 1. 12 specifies this knowledge as immediate liberation (*sadyomukti*), as opposed to gradual (*krama*) liberation that arises from "meditation" (*upāsana*)—I will say more on this later.

15. This point is significant in part because of Śaṅkara's wish to decouple knowledge and action.

16. In *BāU* IV. 4. 7, he reiterates that one attains *brahman* here, so liberation is not dependent on going to some other place (like heaven).

17. Still, the *mukta* is at the end of the body series and does not transmigrate as before.

18. Unlike the attainment of a heavenly world that is uncertain, since it happens only after one experiences the fruits of actions.

19. There are a few brief indications of his view in the *Upaniṣad* commentaries, such as *BāU* IV. 4. 6, which says the *mukta* is both desireless and has attained all desires (since he has attained the self). This passage speaks of the knower as *ātmakāma, āptakāma, niṣkāma, and akāma*. Desire is the root of transmigratory existence, causing limitation and connection with *karma*, while desirelessness causes liberation. *BāU* I. 4. 2 describes Prajāpati as knowing unity while in human form, since all sins caused by the opposite of *dharma*, knowledge (*jñāna*), renunciation (*vairāgya*), and *aiśvarya* (supernatural powers) are burnt. He now has excellence in memory, intelligence, and insight.

20. Other qualities indicate proper understanding of caste and life stage. This is, of course, reminiscent of, and expands on, the fourfold *sādhana*, discussed in *BS bhāṣya* I. 1. 1.

21. A little later in the passage, Śaṅkara writes he should teach *śrutis* instructing the unity of the self, such as "this being is one without a second" (*ChU* VI. 2. 1), "the self is all this" (*ChU* VII. 25. 2), "all this is *brahman*" (*ChU* III. 14. 1), and so on.

22. See also *Muṇḍaka* III. 2. 6 on the *jīvanmukta* as *saṃnyāsin*.

23. For a good introduction to this issue, see Yoshitsugu Sawai, "Śaṅkara's Theory of *Saṃnyāsa*." *Journal of Indian Philosophy* 14 (1986): 371–87.

24. Śaṅkara substitutes the term "*mokṣa*" for "*nirvāṇa*" in V. 24, 25, and 26, as well as II. 71–72. He is clearly not comfortable with "*brahma-nirvāṇa*."

25. Something similar is said in *ChU* VIII. 12. 1: *aśarīratva* is from *vidyā* and *saśarīratva* is from *avidyā*.

26. This idea is emphasized in Śaṅkara's best-known noncommentatorial work, the *Upadeśasāhasrī*. Verse X. 6 states that since bodiless, I have neither virtue nor vice, caste nor life stage. Verse XV. 6 says bodilessness is not a fruit of action (which causes connection with the body). According to Verse XVII. 6, actions are based on caste, which belongs to the body.

27. Both Vācaspati Miśra's Bhāmatī and Ānandagiri follow Śaṅkara rather closely here. They elaborate some points and add some illustrations, but little new ground is broken. In Vācaspati Miśra's case, this seems to indicate a certain lack of interest in the *jīvanmukti* doctrine, since he does not follow Śaṅkara so closely on every issue.

28. Ānandagiri here says that such a being is a *jīvanmukta,* in a body (*dehastha*), but not transmigrating (a *saṃsārī*).

29. Here as elsewhere, *Upaniṣadic* language links knowledge and cessation of desire with immortality, a physical state Śaṅkara wants to deemphasize.

30. This account appears in numerous places, including *BS* III. 3. 32, IV. 1. 15, 19, *BāU* I. 4. 7, 10, IV. 4. 6–7, and *ChU* VI. 14. 2.

31. *BS* IV. 1. 15, *BāU* I. 4. 10. Further, future evil notions do not arise for the knower, since they have no support.

32. The terminology for kinds of *karma* is later formalized as *āgamī* (future fruit-producing activity), *prārabdha* (currently manifesting actions), and *saṃcita* (the mass of previously accumulated actions).

33. *ChU* VI. 14. 2 adds that *anārabdha karma* is also burnt by expiatory acts (*prāyaścitta*).

34. Here suggesting final release, later called *videhakaivalya* or *videhamukti.*

35. This is called *kṣema* or "ease" in IV. 1. 15.

36. This analogy also is used in *BS* III. 3. 32 and *BāU* I. 4. 7 and 10.

37. He quotes *Gītā* IV. 37 here: "The fire of knowledge turns all actions to ashes."

38. This view is echoed strongly in Vidyāraṇya's *Jīvanmuktiviveka*. We shall look at the relationship between knowledge and action more closely later.

39. Śaṅkara, rather uncharacteristically, mentions yogic practice in I. 4. 7, stating that when knowledge is weaker than already commenced *karma*, the stream of recollection of *ātma-jñāna* must be regulated by the power of *sādhanas* like renunciation and detachment. This action-centered approach is of course only enjoined as an alternative, depending on the circumstance. For more, see the endnote on Śaṅkara and *Yoga*.

40. In *BS* IV. 1. 19, Śaṅkara adds that although seeing difference continues after full insight, it will not continue after the body falls, since the cause of seeing difference before the body falls (the enjoyment of *prārabdha karma*) ceases at death.

41. The late Advaitin Madhusūdana Sarasvatī also mentions these passages. See chapter 8.

42. B. N. K. Sharma. *The Brahmasūtras and Their Principal Commentaries.* Vol. III. Bombay: Bharatiya Vidya Bhavan, 1978.

43. See also the brief reference to commenced *saṃskāras* in *ChU* III. 14. 4. Vācaspati Miśra here mentions the later often-used analogy of *saṃskāras* being like the trembling that continues awhile, even after a snake is realized to be truly a rope. Trembling and *saṃskāras* inevitably but only gradually cease after fear and *karma* cease.

44. In *BS* II. 1. 8, Śaṅkara adds *muktas* are not reborn, since right insight removes delusive "knowledge" (*mithya-jñāna*). This is as opposed to deep sleep or a world dissolution (*pralaya*) in which ignorance and its adjuncts (*upādhi*) remain.

45. This passage and issue are largely ignored in later Advaita, being mentioned only briefly in Dharmarāja's *Vedāntaparibhāṣa*. (IX. 55) and *Pañcadaśī* VII. 252 ff.

46. Vācaspati Miśra follows Śaṅkara rather closely here. He stresses the necessity of experiencing the fruits of *prārabdha karma* before gaining liberation. He also uses unŚaṅkaran terminology in emphasizing the immediate experience (*anubhava, sākṣātkāra*) of nondual reality (*Advaita-tattva*).

47. This topic is addressed in similar fashion in *BS* IV. 1. 19. *Karma* can produce other fruits after the fall of the body only when supported by *mithya-jñāna*. False "knowledge" has been burnt away by full insight, however. Thus, when a knower's already commenced activity ceases, *kaivalya* is inevitable.

48. Ānandagiri underlines that *jñāna*, and not *aiśvarya*, brings liberation.

49. He then describes some of the "thousands of attachments" of the ignorant person who thinks "I am son of *x* and related to *y*, I am happy/sad, foolish/wise, born/aged/dead; my son is dead, wealth gone, I am destroyed. How shall I live? Where shall I go? Etc."

50. Teaching others can be seen as an aspect of "social service" (i.e., Western-style "doing good"), or in more Indian terms, protecting (*saṃgraha*) and favoring (*anugraha*) the world order. Many neo-Vedantins in particular have argued that *jīvanmuktas* are socially concerned, performing good works for others. Much will be said about this issue in Chapter 12, including the fact that Śaṅkara does not emphasize the knower's solicitude for others, although he does refer to it on occasion. Here I will only say that while teaching can be regarded as spiritual service, active social service is not emphasized in the classical Advaita tradition, and one could argue that when one sees no duality, there are no others (or "society") to be concerned about.

51. *BāU* IV. 3. 36. A similar statement on the body as the seat for experiencing the fruits of *karma* appears in BS II. 2. 1. We also have seen that the *Gītā* points out that even the advanced *yogin* takes many lives to gain perfection (VI. 42–45).

52. He makes a related point in comments on *BāU* IV. 4. 22. Ritual actions cause purification, and when purified, one can know the self revealed by the *Upaniṣads* without impediment. Still the main means (*mukhya sādhana*) to the world of the self is renouncing all activity; those desiring this world should, like the wise, renounce (*pravraj*).

53. Among the many passages where Śaṅkara argues at length for the utter separation between knowledge and karmic activity, one can look at *BāU* III. 3. 1 or IV. 5. 15. It will suffice here to mention that the latter commentary points out that activity is for the ignorant, although while ignorance persists, mendicancy and performing rites are recommended for those desirous of liberation. Since non-Brahmins are not entitled to mendicancy, they should definitely perform rites throughout their lives. See also *BS* III. 4. 20 (which emphasizes that only *saṃnyāsins* should pursue attaining *brahman* while those in other life stages should continue to follow all appropriate duties), and *ChU* II. 23. 1 on this issue.

54. On the other hand, Śaṅkara does say, in *BāU* IV. 4. 8 and elsewhere, that *brahman*-knowers, being free, go to heavenly worlds after the fall of the body.

55. *Kaṭha* VI. 14 actually refers to the departing of the heart's desires, which Śaṅkara says are seated in the intellect (*buddhi*) and not the self.

56. See related passages in chapter 1. *Muṇḍaka* II. 1. 10 puts it the other way: One who knows the supreme immortal *brahman* existing in the heart destroys the knot of ignorance here (i.e., while living). Both the *Kaṭha* VI. 14 and *Muṇḍaka* III. 2. 6 commentaries say that becoming *brahman* here is like the blowing out of a lamp.

57. Śaṅkara refers back to *BāU* IV. 4. 6 here: being *brahman,* he merges in *brahman. Muṇḍaka* II. 2. 8 (and Śaṅkara's commentary on it) largely echo the *Kaṭha* VI passage. It adds all doubts are cut, and Śaṅkara reiterates that actions with uncommenced fruits are destroyed, but not those with fruits now manifesting.

58. A similar notion is mentioned in his commentary on the *sthita-prajña* in the *Gītā*.

59. This passage also says, following *Māṇḍūkya Upaniṣad* 10 (and *Gītā* VI. 41–42) that no non-knower of *brahman* is born in the knower's family.

60. In addition to knowing *brahman*, the liberated being is said to be desireless, detached from works, and concerned for others.

61. Such a being might now have and use supernatural powers, but these powers are not as significant as or essential to *brahma-jñāna*.

62. See "Śaṅkara the Yogin and Śaṅkara the Advaitin: Some Observations" in *Philology and Confrontation*. In *Tradition and Reflection,* Wilhelm Halbfass disagrees with Hacker's view that Śaṅkara wrote a *Yogasūtra* commentary. For more on this issue and on the role of *yoga* and meditation in Śaṅkara's thought, see J. Bader, *Meditation in Śaṅkara's Vedanta* (New Delhi: Aditya Prakashan, 1990).

63. "The Question of the Importance of *Samādhi* in Modern and Classical Advaita Vedanta," *Philosophy East and West* 43 (January 1993): 19–38.

64. For example, see his remarks on the value of meditation on the *om mantra* in *BS* I. 3. 13 and *BāU* I. 3. 9.

65. In comments on *BāU* III. 5. 1, he writes that the contemplative sage (*muni*) becomes a *yogin* from the strength (*bālya*) of knowing the self and from scholarship (*pāṇḍitya*). Having removed all ideas of the non-self, all is accomplished (*kṛtakṛtya*), and one becomes a *yogin*.

66. Incidentally, Śaṅkara has no reservation about granting the existence of supernatural yogic powers. See *BS* II. 1. 25, III. 2. 5, III. 3. 32, or IV. 4. 15.

67. Śaṅkara also refers to *upāsana* as a continuous stream (*pravāha-karaṇa*) of similar thoughts (*samāna-pratyaya*) in *BS* IV. 1. 7.

68. Honolulu: University of Hawaii Press, 1994. See also Coman's article, pp. 19–21 and 30.

69. *Limits of Scripture*, p. 65 ff.

70. Ibid., p. 97.

Chapter 3

1. One of these pupils, Padmapāda, mentions living liberation briefly; he seems to follow Śaṅkara's comments on *BS* IV. 1. 15. Padmapāda states that knowledge ends all attachment and transmigratory existence, but the apparent consciousness of sense-objects endures, due to the continuance of residual *karma* for this life, like the moon continues to appear twofold to one with an eye defect. See *Padmapāda's Pañcapādika*. Translated by R. D. Venkataramiah. Gaekwad's Oriental Series, Vol. 107. (Baroda: Oriental Institute, 1948), p. 328.

2. Though dating these figures exactly is, of course, problematic.

3. For a brief comment on the Maṇḍana-Sureśvara identity controversy, see the beginning of the next section.

4. Edited by S. Kuppuswami Sastri. (Delhi: Sri Satguru Publications, 1984). *Jīvanmukti* is discussed on pp. 129–33. For more on Maṇḍana and this text, see Allen Thrasher, *The Advaita Vedanta of the Brahmasiddhi* (Delhi: Motilal Banarsidass, 1993).

5. That is, experiencing karmic fruits until completion.

6. *Tasya tāvad eva ciram yāvan na vimokṣa*. An alternate reading could be: "There is a delay (in liberation) only as long as I am not free (from the body)," which would have very different implications.

7. An image used by Sureśvara, Vācaspati, and Vimuktātman.

8. On the other hand, we shall see Vimuktātman make an eloquent critique of this idea.

9. This example first appears in *Sāṃkhya kārikā* 67, and is used by Śaṅkara in his *BS bhāṣya* IV. 1. 15.

10. And, he twice states that there is no other cause of the effect ceasing.

11. This is perhaps the first usage of this term in Advaita.

12. He repeats here that although *prārabdha karma* (the cause) ceases, *saṃskāras* (the effect) remains awhile, causing continued embodiment as the potter's wheel and trembling continue after their causes (potter and fear) cease.

13. S. Kuppuswami Sastri calls them "extremely attenuated and entirely powerless" to cause any binding (*ibid.*, p. xxxix).

14. Nor will one desire anything appearing in *māyā*.

15. This last phrase also can be understood to say "since the highest knowledge destroys the appearance of both these in the self."

16. Like a jewel that is only reflected in a mirror.

17. *The Bhāmatī of Vācaspati Miśra.* Edited and translated by S. Suryanarayana Sastri and C. Kunhan Raja. (Adyar: Theosophical Publishing House, 1933), p. xliii.

18. For a brief summary of the issue and further reference, see Potter, pp. 346–47, or S. Kuppuswami Sastri's introduction to the *Brahmasiddhi*, pp. xxiv–xlvii. Incidentally, both the Kanchi and Sringeri *pīthas* claim Sureśvara as a founding *Śaṅkarācārya*.

19. *The Naiṣkarmyasiddhi of Sureśvara.* Edited and translated by R. Balasubramanian (Madras: University of Madras Press, 1988).

20. See *Naiṣkarmyasiddhi* IV. 56 ff.

21. Sureśvara's use of this example (unmentioned by Śaṅkara) may in fact be a reference to Maṇḍana.

22. Edited by S. Subrahmanya Sastri. (Varanasi: Mahesh Research Institute, 1982).

23. For example, *Muṇḍaka* II. 2. 8, *Gītā* IV. 37 (the fire of knowledge burns all to ashes).

24. For more on Śaṅkara on *ChU* VI. 14. 2, see chapter 2.

25. While this issue is surprisingly little discussed in Advaita writings, one can refer to Prakāśātman and Sadānanda in chapter 4 and *Pañcadaśī* IV. 54–57 in chapter 8.

26. He quotes Śaṅkara's *Upadeśasāhasrī* 18. 231–32.

27. Edited and translated by N. Veezhinathan (Madras: University of Madras, 1972).

28. *Aitareya* II. 1. 5. He also refers to *Gītā* VI. 41, which points out that no right practice is wasted. Śaṅkara gives the same examples in *BS* III. 4. 51. See also *PD* IX. 35.

29. This perhaps expands on Śaṅkara's *BS* III. 5. 1 commentary; see chapter 2.

30. A surprising echo of this is found in Ramana Maharshi's teaching. See *The Teachings of Bhagavan Sri Ramana Maharshi in His Own Words*. Edited by Arthur Osborne. Fifth edition. (Tiruvannamalai: Sri Ramanashramam, 1988), p. 28.

31. For Śaṅkara's analysis of this passage, see chapter 2.

32. The usual term Sarvajñātman uses for ignorance is *tamas*.

33. *SS* IV. 47–48 add that the *mukti* of *Brahmā*, and so on, via the path of the gods mentioned in *śruti,* is not connected with knowledge of *nirguṇa brahman* but with a lower *vidyā*; see also chapter 2. Vimuktātman will make a similar argument.

34. For more on this, see Prakāśānanda as *pūrvapakṣin* and *siddhāntin* in chapter 4.

35. This text mentions the experience of two apparent moons that persists in the diseased eye even after one knows only one is real. This passage also is the one place Śaṅkara refers to the *brahman*-knower who is convinced in his heart of hearts (i.e., his "experience") that he is *brahman* and yet remains in a body.

36. The remnant also is called scent (*gandha*), shadow (*chāya*), or impression (*saṃskāra*).

37. Though, notably, neither Śaṅkara nor Sarvajñātman claim such experience themselves.

38. The exact meaning of this *śruti* will be discussed in more detail by Citsukha and especially Madhusūdana Sarasvatī in chapter 4.

39. In IV. 3, apparently following Śaṅkara on *ChU* VI. 14. 2, the teacher is said to be "the one marked with compassion" who brings knowledge to the disciple ("the one to be led").

40. This point is in fact largely worth making because the text translator, N. Veezhinathan, makes a claim common to neo-Vedantins that "the perogative of the *jīvanmukta* is to keep alive the Advaitic tradition for the benefit of posterity (p. 138)." For more on this topic, see chapter 12.

41. Edited and translated by P. K. Sundaram. Two vols. (Madras: Swadharma Swaraajya Sangha, 1980).

42. See pp. 74–78 (text) and 77–81 (translation).

43. The body continues since it requires food and drink, which depends on seeing duality, which is based on ignorance.

44. This follows Śaṅkara, and does not mention Maṇḍana's point about the brevity of delay.

45. For *śruti* support of this position, see Prakāśānanda *pūrvapakṣin* in chapter 4.

46. For a similar analysis, see Citsukha in chapter 4.

47. This passage is not completely clear. It also may suggest that these actions cause the teacher to remain to "protect" the continuity of knowledge (which would cease if the teacher died before passing it on).

48. Vimuktātman also argues against *saṃskāras* alone remaining for a *jīvanmukta* (p. 335 text; p. 411, translation). He says illusion does not come from and is not merely impressions. If it were, when *saṃskāras* disappear, so does the teacher, and (as said earlier) a teacher is necessary for liberation.

49. He does not address Maṇḍana's idea that an effect is weaker than its cause.

50. This seems to conflict with *BS* III. 3. 32, which Śaṅkara's *bhāṣya* reluctantly supports; see chapter 2.

51. These refer to the continuation of commenced fruits of action, which must be experienced before *brahman* is attained, as mentioned in chapter 2.

52. For a similar, but more extended, analysis, see chapter 2.

Chapter 4

1. *The Pañcapādikā of Śrī Padmapādācārya with the Pañcapādikā-vivaraṇa of Śrī Prakāśātman*, edited by S. Srirama Sastri and S. R. Krishnamurthy Sastri (Madras: Government Oriental Series, Vol. 155, 1958).

2. There is an English translation of this text by S. S. Suryanarayana Sastri and Saileswar Sen. Andhra University Series No. 24. (Kumbakonam: Sri Vidya Press, 1941).

3. This term may refer back to Sarvajñātman's conception of the imagined teacher.

4. This seems to be stronger than the subordinate but still relevant place Śaṅkara gives ritual activity.

5. The *VPS* adds that the accumulated mass of evil actions are destroyed by *jñāna*.

6. Sadānanda will concur with this.

7. Page 105 in the edition referenced above.

8. As opposed to only in memory (*smṛti*), since a *saṃskāra*, a residual trace of ignorance, should only be possible after direct experience is gone.

9. Upon this destruction, the *avidyā-leśa* ceases due to knowledge of the real.

10. I used the Kāśī Sanskrit Series edition, No. 242 (Varanasi: Chaukhambha Sanskrit Sansthan, 1987).

11. For a good basic summary, see V. A. Sharma's *Citsukha's Contribution to Advaita* (Mysore: Kavyalaya Publishers, 1974). Among other things, Citsukha argues

that *śruti* is the means to direct knowledge of *brahman* (assisted by *manana* and *nididhyāsana*), that *brahman* is the locus of ignorance, and that there is no *jñāna-karma-samuccaya.*

12. He significantly calls this the name for various forms of illusion (*moha*).

13. Madhusūdana Sarasvatī will expand on this conception.

14. The third form is *aparokṣa-pratibhāsa-viṣayākāra-kalpaka.*

15. To use other Advaitic language, one could say the *āvaraṇa* (concealing) forms of *avidyā* are now removed.

16. *aparokṣa-pratibhāsa-yogyārthābhāsa-janaka.*

17. For an interesting discussion of Madhva's teaching about *aparokṣa jñāna* as direct knowledge of God, see the chapter by Daniel Sheridan in *Living Liberation in Hindu Thought.*

18. Citsukha, later in this passage, argues again that a form (the threefold *avidyā-leśa*) can remain after its substratum (*avidyā*) ceases, since when a particular aspect of something consisting of both particular and general ceases, the general form (*prārabdha karma*) remains. He here is disputing the *Nyāyā* position on the difference between the general (*sāmānya*) and the particular (*viśeṣa*).

19. Chapter 3.

20. A passage also mentioned by Vimuktātman.

21. Which arises from the repeated practice of virtue (*abhyāsaśīla*).

22. Also mentioned by Sarvajñātman (*SS* IV. 46) and Madhusūdana Sarasvatī.

23. Lance Nelson has done some valuable work on Madhusūdana's views about the role of *bhakti* in Advaita. See "Madhusūdana Sarasvatī on the 'Hidden Meaning' of the *Bhagavad-Gītā*: *Bhakti* for the Advaitin Renunciate" in *Journal of South Asian Literature* 23 (1988): 73–89 and "*Bhakti-Rasa* for the Advaitin Renunciate: Madhusūdana Sarasvatī's Theory of Devotional Sentiment," *Religious Traditions* 12 (1989): 1–16.

24. Edited by N. S. Ananta Krishna Sastri (Delhi: Parimal Publications, 1988). Pp. 890–92.

25. He also wrote a commentary called *Sāra-saṃgraha* on Sarvajñātman's *Saṃkṣepa-ṣārīraka*, which can be found in Kashi Sanskrit Series 18, edited by Bhau Sastri Vajhe. (Benares: Vidya Vilas Press, 1924).

26. *Bhagavad-Gītā with Gūḍārthadīpikā of Madhusūdana Sarasvatī.* Edited by Hari Narayana Apte. (Anandasrama Sanskrit Series No. 45. Poona, 1912). Refer also to *Madhusūdana Sarasvatī on the Bhagavad-Gītā.* Sisir Kumar Gupta, translator (Delhi: Motilal Banarsidass, 1977).

27. I am particularly grateful to Dr. R. Krishnamurthi Sastry of the Madras Sanskrit College for his assistance in untangling Madhusūdana's thought here.

28. *jīvanmuktaśca tattvajñānena nivṛttāvidyoʃpyanuvṛttadehādipratibhāsah.*

29. When discussing the topic of the self not being the body (p. 617), Madhusūdana refers to *jīvanmukti* in a single sentence. He states that in living liberation superimposition (*adhyāsa*) based on the concealing power (*āvaraṇa-ṣakti*) of ignorance is absent, but superimposition based on *avidyā*'s projective (*vikṣepa*) power is still possible. These powers of ignorance in connection with *jīvanmukti* are unelaborated here and unmentioned in the major passage discussed below. In the *Sāra-saṃgraha* commentary on *SS* IV. 41–43, Madhusūdana says a number of times that the *avidyā-leśa* possesses the power of projecting appearance, despite the cessation of the concealing power.

30. Madhusūdana confirms this in comments on *SS* IV. 41–43.

31. This text can be taken in quite a different way if one focuses on the prior line in *śruti*: "due to attending to (*abhidhyāna*), yoking with (*yojana*), and knowing the reality of (*tattvabhāva*) the lord (*deva*) more and more (*bhūyas*), at the end, all world illusion (*māyā*) ceases." Madhusūdana argues that "*bhūyas*" should go with the last portion of the line, instead of being an intensifier referring to the practices mentioned at the line's beginning. If "*bhūyas*" was combined with "*yojana*," then the text would not point to the continuity of the trace of *avidyā* until the body ends (which is the desired meaning). He says "*bhūyas*" goes with "*nivṛtti*" (cessation) for three reasons: words properly combine with the main noun (which is *nivṛtti*) "*tattvabhāva*" is not connected with "*bhūyas*" (and it intervenes between *yojana* and *bhūyas*), and if "*bhūyas*" is connected with "*yojana*," then "*ante*" is useless (which is undesirable in *śruti*).

In *Sāra-saṃgraha* IV. 46, which also refers to this passage, Madhusūdana writes that by direct experience from ripened meditation, the *māyā-leśa*, which causes the illusion of *vyavahāra*, ceases "at the end." That is, when duality is destroyed by experiencing out all *prārabdha karma*, one becomes fully identified with *ātman/ brahman*. Thus, at the end, "all *māyā* ceases" (including the third form that produces illusory object appearance) by knowing the real.

32. Or it allows one to conform to the the imagined body (until commenced *karma* ceases).

33. Edited and translated by Arthur Venis (Varanasi: Chaukambha Orientalia, 1975), pp. 137–142.

34. For more on Prakāśānanda's *dṛṣṭi-sṛṣṭi-vāda*, see S. Dasgupta, *A History of Indian Philosophy* (Delhi: Motilal Banarsidass, 1975), vol. II, pp. 17–19 and 221–25.

35. Still, unlike Lance Nelson in *Living Liberation in Hindu Thought*, I think he does finally argue for *jīvanmukti*.

36. More will be said about this later.

37. This perhaps responds to Madhusūdana's image of the cloth form remaining after the cloth is burnt.

38. Perhaps refering to Madhusūdana.

39. This is similar to the "Sāṃkhya/Yoga Vedantin" Vijñānabhikṣu's reference to blind tradition in chapter 5.

40. One might, of course, wonder how a false teaching would, in the long run, breed trust.

41. Chapter 3.

42. Edited by S. R. Krishnamurti Sastri and N. Veezhinathan. (Secunderabad: Srimad-Appayya-Diksithendra-Granthavali Prakashana-Samiti, 1973). See pp. 364–66.

43. Edited and translated by M. Hiriyanna. 2d ed. Poona Oriental Series No. 14. (Poona: Oriental Book Agency, 1962).

44. For a number of good *Upaniṣadic* quotations on how a liberated being is free to do evil (inc. *Kauṣitaki* III. 1, *BāU* IV. 3. 22 and IV. 4. 23, and *ChU* IV. 14. 3), see G. A. Jacob's translation, *A Manual of Hindu Pantheism: The Vedantasāra* (Varanasi: Bharat-Bharati, 1972), pp. 128–29. These passages are ignored here and by Sureśvara.

45. Edited and translated by S. S. Suryanarayana Sastri. (Madras: Adyar Library, 1971).

46. Suryanarayana Sastri has a useful footnote on the development of Advaita responses to this problem in endnote 85, pp. 216–17.

47. Dharmarāja quotes a supporting text by Vācaspati Miśra, but one might note that Vācaspati states that the commission is assigned by God (*īśvara*), not caused by *prārabdha karma*.

48. "A Note on Liberation in Bodily Existence,"*Philosophy East and West* 5 (1955): 69–74.

49. For a rather different interpretation than the one given here, see Lance Nelson on the *jīvanmukta*'s similarity to *īśvara* in *Living Liberation in Hindu Thought*.

50. This question of being arises in S. K. Ramachandra Rao's book *Living Liberation* (Bangalore: IBH Prakashana, 1979), in which he introduces, but does not pursue, conceptualizing *jīvanmukti* in Heideggerian language (pp. 8–10). If, as he suggests, liberation is pure Being, one might ask how a liberated person could simply be while "in the world"? While embodied, is not our being always conditioned "being-in-the-world"?

Chapter 5

1. For an extended analysis of Rāmānuja's views on *jīvanmukti,* see Kim Skoog's "Is the *Jīvanmukti* State Possible? The Perspective of Rāmānuja," in *Living Liberation in Hindu Thought.*

2. Much of the Dvaita Vedantin theologian Madhva's writings on living liberation are also devoted to anti-Advaita polemics. See Daniel P. Sheridan's "Direct Knowledge of God and Living Liberation in the Religious Thought of Madhva," also in *Living Liberation in Hindu Thought*. Sheridan makes a persuasive case that the role of direct and immediate knowledge (*aparokṣa-jñāna*) in Madhva's thought is functionally similar to that of *jīvanmukti* in Śaṅkara's Advaita, though their substantive views of *brahman* and liberation are very different.

3. In *ŚB* IV. 4. 4, Rāmānuja writes that the self, when liberated, is a mode (*prakāra*) of *brahman.* The self is inseparable but conscious of its nonseparateness, one but not identical with *brahman,* and equally pure but not nondual.

4. For more on this point, see Yoshitsugu Sawai, "Rāmānuja's Theory of *Karman*," *Journal of Indian Philosophy* 21 (1993): 11–29.

5. Skoog's essay, pp. 66–68, is particularly helpful here.

6. I have noted elsewhere that this passage may be read in different ways, for that which one is released from and to remain unstated; see chapter 1.

7. In Fort and Mumme, Eds., *Living Liberation in Hindu Thought,* p. 127.

8. For more detail, see *The Sāṃkhya Philosophy (with the Sāṃkhya-pravacana sūtra, Aniruddha's vṛtti, and Vijñānabhikṣu's bhāṣya),* Nandalal Sinha, translator (1915. Reprint; New Delhi: Munshiram Manoharlal, 1979), pp. 352–60 and the *Sāṃkhya* volume of the *Encyclopedia of Indian Philosophies,* edited by Gerald Larson and R. S. Bhattacharya (Princeton: Princeton University Press, 1987), pp. 327–29, 352–53.

9. Vijñānabhikṣu says middling discrimination rises by *saṃprajñāta yoga*, and perfect *viveka* by *asaṃprajñāta yoga.*

10. Larson and Bhattacarya, pp. 411–12.

11. One reason might be, as Chapple points out *(Living Liberation*, p. 116), that in the *Yoga* tradition, publicly available texts about liberation are not important; instead, a student should be part of a lineage in which the master personally discerns and guarantees authentic liberation.

12. *kleśa-karma-nivṛttau jīvanneva vidvān vimukto bhavati.* Chapple indicates (p. 124) that the absence of afflicted action also is associated with *Īśvara*, or God (*YS* I. 24).

13. See *Yogavārttika of Vijñānabhikṣu.* Translated and annotated by T. S. Rukmani. Four vols. (Delhi: Munshiram Manoharlal, 1978–89).

14. Rukmani points out that this allows for *prārabdha karma* to both exist and cease without the presence of *kleśa.*

15. While ranging a bit afield from Advaitic *jīvanmukti*, Vijñānabhikṣu's commentary on *YS* II. 27, which mentions seven kinds of *prajñā,* is rather interesting. This passage has echoes of, but no clear references to, the sevenfold *jñānabhūmi* model that appears in the *YV* and *JMV*. He begins that in *nirodha* or *asaṃprajñāta*

samādhi (the third kind of *prajñā*), which rises from the destruction of ignorance, one has the direct experience (*sākṣātkāra*) of sorrow-free *mokṣa* to come. This will arise after the body falls. This view raises the questions: How can one experience this perfection while still embodied? How can there be unconditioned *samādhi* in a body?

While not addressing this directly, Vijñānabhikṣu says that *jīvanmukti* is the completion of what is to be done and liberation from action. He asserts that having *tattva-jñāna* (see the *JMV*), known as *prajñā,* the aforementioned is the first stage of mental destruction (*citta-nāśa*), which has the form of higher detachment (*vairāgya*). *Citta-mukti* is called the highest liberation, *prajñā*'s object, and is threefold, not dependent on any means (*sādhana*). The intellect (*buddhi*) here has completed both enjoyment (*bhoga*) and release (*apavarga*). (See also II. 18 on *apavarga* and *bhoga.* The former is called *jīvanmukti* and the latter bondage when the *buddhi* separates from *puruṣa*.) After *paravairāgya* (stage one), the *buddhi-guṇas* like joy and sorrow merge with *prakṛti* in stage two (and the *liṅga-śarīra* is destroyed), and finally (stage three) the *puruṣa* is not connected with the *guṇas* and *buddhi*, is just the form of light (*jyotis*), objectless, flawless, and solitary (*kevalī*), undivided among liberated isolates. This final stage of bodiless (*videha*) *kaivalya* is attainment of utter absorption (*laya*). This threefold *citta-bhūmi* to come is, Vijñānabhikṣu concludes, directly experienced by the pure-minded *yogī* in the *jīvanmukti* state.

He continues that the *jīvanmukta* sees *prajñā,* a *buddhi-vṛtti,* only as witness (*sākṣin*), without selfish desire (*abhimāna*). This is distinct from the highest *mukta* (i.e., *puruṣa*) due to the flaw of *pratiprasava*, that is, although the mind is absorbed, there is still pleasantness (*kuśala*), that is, *kuśala guṇas* without *duḥkha* or *sattva.* While anything unpleasant is annulled in the *jīvanmukti* state, *kuśalatva* is secondary (*gauna*) but still present. Thus, it seems that *jīvanmukti* is not quite equal to *kaivalya,* since pleasantness *guṇas* remain.

Chapter 6

1. The sleeper (*suṣupta*) rests in the self, while waking, the realm of delusory objects is not present.

2. *yathāsthitam idaṃ yasya vyavahāravatoʃpi ca*
astaṃ gataṃ sthitaṃ vyoma jīvanmuktaḥ sa ucyate

bodhaikaniṣṭhatāṃ yāto jāgraty eva suṣuptavat
ya āste vyavahartaiva jīvanmuktaḥ sa ucyate

nodeti nāstamāyāti sukhe duḥkhe mukhaprabhā
yathā prāptasthiter yasya jīvanmuktaḥ sa ucyate

yo jāgarti suṣuptastho yasya jāgranna vidyate
yasya nirvāsano bodhaḥ sa jīvanmukta ucyate

rāgadveṣabhayādīnām anurūpaṃ carannapi
yoʃntarvyomavad acchasthaḥ sa jīvanmukta ucyate

yasya nāhaṃkṛto bhāvo yasya buddhir na lipyate
kurvato∫kurvato vāpi sa jīvanmukta ucyate

yasyonmeṣanimeṣārdhād vidaḥ pralayasaṃbhavau
paśyettrilokyāḥ svasamaḥ sa jīvanmukta ucyate

yasmānnodvijate loko lokānnodvijate ca yaḥ
harṣāmrṣabhayonmuktaḥ sa jīvanmukta ucyate

śāntasaṃsārakalanaḥ kalāvānapi niṣkalaḥ
yah sacittopi niṣcittaḥ sa jīvanmukta ucyate

yaḥ samastārthajāteṣu vyavahāryapi śītalaḥ
padārtheṣvapi pūrṇātmā sa jīvanmukta ucyate

Utpatti khaṇḍa 9. 4–13. For references to passages using similar terms, see chapter 8. Other good summaries of the nature of *jīvanmukti* appear in *Upaśama* 70. 1–10 and 77. 1–44.

3. The *Yogavāsiṣṭha of Vālmīki*. Vasudeva Laxmana Sharma Pansikar, Ed. 2 vols. 3rd edition (Bombay: Nirnaya Sagar Press, 1918. Reprint; Delhi: Motilal Banarsidass, 1984).

4. I abbreviate the *khaṇḍa* names below as follows:

V = *Vairāgya*	Up = *Upaśama*	M = *Mumukṣu*
P = *Pūrvanirvāṇa*	U = *Utpatti*	Ut = *Uttaranirvāṇa*
S = *Sthiti*		

5. The *Yogavāsiṣṭha* has many cosmogonic passages that make extensive use of *Sāṃkhya* categories, but when *jīvanmukti* is considered, the Advaita framework predominates.

6. Readers interested in the Puranic dimension should look at Mackenzie Brown's chapter in *Living Liberation in Hindu Thought* on Śuka as *jīvanmukta* in the *Mahābhārata* and the *Bhāgavata* and *Devī-Bhāgavata Purāṇas*.

7. The text also mentions many other kinds of sages: *muni*, *siddha*, *guru*, *yogin*, *sādhu*, and *jñānin*. We will focus on passages where the term *jīvanmukta* is specifically used.

8. One of the distinctive characteristics of the *Yogavāsiṣṭha* is its (often literally) flowery language. Many chapters include luxuriant descriptions of natural phenomena, which are then called illusory and necessary to renounce. Natural metaphors abound: wisdom is said to "blossom like flowers" and "shine like the full moon's beams" in the "forest of awakening" (Up 18. 4–5). The world is ultimately "burnt in the fire of the intellect," and clear minds do not "sprout illusion" like burnt seeds sprout no plants (P 2. 46–49).

The *jīvanmukta* (or his mind) is often termed "clear" or "empty," like the cloudless (autumn) sky (U 9. 8, Up 17. 18, 18. 25, 53. 74, 77. 33, 89. 19, P 56. 2). A typical image appears in Ut 125. 63–65: the *jīvanmukta* sees all characteristics without any difference, like "space" (*akāśa*) in the sky, and knows a brilliant rainbow, like all visible objects, is really only an empty reflection.

9. V 3. 1–3, Up 18. 28–30, Ut 95. 17–21, 125. 65–68.

10. Up 18. 13–15. The *JMV* will reiterate this theme, and those that follow.

11. The point seems to be, as Ut 125. 36 says, that the mind is bound and burning whether sad (having body cut up) or happy (sitting on a throne).

12. Up 17. 5, 93. 84, 87, P 120. 18–19.

13. Ut 95. 26, 199. 34–35.

14. U 8. 16, Up 18. 30, 34. A common synonym for *jīvanmukta* is *mahātma* ("great self"); both are detached, have a controlled mind, and so on.

15. U 9. 2, S 46. 23–24, Up 12. 15–16, 75. 45.

16. A point also made by the texts Mackenzie Brown studies in his chapter in *Living Liberation in Hindu Thought*.

17. As with traditional Advaita, we shall see that the key to liberation lies with neither the body's presence or absence, nor performance of action or nonaction, nor supernatural powers (*siddhi*).

18. In Ut 95. 16, Vasiṣṭha says he is here teaching among us since he did not reach *brahman*-hood. One wishes for further elaboration on this admission.

19. Various forms of the root *śam*, indicating peacefulness, also appear frequently.

20. Up 53. 80, 68. 5, 70. 24, 86. 5, 93. 93, Ut 125. 56.

21. Up 68. 9, Ut 199. 32.

22. Up 68. 4, 70. 1, 93. 90–91.

23. Up 70. 1, P 101. 30, Ut 199. 9. We shall later consider liberated beings' detachment from supernatural powers (Up 89) and impure *vāsanās* (Up 93).

24. U 118. 18, Up 12. 8–10, 16. 18, 68. 7, 77. 26, and so on. Both the *JMV* and the *Gītā* speak of the highest *yogin* in similar terms.

25. Up 74. 37, 77. 12, 32.

26. Up 18. 24, Ut 125. 37. It is also often said that the *jīvanmukta* smiles while internally detached.

27. Up 16. 19–20, 71. 10, 77. 43.

28. Up 18. 27–29, 17. 8, 77. 19–20.

29. There are a few passages that suggest that he does not act at all: the detached man completely abandons all actions and fruits (Up 68. 8), all hopes and undertakings (Up 74. 38), and the Self-knower does and desires nothing (Up 89. 17).

However, the overwhelming emphasis in the *Yogavāsiṣṭha* is on detachment, not non-action.

30. The "inner cool" (*antaḥśītalatā*) of the *jīvanmukta* is often mentioned (this term also appears in the *JMV*). In general, inner coolness is linked to detachment in action and lack of delusion or *vāsanā* (U 9. 13, Up 16. 9, 18. 11, 53. 82, 70. 22, 75. 26, P 56.1, Ut 125. 35). It also rises from investigating the *Yogavāsiṣṭha* (Ut 95. 28).

31. U 9. 4, Up 18. 18–19, 77. 10, 93. 97.

32. U 9. 6, Up 12. 2, 17. 4, 70. 18, 93. 93.

33. Up 18. 18–22, 77. 9, 27.

34. Up 77. 11, P 56. 5.

35. Up 70. 19–20, 77. 8.

36. U 22. 8, 118. 28, Ut 125. 33. This also is the case with Janaka in the *Devī-Bhāgavata Purāṇa*.

37. I translate the root *vi-hṛ*, which appears repeatedly in passages that discuss *jīvanmukti*, as "wander." *Vi-hṛ* suggests both detached roaming *in* the world and withdrawal or separation *from* the world. For example, it is said the sage with *jīvanmukti*-mind roams the world following all customs yet indifferent to all, and wanders detached and even-minded while in everyday activity (Up 18. 17–26, 93. 92–93, P 101. 30, Ut 199. 9). Sage Nārada and Lord Viśvamitra are said to wander the world as *jīvanmuktas* (Up 75. 22, 86. 9).

38. We see the Puranic element of the *YV* clearly here. Gods are also called *videhamuktas* in note 45.

39. Up 12. 1–9, 16. 9–13, 75. 47, Ut 125. 59. For more (and for conflicting reports) on Janaka's character, see Mackenzie Brown's article in *Living Liberation in Hindu Thought*.

40. Māndhātā's liberation while living is also mentioned in Ut 125. 60.

41. Up 42. 17 says Prahlāda rested within himself with his own pure *sattva vāsanā* until awoken by a conch.

42. Ut 125. 51 adds that Viṣṇu, creator and destroyer, is a *jīvanmukta*.

43. Up 75. 50, P 120. 11.

44. Up 17. 13 says the body made by parents is unreal, and S 33. 66 states that the highest goal is knowing that the notion of a body-based "I" (*ahaṃkāra*) is unreal.

45. Ut 9. 16–21 continues that the *videhamukta* is pervasive, controlling all—as sun, he rules three worlds like the *trimūrti*; as sky, he supports the gods; as earth, he supports animals and plants; as fire and water, he burns and melts; he also becomes light and darkness and makes animals and mind move. Elsewhere (P 126. 71–73), it is said that the peaceful and incomprehensible *videhamukta* is called Śiva, Brahma,

or *prakṛti*, according to how others imagine the self. These passages are representative of several (see p. 10 ff.) that suggest that the *jīvan-* or *videha-mukta* is a god or supreme being, rather than an "individual" liberated spirit.

46. This also appears in the *JMV* (128, 365). See chapter 7 and chapter 8.

47. P 126. 70–71 makes this same point in a different model: the sixth (of seven) stages is *jīvanmukti*; the seventh stage, called *videhamukti*, is utterly peaceful and unreachable by words.

48. I could find no consistent definitional differentiation among these terms.

49. P 2. 43, 47–49, P 101. 24, 27–28, Up 90. 15.

50. Up 77. 21–22, 86. 12, 93. 94–95, P 2. 4–5. These *jīvanmuktas* are said to wander detached from joy and sorrow, solely intent on knowing the self, at peace and unaffected by *saṃsāra* (Up 68. 5–6, 70. 1–9, P 101. 30).

51. U 9. 9, 22. 11, Up 16. 20, 18. 25.

52. This idea is one of several passages apparently influenced by Buddhist ideas in which *jīvanmukti* appears. While Buddhist terms occasionally are mentioned in the *jīvanmukti* context, almost no Buddhist technical language is used. Most common is the word "*nirvāṇa*"; generally, it designates the highest goal, often *videhamukti* (U 9. 25, V 3. 5–6, Up 53. 75, P 120. 6). The detached but "in the world" *jīvanmukta* might be influenced by the concept of the *bodhisattva*, but no explicit connection is made.

53. See chapter 7.

54. P 2. 43, 101. 28.

55. Up 93. 84, 87, P 120. 18–19.

56. Up 93. 85, P 120. 20.

57. V 3. 8–9, U 22. 8, P 2. 45, P 55. 42–45, P 56. 1, P 101. 34. Sleep without *vāsanās* also brings inner coolness and liberation (called *turīya* here). Sleep is said to arise from the *vāsanā*-less dream state, and liberation from *vāsanā*-less waking state (U 22. 4, Up 70. 22, 26, P 126. 64–65).

58. Refer here also to P 2. 44 and Up 18. 3.

59. Up 42. 14–17, P 101. 29.

60. U 22. 5, P 2. 42–43, 47–49, 101. 31.

61. Up 90. 17, 21–25, P 101. 30, 33. This also appears in *JMV* 128, 365 (and is taken from the *LYV*).

62. This topic also appears in the *JMV* (103, 327), also taken from the *LYV*; see chapter 7.

63. A list of oft-repeated terms describing the *jīvanmukta* follows: eternally satisfied (*nitya-tṛpta*), tranquil self (*praśāntātma*), passions ceased (*vītarāga*), and without *vāsanās*.

64. U 9. 5–7, Up 12. 2, 13, 16. 19, 22, 60. 20, 70. 10, 16, 19, 77. 8, 86. 6, P 56. 6.

65. For more on this doctrine, in the *Yogavāsiṣṭha* and Advaita thought in general, see my book *The Self and Its States* (Delhi: Motilal Banarsidass, 1990).

66. References to dream can be found in U 22. 1–4 and Ut 95. 17, 23–24. The theme is that dreams and their objects are unreal, and cease with knowledge. Waking is "real" only relative to dreams.

67. Up 42. 15, 70. 22, 77. 3–4.

68. See also Up 70. 26: When fully established in sleep from repeated yogic practice, this is *turīya*, and Up 71. 4: Having enjoyed the worldly condition in sleep state, one then goes to the fourth.

69. U 118. 15, Up 70. 27–33, 71. 1.

70. U 118. 16, Up 70. 32, 71. 5. One passage, in contrast, says one resting in the fourth abides there dead (*kayānta*) *or* in bodily state (Up 86. 6).

71. For more on this, and connections between the *Yogavāsiṣṭha* and the *Jīvanmuktiviveka*, see J. F. Sprockhoff's "Der Weg zur Erlosung bei Lebzeiten . . . " in *Wiener Zeitschrift fur die Kunde Sud und Ostasiens* 14 (1970), p. 137 ff.

72. The *JMV* refers to this passage (see chapter 7) as well as a third seven-stage model in U 118, which says those in the seventh stage are great selves (*mahātma*), great enjoyers (*mahābhāga*), and enjoyers of the self (*ātmarāma*). The latter is a common synonym for *jīvanmukti*; U 118. 20, for example, states that the enjoyer of the self takes no pleasure in worldly activity like those asleep take no pleasure in beautiful women around them.

Chapter 7

1. This chapter is a revision of my essay "Liberation While Living in the *Jīvanmuktiviveka:* Vidyāraṇya's 'Yogic Advaita,'" in *Living Liberation in Hindu Thought.*

2. Edited and Translated by S. Subrahmanya Sastri and T. R. Srinivasa Ayyangar (Madras: Adyar Library and Research Center, 1978). Translations cited are mine. Page references that follow indicate text and translation, that is, (33, 178).

3. There has been some debate about the relationship of the *JMV* author to Sāyaṇa, Mādhava, Bhāratītīrtha, and the Vidyāraṇya of the *Pañcadaśī* (including whether they are different people or the same person at different stages of life). As I will discuss in the chapter on the *Pañcadaśī*, it is unlikely that the Vidyāraṇya of the *JMV* is the same Vidyāraṇya who authored the *Pañcadaśī,* whom I shall call Bhāratītīrtha.

4. For an excellent summary and analysis of this text, one can consult J. F. Sprockhoff's two-part article on the *Jīvanmuktiviveka,* "Die Weg zur Erlösung bei

Lebzeiten, Ihr Wesen and Ihr Wert, nach dem *Jīvanmuktiviveka* des Vidyāraṇya." *Wiener Zeitschrift fur die Kunde Sud- und Ost-asiens* 8 (1964): 224–62 and 14 (1970): 131–59. A more recent work focusing on living liberation in the *JMV* is L. K. L. Srivastava's *Advaitic Concept of Jīvanmukti* (Delhi: Bharatiya Vidya Bhavan, 1990). This book is less satisfactory than Sprockhoff's work, as it is heavily neo-Vedantic and lacking in critical analysis. For more on Srivastava, see chapter 12.

5. Translated by K. Narayanaswami Aiyer (Madras: Adyar Library and Research Center, 1971).

6. See, for example, pp. 30, 224; 72, 285.

7. "*Jivataḥ puruṣasya kartṛtva-bhoktṛtva-sukhaduhkhādi-lakṣaṇaś citta-dharmaḥ kleśa-rūpatvād bandho bhavati, tasya nivāraṇaṃ jīvanmuktih.*" (10, 194). See also *Muktika Upaniṣad* 11.

8. Vidyāraṇya discusses mental impressions at some length, devoting an entire chapter to the destruction of impressions (*vāsanā-kṣaya*) as a means for attaining *jīvanmukti*. He adopts the *LYV* definition of *vāsanās* as an intense binding to a thing, which, because of strong attachment, causes one to think one's delusory impression is the real thing (*sadvastu*) (52, 256). The rest of the chapter describes various kinds of pure (*śuddha*) and impure (*malina*) *vāsanās*. Pure *vāsanās* are sense activity that merely keeps the body alive, without causing rebirth (56, 261). Impure mental impressions that have the form of profound ignorance and intense egoism are of three types: *loka* (desire for the world's praise), *śāstra* (addiction to, and pride in, mere textual study and ritual observance) and *deha* (the threefold illusion that the body is the self, that it can be beautified, and that its flaws can be removed) (56, 261 ff.).

9. See note on Śaṅkara and *Yoga* in chapter 2. Still, we have seen that Śaṅkara does, on rare occasions, speak of the value of mental concentration as a preparatory stage, encouraging the rise of knowledge.

10. Still following the *Gītā*, Vidyāraṇya goes on to describe the *jīvanmukta* as a detached and content devotee of the Lord (*bhagavad-bhakta*) and as one who has gone beyond the threefold qualities (*guṇātīta*) (25, 218 ff.). Here we see Vidyāraṇya's commingling of devotional, yogic, and nondualistic strands of Indian thought. He writes that the discriminating *guṇātīta* is beyond activity or superimposing the "I" on action. The one beyond qualities aims to serve the self by knowledge, repeated meditation, and unswerving devotion (a theme clearly emphasized in the *Gītā*).

11. Vidyāraṇya here (pp. 43, 241 ff.) also goes over the divine (*daiva*) and demonic (*āsura*) qualities leading to and from *jīvanmukti*, again taking his lead from the *Gītā* (XVI.1–4). He also speaks of two types of bondage, sharp (*tīvra*) and mild (*mṛdu*), with their *guṇa*-based *vṛttis*, which are removed by *mano-nāśa* and *vāsanā-kṣaya.*

12. Sprockhoff (1964) has a detailed analysis of this portion of the text, and points out that Vidyāraṇya, while following Patañjali in many ways, has his own version of yogic limbs (p. 251).

13. The passage quoted is from *LYV* 28. 1–9. See also *Yogavāsiṣṭha Upaśama khaṇḍa* 89. 9-21 (chapter 6).

14. A similar call to go beyond a yogic *samādhi* appears in the chapter on destroying *vāsanās*, which closes calling for cultivation of the "consciousness only" (*cinmātra*) *vāsanā,* then impressionless (*nirvāsanā*) *samādhi*. As the *LYV* says (16. 45–46, 5. 92, 18. 26–29 [pp. 83, 299]), the real *jīvanmukta* is free from any *vāsanā* at all. He is "asleep while awake," beyond *karma* or efforts of any sort (ritual, meditation, or textual study). The utterly detached *jīvanmukta* thus illustrates the benefits of destruction of mental impressions.

On the other hand, a little later (pp. 116, 347) Vidyāraṇya quotes (and agrees with) *Gītā* VI. 46, which asserts that *yoga* is superior to asceticism and knowledge. The kind of knowledge referred to here is not clear. It is never termed *brahma-jñāna*. Also, on pages 127 and 364, Vidyāraṇya states that the mind is extinguished when extremely ascetic *yogins* attain *asaṃprajñāta* (undiscriminated) *samādhi.* At this point, *jīvanmukti* is said to be firmly established.

15. The closest equivalent for this term in scholastic Advaita is *videha-kaivalya.*

16. *jīvanneva dṛṣṭabandhanāt kāmāder-viśeṣeṇa muktaḥ san dehapāte bhāvibandhanād-viśeṣaṇena mucyate* (15, 202).

17. He here gives many examples of *Upaniṣadic jñāna-śāstra*: *Muṇḍaka* II. 2. 8 and 10, III. 2. 9, *Kaṭha* III. 8, *Bṛhadāraṇyaka Upaniṣad* I. 4. 10, and so on.

18. Vidyāraṇya here quotes a pseudo-Śaṅkaran text, *Vākyavṛtti* 52–53, which says (following *ChU* VI. 14. 2 and mainstream Advaita) that one is a *jīvanmukta* (i.e., has knowledge while living) while currently manifesting *karma* causes the body to continue, and when this *karma* is used up, one then attains blissful *kaivalya* (i.e., *videhamukti*).

19. Śaṅkara's discussion of *aśarīratva* (bodilessness) in *Brahmasūtra bhāṣya* I. 1. 4 is exemplary here.

20. To this mainstream Advaita position, he adds a familiar Yogic Advaita point: Knowledge of the truth is the main, direct means to *mukti* (here "bodiless"), while destroying both the mind and impressions are means to knowledge. Though inferior, they are still necessary (49, 252).

21. Found also in *Muktika Upaniṣad* II. 32 ff. and *Annapūrṇa Upaniṣad* IV. 14–20.

22. Vidyāraṇya argues that doubt is even worse than error (such as the erroneous belief that ritual action can bring release). One can at times be happy when ignorant or in error, but doubt prevents worldly enjoyment as well as liberation, thus allowing no satisfaction on either level.

23. See chapter 6. These stages of knowledge are said to be preceded by asceticism (*vairāgya*). The first three stages include desiring purity, reflection (*vicāraṇa*), and accomplishing good acts (*sadācāra*) while reducing mental activity (*tanumanasā*).

Since these stages do not remove all trace of duality, they are only a means to knowledge, not *brahmavidyā* proper.

24. In describing degrees of living liberation, Vidyāraṇya seems to be trying to address a controversy about the necessity post-knowledge of "departing" or "rising" from (*vyutthāna*) *samādhi*, and the extent of one's control over *samādhi*. In the fifth stage, the "preferred" *brahman*-knowing *yogin* leaves the highest *samādhi* on his own; in the sixth stage, the "better" *brahman*-knowing *yogin's samādhi* is so concentrated that he only leaves it with a companion's assistance. The meditative enstasis of these *yogins* is so profound that it seems like deep sleep, free from a sense of diversity or even unity. Finally, the "best" *brahman*-knowing *yogin* never departs from nonconceptual *samādhi* at all; all texts describing yogic states are said to end here. This sevenfold model reappears in Madhusūdana Sarasvatī's *Gītā* commentary, the *Gūḍārthadīpikā* III. 18 and VI. 43.

25. In response to the latter point, Vidyāraṇya argues that even killing a Brahmin does not bar liberation; no act can bar liberation, since, after all, we are not our bodies or attendant actions.

26. More will be said on this distinction later.

27. There is another way that the *yogin*'s personal (but not body-based) austerity affects many. As *Sūtasaṃhitā* II. 20. 45 says, by knowing *brahman*, he saves his ancestors from rebirth, sanctifies all of his family, and purifies the whole earth. By transforming his consciousness, he transforms his entire lineage.

This can be seen as an excellent example of the difference between Christian "doing good" by serving others and Hindu "doing good" by allowing others to serve you. The *guru* serves by "being," not "doing." In the final chapter, I will suggest that later Advaita scholars, in part trying to show that Advaita includes the Christian notion, are not always sufficiently aware of this distinction.

28. Furthermore, he does not argue with doctrinaire "text lovers" (*śāstra-prema*), since he acts in accordance with Vedic texts that say not to challenge other schools of thought, nor care to establish one's own views. Seeing your "opponent" as yourself, what is the point? In one of his most extreme attempts to syncretize (144, 387), Vidyāraṇya then makes an interesting, and certainly debatable, assertion: all thinkers (*tairthika*) except Lokāyatas (but including Buddhists, Jainas, and Śāktas, among others) agree on (*aṅgī-kṛ*) liberation (*mokṣa*) and would not dispute that yogic conduct (*yogicārita*), that is, the *yogin*'s eight-limbed path, is the way to liberation, even if the topics on which these thinkers expound differ. While it may be true that practices often are more similar than doctrines, Vidyāraṇya's assertion here certainly oversimplifies the great diversity of Indian practices toward liberation. In any case, the point he wants to make here is that the Advaitic *yogin* is honored by all, leaving no room for dispute.

One can here point out that nondisputation is certainly not a goal of mainstream Advaita, nor an attribute of Śaṅkara, himself often called a *jīvanmukta*.

29. It does not seem that one can be so detached about women, however. Vidyāraṇya claims they are forbidden (*pratiṣiddha*) and disgusting (*jugupsitā*), like

corpses. They overcome men by causing desire, despite having vaginas like oozing sores, and so on (32, 227).

30. This is reminiscent of the figure Śuka in the *Purāṇas*. For more, see Mackenzie Brown's chapter in *Living Liberation in Hindu Thought*.

31. Still, Vidyāraṇya states, after liberation, completing these duties will not cause future births. Injunctions to study, meditate, and assimilate remove obstacles to *brahma-jñāna* but do not add *karma/apūrva* (154, 403).

32. See also the Introduction on this matter.

33. Further, as we saw in Vidyāraṇya's discussion of austerity (*tapas*), at this highest level of detachment, the *jīvanmukta* can allow others to follow and serve him, freeing them and purifying the world by his injunction-transcending austerity.

34. Asceticism is prescribed through the rest of this chapter, and a mendicant is described as being beyond *mantra* or *dhyāṇa*, beyond textual debates and the distinction of "I" and "you." One with the stick (*daṇḍa*) of knowledge is abodeless, only sky-clad, greets no one, and does not propitiate ancestors (166, 422). Abodelessness is important because even living in a monastery reinforces the "I," as does possession of utensils and plates. This renouncer shuns students, rejects gold, and remains always detached. He simply rests in *brahman*, avoiding all mixing with the world.

35. Vidyāraṇya's views here represent a common theme in religious literature: after rejecting the world, one can return, and be "in" but not "of" the world. When ignorant, one thinks one must get from "here" (the world of suffering and attachment) to "there" (liberation). From the liberated viewpoint, however, the duality of "here" and "there" is an illusion. *Jīvanmukti* is in part predicated on the idea that you can be both here *and* there.

Chapter 8

1. *Panchadashi*. Hari Prasad Shastri, Ed. and Trans. (London: Shanti Sadan, 1965).

2. In the Sringeri *Śaṅkarācārya* tradition, Bhāratītīrtha is held to be the younger brother (though senior in taking *saṃnyāsa)* of Vidyāraṇya.

3. T. M. P. Mahadevan, *The Philosophy of Advaita with Special Reference to Bhāratītīrtha-Vidyāraṇya*. (Madras: Ganesh and Co., 1957), pp. 1–8. See also L. K. L. Srivastava's *Advaitic Concept of Jivanmukti* (Delhi: Bharatiya Vidya Prakashan, 1990), pp. 30–38. S. N. Dasgupta argues for joint authorship of the *PD* by Bhāratītīrtha and (Mādhava) Vidyāraṇya in *History of Indian Philosophy* (Delhi: Motilal Banarsidass, 1975), Vol. II, p. 216n.

4. Dasgupta argues the latter is later, *History*, Vol. II, p. 251n.

5. The *Gītā* is also quoted or referred to in this context in IV. 59–62, VII. 156–61, and IX. 46–60.

6. This point is echoed in *PD* VII. 2, which says that the satisfaction *(tṛpti)* of the *jīvanmukta* is clearly known by studying a *śruti* (*BāU* IV. 4. 42), which ends desire by teaching knowing the "I" as the self.

7. 37, 232 ff.; chapter 7.

8. VI. 13–14 reiterates that realization *(bodhi)* is knowing the falsity (*mithyātva*) of the world and *jīva*, and certainty that the highest self remains and is real—thus supporting living *(jīvan)mukti.*

9. This answer again raises the thorny problem of how the knower can be deluded.

10. Verses 253–70 are repeated in XIV. 40–57.

11. IX. 76 repeats this point.

12. As seen in portions of the *Upadeśasāhasrī,* and later in Prakāśānanda (chapter 4).

13. *PD* IX. 97 ff. also state that meditation is optional for the truth-knower.

14. In his translation, Shastri adds a neo-Vedanta footnote here: "The illumined sage does not pose as a superior man, but behaves like a thorough gentleman (p. 258)." The prior verses hardly seem typical of a British gentleman.

15. This is an interesting, but isolated, reference to concern for the world's welfare, again probably related to the *Gītā* (III. 20).

16. "Die Idee der *Jīvanmukti* in den Späten *Upaniṣads,*" *WZKSO* 7 (1963): 190–208.

17. *The Sāmānya-Vedānta Upaniṣads*. Edited by A. Mahadeva Sastri. (Madras: Adyar Library, 1916).

18. Particularly *Pūrvanirvāna* 115; see Sprockhoff, p. 193, and beginning of chapter 6.

19. In this context, see also *Tejobindu Upaniṣad* IV 33 ff., which exalts bodiless liberation as the highest bliss, and so on.

20. Sprockhoff, p. 196.

21. *JMV* 10, 194; see chapter 7.

22. *upādhi-vinirmukta-ghaṭākāśavat prārabdha-kṣayād videhamuktiḥ*.

23. *Saṃnyāsa Upanisads* (New York: Oxford University Press, 1992), p. 80, note 25.

24. See Olivelle, pp. 246–50.

25. On the earlier group of verses, see the section on the *Pañcadaśī*.

26. Lance Nelson offers a valuable description of Madhusūdana's different messages for different audiences on the role of *bhakti* in Advaita in his "Madhusūdana

Sarasvatī on the 'Hidden Meaning' of the *Bhagavad-Gītā*: Bhakti for the Advaitin Renunciate" in *Journal of South Asian Literature* 23 (1988): 73–89.

27. In IV. 23, Madhusūdana states that Janaka and others, as *sthita-prajñas*, know they are not doers and have all ignorance removed, but perform sacrifices and do good acts due to *prārabdha karma.*

28. *LYV* 13. 113–14. See *JMV* 134–36, 373–75.

29. He homologizes each stage to a state of consciousness, saying here, for example, that *yogins* call these three stages the waking state, since the world now appears as differentiated.

30. The fourth stage is called the dream state, since it displays the falsity of the whole world. The fifth and sixth are called deep sleep *(suṣupti)* and profound *(gāḍha)* deep sleep.

31. *brahmavid-vara, -varīyas,* and *-variṣṭha.*

32. See chapter 7, particularly footnote 24.

33. A little earlier, VI. 27 describes the *yogin* with peaceful mind *(praśānta-mānasam)*, and Madhusūdana holds that this *yogin*, convinced that "having become *brahman*, all is indeed *brahman*," obtains *brahman*, is a *jīvanmukta*, and goes to the highest bliss (*uttama sukha*).

34. See *JMV* 134–35, 373–74.

35. He adds that the *saṃnyāsin* who, due to the strength of the mental impression of detachment (*vairagya-vāsanā),* which manifests by the Lord's grace, has only a weak desire for more enjoyment (*bhoga*) at death will be born in a family of *brahman*-knowers. Such a renouncer will surely gain liberation.

36. See *Gītā* II. 54 ff. in chapter 1.

37. We also noted that in scholastic Advaita, Maṇḍana Miśra introduces (but does not clearly settle) the issue of whether the one with firm wisdom is a *siddha* ("accomplished being," and a *jīvanmukta)* or "merely" a highly advanced student (*sādhaka)*. In brief references, Vimuktātman and Citsukha hold the *sthita-prajña* (and the *guṇātīta)* to be liberated while living, and not just a *sādhaka*.

Chapter 9

1. I also remind the reader that I recognize that such broad categories like "India," "Hindu," and "the West" both conceal and reveal. Still, such terms can be useful, and are in fact inevitable.

2. (Albany: State University of New York Press, 1988).

3. Halbfass has closely read Heidegger (and Gadamer), and holds J. L. Mehta, one of Heidegger's foremost interpreters (and of course an Indian), in high esteem. One can also notice Paul Hacker's influence on Halbfass' thought.

4. For more, interested readers should look at *India and Europe* (particularly pp. 16–17 and 434–42) and the recent volume *Beyond Orientalism: The Work of Wilhelm Halbfass and Its Impact on Indian and Cross-Cultural Studies*, edited by Eli Franco and Karin Preisendanz, Poznan Studies in the Philosophy of Sciences and Humanities No. 59 (Amsterdam/Atlanta: Editions Rodopi, 1997). One might also refer with profit to *Tradition and Reflection*, and his translation of Paul Hacker's writings, *Philology and Confrontation*.

5. Though they also think they go beyond "mere" scholastic Advaita.

6. S. K. Ramachandra Rao's book on living liberation is a good example of the use of modern psychological language. He states that the *jīvanmukta* knows the "essential unity of all experience," and calls *jīvanmukti* an "altered state of consciousness (58)," "authentic living (69)," and "intense awareness of a new dimension of being (7)."

7. A further elaboration of what is generally "Western" and what is more specifically Christian is interesting and important, but beyond my scope here. Much more could also be said about the sociopolitical realities that brought about neo-Vedanta, but again this is not my focus.

8. I document an example of this phenomenon in "Neither East Nor West: A Case of Neo-Vedanta in Modern Indian Thought," *Religious Studies Review* 18 (April 1992): 95–100, which considers L. K. L. Srivastava's *Advaitic Concept of Jīvanmukti*. This book covers the Advaita concept of living liberation in greater breadth (though not in greater depth or rigor of analysis) than any prior work, focusing particularly on the *Jīvanmuktiviveka*. While ostensibly about *jīvanmukti* in the Advaita tradition, this book is also an attempt to make this concept relevant to modern Western concerns, such as psychological well-being and social service. At times, one gets more of the neo-Vedanta view of living liberation than the "Advaitic Concept of *Jīvanmukti*." For more, particularly concerning social ethics issues, see chapter 12.

9. I should mention that there is an ongoing delegitimation of the neo-Vedantic worldview of Vivekananda and Radhakrishnan in modern India, which is one of the reasons behind the rise of the ideology of "Hindutva." I consider this ideology both destructive and at least as intellectually removed from traditional Indian thought as neo-Vedanta. It is certainly more inimical to the humanistic values that I personally and professionally hold dear. I will regret if my criticisms here contribute to the loss of neo-Vedantic values like tolerance and inclusion.

10. *The Limits of Scripture* (Honolulu: University of Hawaii Press, 1994), p. 133. Rambachan writes that Vivekananda was an early and extremely important proponent of the notion that the highest truth in Hinduism (and all religions) is known by direct "intuitive" experience (often called *samādhi*), unlike Śaṅkara's view that *apauruṣeya śruti* is the definitive source for knowing the real (*brahman*).

L. K. L. Srivastava shows a typically neo-Vedantic individualistic and experience-based psychologism quite foreign to traditional Indian thought; for him, "true" religion must be "experiential," that is, "something inward and personal [which] unifies all values and organizes all experience (3)." The "ethical or ritualistic aspect of religion" is "secondary," but a "prerequisite to the art of conscious self-revelation or contact with the Divine" (4). Śaṅkara, on the other hand, talks of the authority of *śruti*, not of "religion," and of immediate knowledge of *ātman/brahman*, not of "experience" as a state of awareness.

11. Still, modern Vedantins certainly seem less committed than traditional Advaitins to the notion that empirical experience is always a limitation or a defect (like an eye disease), and utter isolation and bodiless liberation our final goal.

12. As mentioned in the Introduction, "accurate representation" falls within a range of understandings.

Chapter 10

1. *Ramana Maharshi: The Sage of Arunacala* (London: George Allen and Unwin, 1977).

2. A number of books record his life. In addition to Mahadevan's book, mentioned in the prior note, see also Arthur Osborne's *Ramana Maharshi and the Path of Self-Knowledge* (London: Ryder and Co., 1954), or K. Swaminathan's *Ramana Maharshi* (Delhi: National Book Trust, 1975). Each of these books is rather hagiographic; for a good brief summary, see David Kinsley's *Hinduism: A Cultural Perspective* (Englewood Cliffs, N. J.: Prentice-Hall, 1993).

3. *The Teachings of Bhagavan Sri Ramana Maharshi in His Own Words.* Edited by Arthur Osborne. 5th ed. (Tiruvannamalai: Sriramanashrama, 1988), p. 2.

4. See his *A Search in Secret India* (London: Ryder and Co., 1964). There are some references to interviews between Ramana and the Tibetologist Evans-Wentz in the *Teachings.* Some research into their discussions would be a welcome addition to Ramana scholarship.

5. I had the opportunity to be a guest at the ashram in January 1990 and December 1996. I found a slightly larger number of visitors and additional buildings during my second visit.

6. At the back of this central shrine is a statue of Ramana, with a plaque indicating that Indira Gandhi was present at its installation in 1980.

7. *The Collected Works of Ramana Maharshi.* Arthur Osborne, Ed. 5th edition. (Tiruvannamalai: Sri Ramanasramam, 1979).

8. A short chapter of Mahadevan's *Ramana Maharshi: The Sage of Arunacala* compares Śaṅkara and Ramana. Mahadevan argues that their views are very similar and gives two examples of Ramana's and Śaṅkara's kinship of thought. The first is that both hold that there are levels of understanding, the highest being that all is nondual (127). The second example quotes a passage just mentioned, where Ramana tells a questioner that his teaching expresses his own experience, while "[o]thers find

that it tallies with Sri Shankara's." Ramana then adds that "[a] realised person will use his own language (128)." While Mahadevan claims that this indicates Ramana finds their teachings in "complete identity," one could argue instead that Ramana here explicitly avoids making such a statement. Mahadevan here seems to be attempting to show more continuity than exists, a goal shared by many thinkers over the centuries, who want to argue that Advaitic thought is a seamless web. An attempt to find distinctions can be seen, from this perspective, as exhibiting a lower level of understanding.

9. *Teach*, 10, 106, 235. J. Jayaraman also used this analogy in our conversation.

10. Osborne follows this with a paragraph on the nature of "religion," a modern Western term with no exact equivalent in Advaita. We should here be especially careful in uncritically accepting Osborne's translations.

11. This view was explicitly endorsed by Kunju Swami.

12. See "Self-Enquiry" in *Collected Works*, pp. 29–32. He here makes a distinction between yogic and *"jnanic"* breath and mind control, which is not found elsewhere.

13. According to N. Veezhinathan, in his manuscript, "Bhagavan Ramana—A Jivanmukta," Ramana said that "atma-siddhi is the highest siddhi (11)."

14. This view was firmly endorsed by both Kunju Swami and J. Jayaraman.

15. Ramana takes a similar position concerning nationalism. When asked if it is one's duty to be a patriot, he is said to respond, "It is your duty to BE and not to be this or that (*Teach*, 103)." As far as working for the country's welfare goes, he states, "[f]irst take care of yourself and the rest will naturally follow (104)." However, his view of Gandhi is said to be that "Gandhiji has surrendered himself to the Divine and works accordingly with no self-interest (104)."

16. From *Bhagavan Sri Ramana: A Pictorial Biography* (Tiruvannamalai: Sri Ramanasramam, 1981), p. 96. This is also quoted by R. Balasubramanian in his article on Ramana as a *jīvanmukta,* mentioned later.

17. *Ramana Maharshi*, pp. 62–63.

18. Balasubramanian has been chair of the philosophy department at the University of Pondicherry and head of the Centre for the Advanced Study of Philosophy at the University of Madras.

19. "Ramana Maharshi, The Liberated-in-Life," *Indian Philosophical Annual* 17 (1984–85), p. 230.

20. *Ibid.*, pp. 230–31. For more on this passage, including Balasubramanian's views of it, see chapter 12.

21. This book is later than, and includes parts of, Mahadevan's *Ramana Maharshi and his Philosophy of Existence* (Tiruvannamalai: Sri Ramanashramam,

1967). One might characterize this latter book (and the second half of the former) more accurately as Mahadevan's philosophy of existence, with support from Ramana Maharshi. Mahadevan also wrote a book on South Indian holy men called *Ten Saints of India* (Bombay: Bharatiya Vidya Bhavan, 1971), and he includes *bhakti* poet–saints, as well as Vedantins. It is revealing that of ten biographies the longest two are those of Śaṅkara and Ramana.

22. For example, see previous note 8.

23. Given to me by the author in manuscript form.

24. He also writes that Ramana, like Jacob Boehme, gained a sudden but full "mystical" illumination at a young age. In a comparison within the Hindu tradition, Veezhinathan says, "as in the case of Vamadeva of the Upanisadic fame, in the case of Bhagavan [Ramana] too, self-realization came as a flash (6)."

25. *Videhamukti* is then called "transcendent" attributeless *Brahman* and *Turiya*.

26. This view was explicitly supported by J. Jayaraman.

27. *Talks with Sri Ramana Maharshi* (Tiruvannamalai: Sri Ramanashramam, 1978), pp. 422–23.

28. However, he refers to the mark as an animal that departs and is replaced by another. This part of the analogy is not part of traditional Advaita and is unclear to me.

29. It would be valuable to know to what Ramana is referring in his mention of "with *and* without form."

30. This last comment could indicate his familiarity with Vidyāraṇya's *Jīvanmuktiviveka,* though there is no clear evidence of his knowledge of this text. Also, Kunju Swami told me that one is a *videhamukta* while living, when not thinking dualistically.

31. Both the stages of *brahman*-knowing and their ultimately singular nature were stressed by Kunju Swami.

32. I am grateful to Professor Arabinda Basu of the Aurobindo Ashram for clarifying my understanding here.

33. He further states that the *jīvanmukta* "is made one with the luminous shadow of Parabrahman, which we call the Sachchidananda (XII, 460)." All references are to the Sri Aurobindo Birth Centenary Library (Pondicherry: Sri Aurobindo Ashram Press), 1970–73.

34. Elsewhere he states that "[a] man may be a great Rishi or Yogi without being a Jivanmukta. Yoga and spiritual learning are means to Mukti, not Mukti itself (XII, 463)." This seems to accord with the *Jīvanmuktiviveka* and other Yogic Advaita texts.

35. A novel image, and an interesting choice for a former political prisoner.

Chapter 11

1. For an excellent introduction to the *Śankarācārya* tradition, see William Cenkner's *A Tradition of Teachers* (Delhi: Motilal Banarsidass, 1983). For an interesting social scientific perspective on the Kanchi *Śankarācāryas*, particularly the reigning *Śankarācārya,* Jayendra Sarasvati, see Mattison Mines and Vijayalakshmi Gourishankar, "Leadership and Individuality in South Asia: The Case of the South Indian Big-Man," *Journal of Asian Studies* 49: 4 (November 1990): 761–86.

2. Cenkner, p. 123. Jayendra Sarasvati, Candrasekharendra's successor, compares him to Ramana and Śaṅkara himself.

3. "The Sage of Kanchi (henceforth, "Sage")," which appears in a book he edited called *Spiritual Perspectives: Essays in Mysticism and Metaphysics* (New Delhi: Arnold-Heinemann, 1975), p. 15. One must note that to an extraordinary degree, the image Mahadevan's words cast here is that of Christ, not Śaṅkara.

4. "Renowned Hindu Saint Begins Hundredth Year," *Hinduism Today* 15: 5 (May, 1993), p. 1. Interestingly, both Mahadevan and the article's writer refer to Candrasekharendra as a "pontiff."

5. One might note that, according to Advaita tradition, Ādi Śaṅkara established four teaching *pīṭhas* (seats) in the four corners of India, and it is generally agreed that the southern seat was founded at Sringeri in present-day Karnataka. Thus, there is a good deal of controversy about whether the Kanchipuram *maṭha* (monastic institution) should count as a *Śaṅkarācārya*'s seat (see Cenkner, p. 109 ff.). Followers of Candrasekharendra not only claim this to be a *Śaṅkarācārya* seat, but say it is the one from which Śaṅkara himself presided. This debate is not central to our aims; it suffices here to say that the Kanchi *pīṭha* is currently one of the best-known and most active *Śaṅkarācārya* seats and has been for many decades. The Kanchi *maṭha* (like that of Sringeri) has affiliated temples, schools, a library, and additional satellite institutions. In his article referenced in note 3, Mahadevan does not mention the controversy between the Sringeri and Kanchi *Śaṅkarācāryas,* but R. Sankaranarayan in *The Holy Advent* (Madras: Sri Surabhi Printers, 1982) writes that in 1925, they performed *pūjās* five miles from each other (27), and that Candrasekharendra stayed in Sringeri in 1927 (35). One point of contention has been the current Kanchi *Śaṅkarācārya*'s increasing rejection of caste barriers.

6. One of whom was Professor Russell Blackwood of Hamilton College, who has been generous in sharing his perspective and other material on the Kanchi *Śaṅkarācārya*.

7. These scholars include Mahadevan, R. Balasubramanian, P. K. Sundaram, and N. Veezhinathan.

8. As this indicates, there are in fact currently two *Śaṅkarācāryas* at Kanchi: Jayendra is ruling, and his successor, Vijayendra, is in training.

9. Biographical facts are based on T. M. P. Mahadevan's aforementioned 1975 biography, "The Sage of Kanchi," R. Sankaranarayan's *The Holy Advent* (Madras: Sri

Surabhi Printers, 1982), and the Kuppuswami Sastri Research Institute's *Journal of Oriental Research* (henceforth *JOR*) 34–35 (1964–1966) volume dedicated to Candrasekharendra. These writings largely agree in fact and interpretation about Candrasekharendra's life.

10. This openness has been continued and extended by Jayendra Sarasvati, who, it would be fair to say, is something of a political or social activist. Jayendra has rejected untouchability and caste distinctions to a greater degree than did Candrasekharendra and started the Jan Kalyan (People's Welfare) group for vocational and moral training of *harijans*. See Mines and Gourishankar (1990) and *India Today* (June 30, 1988), pp. 83–84. The *India Today* article discusses the new social activism of a variety of *maṭhas*, and quotes Jayendra as saying, "[T]he reason for our social work is to sincerely do social service to the people. Another motive is to spread the feeling of humanitarianism. The third, most important, reason is to dispel the impression that only other religions do missionary and social work (84)." This indicates clearly how deeply neo-Vedanta has entered the most traditional bastion of Vedantic and *Smārta* Hinduism.

11. *JOR*, 170.

12. Quoted both by Mahadevan (33) and Slater (171).

13. *JOR*, 178.

14. In 1933, Candrasekharendra began a year-long pilgrimage on foot to Banaras via Andhra Pradesh and Prayaga (Allahabad). He spent six months in Banaras, then proceeded to Calcutta. Throughout his journey, he regularly performed *pūjās* and consecrations (*abhiṣekha*), and gave many public discourses. On his journey back southward during 1936, he stopped at Puri, another *Śaṅkarācārya* seat, without, however, meeting with the Puri *Śaṅkarācārya*. He finally returned to Kanchi and Kumbakonam in 1939.

15. The *Hinduism Today* article mentions that Indira Gandhi visited the *Śaṅkarācārya* during Emergency rule and tried to defend her position. In response, Candrasekharendra was said to have asked, "If you say that whatever you have done is for the good of the country, then why are even your own partymen opposed to you?" (p. 7).

16. There are two overlapping collections of discourses compiled from presentations given in Madras in 1957–1958, *Aspects of Our Religion* (Bombay: Bharatiya Vidya Bhavan, 1988; henceforth *Aspects*) and *The Call of the Jagadguru: Sri Sankaracarya of Kanchi*. Compiled by P. Sankaranarayan. (Madras: Ganesh and Co., 1958; henceforth *Call*). This latter collection often expands on themes introduced in the former, giving more examples from the tradition.

17. While beyond the scope of this paper, one wonders if the *Śaṅkarācārya* was at all influenced by Swami Vivekananda's views.

18. See also *Call*, p. 69 ff.

19. Here and elsewhere in *Aspects*, the text uses double vowels (aa) for a long vowel in Sanskrit (e.g., saastra, aatman, jnaani); in the interest of easier reading, I have simply used the single consonant.

20. He seems to have been to some extent successful as a world teacher. Mahadevan claims that all Candrasekharendra's visitors experience "an inner transformation" and "a noble revolution in their soul (16)," and quotes a variety of foreign seekers and scholars, including Paul Brunton, Arthur Koestler, and S. H. Nasr, about the effect meeting Candrasekharendra had on them. Typical are Robert Slater's comments: the *Śaṅkarācārya* had both "saintly serenity" and "concerned interest" in the world, as well as an "ecumenical outlook." See his "There is no bar in religion," *JOR,* p. 170–71.

21. See also *Call*, 84 ff.

22. Blackwood writes that the *Śaṅkarācārya* even asked him about American Indian religions ("The Two Shankaracharyas of Kanchi Kamakoti Peetham," paper delivered at Colgate University, April 1991, p. 6). Slater also mentions this (*JOR*, p. 171).

23. For an excellent article contesting many of these points, see Heinrich von Stietencron's "Religious Configurations in Pre-Muslim India and the Modern Concept of Hinduism," in *Representing Hinduism: The Construction of Religious Traditions and National Identity*. Edited by Vasudha Dalmia and H. von Stietencron (Delhi: Sage Publications, 1995).

24. According to Cenkner, the *Śaṅkarācārya maṭha* schools (*paṭhaśala*) have students in the few dozens. They focus on Vedic memorization and recitation and on studying the commentaries (*bhāṣya*) of Śaṅkara (pp. 118–21). And while the Kanchi *Śaṅkarācāryas* have become more open to all castes, the *maṭha* schools are still populated only by *Smārta* Brahmins.

25. Mahadevan quotes these in "Sage," pp. 48–49.

26. See, for example, Manu's hierarchical differentiation of *varṇas* in I. 87–88, or his famous remarks on women's dependence on father, husband, and son in V. 148.

27. "Veda and Vedanta—Are They Contradictory?" *The Voice of Sankara* 13. 4 (February 1989), pp. 7–8.

28. *Ibid.*, p. 7.

29. On 1/9/90, I had the opportunity to interview Jayendra individually about *jīvanmukti*, but, regretfully, not Candrasekharendra himself. One can infer, however, both from Candrasekharendra's existing comments and Jayendra's rather traditional understanding, that Candrasekharendra's views remain in the Advaita mainstream.

30. "There is no bar in religion," *JOR*, p. 170–71.

31. Mahadevan (1975), pp. 85–90.

32. He first gives the model of seven stages of knowledge (*jñānabhūmis*) seen in the *YV* and *JMV* (but not mentioned by Candrasekharendra himself). Veezhinathan then turns to the *sthita-prajña* in the *Gītā*, calling him "a *jivanmukta* in the state of *samadhi* (88)," and elaborates by way of Madhusūdana Sarasvatī's *Gītā* commentary.

33. *Tamevaṃ vidvān-amṛta iha bhavati.* I was unable to determine the text in which this appears.

34. Cenkner's book and subsequent conversations with him have assisted me greatly here.

35. Cenkner, pp. 182, 186. While adherence to the traditional Brahminical model may be lessening, the *Śaṅkarācāryas* themselves are still generally greatly honored. They continue to provide a comforting link to the tradition for many otherwise rather Westernized Hindus.

36. Interview, 1/9/90.

37. He agreed that *vāsanās* might remain for a short time after *prārabdha karma* disappears.

38. He said the prospect must pray, talk, train, and then take *saṃnyāsa*. Even after all this preparation, sometimes the trainee leaves; in some *pīṭhas*, no one is ready (though he added the Kanchi *pīṭha* was ready).

39. As mentioned earlier (chapter 8), the exact relationship of these two is uncertain.

40. See, for example, the standard introduction to the Sringeri *maṭha*, *The Greatness of Sringeri* (Bombay: Tattvaloka Press, 1991).

41. Some have questioned his mental stability, especially in light of his apparent suicide by drowning in the Tunga River.

42. See, for example, *The Call of the Jagaduru* by R. Krishnaswami Aiyar (Madras: Ganesh and Co., 1961), *Dialogues with the Guru,* compiled by R. Krishnaswami Aiyar (Bombay: Chetana Pubs, n.d.), or *Our Duty* by Chandrasekhara Bharati (Bombay: Bharatiya Vidya Bhavan, 1982).

43. See S. Y. Krishnaswamy, *The Saint of Sringeri in Sacred India* (Madras: Sringeri Jagadguru Sanatana Dharma Vidya Samiti, 1968) and Cenkner's *A Tradition of Teachers*.

44. For a fascinating description of this occasion with interpretive comments, see Glenn Yocum, "The Coronation of a Guru: Charisma, Politics, and Philosophy in Contemporary India," in *A Sacred Thread: Modern Transmission of Hindu Traditions in India and Abroad,* Raymond Brady Williams, Ed. (Chambersburg, Penn.: Anima Publications, 1992): 68–91.

45. When asked if Ramana Maharshi was a *jīvanmukta*, he stated that while perhaps not a living liberated being, certainly he was a *mahant* (and he added, in English, a "great person").

46. And responding affirmatively to my question if the *jīvanmukta* was a *sthita-prajña*.

47. Before leaving, I also asked what he thought his most important duty as a *Śaṅkarācārya* today was. He held it was most important to "protect the practices (*pracāra*) of the *sanātan dharm*." To this end, he said, his teacher (Abhinava Vidyatirtha) directed him to establish schools, conduct rituals, undertake tours (*yātra*), and encourage discourses and meetings of teachers. All, he concluded in English, "to propagate the *sanātan dharm*."

Chapter 12

1. This chapter (and part of chapter 9) is a revision of my essay "*Jīvanmukti* and Social Service in Advaita and Neo-Vedanta," in *Beyond Orientalism*.

2. A good example of these tendencies is S. Radhakrishnan's *Brahmasūtra* "commentary," *The Brahma Sutra: The Philosophy of Spiritual Life* (London: George Allen and Unwin, 1960).

3. On the issue of caste in the Hindu tradition, see chapter 10 in Halbfass' *Tradition and Reflection*.

4. On this, see Lance Nelson, *Purifying God's Earthly Body: Ecological Concern in India's Religious Traditions* (Albany: State University of New York Press, 1998).

5. See his "*Jīvanmukti* and Social Concerns." *India Philosophical Annual* 2 (1966): 119-24. When conversing with K. Kunjunni Raja of the Adyar Library in Madras, I found he largely agreed with Pandeya's view.

6. K. Kunjunni Raja added that while one can argue that seeing oneness will lead to helping others, this view is not made explicit in traditional Advaita (personal interview, 1/22/90).

7. Like Śaṅkara, Rāmānuja holds that *śūdras* are not competent to know *brahman,* for they are not eligible to study or hear the Veda, so cannot understand it or perform rites mandated there. He also agrees that they can eventually get liberation by hearing the histories and *purāṇas* (See *ŚB* I. 3. 38). However, in comments on I. 3. 39, he goes on to claim that Advaitins cannot prove the *śūdra*'s ineligibility. His own argument against *śūdra* competence is that injunctions on meditation that give ignorance-ending love of the Lord are learned only from Veda study of one rightly initiated. Since *śūdras* cannot be initiated, they cannot learn the Vedic injunctions. On the other hand, in commenting on *BS* III. 4. 36–37, both Śaṅkara and Rāmānuja hold that one outside the life stages (*anāśramin*) is eligible for knowledge via prayer (*japa*), donation (*dāna*), and fasting (*upavāsa*).

Neo-Vedantins, of course, claim that Śaṅkara's views were very different. In his biography of Śaṅkara (based on the traditional *Śaṅkara-digvijaya* of Mādhava), the neo-Vedantin I. S. Madugula asserts a *caṇḍāla* (really Śiva in disguise) teaches Śaṅkara a lesson in "practical Vedanta" by pointing out that one should identify only with the nondual Self and not with the body or Brahmin caste. After this instruction, Madugula writes, Śaṅkara "realized his error which was the result of his social conditioning and his upbringing but entirely contrary to his conviction." *The Ācārya: Śaṅkara of Kaladi* (Delhi: Motilal Banarsidass, 1985), p. 26.

8. *Tradition and Reflection*, p. 385.

9. Chapter 2.

10. *Iṣṭasiddhi*, pp. 74–78; see chapter 3. Sarvajñātman's *Saṃkṣepaśārīrika* (II. 225–27) and Prakāśānanda's *Vedānta-siddhānta-muktāvalī* state that there is an imagined teacher who, when thought to be omniscient, brings knowledge to the ignorant in accordance with the *śāstras*.

11. S. K. Ramachandra Rao, *Jīvanmukti in Advaita* (Bangalore: IBH Prakashana, 1978), p. 61, S. Radhakrishnan, *Indian Philosophy*, Vol. II, p. 644, and P. K. Sundaram in conversation. For Śaṅkara's views, see chapter 2.

12. The idea that despite having no aims of one's own after liberating knowledge one continues to act to uphold the world order also appears in Śaṅkara's commentary on *Gītā* II. 10 and IV. 20.

13. The liberated being's concern for others is somewhat of an issue in *yoga*-influenced Advaita texts like Vidyāranya's *Jīvanmuktiviveka*, however. See especially his description of austerity (*tapas*), the second purpose of attaining *jīvanmukti,* in chapter 7.

14. This conclusion is supported by Satya P. Agarwal's recent *The Social Role of the Gītā: How and Why* (Delhi: Urmila Agarwal [Motilal Banarsidass], 1993). Agarwal favors the neo-Vedanta conception of *loka-saṃgraha*, but acknowledges that this conception has been "elaborated, modified, and updated to suit the changing sociopolitical needs" of today (p. 442), primarily by Vivekananda, B. G. Tilak, Aurobindo, and Gandhi.

15. *What Religion Is in the Words of Swami Vivekananda*. John Yale, Ed. (London: Phoenix House, 1962), p. 74. The best statement of Vivekananda's views on numerous topics relevant here is probably his four lectures on "Practical Vedanta." See *The Yogas and Other Works* (New York: Ramakrishna-Vivekananda Center, 1953), pp. 338–77.

16. For example, his usage of "freedom" sometimes suggests Mill more than *mokṣa,* and "evolution" Spencer more than *Sāṃkhya*.

17. In fact, Paul Hacker argues that Vivekananda propagates neo-Vedanta views largely for nation-building purposes, to bring pride to and unify India around "Hinduism" broadly and Vedanta in particular. See "Vivekananda's Religious Nationalism" in *Philology and Confrontation*.

18. *What Religion Is*, p. 32.

19. *India and Europe*, p. 239. For a further discussion of whether there can be "nondualistic ethics" if no relationships truly exist, see Hacker's "Schopenhauer and Hindu Ethics" in *Philology and Confrontation*, pp. 273 ff, and Halbfass' "Practical Vedanta" in *Representing Hinduism*, pp. 211–23.

20. *What Religion Is*, pp. 46–47. He also writes that while Śaṅkara made Vedanta "rationalistic," and stressed the "intellectual" side of Vedanta, the Buddha emphasized the "moral" side (*The Yogas*, p. 249). This notion will reappear in Radhakrishnan's thought.

21. *The Yogas*, p. 333.

22. *What Religion Is*, pp. 84–85.

23. *The Yogas*, pp. 334–35.

24. He eventually became president of India as well.

25. See "A Prasthānatraya Commentary of Neo-Hinduism: Remarks on the Work of Radhakrishnan," in *Philology and Confrontation.*

26. (Albany: State University of New York Press, 1987), p. 131 ff.

27. Radhakrishnan writes extensively on the caste system, in part defending it and in part agreeing with its critics. His position is that caste is, *or should be,* based on temperament or character and natural capacity, not on heredity (thus offering "equal opportunity" given our unequal dispositions). However, in his clearest statement on caste, the last lecture in *The Hindu View of Life* (London: George Allen and Unwin, 1927), he claims that caste does discourage "indiscriminate racial amalgamation (98)." He defends castes as customary social groupings that emphasize mutual benefit and cooperation, and are "functional" in a complex society. The caste system also gives a feeling of solidarity to a society, as opposed to Western individualism and competitiveness. Radhakrishnan shows his Brahmin solidarity here, emphasizing caste members' spiritual development and holding that Brahmins are "said to be above class interests and prejudices," being "freed from the cares of existence" to perform duties like developing and broadcasting "spiritual ideals (18)." See also his *Eastern Religions and Western Thought* (London: Oxford University Press, 1940), pp. 351–78, and Robert Minor's insightful "Radhakrishnan as Apologist for the Class/Caste System as a Universal Religion-Social System," delivered at the August 1994 Congress on Vedanta in Oxford, Ohio.

Incidentally, Radhakrishnan distorts Śaṅkara's views on the *varṇāśrama-dharma*, repeatedly suggesting that Śaṅkara was merely meeting "the common beliefs of his age (616)." In *Indian Philosophy*, (Vol. II. Rev. 2nd ed. London: George Allen and Unwin, 1931), he claims that while "the efficacy of caste institutions has ceased to be vital for Samkara, he allows room for belief in it (616)." He admits that Śaṅkara privileges Brahmins and *saṃnyāsins*, yet argues that overall "Samkara undermined the belief of the exclusive right of the upper classes to salvation (617)." (He passes over the exclusion of women in one sentence.) Radhakrishnan's interpretation of the relevant *Brahmasūtra* commentary here demonstrates both his attempt to represent the text accurately and his desire to make the text fit his view of what Hinduism/ Vedanta/Śaṅkara *should* say.

28. He here asserts the common neo-Vedantic view that Śaṅkara was "rational," a "philosopher," and a "social idealist" aiming to unify earlier "Hindu" thought (pp. 655–58).

29. *Eastern Religions and Western Thought*, p. 11.

30. Pp. 215–18, 222.

31. He also mentions currently manifesting *karma* and the two moons analogy (in which one knows only one moon exists, but sees two from eye disease, found in *Brahmasūtra bhāṣya* IV. 1. 15).

32. He makes a number of similar, but less focused comments on the nature of the liberated being in the introduction to his translation of the principal *Upaniṣads* (London: George Allen and Unwin, 1953), pp. 121 ff. Minor writes that Radhakrishnan, when speaking on the *Dhammapada*, called the Buddha a *jīvanmukta* who realized *tat-tvam-asi* and then returned to the world as a social reformer and prophet of Vedanta (97). Radhakrishnan was not always quite this "ecumenical."

33. Other comments on good and evil appear in *Eastern Religions and Western Thought*, pp. 12–13.

34. *Liberated Life* (Madurai: Dialogue Series, 1980), pp. 162–64.

35. Veezhinathan, pp. 138–39.

36. This and the following quotations come from their essay that immediately follows the Pandeya article mentioned earlier, called "The Social Concern of the *Jīvanmukta*," *India Philosophical Annual* 2 (1966): 125–30.

37. *A Comparative Study of the Concept of Liberation in Indian Philosophy* (Burhanpur: Gindharlal Keshavdas, 1967), pp. 118–19.

38. *The Naiṣkarmyasiddhi of Sureśvara,* p. 385.

39. Personal interview, 1/19/90.

40. Personal interview, 1/10/90.

41. See chapter 9, note 6.

42. Later, Srivastava writes that the *jīvanmukta*'s "spiritual enlightenment is only for doing good for people. It is with the same view that Śaṅkara says that *jīvanmuktas* are reincarnated to save the world." (264). (This is at the least a distortion of Śaṅkara's position, presumably in *BS* III. 3. 32).

43. In fact, when Srivastava goes over *loka-saṃgraha* in the *Gītā,* he turns for support not to Advaitins, but to the modern *Gītā-Rahasya* commentary of B. G. Tilak.

44. He calls the *tīrthaṃkara* a compassionate *karma yogin* (85), and says the Buddha taught a "wise and reasonable ethical system." The Buddha's "ideal of life" was "service to all sentient beings (87)."

45. Srivastava finds Śaṅkara puts more emphasis on *jīvanmukti*'s "ethical aspects" (i.e., *lokasaṃgraha*) than does Vidyāranya. Again offering a neo-Vedantic perspective, he says that Śaṅkara's own life "shows how, after attaining the highest spiritual illumination, he engaged himself in active service of humanity . . . only to spread the Truth." Vidyāranya, on the other hand, is more "negative," ignoring the *Yogavāsiṣṭha*'s "ethical implications" regarding *jīvanmukti* (i.e., internal renunciation of results, not action) (276). Srivastava psychologizes that Vidyāranya, post-*saṃnyāsa,* "felt disillusionment with regard to the possibility of benefitting societies through sociopolitical action (277)." Without some textual evidence, such speculation could be argued to represent Srivastava more than Vidyāranya.

46. Vivekananda was also mentioned by P. K. Sundaram.

47. An interesting piece of evidence for this claim could be seen at the 1992 International Congress on Vedanta in Oxford, Ohio, which was dedicated to Vivekananda. These meetings regularly attract many neo-Vedantins, both Indian and Western. In 1992, Vivekananda's "practical Vedanta" was praised often and at length.

48. Found in Vivekananda's *Complete Works*, Vol. II, p. 284.

Bibliography

Sanskrit Texts and Translations

Appayya-Dīkṣita. *Śāstra-Siddhāntaleśa-saṃgraha*. Edited by S. R. Krishnamurti Sastri and N. Veezhinathan. Secunderabad: Śrīmad-Appayya-Dīkṣithendra-Granthāvali Prakāśana-Samiti, 1973.

The Bhagavad-Gita: Krishna's Counsel in Time of War. Translated by Barbara Stoler Miller. New York: Bantam Books, 1986.

The Bhagavadgītā in the Mahābhārata: A Bilingual Edition. Edited and translated by J. A. B. van Buitenen. Chicago: University of Chicago Press, 1981.

Bhāratītīrtha-Vidyāraṇya. *Vivaraṇa-prameya-saṃgraha*. Translated by S. S. Suryanarayana Sastri and Saileswar Sen. Andhra University Series No. 24. Kumbakonam: Sri Vidya Press, 1941.

Citsukha. *Tattvapradīpikā*. Kāśī Sanskrit Series Edition No. 242. Varanasi: Chaukhambha Sanskrit Sansthan, 1987.

Dharmarāja Adhvarin. *Vedāntaparibhāṣa*. Edited and translated by S. S. Suryanarayana Sastri. Madras: Adyar Library and Research Centre, 1971.

Gauḍapāda. *The Āgamaśāstra of Gauḍapāda*. Edited and translated by Vidhushekara Bhattacharya. 1943. Reprint, Delhi: Motilal Banarsidass, 1989.

Laghu Yogavāsiṣtha. Translated by K. Narayanaswami Aiyer. Madras: Adyar Library and Research Centre, 1971.

Madhusūdana Sarasvatī. *Advaitasiddhi*. Edited by N. S. Ananta Krishna Sastri. Delhi: Parimal Publications, 1988.

———. *Bhagavad Gītā with Gūḍārthadīpikā of Madhusūdana Sarasvatī*. Edited by Hari Narayana Apte. Anandasrama Sanskrit Series No. 45. Poona, 1912.

———. *Madhusūdana Sarasvatī on the Bhagavad Gītā*. Translated by Sisir Kumar Gupta. Delhi: Motilal Banarsidass, 1977.

———. *Sāra-saṃgraha* on Sarvajñātman's *Saṃkṣepa-śārīraka*. Edited by Bhau Sastri Vajhe. Kashi Sanskrit Series 18. Benares: Vidya Vilas Press, 1924.

Maṇḍana Miśra. *Brahmasiddhi*. Edited by S. Kuppuswami Sastri. 2d ed. Delhi: Sri Satguru Publications, 1984.

Padmapāda. *Pañcapādikā*. Translated by R. D. Venkataramiah. Gaekwad's Oriental Series Vol. 107. Baroda: Oriental Institute, 1948.

Prakāśānanda. *Vedānta-siddhānta-muktāvalī*. Edited and translated by Arthur Venis. Varanasi: Chaukambha Orientalia, 1975.

Prakāśātman. *The Pañcapādikā of Śrī Padmapādācārya with the Pañcapādikā-vivaraṇa of Śrī Prakāśātman*. Edited by S. Srirama Sastri and S. R. Krishnamurthy Sastri. Madras: Government Oriental Series Vol. 155, 1958.

The Principal Upaniṣads. Edited and translated by S. Radhakrishnan. London: George Allen and Unwin, 1953.

Rāmānuja. *Brahmasūtra with Śrībhāṣya* (in Sanskrit). Two vols. Madras: Sreevathsa Press, 1963–64.

———. *The Vedānta Sūtras with Rāmānuja's Śrībhāṣya*. Translated by George Thibaut. Sacred Books of the East Vol. 48. 1904. Reprint, Delhi: Motilal Banarsidass, 1962.

Sadānanda. *Vedāntasāra*. Edited and translated by M. Hiriyanna. 2d ed. Poona Oriental Series No. 14. Poona: Oriental Book Agency, 1962.

———. *The Vedāntasāra: A Manual of Hindu Pantheism*. Edited and translated by G. A. Jacob. Varanasi: Bharat-Bharati, 1972.

The Sāmānya-Vedānta Upaniṣads. Edited by Pandit A. Mahadeva Sastri. Madras: Adyar Library and Research Centre, 1916.

The Sāṃkhya Philosophy (with the Sāṃkhya-pravacana sūtra, Aniruddha's vṛtti, and Vijñānabhikṣu's bhāṣya). Translated by Nandalal Sinha. New Delhi: Oriental Books Reprint Corp. (Munshiram Manoharlal), 1979.

The Sāṃkhyakārikās of Īśvara Kṛṣṇa. Edited and translated by S. S. Suryanarayana Sastri. 2d ed., revised. Madras: University of Madras, 1935.

The Saṃnyāsa Upanisads. Edited by T. R. Chintamani Dikshit. Adyar: Adyar Library and Research Centre, 1966.

Saṃnyāsa Upaniṣads. Translated by Patrick Olivelle. New York: Oxford University Press, 1992.

Śaṅkara. *Bhagavad Gītā with Śaṅkarabhāśya.* (in Sanskrit). Edited by Wasudev Laxman Śāstrī Panśīkar. 2d ed. Delhi: Munshiram Manoharlal Publications, 1978.

———. *Bhagavad Gītā Bhāśya.* Translated by A. G. Krishna Warrier. Madras: Ramakrishna Math, 1983.

———. *Brahmasūtra-Śaṅkarabhāṣyam.* J. L. Shastri, Ed. Delhi: Motilal Banarsidass,1980.

———. *Brahmasūtra Bhāṣya of Śaṅkarācārya.* Translated by Swami Gambhirananda. 3rd ed. Calcutta: Advaita Ashrama, 1977.

———. *The Bṛhadāraṇyaka Upaniṣad with the Commentary of Śaṅkarācārya.* Translated by Swami Madhavananda. 5th ed. Calcutta: Advaita Ashrama, 1975.

———. *Eight Upaniṣads with the Commentary of Śaṅkarācārya,* Vol. I. Translated by Swami Gambhirananda. Calcutta: Advaita Ashrama, 1957.

———. *Īśādidaśopaniṣadaḥ Śaṅkarabhāṣyasametah.* Delhi: Motilal Banarsidass, 1978.

———. *A Thousand Teachings: The Upadeśasāhasrī of Śaṅkara.* Translated and edited by Sengaku Mayeda. 1979. Reprint, Albany: State University of New York Press, 1992.

———. *Upadeśasāhasrī of Śrī Śaṅkarācārya.* Edited and translated by Swami Jagadananda. 7th ed. Madras: Ramakrishna Math, 1984.

———. *The Vedānta Sūtras with Śaṅkarācārya's Commentary.* Translated by George Thibaut. Sacred Books of the East, Vols. 34 and 38. Reprint, Delhi: Motilal Banarsidass, 1890, 1896.

Sarvajñātman. *Saṃkṣepa-śārīraka.* Edited and translated by N. Veezhinathan. Madras: University of Madras, 1972.

Sureśvara. *Bṛhadāraṇyakopaniṣad Bhāṣyavārtikam.* Edited by S. Subrahmanya Shastri. Varanasi: Mahesh Research Institute, 1982.

———. *The Naiṣkarmyasiddhi of Sureśvara.* Edited and translated by R. Balasubramanian. Madras: University of Madras Press, 1988.

The Thirteen Principal Upaniṣads. Translated by R. E. Hume. 2d edition, revised. New York: Oxford University Press, 1931.

Upaniṣads. Translated by Patrick Olivelle. World Classics Series. New York: Oxford University Press, 1996.

Vācaspati Miśra. *The Bhāmatī of Vācaspati Miśra.* Edited and translated by S. Suryanarayana Sastri and C. Kunhan Raja. Adyar: Theosophical Publishing House, 1933.

Vidyāraṇya. *Jīvanmuktiviveka.* Edited and translated by S. Subrahmanya Sastri and T. R. Srinivasa Ayyangar. Madras: Adyar Library and Research Centre, 1978.

———. *Pañcadaśī: A Treatise on Advaita Metaphysics.* Translated by Hari Prasad Shastri. London: Shanti Sadan, 1965.

Vimuktātman. *Iṣṭasiddhi.* Edited and translated by P. K. Sundaram. 2 vols. Madras: Swadharma Swaraajya Sangha, 1980.

The Yoga Upaniṣads. Edited by Pandit A. Mahadeva Sastri. 1920. Reprint, Madras: Adyar Library and Research Centre, 1968.

Yogavārttika of Vijñānabhikṣu. Translated and annotated by T. S. Rukmani. 4 vols. Delhi: Munshiram Manoharlal, 1978–89.

The *Yogavāsiṣṭha of Vālmīki.* Edited by Vasudeva Laxmana Sharma Pansikar. 2 vols. 3rd edition. Bombay: Nirnaya Sagar Press, 1918. Reprint, Delhi: Motilal Banarsidass, 1984.

Secondary Sources

Agarwal, Satya P. *The Social Role of the Gītā: How and Why.* Delhi: Urmila Agarwal (Motilal Banarsidass), 1993.

Aurobindo (Ghose), Sri. Sri Aurobindo Birth Centenary Library. Pondicherry: Sri Aurobindo Ashram Press, 1970–73.

Bader, J. *Meditation in Śaṅkara's Vedānta.* New Delhi: Aditya Prakashan, 1990.

Balasubramanian, R. "Ramana Maharshi, The Liberated-in-Life," *Indian Philosophical Annual* 17 (1984–85): 218–32.

Bharati, Chandrasekhara. *Our Duty.* Bombay: Bharatiya Vidya Bhavan, 1982.

———. *Dialogues with the Guru.* Compiled by R. Krishnaswami Aiyar. Bombay: Chetana Pubs, n.d.

Blackwood, Russell. "The Two Shankaracharyas of Kanchi Kamakoti Peetham," paper presented at Colgate University, April 1991.

Breckenridge, Carol, and Peter van der Veer, Editors. *Orientalism and the Postcolonial Predicament: Perspectives on South Asia.* Delhi: Oxford University Press, 1994.

Brunton, Paul. *A Search in Secret India.* London: Ryder and Co., 1964.

Candrasekharendra Sarasvati. *Aspects of Our Religion.* Bombay: Bharatiya Vidya Bhavan, 1988.

———. *The Call of the Jagadguru: Sri Sankaracarya of Kanchi.* Compiled by P. Sankaranarayan. Madras: Ganesh and Co., 1958.

———. "Veda and Vedanta—Are They Contradictory?" *The Voice of Sankara* 13. 4 (February 1989).

Cenkner, William. *A Tradition of Teachers: Śaṅkara and the Jagadgurus Today.* Delhi: Motilal Banarsidass, 1983.

Clooney, Francis X. *Theology After Vedanta: An Experiment in Comparative Theology*. Albany: State University of New York Press, 1993.

Comans, Michael. "The Question of the Importance of *Samādhi* in Modern and Classical Advaita Vedānta,"*Philosophy East and West* 43: 1 (January 1993): 19–38.

Dalmia, Vasudha, and Heinrich von Stietencron, Editors. *Representing Hinduism: The Construction of Religious Traditions and National Identity*. New Delhi: Sage Publications, 1995.

Das, A. C. "Advaita Vedanta and Bodily Liberation." *Philosophy East and West* 4 (1954): 113–24.

Dasgupta, Surendranath. *A History of Indian Philosophy*. 1922. 5 vols. Delhi: Motilal Banarsidass, 1975.

Deussen, Paul. *The Philosophy of the Upanishads*. A. S. Geden, Trans. 1906. Reprint, New York: Dover Publications, 1966.

———. *The System of the Vedānta*. Charles Johnston, Trans. 1912. Reprint, New York: Dover Publications, 1973.

Fort, Andrew O. *The Self and Its States*. Delhi: Motilal Banarsidass, 1990.

———. "Neither East Nor West: A Case of Neo-Vedanta in Modern Indian Thought," *Religious Studies Review* 18 (April 1992): 95–100.

———, and Patricia Y. Mumme, *Living Liberation in Hindu Thought*. Albany: State University of New York Press, 1996.

Franco, Eli, and Karin Preisendanz, Editors. *Beyond Orientalism: The Work of Wilhelm Halbfass and Its Impact on Indian and Cross-Cultural Studies*. Poznan Studies in the Philosophy of Sciences and Humanities No. 59. Amsterdam/Atlanta: Editions Rodopi, 1997.

Frykenberg, Robert. "Constructions of Hinduism at the Nexus of History and Religion," *Journal of Interdisciplinary History* 23: 3 (winter 1993): 523–50.

Gowri Sankar, "Renowned Hindu Saint Begins Hundredth Year," *Hinduism Today, North America Edition* 15: 5 (May 1993), p. 1.

The Greatness of Sringeri. Bombay: Tattvaloka Press, 1991.

Hacker, Paul. See Wilhelm Halbfass.

Halbfass, Wilhelm. *India and Europe: An Essay in Understanding*. Albany: State University of New York Press, 1988.

———. *Tradition and Reflection: Explorations in Indian Thought*. Albany: State University of New York Press, 1991.

———. Editor and translator. *Philology and Confrontation: Paul Hacker on Traditional and Modern Vedanta*. Albany: State University of New York Press, 1995.

Hawley, John S., "Naming Hinduism," *Wilson Quarterly* (summer 1991): 20–34.

Jacob, G. A. *A Concordance to the Principal Upaniṣads and Bhagavadgītā.* 1981. Reprint, Delhi: Motilal Banarsidass, 1971.

Kinsley, David. *Hinduism: A Cultural Perspective.* Englewood Cliffs, N. J.: Prentice-Hall, 1993.

Krishna Warrier, A. G. *The Concept of Mukti in Advaita Vedānta.* Madras: University Madras, 1961.

Krishnaswami, S. Y. *The Saint of Sringeri in Sacred India.* Madras: Sringeri Jagadguru Sanatana Dharma Vidya Samiti, 1968.

Krishnaswami Aiyar, R. *The Call of the Jagadguru.* Madras: Ganesh and Co., 1961.

Lad, A. K. *A Comparative Study of the Concept of Liberation in Indian Philosophy.* Burhanpur: Gindharlal Keshavdas, 1967.

Larson, Gerald James, and Ram Shankar Bhattacharya, Editors. *Sāṃkhya: A Dualist Tradition in Indian Philosophy.* Volume IV. *Encyclopedia of Indian Philosophies.* Princeton: Princeton University Press, 1987.

———, and Eliot Deutsch, Editors. *Interpreting Across Boundaries: New Essays in Comparative Philosophy.* Delhi: Motilal Banarsidass, 1989.

Madugula, I. S. *The Ācārya: Śaṅkara of Kaladi.* Delhi: Motilal Banarsidass, 1985.

Mahadevan, T. M. P. *The Philosophy of Advaita with Special Reference to Bhāratītīrtha-Vidyāraṇya.* Madras: Ganesh and Co., 1957.

———. *Ramana Maharshi and His Philosophy of Existence.* Tiruvannamalai: Sri Ramanashramam, 1967.

———. *Ramana Maharshi: The Sage of Arunacala.* London: George Allen and Unwin, 1977.

———. *Spiritual Perspectives: Essays in Mysticism and Metaphysics.* New Delhi: Arnold-Heinemann, 1975.

Maharshi, Ramana. See Ramana Maharshi.

Malkani, G. R. "A Note on Liberation in Bodily Existence." *Philosophy East and West* 5 (1955): 69–74.

Mines, Mattison, and Vijayalakshmi Gourishankar. "Leadership and Individuality in South Asia: The Case of the South Indian Big-Man," *Journal of Asian Studies* 49: 4 (November 1990): 761–86.

Minor, Robert. *Radhakrishnan: A Religious Biography.* Albany: State University of New York Press, 1987.

———. "Radhakrishnan as Apologist for the Class/Caste System as a Universal Religion-Social System," paper presented at the Congress on Vedanta in Oxford, Ohio, August 1994.

Nelson, Lance. "*Bhakti-Rasa* for the Advaitin Renunciate: Madhusūdana Sarasvatī's Theory of Devotional Sentiment," *Religious Traditions* 12 (1989): 1–16.

———. "Madhusūdana Sarasvatī on the 'Hidden Meaning' of the *Bhagavad-Gītā*: Bhakti for the Advaitin Renunciate," in *Journal of South Asian Literature* 23 (1988): 73–89.

———. *Purifying God's Earthly Body: Ecological Concern in India's Religious Traditions.* Albany: State University of New York Press, 1998.

Osborne, Arthur. *Ramana Maharshi and the Path of Self-Knowledge.* London: Ryder and Co., 1954.

Pandeya, R. C. "*Jīvanmukti* and Social Concerns." *Indian Philosophical Annual* 2 (1966): 119–24.

Potter, Karl, Editor. *Advaita Vedānta up to Śaṃkara and his Pupils.* Vol. III. *The Encyclopedia of Indian Philosophies.* Delhi: Motilal Banarsidass, 1981.

Radhakrishnan, Sarvepalli. *The Brahma Sutra: The Philosophy of Spiritual Life.* London: George Allen and Unwin, 1960.

———. *Eastern Religions and Western Thought.* London: Oxford University Press, 1940.

———. *The Hindu View of Life.* London: George Allen and Unwin, 1927.

———. *Indian Philosophy.* Rev. 2d ed. London: George Allen and Unwin, 1931.

Ramachandra Rao, S. K. *Jīvanmukti in Advaita.* Bangalore: IBH Prakashana, 1979.

Ramachandran, T. P., and N. Veezinathan. "The Social Concern of the *Jīvanmukta*," *India Philosophical Annual* 2 (1966): 125–30.

Ramana Maharshi. *The Collected Works of Ramana Maharshi.* Edited by Arthur Osborne. 5th edition. Tiruvannamalai: Sri Ramanasramam, 1979.

———. *Bhagavan Sri Ramana: A Pictorial Biography.* Tiruvannamalai: Sri Ramanasramam, 1981.

———. *Talks with Sri Ramana Maharshi.* Tiruvannamalai: Sri Ramanashramam, 1978.

———. *The Teachings of Bhagavan Sri Ramana Maharshi in His Own Words.* Edited by Arthur Osborne. 5th edition. Tiruvannamalai: Sri Ramanashramam, 1988.

Rambachan, Anantanand. *The Limits of Scripture.* Honolulu: University of Hawaii Press, 1994.

Sankaranarayan, R. *The Holy Advent.* Madras: Sri Surabhi Printers, 1982.

Sarasvati, Candrasekharendra. See Candrasekharendra Sarasvati.

Sastri, P. S. "*Jivanmukti* and *Avidya*." *Prabuddha Bharata* 57 (1952): 345–49.

Sawai, Yoshitsugu. *The Faith of Ascetics and Lay Smārtas: A Study of the Śaṅkaran Tradition of Śṛṅgeri*. Publications of the De Nobili Research Library. Vol. 19. Vienna: Sammlung De Nobili, 1992.

———. "Rāmānuja's Theory of *Karman*," *Journal of Indian Philosophy* 21 (1993): 11–29.

———. "Śaṅkara's Theory of *Saṃnyāsa*." *Journal of Indian Philosophy* 14.4 (December 1986): 371–87.

Sharma, B. N. K. *The Brahmasūtras and Their Principal Commentaries*. Vol. III. Bombay: Bharatiya Vidya Bhavan, 1978.

Sharma, V. A. *Citsukha's Contribution to Advaita*. Mysore: Kavyalaya Publishers, 1974.

Sinha, J. *A History of Indian Philosophy*. Vol. III. Calcutta: Sinha Publishing House, 1971.

Slater, Robert. "There Is No Bar in Religion," Kuppuswami Sastri Research Institute's *Journal of Oriental Research* 34–35 (1964–66), p. 170–71.

Sprockhoff, J. F. "Die Idee der *Jīvanmukti* in den Späten *Upaniṣads*." *Wiener Zeitschrift fur die Kunde Sudasiens* 7 (1963): 190–208.

———. "Die Vorbereitung der Vorstellung von der Erlösung bei Lebzeiten in den *Upaniṣads*." *Wiener Zeitschrift fur die Kunde Sudasiens* 6 (1962): 151–78.

———. "Der Weg zur Erlösung bei Lebzeiten, Ihr Wesen, and Ihr Wert nach dem *Jīvanmuktiviveka* des Vidyāraṇya." *Wiener Zeitschrift fur die Kunde Sudasiens* 8 (1964): 224–62 and 14 (1970): 131–60.

Sri Aurobindo. See Aurobindo, Sri.

Srivastava, L. K. L. *Advaitic Concept of Jivanmukti*. Delhi: Bharatiya Vidya Prakashan, 1990.

———. "The Purpose of Attaining *Jīvanmukti*." *Darshana* 14.4 (1974): 1–8.

Sundaram, P. K. "Reflections on *Jīvanmukti* in Advaita." *Journal of Madras University* 30 (1958): 121–34.

Suryanarayana Sastri, S. S. "*Jīvanmukti* " in *Collected Papers of S. S. Suryanarayana Sastri*. Edited by T. M. P. Mahadevan. Madras: University of Madras, 1961.

Swaminathan, K. *Ramana Maharshi*. Delhi: National Book Trust, 1975.

Thrasher, Allen. *The Advaita Vedānta of Brahma-siddhi*. Delhi: Motilal Banarsidass, 1993.

Timm, Jeffrey, Editor. *Texts in Context: Traditional Hermeneutics in South Asia*. Albany: State University of New York Press, 1992.

Valiaveetil, Chacko. *Liberated Life*. Madurai: Dialogue Series, 1980.

Veezhinathan, N. "Bhagavan Ramana—A Jivanmukta." Unpublished manuscript given to author, 1990.

Vivekananda, Swami. *What Religion Is in the Words of Swami Vivekananda*. Edited by John Yale. London: Phoenix House, 1962.

———. *The Yogas and Other Works*. New York: Ramakrishna-Vivekananda Center, 1953.

von Stietencron, Heinrich. "Hinduism: On the Proper Use of a Deceptive Term," in *Hinduism Reconsidered*. Edited by Gunther Sontheimer and Hermann Kulke. Delhi: Manohar Munshiram, 1989.

Yocum, Glenn. "The Coronation of a Guru: Charisma, Politics, and Philosophy in Contemporary India." In *A Sacred Thread: Modern Transmission of Hindu Traditions in India and Abroad,* Raymond Brady Williams, Ed. (Chambersburg, Penn.: Anima Publications, 1992): 68–91.

Index

A

B

T

U

V

Y